Genetic Resources, Equity and International Law

NEW HORIZONS IN ENVIRONMENTAL AND ENERGY LAW

Series Editors: Kurt Deketelaere, *Professor of Law, University of Leuven, Belgium and University of Dundee, Scotland and* Zen Makuch, *Reader in Law, Barrister, Imperial College, London, UK*

Environmental law – including the pressing considerations of energy law and climate change – is an increasingly important area of legal research and practice. Given the growing interdependence of global society and the significant steps being made towards environmental protection and energy efficiency, there are few people untouched by environmental and energy lawmaking processes.

At the same time, environmental and energy law is at a crossroads. The command and control methodology that evolved in the 1960s and 1970s for air, land and water protection may have reached the limit of its environmental protection achievements. New life needs to be injected into our environmental protection regimes – perhaps through the concept of sustainability in its environmental, economic and social forms. The same goes for energy policy and law, where liberalisation, environmental protection and security of supply are at the centre of attention. This important series seeks to press forward the boundaries of environmental and energy law through innovative research into environmental and energy law, doctrine and case law. Adopting a wide interpretation of environmental and energy law, it includes contributions from both leading and emerging international scholars.

Titles in the series include:

Conservation, Biodiversity and International Law
Alexander Gillespie

Comparative Ocean Governance
Place-Based Protections in an Era of Climate Change
Robin Kundis Craig

Environmental Governance of the Great Seas
Law and Effect
Joseph F.C. DiMento and Alexis Jaclyn Hickman

Conservation on the High Seas
Harmonizing International Regimes for the Sustainable Use of Living Resources
Simone Borg

Global Environmental Governance
Law and Regulation for the 21st Century
Louis Kotzé

Climate Law in EU Member States
Towards National Legislation for Climate Protection
Edited by Marjan Peeters, Mark Stallworthy and Javier de Cendra de Larragán

International Law and Freshwater
The Multiple Challenges
Edited by Laurence Boisson de Chazournes, Christina Leb and Mara Tignino

Genetic Resources, Equity and International Law
Camena Guneratne

Genetic Resources, Equity and International Law

Camena Guneratne

Professor, Open University of Sri Lanka

NEW HORIZONS IN ENVIRONMENTAL AND ENERGY LAW

Edward Elgar

Cheltenham, UK • Northampton, MA, USA

Published by
Edward Elgar Publishing Limited
The Lypiatts
15 Lansdown Road
Cheltenham
Glos GL50 2JA
UK

Edward Elgar Publishing, Inc.
William Pratt House
9 Dewey Court
Northampton
Massachusetts 01060
USA

A catalogue record for this book
is available from the British Library

Library of Congress Control Number: 2012942513

FSC
www.fsc.org
MIX
Paper from
responsible sources
FSC® C018575

ISBN 978 0 85793 494 9

Typeset by Columns Design XML Ltd, Reading
Printed and bound by MPG Books Group, UK

Contents

Acknowledgements

Many people have had an input into this manuscript and offered advice, encouragement and guidance along the way. I am grateful to Barry Barton, Kate Bjork, Al Gillespie, Raja Goonesekere and Arjun Guneratne who read drafts and provided helpful criticisms on various aspects of the book as it gradually evolved. Any shortcomings which remain are, of course entirely my own responsibility.

I thank the many friends, both within and outside Sri Lanka whose affection and support have seen me through the time it took me to produce this manuscript. I would also like to record my appreciation of my lawyer friends in Sri Lanka, particularly Jagath Gunewardena and Ruana Rajepakse, who have over the past two decades spent much of their time and energy in litigating public interest cases on issues of environment and development, human rights and justice. The cases they have fought have contributed in no small measure to ensuring equitable and sustainable development in Sri Lanka in many spheres.

Last, but not least, I thank Savitri Goonesekere for being a guide and role model and for giving me many years of mentoring, friendship and support.

I dedicate this book to my mother, Erica Guneratne, and to the memory of my father, Upali Ananda Guneratne.

Abbreviations

ABS	Access and Benefit Sharing
AIPPI	International Association for the Protection of Industrial Property
ASEAN	Association of South East Asian Nations
ASSINSEL	International Association of Plant Breeders
CBD	Convention on Biological Diversity
CDIP	WIPO Committee on Development and Intellectual Property
CGIAR	Consultative Group on International Agricultural Research
CGRFA	Commission on Genetic Resources for Food and Agriculture
CHH	Common Heritage of Humankind
CoP	Conference of the Parties to the Convention on Biological Diversity
CPRs	Common Property Resources
EFTA	European Free Trade Association
EU	European Union
FAO	Food and Agriculture Organization
FAO Treaty	FAO International Treaty on Plant Genetic Resources for Food and Agriculture
FOD	Group of Friends of Development
FTA	Free Trade Agreement
GATT	General Agreement on Tariffs and Trade
GRAIN	Genetic Resources Action International

GURTs	Genetic Use Restriction Technology
HYVs	High Yielding Varieties
IARCs	International Agricultural Research Centre
ICCPR	International Covenant on Civil and Political Rights
ICESCR	International Covenant on Economic, Social and Cultural Rights
IGC	Intergovernmental Committee on Intellectual Property and Genetic Resources, Traditional Knowledge and Folklore
ILM	International Legal Materials
ILO	International Labour Organization
IP	Intellectual Property
IPGRI	International Plant Genetic Resources Institute
IPRs	Intellectual Property Rights
IRRI	International Rice Research Institute
ITO	International Trade Organization
LDCs	Lesser Developed Countries
LMMC	Group of Like Minded Megadiverse Countries
MATs	Mutually Agreed Terms
MDGs	Millennium Development Goals
MFN	Most Favoured Nation Treatment
MLS	Multilateral System
MNC	Multinational Corporation
MTA	Material Transfer Agreements
OAS	Organisation of American States
OAU	Organisation of African Unity
OECD	Organisation for Economic Co-operation and Development
PBRs	Plant Breeders' Rights

PCDA	Provisional Committee on Proposals Related to a WIPO Development Agenda
PCIPD	Permanent Committee on Co-operation on Development Related to Intellectual Property
PCT	Patent Co-operation Treaty
PGRFA	Plant Genetic Resources for Food and Agriculture
PIC	Prior Informed Consent
PLT	Patent Law Treaty
PVP	Plant Variety Protection
PVPA	US Plant Variety Protection Act
SBSTTA	Subsidiary Body on Scientific, Technical and Technological Advice
SCP	Standing Committee on the Law of Patents
SMTA	Standard Material Transfer Agreement
SPLT	Substantive Patent Law Treaty
TEK	Traditional Ecological Knowledge
TEKW	Traditional Ecological Knowledge and Wisdom
TK	Traditional Knowledge
TRIPS Agreement	Agreement on Trade Related Aspects of Intellectual Property Rights
TRIPS Council	Council for Trade Related Aspects of Intellectual Property Rights
UDHR	Universal Declaration on Human Rights
UN	United Nations
UNCED	United Nations Conference on Environment and Development
UNCLOS	United Nations Convention on the Law of the Sea
UNCTAD	United Nations Conference on Trade and Development
UNEP	United Nations Environment Programme

UNESCO	United Nations Education, Cultural and Scientific Organization
UPOV Convention	Convention for the Protection of New Varieties of Plants
UPOV	International Union for the Protection of New Varieties of Plants
USPTO	US Patent and Trademark Office
WG8J	Working Group on Article 8(j) and Related Provisions of the Convention on Biological Diversity
WG-ABS	*Ad hoc* Open-Ended Working Group on Access and Benefit Sharing
WIPO	World Intellectual Property Organization
WTO	World Trade Organization

1. Introduction

The International Treaty on Plant Genetic Resources for Food and Agriculture defines 'plant genetic resources for food and agriculture' (PGRFA) as 'any genetic material of plant origin of actual or potential value for food and agriculture.' In essence, the term is used to refer to the diversity of crop plants, both wild varieties, and those modified, developed and used by humans throughout history, and which have now accumulated in a vast resource of agricultural plant diversity. This resource has been drawn upon to meet basic human needs of food and nutrition, and has sustained agricultural systems throughout the world for centuries.

In the last few decades certain developments have brought about changes, not to the nature of PGRFA, but to the conception of their values. The first such development is the progress of biotechnology which now enables the genetic manipulation of plants, including the accelerated development of new crop varieties. This has resulted in an immense escalation in the value of PGRFA. Aside from their historic uses as a source of food and nutrition, such plants have now become a significant commercial asset, particularly for corporate interests working in the field of plant development.

A second related issue in this narrative is the increased interest in the knowledge systems of traditional communities, including indigenous peoples and farming communities, particularly in regard to the uses of plants for food and medicine. It has become a matter of concern that the knowledge related to these resources is being used to search for plants which can then be appropriated for further development and commercialized, and retained within the exclusive control of a few. These two issues have now become inextricably linked to the debate on the international regulation of the uses of PGRFA.

In order to successfully market new crop varieties produced by the use of biotechnology, it is necessary to acquire exclusive legal rights over them. This objective has been facilitated by concurrent developments in international intellectual property and trade law, which require all nations to adhere to a global legal framework which enforces private property rights over, *inter alia*, crop plant varieties, which were hitherto generally accessible to everybody. On the other hand, an international environmental conservation regime has concurrently evolved, which calls for equitable access to and benefit sharing of these resources.

This book is a study of these international law developments in the regulation of the uses of PGRFA, and asks a specific question: does the present international legal system regulating the uses of plant genetic resources for food and agriculture ensure equitable access to these plants and to the benefits which arise out of them to the global community?

This question takes on a particular significance in the current context of sustainable development and environmental conservation in developing countries. Access to plant genetic resources will impact on the ability of these countries to meet the Millennium Development Goals within the next three years, particularly, eradicating extreme poverty and hunger and ensuring environmental sustainability. Adaptation to climate change, especially in sustainable agriculture, is yet another challenge which requires the free availability of these resources. The Bali Ministerial Declaration on the International Treaty on Plant Genetic Resources for Food and Agriculture of 2011 has expressed concern 'over current global challenges, in particular the continuing erosion of agricultural biodiversity, the threats posed by food insecurity, extreme poverty and the effects of climate change,' and recognized 'the importance and unique role of plant genetic resources for food and agriculture in addressing these challenges.'

Under the circumstances it is of critical importance that these resources be kept in the public domain, freely accessible to all. As observed above, the diversity of plant crops now available to humans was largely due to the efforts of generations of farmers and other agriculture-based communities in developing and conserving them to suit their particular environments and nutritional needs. These crops have, until these recent developments, been freely available and have contributed to a continuous process of agricultural development over time. A legal regime that now permits these plants or their components to be acquired by vested interests to the exclusion of all others, including those who originally developed and used them, raises questions of equity and justice. This book will explore this international legal regime and analyze the various rights, both property rights and human rights, which define access to these resources.

THE STRUCTURE OF THE BOOK

This book will consist of factual introductions to the issues, an analysis of the various forms of property which are potentially applicable to plant genetic resources, and an examination of the international intellectual property rights and environmental conservation regimes which embody these property systems. In doing so it will review the international debate on PGRFA as it has been played out in the international fora which administer these agreements. It will contain a detailed analysis of the provisions of the treaties, and examine the records of the debates in their implementing institutions so as to consider the question whether they achieve equity in the use of PGRFA. These debates reflect the perspectives of the various stakeholders involved and strategies to negotiate contentious points, and illustrate the economic and political realities underlying this discourse.

Chapter 2 contains an overview of PGRFA and its location, importance and the causes of its loss. A related element of diversity, namely human cultural diversity and its link to natural resources is also considered. This explanation feeds into the later discussion on traditional knowledge. Chapter 3 contains a discussion of how modern biotechnology has changed the institutional framework within which PGRFA is used, for example the changes it has made to agricultural systems, particularly in developing countries. It also discusses matters of concern which have arisen as a result of biotechnological processes, importantly, the appropriation of plant resources as raw material for this purpose. This section provides a historical perspective on the impacts of agricultural biotechnology on the agricultural systems and economies of developing countries.

PGRFA is now susceptible to private ownership and international law has, in a range of treaties, devised several forms of ownership which can be applied to these resources. Therefore it is important to analyze the concepts underpinning the notion of property in general, and the property rights applicable to PGRFA in particular. Accordingly, Chapter 4 discusses the philosophical foundations of property regimes over natural resources. It then examines, more specifically, the property regimes contained in the international agreements which regulate the uses of these resources. These concepts are important as they form the basis of the debate regarding which form of property rights, if any, should be applied to crop plants.

Chapter 5 contains a historical overview of the international environmental/conservation regime. The focus of these treaties is not limited to the conservation of natural resources as they also contain provisions on access to genetic resources and sharing of the benefits of their uses. It is this latter aspect that is important for the present discussion. The chapter then provides a brief overview of PGRFA in the context of this international environmental regime.

Chapter 6 deals with issues relating to agriculture-based communities which are also addressed in the international environmental treaties, and which are intrinsically linked to the discourse on access to and benefit sharing of PGRFA. Specifically, it considers the international discourse on the rights of farmers and indigenous peoples respectively. It examines a range of international documents, including human rights documents, in analyzing the nature, scope and extent of the rights of these communities in regard to PGRFA and their linkage to this debate. The last section of this chapter deals with the question of traditional knowledge. The appropriation of this knowledge often runs parallel with the appropriation of genetic resources and is thus an interface between these communities and PGRFA issues.

Chapters 7 and 8 deal with the international property rights regime, which conversely seeks to restrict access and to facilitate private ownership of plants. Chapter 7 provides a historical perspective on the nature and structure of these agreements, and importantly the political basis of their negotiation and implementation. This is necessary in order to set the context for the more detailed analysis of their provisions which have contributed to the controversy over PGRFA which is discussed in Chapter 8.

Having defined the parameters of the debate, Chapters 9 to 12 deal with four specific questions which have been raised in international fora to address questions of access and benefit sharing of PGRFA. These questions largely constitute the points of reference in the negotiations on the nature and extent of access to these resources and the application of property rights over them. They have been raised by countries within which genetic resources are located as measures to ensure equity and fairness in sharing of the benefits to be derived from them, and can be considered to be the benchmarks by which to determine whether such equity will be achieved.

The concluding chapter summarizes the analysis and arguments in the book, and based upon them, attempts to offer an answer to the question which was posed. This book does not seek to provide practical solutions to the problem or strategies for further action. Its purpose is rather to analyze the current trends and issues, and their impacts upon the various stakeholders involved and to raise points of concern.

2. Overview of plant genetic resources for food and agriculture

Biological diversity has in practice been defined at three levels – ecosystem, species and genetic diversity – in descending order.[1] In addition, a further form of diversity, namely human cultural diversity, has been cited as being inextricably linked to the conservation and sustainable use of natural resources. The term 'biological resources' refers more specifically to the physical manifestations of biodiversity which have actual or potential value for humanity.[2] Biological resources can be managed, i.e. they can be consumed or replenished and conserved. The way biological resources are managed enhances or reduces biodiversity.[3]

The world's biodiversity is not evenly distributed, and generally species' richness increases with decreasing latitude. Thus species diversity is greatest in the tropics, less in temperate regions and decreases further in polar regions.[4] The largest concentration of biodiversity is in the tropical forests which comprise about 7 per cent of the land surface of the Earth and which are estimated to hold more than 50 per cent of all species.[5] Many of the

---

[1] *Convention on Biological Diversity* (1992) 31 ILM 818, Article 2 (hereinafter CBD). See also World Resources Institute, International Union for the Conservation of Nature and United Nations Environment Programme, *Global Biodiversity Strategy* (1992) Box 1 at 2 (hereinafter *Global Biodiversity Strategy*). Jeffrey A McNeely, Kenton R Miller, Walter V Reid, Russell A Mittermeier and Timothy B Werner, *Conserving the World's Biological Diversity* (1990) 11.

[2] *Conserving the World's Biological Diversity*, above n 1, 18. Article 2 of the CBD defines it as including 'genetic resources, organisms or parts thereof, populations, or any other biotic component of ecosystems with actual or potential use or value to humanity.'

[3] *Conserving the World's Biological Diversity*, above n 1, 18.

[4] Brian Groombridge (ed), *Global Biodiversity – Status of the Earth's Living Resources, A Report compiled by the World Conservation Monitoring Centre* (1992) 43.

[5] Thomas E Lovejoy, 'Biodiversity: What is it?' in Marjorie L Reaka-Kudla, Don E Wilson and Edward O Wilson (eds), *Biodiversity II Understanding and Protecting Our Biological Resources* (1997). See also *Conserving the World's*

countries in which this diversity is concentrated are located in the southern hemisphere and are also those which are economically less developed.[6]

Agricultural diversity, being a component of biodiversity, is also considered within the three levels of ecosystem, species and genetic diversity.[7] One of the primary categories of ecosystems is agricultural ecosystems or agroecosystems, managed by people to meet food, fibre and fuel needs. They have been described as follows:

> Agricultural ecosystems, or agroecosystems, are ecosystems in which naturally occurring plants and animals have been replaced by crop plants and livestock animals deliberately selected by human beings. The degree of disruption of the natural system varies widely with different types of agriculture.[8]

Agriculture is one of the most common uses of land, and estimates of the areas of agricultural ecosystems range from 24 per cent to 38 per cent of the earth's land area. It has been said that as a managed ecosystem, agriculture plays a unique role in supplying ecosystem services, i.e. provisioning, regulating, and cultural services, as well as demanding supporting services to enable it to be productive.[9]

The second level of diversity is species diversity and a species has been defined as 'a group of organisms capable of inter breeding freely with each

---

Biological Diversity, above n 1, 86 and Norman Myers, *The Primary Source, Tropical Forests and Our Future* (1984).

[6] Russell A Mittermeier, Norman Myers, Jorgen B Thomsen, Gustavo A B da Fonseca and Silvio Olivieri, 'Biodiversity Hotspots and Major Tropical Wilderness Areas: Approaches to Setting Conservation Priorities' (1998) 12(3) *Conservation Biology* 516. For a discussion on legal protection of hotspots see John Charles Kunich, 'Fiddling around While the Hotspots Burn Out' (2001) 14 *Georgetown International Environmental Law Review* 179.

[7] For a definition of ecosystems see CBD, Article 2. This definition is echoed in the World Resources Institute, *Millennium Ecosystem Assessment, 2005 – Ecosystems and Human Well-being: Biodiversity Synthesis*, Preface, page iii (hereinafter *Millennium Ecosystem Assessment*).

[8] UNEP/CBD/SBSTTA/2/10 – Subsidiary Body on Scientific, Technical and Technological Advice, Second Meeting, 2–6 September 1996, *Agricultural Biological Diversity*, 12 August 1996.

[9] Scott M Swinton, Frank Lupi, G Philip Robertson and Stephen K Hamilton, 'Ecosystem services and agriculture: Cultivating agricultural ecosystems for diverse benefits' (2007) 64(1) *Ecological Economics* 245. See also World Resources Institute, *Peoples and Ecosystems, The Fraying Web of Life* (2000) 53–68 (hereinafter *Peoples and Ecosystems*); CGRFA-11/07/Inf.17 – CGRFA, Eleventh Regular Session, 11–15 June 2007, *Environment and Agriculture*.

other but not with members of other species.'[10] Species diversity refers to the variety of such groups of organisms on earth and also includes domestic and cultivated species in agriculture.[11] The Global Biodiversity Strategy notes the value of variety in agriculture and points out that for generations, people have raised a wide range of crops and livestock to enhance productivity. These have contributed to watershed protection, maintenance of soil fertility and pest management strategies.[12] However, modern agricultural practices which are dependent on a few high yielding varieties are largely eroding this heterogeneity. As the number of crop species declines, the species which co-evolved with traditional agricultural systems also diminish.

The third level of diversity is genetic diversity which has been defined as the 'variation of genes within species.'[13] This includes distinct populations of the same species[14] and the genetic variation within a particular population.[15] 'Genetic resources' are those elements of genetic diversity which are beneficial to humans,[16] and of the earth's natural resources these are perhaps the most critical to humanity. It has been noted that '[t]he genetic

---

[10] *Global Biodiversity Strategy*, above n 1, 230. See also Edward O Wilson, *The Diversity of Life* (1992) 38. It has also been noted that species diversity is a difficult concept to define and measure – Andrew J Hamilton 'Species Diversity or Biodiversity' (2005) 75 *Journal of Environmental Management* 89.

[11] The CBD defines domestic or cultivated species as 'species in which the evolutionary process has been influenced by humans to meet their needs' – CBD, Article 2.

[12] *Global Biodiversity Strategy*, above n 1, 4.

[13] Ibid at 2.

[14] The example cited is the thousands of traditional rice varieties in India – *Global Biodiversity Strategy*, above n 1, 2.

[15] The United Nations Environment Programme, *Global Biodiversity Assessment* (1995) defines this as the 'variation in the genetic composition of individuals within or among species; the heritable genetic variation within and among populations' at 1110 (hereinafter *Global Biodiversity Assessment*). For example, genetic variation is very high among Indian rhinos and very low among cheetahs – *Global Biodiversity Strategy*, above n 1, 2. See also *Conserving the World's Biological Diversity*, above n 1, 17.

[16] *Global Biodiversity Assessment*, above n 15, defines genetic resources as the 'genetic material of plants, animals or microorganisms, including modern cultivars and breeds, primitive varieties and breeds, landraces and wild/weedy relatives of crop plants or domesticated animals of value as a resource for future generations of humanity' at 1110. The CBD defines 'genetic material' as 'any material of plant, animal, microbial or other origin containing functional units of heredity' and 'genetic resources' as 'genetic material of actual or potential value' – CBD, Article 2.

diversity of plants, animals, insects, and microorganisms determines agro-ecosystems' productivity, resistance to pests and disease, and, ultimately, food security for humans.'[17]

The importance of genetic diversity is not confined to its direct values for humans and it is also an essential aspect of ecological processes. As crops evolved for agriculture over centuries they became diversified into countless 'landraces.'[18] These landraces form the second category of genetic resources and are part of traditional agricultural systems. They were adapted to varied environmental conditions, cropping systems, human uses and preferences. These traditional systems are an extension of natural ecosystems and, like the former, achieve sustainability and balance through genetic diversity, which enables them to constantly adapt to changing conditions. This function serves the purpose not only of maximizing yields but also of ensuring yield security.[19]

HUMAN CULTURAL DIVERSITY

The subject of cultural diversity is introduced into this chapter because it is closely linked with biodiversity, including PGRFA. Cultural diversity is measured by the attributes of human society including language, religious beliefs, land management practices, art, music, social structure, crop selection, diet and others.[20] Cultural diversity obviously does not pertain only to 'local, indigenous and traditional cultures and groups but must be understood and recognised as a dynamic source of exchange, creativity and innovation in any culture'[21] in both the developing and developed

---

17 *Peoples and Ecosystems*, above n 9, 14.

18 Landraces are 'a crop cultivar or animal breed that evolved with and has been genetically improved by traditional agriculturalists, but has not been influenced by modern breeding practices', *Global Biodiversity Assessment*, above n 15, 1112.

19 J J Hardon, 'Conservation and Use of Agro-Biodiversity' (1996) 3(3) *Biodiversity Letters* 92.

20 *Global Biodiversity Strategy*, above n 1, 3. See also UNEP/GC.22/INF/16 – United Nations Environment Programme, *Summary Report of the High-Level Roundtable on Cultural Diversity and Biodiversity for Sustainable Development* (20 December 2002); UNEP/GC.23/INF/23 – United Nations Environment Programme, *Report on the Implementation of Governing Council Decision 22/16 on Environment and Cultural Diversity* (2005) footnotes 14 and 15.

21 UNEP/GC.23/INF/23, above n 20, 7. See also *UNESCO Convention on the Protection and Promotion of the Diversity of Cultural Expressions*, CLT-2005/CONVENTION DIVERSITE-CULT REV 20 October 2005 – Article 4 for the definition of cultural diversity.

worlds.[22] However, a direct correlation between environment and cultural diversity has been identified in the tropical countries, which also have the highest concentrations of both biological and cultural diversity.[23]

A specific aspect of cultural diversity which is examined below is that of the traditional knowledge of communities and peoples located throughout the world which relates to the uses of plants for human benefit. The fact that this knowledge is sometimes utilized by those outside these communities, and commercial benefits derived from it, has become a contentious issue in the international debate on the conservation and sustainable use of biodiversity including agricultural diversity.

It is significant that the CBD has recognized the link between cultural diversity and biodiversity, noting 'the close and traditional dependence of many indigenous and local communities embodying traditional lifestyles

---

[22] The developing countries which are predominantly located in the southern hemisphere have been tagged with the term 'third world.' This term has been discussed in Karin Mickelson, 'Rhetoric and Rage: Third World Voices in International Legal Discourse' (1998) 16 *Wisconsin International Law Journal* 353. The author notes that '[i]n a purely descriptive sense, "Third World" is frequently used interchangeably with other terms such as "less-developed," "developing," or "underdeveloped" countries, and, increasingly, "the South." The referent are the countries of Africa, Asia, and Latin America that have traditionally been classified as lagging behind the "West," "North," "First World" or "developed countries" in terms of economic growth and indicators of economic prosperity' (at 356). The terms also refer to the countries which have been marginalized within the international community. From another perspective the term would refer to a political coalition of nations in pursuit of common goals. Such a grouping was formalized in the Non-aligned movement and the Group of 77. The author argues that this conceptualization is dubious as there is a growing diversity among these countries and they are often fractured politically. However, for the sake of clarity these terms will be used to refer to the countries which have a general common interest in protecting their PGRFA and traditional knowledge and which are predominantly, but not all, located in the southern hemisphere.

[23] UNEP/GC.23/INF/23, above n 20, 6. See also Darrell A Posey (ed), *Cultural and Spiritual Values of Biodiversity* (1999), Introduction (at 3) where it is noted that 'of the nine countries which together account for 60 percent of human languages, six of these centres of "cultural diversity" are also "megadiversity" countries with exceptional numbers of unique plant and animal species.' An example of the extent of cultural diversity which may be present within one nation (India) is provided by Shalini Bhutani and Ashish Kotari, 'The biodiversity rights of developing nations: A perspective from India' (2002) 32 *Golden Gate University Law Review* 587, 594. Jonathan Loh and David Harmon, 'A global index of biocultural diversity' (2005) 5(3) *Ecological Indicators* 231, where the authors identified Papua New Guinea, Indonesia, Cameroon and Columbia as the world's most biodiverse countries; Luisa Maffi, 'Diversity and the Spice of Life' (2002) 25(2) *ReVision* 19.

on biological resources,'[24] and acknowledging that the knowledge, innovations and practices of such communities are relevant for the conservation and sustainable use of biological diversity.[25] However, I will argue in this book that this recognition has not contributed positively to the current controversy over the equitable uses of either biodiversity or the traditional knowledge relating to it.

Traditional Ecological Knowledge

An aspect of cultural diversity which has been gaining increasing recognition is that of Traditional Ecological Knowledge (TEK) or Traditional Ecological Knowledge and Wisdom (TEKW). Modern western science is not the only source of information on biodiversity,[26] and it has been acknowledged that there is a separate store of such knowledge among traditional communities that have an intimate understanding of their immediate environment and its components. TEK has been defined as the knowledge and insights acquired through extensive observation of an area or a species. This may include knowledge passed down through oral traditions, or shared among users of a resource.[27]

The contemporary nature of the knowledge systems of indigenous and local communities has been emphasized by the United Nations Environment Programme (UNEP). It has noted that the term 'traditional knowledge' is problematic as it 'suggests that the body of knowledge concerned, being "traditional," is something of the past, is immutable, and passed on

---

[24] CBD, Preamble Paragraph 12.

[25] CBD, Article 8(j).

[26] However, one view is that the modern science of systematic biology which emerged from the practice of collecting and preserving representative specimens in biological collections remains the ultimate source of knowledge – Stephen Blackmore, 'Knowing the Earth's Biodiversity: Challenges for the Infrastructure of Systematic Biology' (1996) 274 (No 5284) *Science, New Series* 63.

[27] Henry P Huntington, 'Using Traditional Ecological Knowledge in Science: Methods and Applications' (2000) 10(5) *Ecological Applications* 1270. Posey (ed), above n 23, 4. See also Graham Dutfield, 'The Public and Private Domains: Intellectual Property Rights in Traditional Knowledge' (2000) 21 *Science Communication* 274; Jesse Ford and Dennis Martinez, 'Traditional Ecological Knowledge, Ecosystem Science, and Environmental Management' (2000) 10(5) *Ecological Applications* 1249; Francesco Mauro and Preston D Hardison, 'Traditional Ecological Knowledge Traditional Knowledge of Indigenous and Local Communities: International Debate and Policy Initiatives' (2000) 10(5) *Ecological Applications* 1263; Fikret Berkes, Johan Colding and Carl Folke, 'Traditional Ecological Knowledge – Rediscovery of Traditional Ecological Knowledge as Adaptive Management' (2000) 10(5) *Ecological Applications* 1251.

from generation to generation with little or no change.' It notes that on the contrary, the knowledge is clearly contemporary and dynamic and 'subject to a continuous cultural process of adaptation and development and therefore constantly evolving through experimentation and innovation, fresh insight and external stimuli.'[28] However, since it is the term in most common usage it will be used in this book within the meaning as discussed in this section.

The term 'traditional biocultural knowledge' is also in popular use and has been defined as the 'knowledge of the medicinal or other practical uses of plants and animals.'[29] Holders of traditional biocultural knowledge include shamans, healers, bone-setters, midwives, herbalists, and farmers. Farmers are the holders of another subset of traditional knowledge, namely traditional agricultural knowledge. The difference between crop and natural evolution is that the former is controlled by conscious selection. 'Conscious selection implies knowledge systems about the crop and its environment, which are subsets of the more general traditional knowledge and indigenous knowledge.'[30]

The marginalization of communities holding this repository of knowledge and the disinclination on the part of western scientists to acknowledge it as a source of information is often an obstacle to bridging the gap between the two systems. Nevertheless scientists based in industrialized countries are increasingly relying on it for information in many areas, including knowledge regarding crop genetic resources, the medicinal properties of plant species, and the conservation of biological resources.[31]

---

[28] UNEP/GC.23/INF/23, above n 20, 10.

[29] Craig D Jacoby and Charles Weiss, 'Recognizing Property Rights in Traditional Biocultural Contribution' (1997) 16 *Stanford Environmental Law Journal* 74.

[30] Stephen B Brush, 'The Demise of "Common Heritage" and Protection for Traditional Agricultural Knowledge' in Charles McManis (ed), *Biodiversity and the law: intellectual property, biotechnology and traditional knowledge* (2007) Chapter 20. Another term which has been coined is 'traditional knowledge of the uses of plants' (TKUP) – Ikechi Mgbeoji, *Global Biopiracy – Patents, Plants and Indigenous Knowledge*, (2006). See also UNEP/CBD/WG8J/3/INF/4 – Ad Hoc Open-Ended Inter-Sessional Working Group on Article 8(J) and Related Provisions of the Convention on Biological Diversity, Third Meeting, 8–12 December 2003, Composite Report on the Status and Trends Regarding the Knowledge, Innovations and Practices of Indigenous and Local Communities – Regional Report: Australia, Asia and the Middle East, 26.

[31] Stephen B Brush, 'Indigenous Knowledge of Biological Resources and Intellectual Property Rights: The Role of Anthropology' (1993) 95(3) *American Anthropologist, New Series* 653.

The relationship between biological and cultural diversity was first acknowledged at the Earth Summit in 1992. The Rio Declaration,[32] the Earth Charter[33] and Agenda 21[34] refer to it rather obliquely, while the CBD does so in more explicit terms.[35] Since then, the question of conserving and protecting such knowledge from unrestricted use and exploitation by others has been taken up in various international fora and this issue will be further explored in this book.

PLANT GENETIC RESOURCES FOR FOOD AND AGRICULTURE (PGRFA)

While the CBD deals with all three aspects of biological diversity, this book focuses on a specific element of genetic diversity, namely plant genetic resources for food and agriculture (PGRFA). PGRFA constitute a component of agricultural biodiversity or agro-biodiversity and has been defined as:

> that part of biodiversity that feeds and nurtures people. It includes genetic resources for food and agriculture, such as harvested crop varieties, livestock breeds, fish species and non-domesticated resources within field, forest, rangeland and in aquatic ecosystems. It also refers to activities in the fields of agriculture, animal husbandry, aquaculture and agroforestry including pests, microbial resources and the management of agro-ecosystems, wildlife and protected areas. Agro-biodiversity exists because of the wide range of varying climates, habitats and farming practices found within the centres of diversity and the natural selection caused by the presence of different pests and diseases.[36]

---

[32] *Rio Declaration on Environment and Development*, 31 ILM 876.

[33] For a history of the Earth Charter see http://www.earthcharterinaction.org/content/pages/What-is-the-Earth-Charter%3F.html (last accessed 6 July 2012).

[34] Agenda 21, UN Conference on Environment and Development, UN Doc.A/CONF.151/26/Rev.1 (1992).

[35] CBD, Articles 8 (j) and 10 (c).

[36] A P Kameri-Mbote and P Cullet, 'Agro-biodiversity and International Law – a Conceptual Framework' (1999) 11(2) *Journal of Environmental Law* 257, 259. See also Lori Ann Thrupp, 'Linking Agricultural Biodiversity and Food Security: the Valuable Role of Agrobiodiversity for Sustainable Agriculture' (2000) 76(2) *International Affairs* 283. The CBD has identified the features of agricultural biodiversity – CBD/UNEP – *Handbook on the Convention on Biological Diversity* (3rd ed 2005), 584 (hereinafter *CBD Handbook*). See also UNEP/CBD/SBSTTA/13/2 – Subsidiary Body on Scientific, Technical and Technological Advice, Thirteenth Meeting, 18–22 February 2008, *In-Depth Review of the Implementation of the Programme of Work on Agricultural Biodiversity*, 26 November 2007, 7.

PGRFA as a component of agrobiodiversity:

> comprise the diversity of genetic material contained in traditional varieties and modern cultivars, as well as crop wild relatives and other wild plant species that can be used now or in the future for food and agriculture.[37]

Agricultural biodiversity therefore encompasses all levels of biodiversity – ecosystem, species, and genetic – and this book focuses on the third element. However, the terms 'PGRFA' and 'agricultural biodiversity' have been used interchangeably in the literature and where used in this book will indicate the former.

PGRFA comprise wild species of plants as well as cultivated varieties. Wild species are important both as a source of food in themselves, but also as the natural resource base from which other species are developed and improved upon.[38] Cultivated species are broadly classified into 'modern varieties' and 'farmers' varieties.' Modern varieties are the products of 'formal' or 'scientific' systems of plant breeding, usually conducted by private companies or publicly funded research institutes. While these varieties are often 'high yielding varieties' (HYVs), they also typically have a high degree of genetic uniformity.[39]

Traditional or farmers' varieties (or 'landraces') have evolved over centuries of selection and breeding carried out by farmers, either deliberately or not. They have a high level of genetic diversity and are therefore the focus of conservation efforts. They are also often difficult to define precisely or to distinguish as a particular variety. These different characteristics of 'modern' and 'traditional' crop varieties have given rise to disputes in regard to the legal recognition which should be accorded to them in the national and international spheres, and this will be explored further in this book.

The Values of PGRFA

The values of PGRFA are multiple, and the fact that they are a fundamental necessity for food security and human survival need hardly be stated. Much of the potential benefits of biological resources that may be derived for food

---

[37] Food and Agriculture Organization, *The State of the World's Plant Genetic Resources for Food and Agriculture* (1998) 33 (hereinafter *State of the World's PGRFA*) Chapter 1. For a discussion on the links between agriculture and biodiversity see United Nations Environment Programme, *Global Environmental Outlook 4* (2007), 171.

[38] *State of the World's PGRFA*, above n 37, Chapter 1.

[39] Ibid.

production have yet to be exploited. It has been estimated that there are about 300,000 to 500,000 species of higher plants of which about 30,000 are edible. Approximately 7,000 plants have been cultivated or collected for food by humans at some point in history. Of the latter, 20 species provide 90 per cent of the world's food, and three, namely, wheat, maize and rice, supply more than half.[40] Crop plants also have a direct monetary value, as can be seen for example from the fact that agricultural yields in the United States have increased by an estimated value of $1 billion in 50 years as a result of plant breeding and a broader genetic base.[41]

PGRFA are also an intrinsic aspect of human cultures. There is often a nexus between the agricultural practices of traditional societies and their cultural and religious practices.[42] There is, for example, an interconnection between the diversity of PGRFA and traditional food systems among particular communities and in particular locations. Vandana Shiva has observed that '[t]he diversity of soils, climates and plants has contributed to a diversity of food cultures across the world,' and cites the maize-based food systems of Central America, the rice-based Asian systems, the teff-based Ethiopian diet and the millet-based foods of Africa as examples. She notes that in India, a country rich in biodiversity and cultural diversity, people in the arid and semi arid areas of the west live on millets, while eastern India has a rice- and fish-based food culture. Each region also has its specific edible oil.[43] Food diversity and biodiversity thus mutually reinforce each other.

Diversity of PGRFA

While the number of species used in agriculture is small, the diversity within them is extensive. It has been estimated that the number of distinct varieties of the rice species, *Oryza sativa*, may range from thousands of varieties to over 100,000. Similar variations are found in many other

---

[40] Edward O Wilson, *The Diversity of Life*, (1992), 287.

[41] *Global Biodiversity Strategy*, above n 1, 5.

[42] June Starr and Kenneth C Hardy, 'Not by Seeds Alone: the Biodiversity Treaty and the Role for Native Agriculture' (1993) 12 *Stanford Environmental Law Journal* 85, 120. For a discussion of cultural beliefs and practices related to bioresources in Sri Lanka see FAO, Bangkok (Thailand) Regional Office for Asia and the Pacific; MS Swaminathan Research Foundation, Chennai (India) *Sri Lankan Women and Men as Bioresource Managers* (1999) Chapter 6, available at http://www.fao.org/DOCREP/005/AC791E/AC791E00.htm#TOC (last accessed 6 July 2012).

[43] Vandana Shiva, *Stolen Harvest – The Hijacking of the Global Food Supply* (2000).

different crops, such as over 200 varieties of sweet potato which have been identified in the Philippines, and the thousands of varieties of potatoes in the Andes.[44]

Genetic diversity contributes to sustainable agriculture in three ways. First, it provides stability for farming systems by maintaining a range of diversity of crops. Therefore losses caused by the failure of one crop can be made up by the yields of others. Second, genetic diversity provides an option value against future adverse conditions by characteristics which could be adapted to, for example, changing climatic conditions or blights. Over centuries, farmers have tapped the genetic diversity in plants to breed new varieties which increase yields and adapt to external conditions such as drought, salinity or pests. The current threats to global food security brought about by climate change have reinforced the importance of making effective use of plant genetic diversity to maintain agricultural productivity and farmers' livelihoods. Third, such diversity potentially constitutes a repository of unknown resources of use to humanity. The UN Food and Agriculture Organization (FAO) notes that '[t]his is the reason for maintaining both wild ecosystems and traditional farming systems, as plants in these habitats are likely to contain and develop new and valuable genetic characteristics.'[45]

Genetic diversity of PGRFA is of particular importance to small farmers in developing countries. Such farmers often operate in poor natural conditions and are generally unable to afford inputs such as pesticides and fertilizers which are required by the modern varieties. Farmers' varieties are also adapted to difficult environmental conditions, and using a range of crop varieties spreads the risk of crop failure. The FAO has noted that 'farming systems based on diversity also provide a range of products with multiple uses, including varied food and other products,' and that '[f]armers also often use intercropping and agroforestry techniques that employ mixtures of species with complementary requirements, such as cereals with pulses.'[46] Therefore the loss of genetic diversity in PGRFA will have particular impacts on agriculture in developing countries and this is one of the issues which has been raised in the current debate on these resources.

Genetic diversity of PGRFA is also important in modern varieties of crops which have been bred by using the diversity in farmers' landraces, as well as wild species. Landraces have provided individual traits that have been introduced into existing varieties. These in turn have contributed

---

[44] *State of the World's PGRFA,* above n 37, Chapter 1; *Global Biodiversity Strategy*, above n 1, 4.

[45] *State of the World's PGRFA,* above n 37, Chapter 1.

[46] Ibid.

immensely to the commercial value of crop genetic resources and the FAO estimates that the annual turnover of the commercial seed industry in OECD countries is $13 billion.[47]

Location of PGRFA

PGRFA is found both *in situ* and *ex situ*.[48] The CBD has acknowledged that:

> the fundamental requirement for the conservation of biological diversity is the in-situ conservation of ecosystems and natural habitats and the maintenance and recovery of viable populations of species in their natural surroundings.[49]

Most major agricultural crops were domesticated for thousands of years in developing countries, and, historically most genetic diversity was located in them.[50] While *in situ* conservation is obviously the preferable means of maintaining plant genetic diversity, many factors including habitat loss and the increasing uniformity of cultivated crops has reduced the natural diversity of such resources in these locations. Consequently it has become necessary to also ensure that such diversity is maintained *ex situ.*

Ex Situ Collections of PGRFA

Ex situ conservation refers to the conservation of seeds, plants, microbes and other forms of life held outside their natural habitat.[51] Plant collection, transportation and storage in countries other than those of origin had been

---

[47] Ibid.

[48] CBD, Articles 2, 8 and 9.

[49] CBD, Preamble.

[50] There are different theories regarding the identification of centres/areas of diversity. See CGRFA – Background Study Paper No. 12 – *Crops Proposed For the Multilateral System: Centres of Diversity, Locations of Ex Situ Collections, and Major Producing Countries* (2001). See also *State of the World's PGRFA,* above n 37, 20; Cary Fowler, Melinda Smale and Samy Gaiji, 'Unequal Exchange? Recent Transfers of Agricultural Resources and their Implications for Developing Countries' (2001) 19(2) *Development Policy Review* 181; Stephen B Brush, 'Protecting Traditional Agricultural Knowledge' (2005) 17 *Washington University Journal of Law & Policy* 59. For a definition of centres of diversity and centres of origin see the Preamble of the International Treaty on Plant Genetic Resources for Food and Agriculture, adopted at the 31st Session of the FAO Conference on 3 November 2001.

[51] UNEP/CBD/ISOC/4 – Inter Sessional Meeting on the Operations of the Convention, 28–30 June 1999, *Report on the Information on Ex-Situ Collections in Accordance with Decisions IV/8,* 12 May 1999.

carried on for centuries, but the amassing of genetic resources *ex situ* accelerated significantly from the 16th to the 19th centuries, in the period of European colonial expansion. Another period of extensive collection took place in the latter half of the 20th century. Most material stored *ex situ* today was collected during the 1970s and 1980s from developing countries.[52] It has been noted that while the original accumulation was that of species, modern biotechnology has shifted the focus of interest to the genes necessary for breeding new varieties of crops.[53]

International initiatives to systematically collect and conserve PGRFA began in the 1940s and have been carried forward primarily by the FAO. The FAO was established in 1945 as a specialized agency of the United Nations. Its mandate is to 'raise levels of nutrition, improve agricultural productivity, better the lives of rural populations and contribute to the growth of the world economy.'[54] Fowler and Hodgkin record that its work on PGRFA was initiated in the light of the concern which was raised over the conservation, exchange and utilization of these resources. In 1962 the FAO established a Panel of Experts on Plant Exploration and convened international technical conferences on this issue in 1967, 1973, 1981 and 1996. The early conferences recommended the establishment of a global network of genebanks.[55] Although there was an intensification in PGRFA activity in the 1970s, this was done mainly through national genebanks and botanic gardens, sidestepping the FAO and the UN framework. It was only in the 1980s that the FAO assumed the initiative for plant collection.[56] The International Plant Genetic Resources Institute (IPGRI)[57] had the mandate for co-ordinating the global process to collect and conserve PGRFA.[58]

Conservation off site is now carried out by almost every country in the world, and PGRFA are being increasingly stored in collections maintained by various types of institutions – international, regional, national and private. Large collections are located in the International Agricultural

---

[52] Fowler, Smale and Gaiji, above n 50, 186.

[53] Ibid at 182; Cary Fowler and Toby Hodgkin, 'Plant Genetic Resources for Food and Agriculture: Assessing Global Availability' (2004) 29 *Annual Review of Environment & Resources* 143.

[54] See http://www.fao.org/about/en/ (last accessed 6 July 2012).

[55] Fowler and Hodgkin, above n 53, 151.

[56] Gregory Rose, 'International Law of Sustainable Agriculture in the 21st Century: The International Treaty on Plant Genetic Resources for Food and Agriculture' (2003) 15 *Georgetown International Environmental Law Review* 583, 587.

[57] Originally the International Board for Plant Genetic Resources (IBPGR) established in 1974.

[58] Fowler and Hodgkin, above n 53, 151.

Research Centres (IARCs) of the Consultative Group on International Agricultural Research (CGIAR).[59] In addition, many countries have networks of genebanks which can have either a national or local focus.[60] A significant collection of germplasm[61] is also held by the network of private breeders who use plant genetic resources as the raw material for their work. In some instances these collections are more representative than those of public institutions.[62]

There are more than 1,750 genebanks throughout the world located in all continents. Of these, the majority are in North America and Europe, while Asia, Latin America and the Caribbean and Africa also have significant collections. Botanical gardens also comprise important repositories of germplasm. The majority (61 per cent) are located in Europe, the US and the countries of the former Soviet Union. About 11 per cent are privately owned. Worldwide, 47 per cent of botanical gardens can be considered to have germplasm collections. About 75 per cent of the germplasm conserved in botanical gardens is in North America and Europe.[63] The total number of accessions conserved worldwide has increased significantly in the last decade or so, reaching around 7.4 million.[64]

---

[59] The CGIAR was created in 1971 and describes itself as an informal association of public and private sector CGIAR Members from the South and North. It is jointly sponsored by FAO, the International Bank for Reconstruction and Development (World Bank), the International Fund for Agricultural Development (IFAD) and the United Nations Development Programme (UNDP). Its activities are closely focused on enhancing agricultural productivity, and ensuring food security and poverty alleviation in developing countries. See Consultative Group on International Agricultural Research (CGIAR) – The Charter of the CGIAR System, 8 November 2004 and http://www.cgiar.org/who-we-are/history-of-cgiar/ (last accessed 6 July 2012).

[60] UNEP/CBD/ISOC/4, above n 51. For a discussion on the role and functions of genebanks see Nigel J H Smith, 'Genebanks: A Global Payoff' (1987) 39(1) *Professional Geographer* 1.

[61] Germplasm 'refers to seeds, plants or plant parts that are useful in crop breeding, research or conservation because of their genetic attributes' – Fowler, Smale and Gaiji, above n 50, footnote 2.

[62] UNEP/CBD/ISOC/4, above n 51, paragraph 11. There is very little information regarding these collections and the report notes that private breeders were not contacted to obtain it.

[63] *State of the World's PGRFA,* above n 37, 126.

[64] Commission on Genetic Resources for Food and Agriculture, *The Second Report on the State of the World's Plant Genetic Resources for Food and Agriculture*, (2010), xix.

In view of estimates that there is now greater genetic diversity in *ex situ* collections than *in situ*,[65] their importance to national economies and food security cannot be underestimated. The FAO Global Plan of Action[66] had recognized the importance of networks of *ex situ* collections of PGRFA, and its objectives under this section include developing and strengthening national, regional and international networks and ensuring the free flow of germplasm globally. These networks fall into two broad categories – the *Ex situ* Network under the auspices of FAO and other international networks.

The International Network of *Ex Situ* Collections under the Auspices of FAO

In 1989, the Commission on Genetic Resources for Food and Agriculture (CGRFA) called for the development of the FAO International Network, the reason cited being 'the uncertainty of the legal situation of *ex situ* germplasm in genebanks, and of the lack of appropriate agreements to ensure its safe conservation.'[67] Probably the most important collections of the Network are those of the IARCs maintained by the CGIAR. In 1994, 12 of these centres entered into a series of agreements with FAO whereby they placed around 500,000 accessions in the International Network.[68] Through these agreements, the centres decided to hold the designated germplasm 'in trust for the benefit of the international community' and 'not to claim ownership,

---

[65] Fowler, Smale and Gaiji, above n 50, 187.

[66] *Global Plan of Action for the Conservation and Sustainable Utilization of Plant Genetic Resources for Food and Agriculture and the Leipzig Declaration* adopted by the International Technical Conference on Plant Genetic Resources, 17–23 June 1996 – Action 16 and paragraphs 7 and 10.

[67] The Commission on Genetic Resources for Food and Agriculture (CGRFA) is a permanent intergovernmental forum where matters relevant to genetic resources for food and agriculture are discussed. It was originally established in 1983 as the Commission on Plant Genetic Resources (CPGR) by the FAO Conference, (Resolution 9/83) to deal with plant genetic resources. In 1995 it was renamed the CGRFA and by Resolution 3/95 its mandate was broadened to cover all components of agro-biodiversity of relevance to food and agriculture. The European Union and 175 countries are members at present. See the website at http://www.fao.org/nr/cgrfa/cgrfa-home/en/ (last accessed 6 July 2012). See also CGRFA-11/07/Inf.2 – CGRFA, Eleventh Regular Session, 11–15 June 2007, *Statutes of the Commission on Genetic Resources for Food and Agriculture.*

[68] CGRFA-9/02/11 – CGRFA, Ninth Regular Session, 14–18 October 2002, *Report on the International Network of Ex Situ Collections Under the Auspices of FAO*, paragraphs 2–3. See also CGRFA-10/04/6 – CGRFA, Tenth Regular Session, 8–12 November 2004, *Report on the International Network of Ex situ Collections under the Auspices of FAO*, Part 1.

or seek intellectual property rights, over the designated germplasm and related information.' The collection of the International Coconut Genetic Resources Network (COGENT), held by the governments of India, Indonesia and Cote d'Ivoire was subsequently brought into the Network in 1998.[69]

Other International Networks of *Ex Situ* Collections of PGRFA

There are other *ex situ* collections of PGRFA that are not part of the FAO network.[70] These are held in seed genebanks, field genebanks and in vitro collections.[71] A report prepared by Botanic Gardens Conservation International[72] estimates that there are 2,178 botanic gardens throughout the world in 153 countries. They contain a total of 42 million herbarium specimens in botanic garden herbaria and 6.13 million accessions in their living collections. While the majority of botanic gardens are in the developed countries of Europe and North America, significant numbers are also found in developing and tropical countries. Several national collections have been placed within the FAO system and other collections have voluntarily developed principles and guidelines to facilitate access and benefit sharing of their holdings.[73] Many of the significant botanic gardens throughout the world have joined in an initiative to develop a harmonized set of principles in this regard, which include those on best practices on acquisition of such resources.[74] These principles and common policy guidelines will be applicable, where possible, to collections acquired both

---

69 CGRFA-10/04/3 – CGRFA, Tenth Regular Session, 8–12 November 2004, *Overview of the FAO Global System for the Conservation and Sustainable Utilization of Plant Genetic Resources for Food and Agriculture and its Potential Contribution to the Implementation of the International Treaty on Plant Genetic Resources for Food and Agriculture*, paragraphs 15–20.

70 *CBD Handbook*, above n 36, 194. By Decision V/26 C the Conference of the Parties of the CBD had decided to call for information on these collections – *CBD Handbook*, 681.

71 *State of the World's PGRFA,* above n 37, 84.

72 *An International Review of the Ex Situ Plant Collections of the Botanic Gardens of the World: Reviewing the Plant Genetic Resource Collections of Botanic Gardens Worldwide, as a contribution to Decision V/26 on Access to Genetic Resources of the Conference of the Parties to the Convention on Biological Diversity*, available at http://www.biodiv.org./doc/ref/bot-gard-overview.pdf (last accessed 6 July 2012).

73 For an overview of networks see CGRFA – Background Study Paper No 16, Electra Kalaugher and Bert Visser, *A Summary and Analysis of Existing International Plant Genetic Resources Networks* (date not available).

74 *Principles on Access to Genetic Resources and Benefit-sharing for Participating Institutions and Explanatory Text*, document available at http://

before and after the CBD came into force.[75] However, private collections which constitute a significant proportion of material may still exclude themselves.[76]

Together with the shifting of crop diversity from *in situ* to *ex situ* conditions, the flow of crops between developed and developing countries has also become more multi-directional. The FAO International Network and the voluntary placing of accessions in international networks have ensured a certain degree of accessibility to these collections, including by developing countries. In fact, it has been pointed out that developing countries have received more genetic materials than they have contributed to the centres, and an open access system of germplasm flows will materially benefit them.[77] Fowler et al note that while historical transfers were mainly directed at crop introduction, recent flows of PGRFA have been for the purpose of crop improvement.[78] Therefore unimpeded access to these resources is crucial to maintain both food security and crop diversity in all countries.

Loss of Agricultural Diversity

The CBD has noted the loss of agroecosystem diversity, observing that farming system level diversity is particularly important to small farmers for food and economic security. It observes that '[t]he adoption of modern farming systems has often resulted in the reduction of species, activities and landscape features within the agroecosystem.' The consequences of such

---

www.bgci.org/resources/abs_principles (last accessed 6 July 2012). The participants were from 28 botanic gardens from 21 developing and developed countries.

[75] The reason for developing these guidelines is also pragmatic. As pointed out in the Explanatory Text the reasons why botanical institutions should bring themselves in line with the CBD include: continuing to access and exchanging materials, to build partnerships and to attract funding – paragraph 2.1. It should also be noted that these principles are not legally binding. See also UNEP/CBD/WG-ABS/1/INF/1 – Ad Hoc Open-Ended Working Group on Access and Benefit-Sharing, First meeting, 22–26 October 2001, *Results of the Pilot Project for Botanic Gardens: Principles on Access to Genetic Resources and Benefit-Sharing, Common Policy Guidelines to Assist with their Implementation and Explanatory Text*, 12 September 2001.

[76] For a brief overview of networks see Gerald Moore and Witold Tymowski, *Explanatory Guide to the International Treaty on Plant Genetic Resources for Food and Agriculture* (2005) 129. See also *State of the World's PGRFA*, above n 37, Chapters 3 and 4.

[77] Fowler, Smale and Gaiji, above n 50.

[78] Ibid at 182.

loss include the loss of crop species and the opportunities for continued selection by farmers, the loss of biological diversity in agricultural soils and the erosion of the diversity of insects, potentially leading to pest resurgence.[79]

'Genetic erosion' is defined as the loss of genetic diversity including both individual genes and particular combinations of genes, as for instance those in locally bred landraces.[80] Since the data on the genetic diversity of wild species is scarce, it is difficult to estimate the loss, though studies have revealed that there is a decline.[81] The decline of genetic diversity in cultivated species has however, been established, and while there are several reasons for this, the overwhelming cause is the substitution of improved and exotic crops in place of traditional, locally developed varieties.[82] Since the 1960s traditional crops planted by farmers globally have been replaced by more 'modern' varieties, developed through formal breeding systems.[83] Many of these varieties were adopted in the context of the 'Green Revolution.'[84] These crops are often based upon genetic uniformity derived from 'elite germplasm' rather than on genetic diversity.[85] It has been noted that

---

79 UNEP/CBD/SBSTTA/2/10 – Subsidiary Body on Scientific, Technical and Technological Advice, Second Meeting, 2–6 September 1996, Agricultural Biological Diversity, 12 August 1996, 12–14.

80 *State of the World's PGRFA,* above n 37, 33.

81 *Millennium Ecosystem Assessment*, above n 7, 4.

82 *State of the World's PGRFA,* above n 37, 34.

83 About 80 per cent of wheat area in developing countries and 75 per cent of rice in Asia are now planted with the modern varieties. The loss of diversity can be seen in the example of Sri Lanka, where more than 2,000 varieties of rice were found in 1959, but only five major varieties in the 1980s – *Peoples and Ecosystems*, above n 9, 14. See also FAO, Bangkok (Thailand) Regional Office for Asia and the Pacific; M S Swaminathan Research Foundation, Chennai (India) *Sri Lankan Women and Men as Bioresource Managers* (1999) Chapter 5, available at http://www.fao.org/DOCREP/005/AC791E/AC791E00.htm#TOC (last accessed 6 July 2012). Similarly, around 1,500 local rice varieties have become extinct in Indonesia – *Global Biodiversity Strategy*, above n 1, 9.

84 *Global Biodiversity Strategy*, above n 1, 9. The environmental, economic and other impacts of the Green Revolution will be discussed further in Chapter 3.

85 Genetic uniformity is based on crops that have (1) rapid and uniform germination of seeds, (2) nearly simultaneous flowering (3) nearly simultaneous maturation of harvest, (4) stature that promotes mechanical harvest, (5) product uniformity for taste and chemical composition, and (6) year-to-year stability of yield – *Global Biodiversity Assessment*, above n 15, 949.

while uniformity per se is not necessarily dangerous, the hazards of planting large areas with a genetically uniform crop variety must be recognized.[86]

Crop diversity is being increasingly threatened by global climate change. Farmers have to contend with unpredictable weather patterns, drought and floods and a new emergence of pests and disease. This will in turn affect their livelihoods as well as national food and nutrition security. Conversely, climate change adaptation in agriculture is founded on crop diversity, where heterogeneous varieties can be used in changing climatic conditions. In this context the importance of maintaining the genetic diversity of food crops and access to the traditional landraces bred by farmers takes on a greater urgency.

The loss of biodiversity and the loss of cultural diversity are interconnected and the loss of the latter is taking place at significant levels. Cultural diversity has contributed to the diversity of crops, livestock and habitats, and consequently the loss of this diversity can lead to the extinction of species.[87] As discussed above, an important aspect of cultural diversity is the traditional ecological knowledge and wisdom which has been accumulated over a period of over 300,000 years in the search for plant-based food and medicine.[88] The extinction of cultures, and the languages they represent, will necessarily result in the permanent loss of this knowledge base.[89]

The concurrent loss of cultural and biological diversity will have adverse impacts on peoples and communities. A UNEP report has noted that:

> the loss of biological diversity, weakening of cultural diversity and the poverty phenomenon, which have been dealt with separately, are in fact closely connected. Dealing with this requires a holistic and more comprehensive approach for action at all levels, including the respect for culturally diverse societies.[90]

These negative impacts will not be confined to those who possess such diversity, but will also constitute a loss to humanity as a whole. This is

---

[86] *State of the World's PGRFA,* above n 37, 30. For example the Report notes that in European barley, protection against mildew depends on one gene and one fungicide and mutation of the pathogen could destroy this resistance in a 'single evolutionary step.' See also *Global Biodiversity Strategy*, above n 1, 9 for examples of the impacts on crops of genetic diversity loss.

[87] *Global Biodiversity Strategy*, above n 1, 11.

[88] Arturo Gome-Pampa, 'The Role of Biodiversity Scientists in a Troubled World' (2004) 54(3) *BioScience* 217, 220.

[89] For example, it is estimated that almost half of the world's 6,000 languages may die out in the next century. Of the remainder nearly half will probably not last much longer – *Global Biodiversity Strategy*, above n 1, 11.

[90] UNEP/GC.23/INF/23, above n 20, 8.

particularly so in the case of the traditional ecological knowledge held by communities which relate to PGRFA, as well as to other uses of biodiversity. The value of this knowledge to humans has been acknowledged by the CBD in Article 8(j) which promotes the sharing of the benefits arising from it.[91] The fact that this knowledge is being appropriated for commercial gain is a further indication of its value and is one of the contentious issues in the debate on PGRFA.

Issues of Equity in Regard to PGRFA

No country in the world is self sufficient in PGRFA and there is a high level of interdependence among them in regard to these resources. Both developed and developing countries have come to rely heavily on non-indigenous crops to meet their food needs. North America is completely dependent on species from other parts of the world for its major food and industrial crops, while sub-Saharan Africa is estimated to be 87 per cent dependent.[92] Farmers in most countries are dependent on modern improved varieties of crops including rice, wheat and maize. Studies show that in Asia 67 per cent of the rice, 88 per cent of the wheat and 45 per cent of the maize areas are planted with modern varieties. The corresponding figures for Latin America are 58 per cent of the rice, 68 per cent of the wheat and 46 per cent of the maize areas being planted with these varieties. It has been noted that '[a]t one time, a single rice variety, IR36, accounted for 10 per cent of the world's rice area, occupying more than 11 million hectares in its heyday, and selections from a single wheat cross at the International Maize and Wheat Improvement Center (CIMMYT) accounted for one seventh of the area sown to wheat in developing countries.'[93]

Given this interdependence on crop plants, it is essential that the free movement of these resources is maintained. Notwithstanding the fact that there is a certain degree of accessibility to plant germplasm in *ex situ* collections, controversies still remain in regard to the equitable distribution of new varieties. The outflow of crop varieties from the old to the new world during the period of colonial expansion, and then from developing to developed countries in the latter part of the 20th century, was made possible

---

[91] This Article refers to the 'knowledge, innovations and practices of indigenous and local communities embodying traditional lifestyles relevant for the conservation and sustainable use of biological diversity.'

[92] *State of the World's PGRFA*, above n 37, 22. See also CGRFA – Background Study Paper No 7 Rev 1, Ximena Flores Palacios, *Estimation of Countries' Interdependence in the Area of Plant Genetic Resources* (date not available).

[93] Fowler and Hodgkin, above n 53, 147.

in part by the fact that they were in the public domain and access to them was unrestricted. Many modern varieties of crops have been developed using these traditional varieties as a base and they are now in widespread use in all countries.

The inequity in regard to access to and the use of crop plants is alleged to arise from the fact that while the original varieties were freely accessed, property rights are now being claimed over the modern varieties, which are then being marketed in the countries of origin by corporate entities located in technologically developed countries. The expanding use of these varieties has resulted in greater dependence upon them and consequently monopolistic control over them by a few entities would have potential negative consequences on food security, particularly in developing countries. On the other hand, the increased use of these modern varieties to the exclusion of traditional landraces gives rise to the fear that diversity in crop plants will diminish over time. This possibility assumes greater significance in the current scenario of the potential impacts of climate change on agriculture where agrobiodiversity will be a crucial factor in adaptation measures and maintaining resilience in the face of environmental stress.

The impacts of crop diversity loss on farmers and traditional communities have also been identified as a related concern which will be discussed further. This scenario has resulted in calls (mainly from developing countries) for a more equitable system of access to and distribution of these resources. However, as will be argued in this book, international law has put in place a mechanism that facilitates the appropriation and control of crop plants and enables the application of property rights over them by entities engaged in biotechnological processes and agribusiness. The current international debate on PGRFA therefore centres around strategies to counteract this position, and this book will analyze the extent to which this has succeeded.

3. The uses of biological resources

INTRODUCTION

In this chapter I will examine the means by which plant genetic resources for food and agriculture have been utilized for human benefit, focusing on biotechnology and its significance for plant diversity, including PGRFA. Biotechnology is the enabling factor in developing new crop varieties in a relatively short space of time and with specific, desired characteristics. It has also provided the means by which physical control of these varieties can be ensured, supported by the necessary legal framework. These factors have, to a large extent, contributed to the current conflict over the acquisition and subsequent propertization of the natural resources that often form the raw material of this technology.

I will provide a background to these developments, placing in context the use of biotechnology in regard to PGRFA. I will also consider the past impacts of agricultural biotechnology on developing countries (citing the Green Revolution as an illustration), in order to explain the current concerns regarding possible future impacts in this area, which include the methods by which the raw material for this technology is appropriated and the consequent implications for developing countries. This will provide the context for the debate on PGRFA in international fora.

THE DEVELOPMENT OF BIOTECHNOLOGY

Throughout human history people have exploited and used the earth's natural resources for survival and sustenance. In the process they have also adapted and modified many naturally occurring species to produce new varieties of plants and livestock, primarily for agriculture.[1] Traditionally, this process was conducted by trial and error, over a period of time. In the past 50 years or so, due to modern scientific techniques and novel technological developments, the intensity, speed, and accuracy of this process

[1] Bongo Adi, 'Intellectual Property Rights in Biotechnology and the Fate of Poor Farmers' Agriculture' (2006) 9 (1) *Journal of World Intellectual Property* 91.

have increased to extraordinary levels. Consequently, the modifications that can be made to natural species and the uses to which they can be put have also increased.

These developments are largely due to the use of modern biotechnology. Biotechnology has been defined in the Convention on Biological Diversity (CBD) as 'any technological application that uses biological systems, living organisms, or derivatives thereof, to make or modify products or processes for specific use.'[2]

On a broad interpretation of this definition it is obvious that biotechnology has in fact been carried on for centuries for many purposes, including the improvement of domesticated plants and animals, breeding, utilizing micro-organisms in processing food and drink, control of disease by inoculation and the biological control of pests.[3] While the traditional methods involved human intervention within essentially natural processes and environments, modern biotechnology is usually conducted in laboratories and often involves changes in natural species that may not take place in the normal course of events.[4]

It has been noted that biotechnology differs from other technologies in three ways. First, it is not defined by products or services. Rather, it is a means of production for already existing industries by the 'use of microbial, animal, or plant cells or enzymes to synthesize, breakdown or transform

---

[2] *Convention on Biological Diversity* (1992) 31 ILM 818 – Article 2 (hereinafter CBD). The Cartagena Protocol provides a more specific definition of 'modern biotechnology' as meaning the application of '(a) In vitro nucleic acid techniques, including recombinant deoxyribonucleic acid (DNA) and direct injection of nucleic acid into cells or organelles, or (b) Fusion of cells beyond the taxonomic family' – *Cartagena Protocol on Biosafety to the Convention on Biological Diversity,* 29 January 2000, 39 ILM 1027.

[3] United Nations Environment Programme, *Global Biodiversity Assessment* (1995), 677 (hereinafter *Global Biodiversity Assessment*).

[4] Dutfield classifies biotechnology into three generations: the first included traditional technologies such as beer brewing and bread making which goes back centuries. The second begins with the microbiological applications developed by Louis Pasteur, including the mass production by fermentation of antibiotics, tissue culture and modern plant and animal breeding. The third generation includes the various genetic engineering techniques for transferring one life form to another to create new transgenic organisms with specific and useful traits – Graham Dutfield, *Intellectual Property, Biogenetic Resources and Traditional Knowledge* (2004), Chapter 2.

materials.'[5] Biotechnology can therefore be utilized commercially in products and processes in a wide range of industries including pharmaceuticals, chemicals, agriculture, aquaculture, food processing, forestry, and waste disposal.[6] Second, it is heavily dependent on basic research in molecular biology including recombinant DNA and genetic engineering techniques. Third, it is a controversial process due to the uncertainty of its potential effects on people and the environment, and since it often involves the creation and patenting of new life forms.

A very narrow definition of biotechnology restricts it to the sense of gene manipulation, particularly genetic engineering, for commercial gain.[7] The most visible and also the most contentious of the areas involving gene manipulation are those of health and agriculture. The health biotechnology industry is concerned with developing new drugs and diagnostic processes, but particularly with drug discovery which is its main objective.[8] Agricultural biotechnology is concerned with the development of new seed varieties, often with specific, introduced traits.[9] This book focuses on this latter aspect.

THE BIOTECHNOLOGY INDUSTRY

The potential economic gains of biotechnology have transformed scientific research from a primarily academic exercise into an industrial and entrepreneurial one. The breakthrough that took place in DNA technology resulted in the 'commercialization of the biological sciences,' 'the commodification of scientific knowledge' and 'the growth of entrepreneurship in scientific research.'[10] Within ten years from 1973 to 1983, funding of academic research and development in the United States increased from

---

[5] Susan Bartholomew, 'National Systems of Biotechnology Innovation: Complex Interdependence in the Global System' (1997) 28(2) *Journal of International Business Studies* 241 at 245.

[6] The four main categories of biotechnologies are agricultural, pharmaceutical, environmental and industrial – Philip A Reed, 'Bioprospecting' (2005) 64(4) *Technology Teacher* 14.

[7] However, the *Global Biodiversity Assessment* points out that this interpretation disregards its importance for our understanding, management and conservation of biodiversity – *Global Biodiversity Assessment*, above n 3, 677.

[8] Dutfield, above n 4, 15.

[9] Ibid.

[10] Sheldon Krimsky, 'The Profit of Scientific Discovery and its Normative Implications' (1999) 75 *Chicago-Kent Law Review* 15, 18.

$84 million to $370 million, thus cementing the relationship between scientific research and industry.[11] Within two decades 700 biotechnology firms had been established in the US alone.[12]

The commercial development and use of biotechnology and the marketing of its products has varied among countries. To date most of the basic research has been conducted by governments, universities and private foundations. Private sector funding has increased in recent times, particularly in the US, which has also been the most successful in marketing the end products. It has been noted that Europe and Japan lag behind the US in this regard although these countries have exerted themselves to catch up with the latter in the last few decades.[13] A recent phenomenon in the biotechnology industry is the emergence of a transnational global industry whereby large corporations are forging networks across countries to advance their technological capabilities and consequently overriding national technological spheres.[14]

Developing countries are now entering the biotechnology arena but their research and commercial capacities vary to a great extent. Countries such as China, Mexico and Costa Rica are pursuing technological innovations in

---

[11] Ibid at 19. See Lynne G Zucker, Michael R Darby and Marilynn B Brewer, 'Intellectual Human Capital and the Birth of US Biotechnology Enterprises' (1998) 88(1) *American Economic Review* 290, for a discussion on the inter-relationship between the scientific developments and the rise of the industry. See Michael J Phillips, 'Social Science Implications of Agricultural Science and Technology: Discussion' (1983) 65(5) *American Journal of Agricultural Economics* 976 for a discussion of the potential conflicts which may arise in the university industry linkage.

[12] Zucker, Darby and Brewer, above n 11. See also L Christopher Plein, 'Popularizing Biotechnology: The Influence of Issue Definition' (1991) 16(4) *Science, Technology, & Human Values* 474, for a general discussion on the rise of the industry.

[13] Dutfield, above n 4, Chapter 2. The United States, the United Kingdom, Germany and Japan have been identified as the countries that have the largest scale of biotechnology in the world – Bartholomew, above n 5, 242.

[14] Bartholomew, above n 5, 242; Elisa Mutia Buktuanon, 'Globalisation of biotechnology; the agglomeration of dispersed knowledge and information and its implications for the political economy of technology in developing countries' (2001) 20(1) *New Genetics and Society* 25.

agricultural biotechnology,[15] while India and China have made significant progress in the health biotechnology sector.[16]

The potential profits to be derived from biotechnology also influence the directions taken by both research and commercial institutions. As far back as 1999 it was estimated that the annual market for products derived from natural resources was between US$500 and US$800 billion.[17] This involved products from industries such as pharmaceuticals, botanical medicines, agricultural produce, ornamental horticultural products, crop protection products, personal care and cosmetic products. The annual commercial seed market has been estimated at US$32 billion.[18]

The commercial biotechnology sector is largely profit motivated and is working in areas where such profits can be maximized. This includes the agricultural sector and the breeding of new varieties of plants. It is in the interests of the industry to form an international institutional and legal framework to establish property rights over the end products of these processes so as to ensure maximum returns on its investments. This process and the extent of its success will be examined in this book.

THE APPLICATION AND USE OF BIOTECHNOLOGY FOR AGRICULTURAL DEVELOPMENT

Biotechnology is primarily used in the fields of pharmaceuticals, agriculture and industry. To its advocates it is the panacea for the problems of global food scarcity and the health needs of the world's population.[19] These

---

[15] Anne Simon Moffat, 'Developing Nations Adapt Biotech for Own Needs' (1994) 265 (No 5169) *Science, New Series*, 186; Susmita Sengupta, L K Sengupta and P S Bisen, 'Bioengineered crops – the commercial and ethical considerations' (2001) 2 *Current Genomics* 181.

[16] Sarah E Frew, Hannah E Kettler and Peter A Singer, 'The Indian And Chinese Health Biotechnology Industries: Potential Champions Of Global Health?' (2008) 27(4) *Health Affairs* 1029.

[17] Kerry ten Kate and Sarah A Laird, *The Commercial Use of Biodiversity: Access to Genetic Resources and Benefit-Sharing* (1999), Chapter 1.

[18] Devlin Kuyek, *Intellectual property rights: Ultimate Control of Agricultural R&D in Asia* (2001), available at http://www.grain.org/briefings_files/asiaipr.pdf (last accessed 30 June 2012).

[19] Gordon Conway, 'Food for All in the 21st Century' (2000) 42(1) *Environment* 8; Roger Beachy, 'The gene business' (2002) 173(2337) *New Scientist* 52; Roger Beachy and Elizabeth Schell-Fredrick, 'Plant biotechnology in the service of human health' (1995) 43(4) *Diogenes* 93.

are also the spheres that provide the greatest economic returns on investments. A considerable amount of resources in the biotechnology industry has therefore been channeled into the development and production of pharmaceuticals and the creation of new crop varieties.[20] These processes involve tapping the vast resources of species and genetic diversity and engaging in genetic engineering of both plants and animals.

Plant biotechnology is used for the breeding of new plant varieties and involves the crossbreeding of plants to produce new varieties which contain useful characteristics. It can be used for:

> the accurate selection and delivery of desired characteristics, to transfer genes from one species into another, to remove undesirable characteristics such as allergenic and toxic compounds and to produce varieties that require less input of pesticides, fertilisers and even water and energy.[21]

The techniques involved in achieving these objectives include traditional methods such as cross-pollination,[22] but a range of modern techniques such as embryo rescue, cell and tissue culture and molecular genetics are now available to facilitate the process.[23] Genetic engineering now allows breeders to incorporate characteristics from one species into another, a process which could not have happened under natural conditions and within such constricted time frames.[24]

Plant biotechnology is touted by its advocates as the only viable strategy to ensure that global food production keeps pace with population growth and meets the nutritional needs of the world's peoples. Global food security reached a critical point in 2007/2008 and the surge in food prices continues unabated at present. The increases in food production which resulted from the Green Revolution are now diminishing, and degraded agricultural lands and water scarcity, together with the impacts of climate change, make conventional agriculture less productive. Biotechnology can facilitate alternative strategies to achieve food security, such as increasing the nutritional

---

[20] For example, research and development on pharmaceuticals amounted to around US$21.1 billion globally in 1998 and the costs of developing a single drug have been estimated at between US$231 million and US$500 million – ten Kate and Laird, above n 17, Chapter 3.

[21] Ibid at 128.

[22] That is, shaking or brushing pollen from the male plant onto the female plant.

[23] ten Kate and Laird, above n 17, 127.

[24] Examples of this include the introduction of a gene from the flounder fish into wheat to produce a variety of the crop that could withstand cold temperatures – Ibid at 128.

content of staple foods like rice,[25] making crops resistant to drought, pests and virus borne diseases, and producing plants which are more productive with fewer inputs.[26] While the Green Revolution produced high yielding varieties of food crops through conventional plant breeding methods, the 'Gene Revolution,' by way of genetic engineering can produce what are virtually designer crops, much faster.[27] The technology undoubtedly has the potential to make a positive impact on world food production, but the question to be asked is whether this process will in fact materialize and who will benefit from it?

BIOTECHNOLOGY AND AGRICULTURE IN DEVELOPING COUNTRIES

The Green Revolution

Agriculture is perhaps the area in which biotechnology can potentially have the greatest socioeconomic consequences on all countries for better or for worse.[28] The global impacts of agricultural biotechnology were first manifested in the phenomenon known as the Green Revolution, and this was perhaps the precursor to the present debate on this issue in the developing world. The economic and socio-political impacts of the Green Revolution on developing countries are relevant in assessing the possible impacts on them by the new generation of biotechnology.[29]

The Green Revolution was essentially a transition from indigenous or traditional agriculture to industrial or 'scientific' systems. It originated and

---

[25] For example, the Swiss Federal Institute of Technology in Zurich has genetically modified rice so that it contains beta carotene, which is necessary for the human body to produce vitamin A. For information on the benefits of biotechnology see the website of the Council for Biotechnology Information (CBI), available at www.whybiotech.com (last accessed 30 June 2012).

[26] Author not cited, 'Biotechnology and World Hunger' (2001) 80(3) *Congressional Digest* 73.

[27] Conway, above n 19.

[28] The other area in which this would be so is that of health, which is beyond the scope of this book.

[29] See Stephen B Brush, 'Genetically Modified Organisms in Peasant Farming: Social Impact and Equity' (2001) 9 *Indiana Journal of Global Legal Studies* 135, where the author notes that owing to the lack of data on the impacts of genetically modified organisms (GMO), the impacts of the Green Revolution are reviewed as an exercise in what to expect from them.

was fostered in the US, and implemented in Asia and Latin America. It has been described in these terms:

> Narrowly defined, the Green Revolution is the rapid growth in Third World grain output associated with the introduction of a new package of tropical agricultural inputs. The package consists essentially of a combination of improved grain varieties, mainly rice and wheat, heavy fertiliser usage and carefully controlled irrigation. Without fertiliser and without controlled irrigation, the new varieties usually yield no more and sometimes less than traditional strains. With them, they give substantially higher yields per acre.[30]

The Green Revolution has provoked some of the most contentious debates in regard to its actual impacts on developing countries. To its enthusiasts it is 'a validation of the basic ideas of evolutionary or institutional economics,'[31] 'the apotheosis of technology' and only rivaled by the Marshall Plan.[32] It is the development which economically transformed many areas of Asia and Latin America, averted mass starvation in the latter half of the 20th century, and ensured food security for the populations of the developing countries where it was implemented.[33] It has also been argued that it had environmental benefits as it minimized the amount of land brought under cultivation since the high yielding varieties of staple crops (HYV) produced a greater harvest per land area cultivated. Therefore more land could be freed up for other crops or for environmental conservation.[34] However, given its adverse impacts, the question whether the trade-off was ultimately worthwhile is one that has been intensely debated.

It is undeniable that the Green Revolution did result in a dramatic increase in food production in the short term, but its long term costs and

---

[30] Harry M Cleaver, 'The Contradictions of the Green Revolution' (1972) 62(1/2) *American Economic Review* 177, providing a detailed history of the conception and implementation of the Green Revolution. See also Gordon Conway, *The Doubly Green Revolution – Food for all in the 21st Century* (1997).

[31] Thomas R DeGregori, 'Green Revolution Myth and Agricultural Reality?' (2004) 38(2) *Journal of Economic Issues* 503, 507.

[32] Nick Cullather, 'Miracles of Modernization: The Green Revolution and the Apotheosis of Technology' (2004) 28(2) *Diplomatic History* 227.

[33] However, it has been pointed out that if world food production were to be divided by the world's population, each person would receive a daily average of over 2,700 calories of energy which is enough to prevent hunger and sufficient to lead an active and healthy life – Gordon Conway 'Food for All in the 21st Century' (1999) 66(1) *Social Research* 351. See also Peter Straub, 'Farmers in the IP Wrench – How Patents on Gene-modified Crops Violate the Right to Food in Developing Countries' (2006) *Hastings International and Comparative Law Review* 187, 192.

[34] DeGregori, above n 31.

negative impacts may have obviated these benefits. To its detractors, it represents the cultural and technological dominance of the west, which overrode the traditional livelihoods of the peoples of developing countries and which has had detrimental impacts on their agriculture, environment and economies. Its origins have been described as a strategy of US foreign policy which aimed to control the economic and social development of Asian countries.[35] At best its beneficial impacts were temporary, although they continued for a few decades, and there are now diminishing returns on the HYVs.[36] It did enable many developing countries to maintain food production at the same levels as population growth and so avert mass starvation. However, these benefits have been achieved at the expense of economic equity, agricultural stability and sustainability, and environmental degradation.[37]

The traditional crop varieties or landraces developed by farmers over thousands of years formed the backbone of indigenous agriculture until the latter half of the 20th century.[38] Because the success of the Green Revolution was based upon the cultivation of uniform HYVs to the exclusion of the traditional landraces which had been cultivated up till then, it eroded the crop diversity that had been built up over centuries.[39] This has been one of

---

[35] This strategy had two aims. The first was to ensure the expansion of US multinational commercial interests overseas. Secondly, it served to ensure the stability of those markets which were being threatened by social and political upheavals in the countries concerned, as well as by a rapidly growing population – Cleaver, above n 30. See also Cullather, above n 32.

[36] Gordon R Conway and Edward B Barbier, *After the Green Revolution – Sustainable Agriculture for Development* (1990). It has been observed that the term high yielding varieties is a misnomer as it implies that the varieties are high yielding in and of themselves. In actual fact they are highly responsive to key inputs such as fertilizer and irrigation – Vandana Shiva, *Monocultures of the Mind – Perspectives on Biodiversity and Biotechnology* (1993), 42. Conway notes that the increase in production was due to three factors in equal measure, i.e. availability of the new crop varieties, increased fertilizer use and the growth of irrigation – Conway, above n 30, 61.

[37] Conway and Barbier, above n 36, Chapter 1; Conway, above n 30, Chapter 5; C Peter Timmer, 'Biotechnology and food systems in developing countries' (2003) 133(1) *Journal of Nutrition, Bethesda* 3319. For an opposing view see Brush, above n 29.

[38] For a discussion of indigenous as opposed to industrial agriculture see David A Cleveland and Stephen C Murray, 'The World's Crop Genetic Resources and the Rights of Indigenous Farmers' (1997) 38(4) *Current Anthropology* 477, 479.

[39] Vandana Shiva, *The Violence of the Green Revolution – Third World Agriculture, Ecology and Politics* (1991) Chapter 2. See also *Global Biodiversity Assessment*, above n 3, 745.

its most adverse effects. It has also been noted that while it did significantly increase yields, this sometimes came at the expense of crop stability.[40]

The political and socioeconomic repercussions of the Green Revolution are still in evidence today, primarily because its benefits were not shared equitably. To begin with, it was implemented in the best potential lands, which were irrigated. However, since only a small percentage of agricultural lands in developing countries are in fact irrigated, this resulted in marginalizing a large proportion of small scale farmers. Further, even within the areas in which the projects were implemented, given their inherently technical bias, they accentuated inequalities, favouring wealthy landowners over small scale subsistence farmers.[41] As such, the benefits of the Green Revolution in regard to food production and the livelihoods of resource poor farmers have been uneven at best.[42] Finally, it did not solve the problem of large scale hunger since this does not depend on production alone.[43] Wider issues of poverty such as adequate employment and income are also decisive. The conceptualization of the Green Revolution did not address these issues and thus fell short in this respect.

The Gene Revolution

The Green Revolution has been succeeded by what has been dubbed the Gene Revolution, brought about by further developments in agricultural biotechnology. The Gene Revolution refers to the use of genetically engineered, genetically modified, and transgenic crops which have significant impacts on agriculture globally. These crops, which have been created for higher yield, herbicide tolerance or insect-resistance, once again promise higher productivity for farmers, and the means to combat world hunger. In addition, it is also claimed that some varieties have improved nutrient traits that have been incorporated into them to combat specific health and

---

40 Conway and Barbier, above n 36. For a discussion on the importance of plant diversity for food security see Scott C Lucas, 'Halting the downward culture of monoculturisation and genetic vulnerability; towards a sustainable and biodiverse food supply' (2002) 17 *Journal of Environmental Law and Litigation* 161. See also Jack R Kloppenburg, *First the Seed: The Political Economy of Plant Biotechnology, 1492–2000* (1988) Chapter 7.

41 Cleaver, above n 30.

42 Conway, above n 30, Chapter 5.

43 For example it has been pointed out that India is facing a crisis of over production concurrently with starvation – Glenn Davis Stone, 'Both Sides Now' (2002) 43(4) *Current Anthropology* 611. See also Conway, above n 19.

nutritional problems,[44] and that genetic engineering is the answer to the challenges posed to agriculture by climate change. The question is whether this second phase will trigger a repetition of the experiences of the Green Revolution in developing countries.[45]

Genetically modified crop varieties are now in widespread use in both developed and developing countries and the global proportion of transgenic crops has increased rapidly since 1996. Countries that grew more than one million hectares of genetically modified crops include the United States, Argentina, Brazil, Canada, China, Paraguay, and India.[46]

Notwithstanding the potential benefits of genetically modified crops, several concerns have been raised as to their possible negative impacts. These have been generally in regard to food safety and human health, and adverse environmental impacts, particularly on ecosystems,[47] as well as the negative socioeconomic effects on agriculture and farmers in developing countries. While the first two issues are beyond the scope of this book, the third raises questions of equity and will be considered further.[48]

While biotechnology has the potential to enhance food security in developing countries, the technology and the propagation of genetically engineered crops in these countries should be viewed in the realities of their social and political context.[49] In this regard too, past experiences of the Green Revolution would be relevant. Perhaps the most enduring consequence of the Green Revolution was the entrenchment in developing

---

44 See above n 25. Straub, above n 33, 189; Sengupta, Sengupta Bisen, above n 15; Karen A. Goldman, 'Labeling of Genetically Modified Foods: Legal and Scientific Issues' (2000) 12 *Georgetown International Environmental Law Review* 717, 718.

45 Brush, above n 29.

46 See http://www.gmo-compass.org/eng/agri_biotechnology/gmo_planting/194.docu.html (last accessed 30 June 2012).

47 Goldman, above n 44, 719. This issue has now been addressed by the *Cartagena Protocol on Biosafety* UNEP/CBD/ExCOP/1/3, 42 (2000), 39 ILM 1027 (2000) (entered into force 11 September 2003) and the *WTO Agreement on the Application of Sanitary and Phytosanitary Measures (SPS Agreement)* 1867 UNTS 493 (entered into force 1 January 1995).

48 Brush comments that the negative impacts of GMOs will be greater in developing rather than in developed countries because of the formers' social and environmental conditions – Brush, above n 29.

49 Timmer, above n 37; Stone, above n 43. The Food and Agriculture Organization has also expressed its support of genetically modified crops in its report *Agricultural Biotechnology: Meeting the needs of the poor* (2004). For a comment on the report see Robert Paarlberg, 'From the Green Revolution to the Gene Revolution Agricultural Biotechnology: Meeting the Needs of the Poor?' (2005) 47(1) *Environment* 38.

countries of the economic and technological dependence on the west, brought about by the change over from traditional to industrial agriculture. Industrialization of agriculture necessarily increases the capacity of the industrial sector to control agricultural production since it is this sector that provides the inputs such as fertilizers and pesticides necessary to ensure the high yields. While the development of Green Revolution crops was funded by public institutions, the Gene Revolution and its products are, by and large, funded and controlled by corporate interests, also generally based in developed countries.[50] Dependence on these entities would potentially have even greater ramifications for agriculture and food security in developing countries.

The control exerted by corporate interests of developed countries can potentially operate in several ways. The primary motive of private sector organizations is to maximize profits for shareholders. The development of new seed varieties by biotechnology corporations to be used for agriculture is thus motivated by profit rather than the public interest. Therefore the crops and traits that are developed are those that will provide maximum returns on investments and may not necessarily be appropriate for developing countries or resource poor farmers.[51] Further, the marketing of these plant varieties will also enable the marketing of other products. One of the myths of biotechnology is that it will reduce the need for pesticides and herbicides. While the potential to do so exists, it has been noted that biotechnology research is in fact directed at increasing the use of chemicals.[52] Most work in agricultural biotechnology has been undertaken by multinational corporations whose strategy is to develop plant varieties tolerant to specific chemicals, usually which they own.[53] Falcon and Fowler also note that '74 percent of the transgenic crops grown commercially

---

[50] Shari L Boyd, William A Kerr and Nicholas Perdikis, 'Agricultural Biotechnology Innovations versus Intellectual Property Rights. Are Developing Countries at the Mercy of Multinationals?' (2003) 6(2) *Journal of World Intellectual Property* 211.

[51] Mary Arends-Kuenning and Flora Makundi. 'Agricultural Biotechnology for Developing Countries: Prospects and Policies' (2000) 44 *American Behavioral Scientist*, 318.

[52] David S Tilford, 'Saving the Blueprints: The International Legal Regime for Plant Resources' (1998) 30 *Case Western Reserve Journal of International Law* 373, 398.

[53] Shiva, above n 36. An example of such a crop is the genetically engineered soya bean sold as Round Up developed by Monsanto which is resistant to the chemical herbicide glyphosate and which Monsanto developed to increase its herbicides sales – Vandana Shiva, *Biopiracy – The Plunder of Nature and Knowledge* (1997) 37. See also Tilford, ibid.

between 1996 and 2000 had herbicide resistance as the trait of primary interest,' and much of the research of these companies 'has focused on innovations that could generate linked sales of seeds and chemicals.'[54] This therefore serves to increase sales of their supplementary products.

The private sector also needs to protect its products from unauthorized use in order to prevent losses in revenue. While it is promoting such protection by way of a legal and institutional framework (discussed further), new technologies have given biotechnology corporations the technical ability to control the extent to which seeds can be used. Non-hybrid plants reproduce themselves and historically farmers were always able to save seeds for re-use in succeeding years. As a result private seed companies were unable to control the use and re-use of open pollinated crops such as wheat and rice. Therefore they had no incentive to develop new varieties of these crops and this was left to the public sector. In contrast, hybrid varieties have some limitations on re-use as subsequent generations deteriorate, and therefore seed companies could control their use to some extent.[55] The development of DNA technology has enhanced this control since it is now possible to genetically fingerprint seed varieties which can be identified with a high level of certainty and differentiated from others,[56] thus enabling seed companies to track the unauthorized usage of their seeds.

The interests of biotechnology companies in protecting their seed varieties and ensuring a constant market for them has seen the further development of biotechnology based mechanisms which restrict the unauthorized use of genetic material. This technology, known as genetic use restriction technologies (GURTs) prevents the use of genetic material by either causing the subsequent generation of seeds to be sterile (variety use restriction or V-GURTs) or by restricting the use of a specific trait in the seed (T-GURTs). While the principle of restricting the use of seeds is not novel (as noted above, hybrids have similar effects), unlike hybrids, GURTs are

---

[54] W P Falcon and C Fowler, 'Carving up the commons – emergence of a new international regime for germplasm development and transfer' (2002) 27(3) *Food Policy* 197, 205. It has also been asserted that control of biotechnology by chemical companies is a strategy to promote biotechnology products that complement chemical products and the former can be used to enhance demand for the latter – Richard E Just and Darrell L Hueth, 'Multimarket Exploitation: The Case of Biotechnology and Chemicals' (1993) 75(4) *American Journal of Agricultural Economics* 936.

[55] Robert W Herdt, 'Reflections on Keeping Asia's Food Baskets Full' (1998) 80(5) *American Journal of Agricultural Economics* 969. See also Anthony J Stenson and Tim S Gray, *The Politics of Genetic Resource Control* (1999), Chapter 2.

[56] Herdt, above n 55, 970.

perceived as restricting access without adding value to the seeds. Their primary purpose is rather to mitigate the loss of profits to the producers caused by farmers using saved seed for subsequent harvests. Concerns have been raised as to their impacts on biodiversity, agricultural practices, seed security and rural economies, and these technologies have generated a heated debate.[57]

RELATED ISSUES IN THE BIOTECHNOLOGY DEBATE

Bioprospecting

The use of biotechnology is often dependent upon a constant supply of natural resources which are analyzed and manipulated to achieve the desired results. These resources are often (but not always) located in developing countries. The term 'bioprospecting' refers to the search for these natural resources from the wild including plant and animal species, to be screened for their potential application in manufacturing diverse products of use to humans.[58] Bioprospectors range from village shamans to professionally trained botanists in multinational pharmaceutical companies.[59]

---

[57] UNEP/CBD/COP/7/INF/31 – CBD CoP, Seventh meeting, 9–20 and 27 February 2004, *Thematic Programmes of Work: Progress Reports on Implementation and Consideration of Proposals for Future Action: Agricultural Biological Diversity, Potential impacts of Genetic Use Restriction Technologies (GURTs) on Agricultural Biodiversity and Agricultural Production Systems: Report Submitted by the Food and Agriculture Organization of the United Nations*, 12 January 2004, 2. For a comprehensive analysis of GURTs see UNEP/CBD/SBSTTA/4/9/Rev.1 – Subsidiary Body on Scientific, Technical and Technological Advice, Fourth meeting, 21–25 June 1999, Consequences of the Use of the New Technology for the Control of Plant Gene Expression for the Conservation and Sustainable Use of Biological Diversity, 17 May 1999. See also C S Srinivasan and Colin Thirtle, 'Understanding the emergence of terminator technologies' (2000) 12 *Journal of International Development* 1147.

[58] Other terms include 'gene hunting' which is the search for biological resources for use in medicines and agriculture – Valentina Tejera, 'Tripping over Property Rights: Is it Possible to Reconcile the Convention on Biological Diversity with Article 27 of the TRIPS Agreement?' (1999) 33 *New England Law Review* 967, and 'natural products drug discovery' which has been described as 'the search for bioactive compounds contained in natural sources such as plants, fungi, insects, microbes, and marine organisms,' – Edgar J Asebey and Jill D Kempenaar, 'The

Like biotechnology, bioprospecting is not a novel phenomenon and the screening of biological resources for their possible utility is a human activity that has been carried on since time immemorial.[60] Many of these biological resources, including PGRFA, were traded throughout the world for centuries. Modern bioprospecting however, originated with western scientists who accompanied the expeditions to the New World in the last five centuries,[61] and it was with the advent of the European colonial empires that the ensuing products gained extreme economic significance.[62] For centuries, during the period of colonialism, there was a flow of biological resources from the southern countries to the north which continues to the present day.

The search for these raw materials is not objectionable per se, depending on the manner in which it is done and assuming that the interests of the host country and communities are duly accounted for. However, the misappropriation of those resources, and the marginalizing of the peoples and communities who possess and conserve them, have met with increasing resistance.

A comparison has been drawn between present day bioprospecting and past activities involving prospecting for other precious commodities. Biological resources have in fact often proved to be as valuable as these 'non living' and non-renewable resources. Shiva argues that the metaphor suggests that as in the case of prospecting for substances such as gold, in bioprospecting the resources in question are perceived to lie unknown, unused and valueless, until they are 'discovered,' and ownership after discovery then accrues to the prospector. There are situations where the discovery of the benefits of natural resources is based upon the prior traditional ecological knowledge regarding their use held by local or indigenous communities, but this factor is disregarded when granting

---

Intellectual Property Perspective on Biodiversity: Biodiversity Prospecting: Fulfilling the Mandate of the Biodiversity Convention' (1995) 28 *Vanderbilt Journal of Transnational Law* 703.

59 Tejera, above n 58.

60 Thomas Eisner, 'Chemical Prospecting – A Global Imperative' (1994) 138(3) *Proceedings of the American Philosophical Society* 385.

61 Mary Garson, 'Biodiversity and Bioprospecting' in Natalie P Stoianoff (ed), *Accessing Biological Resources: Complying with the Convention on Biological Diversity* (2004), 17.

62 For an account of the rise of agricultural bioprospecting in the colonies see John Merson, 'Bio-prospecting or Bio-piracy: Intellectual Property Rights and Biodiversity in a Colonial and Postcolonial Context' (2000) 15(1) *Osiris* 282.

property rights over the resource to the prospector.[63] Thus the word 'bio-prospecting' in its present context has unpalatable connotations for many, bringing to mind colonialism and the exploitation of the biodiversity rich South by Northern countries.

'Biopiracy'

The unauthorized search for and appropriation of, biological resources in developing countries and the use of traditional knowledge for this purpose, has been dubbed 'biopiracy.' Dutfield defines biopiracy as referring:

> ... either to the unauthorised extraction of biological resources and/or associated traditional knowledge from developing countries, or to the patenting of spurious 'inventions' based on such knowledge or resources without compensation.[64]

According to Shiva, it refers to:

> the use of intellectual property systems to legitimise the exclusive ownership and control over biological resources and biological products and processes that have been used over centuries in non-industrialised cultures.[65]

There are therefore several common elements inherent in the issue of biopiracy. First, it takes place usually, but not invariably, in developing countries. Second, it involves the unauthorized and uncompensated extraction of biological resources for use in biotechnological processes in order to create new products or processes for commercial use. Third, the extraction may involve using the traditional knowledge of local communities in order to obtain leads as to the potential purposes for which these resources can be used. Fourth, exclusive private property rights are asserted over the end product or process to the exclusion of all others, including those from whom the knowledge and/or resource originated. This is done under the aegis of intellectual property systems, which have now become an integral part of both national and international law. This aspect is perhaps the decisive factor in the situation, and that which has the greatest political, social and economic implications for developing countries.[66]

---

[63] Shiva, above n 53, Chapter 4.

[64] Dutfield, above n 4, 52.

[65] Vandana Shiva, *Protect or Plunder – Understanding Intellectual Property Rights* (2001) 49.

[66] Lakshmi Sarma, 'Biopiracy: Twentieth Century Imperialism in the Form of International Agreements' (1990) 13 *Temple International and Comparative Law Journal* 107, 116.

Dutfield observes that the word biopiracy 'is applied somewhat loosely to the extent it is not always clear who the victims actually are, or if indeed there are any.'[67] It is also not a legally defined concept in either national or international law.[68] It is merely an element in the wider scheme of economic dominance by one part of the world over another. Its workings may affect, at different levels, the nation state, the general public, or indigenous and local communities.[69] Nevertheless, as will be seen, it is now an issue that is being intensely debated in international fora in the context of the propertization of plant genetic resources.

The unauthorized appropriation of resources from developing countries takes place in relation to both biological resources as well as the traditional knowledge related to them. An early instance of the clandestine removal of a natural resource from the country of origin occurred in 1876 when an Englishman smuggled 70,000 rubber seeds out of Brazil, and this has often been cited as the first example of modern day biopiracy.[70] More recent examples[71] include that of the hoodia cactus of the Kalahari Desert,[72] the

---

[67] Dutfield, above n 4, 52.

[68] Odek observes that piracy is 'a nebulous expression lacking a precise legal definition. Because international law has not defined the uncompensated extraction of plant genetic resources as piracy, the characterization of such acts as piracy serves as a normative assertion by developing countries that they have an entitlement to their plant genetic resources' – James O Odek, 'Bio-Piracy: Creating Proprietary Rights in Plant Genetic Resources' (1994) 2 *Journal of Intellectual Property Law* 141,145.

[69] Christopher J Hunter, 'Sustainable Bioprospecting: Using Private Contracts and International Legal Principles and Policies to Conserve Raw Medicinal Materials' (1997) 25 *Boston College Environmental Affairs Law Review* 129, 139. The author notes that biopiracy that victimizes individuals involves the exploitation of the ethnopharmacological knowledge of indigenous communities to identify and study the effect of medicinal plants. Unauthorized resource extraction from developing countries victimizes those countries.

[70] Klaus Bosselmann, 'Plants and Politics: The International Legal Regime concerning Biotechnology and Biodiversity' (1996) 7 *Colorado Journal of International Environmental Law and Policy* 111, 121; Kloppenburg, above n 40, Chapter 7.

[71] See generally, Graham Dutfield, *Intellectual Property Rights, Trade and Biodiversity* (2000) Chapter 5; Dutfield, above n 4, Chapter 5. For a list of the better known instances of biopiracy see Naomi Roht-Arriaza, 'Of Seeds and Shamans: The Appropriation of the Scientific and Technical Knowledge of Indigenous and Local Communities' (1996) 17 *Michigan Journal of International Law* 919.

[72] Rachel Wynberg, 'Rhetoric, Realism and Benefit-Sharing Use of Traditional Knowledge of Hoodia Species in the Development of an Appetite Suppressant' (2004) 7(6) *Journal of World Intellectual Property* 851.

neem tree found in South and South East Asia,[73] the quinoa from the Andean countries of South America, the ayahuasca vine from the Amazon[74] and the Enola bean from Mexico.[75]

Examples of the misappropriation of traditionally bred varieties of PGRFA include that of tropical legume seeds developed in Australia which were based on indigenous Kenyan seeds, further developed and then commercially imported into Kenya.[76] The Monellin and Thaumatin plants which African farmers used for centuries as sweeteners and flavour enhancers is yet another instance.[77] The products of these plants are now patented in the US generating a $900 million per year market for low calorie sweeteners. The African farmers were not compensated. Other better known examples of plant patenting involved two varieties of rice – basmati rice traditionally grown in India and Pakistan, and jasmine rice in Thailand – where 'new' variations of these varieties were bred with slight modifications and patented.[78] Although both these patents were challenged with some degree of success by the governments of the countries concerned, they raised concerns about the potential economic impact on the farmers of those countries and the loss of their export markets for these crops.[79] In a more recent incident, Nestlé, the world's largest food company, is accused of misappropriating two plants found in South Africa, namely rooibos and honeybush, after it applied for international patents for using the plants or their extracts for skin and hair conditions. Nestlé had allegedly not received

---

[73] Emily Marden, 'The Neem Tree Patent: International Conflict over the Commodification of Life' (1999) 22 *Boston College International and Comparative Law Review* 279.

[74] Leanne M Fecteau, 'The Ayahuasca Patent Revocation: Raising Questions about Current US Patent Policy' (2001) 21 *Boston College Third World Law Journal* 69.

[75] Gillian N Rattray, 'The Enola Bean Patent Controversy: Biopiracy, Novelty and Fish-and-Chips' (2002) *Duke Law & Technology Review* 8.

[76] Odek, above note 68, 145.

[77] Ibid at 146.

[78] Michael Woods, 'Food for Thought: The Biopiracy of Jasmine and Basmati Rice' (2002) 13 *Albany Law Journal of Science & Technology* 123; Sumathi Subbiah, 'Reaping What They Sow: The Basmati Rice Controversy and Strategies for Protecting Traditional Knowledge' (2004) 27 *Boston College International and Comparative Law Review* 529; Muriel Lightbourne, 'Of Rice and Men. An Attempt to Assess the Basmati Affair' (2003) 6(6) *Journal of World Intellectual Property* 875.

[79] A more recent example is the patent obtained by the University of Hawaii on taro, a staple food crop of the Hawaiian people which was successfully challenged – Walter Rite and Bill Freese 'Haloa' Seedling (2006), available at http://www.grain.org/article/entries/568-haloa (last accessed 30 June 2012).

permits from the South African government to use these plants. Nestlé denies the allegations.[80]

Biopiracy also takes place in relation to the traditional ecological knowledge of indigenous and local communities. Such knowledge is often common knowledge and it is utilized for the benefit of the general community. It is not used for commercial purposes or for the enrichment of a few. It is also relatively unstructured, usually being passed down orally from generation to generation, unprotected by formal legal systems.[81] The fact that it is freely available makes it susceptible to appropriation without recompense to the communities from whom it originated. Writers have argued that western concepts of what constitutes science and technology are based upon formal scientific knowledge systems and the products of these systems are valued as a form of property which gives rise to legal rights. Western trained scientists do not accord a similar status to the more unstructured knowledge systems of other communities,[82] and since these systems are generally in the public domain, they are considered to be freely available for exploitation. This stance is now being resisted by countries and communities where such knowledge is located, and the matter continues to be debated in international trade and environment fora.

CONCLUSION

Chapter 16 of Agenda 21 is devoted to the 'Environmentally Sound Management of Biotechnology.'[83] It makes a distinction between modern and traditional biotechnology and views the concept as the integration of both techniques. The document cautions that it is not the ultimate solution for all the problems of environment and development, but offers promises for better health care, enhanced food security through sustainable agricultural

---

[80] See http://ictsd.org/i/news/bridesweekly/77411/ (last accessed 30 June 2012).

[81] It has been noted that in view of the changes which indigenous communities are undergoing and the consequent loss of traditional knowledge, the documentation of this knowledge is important – Michael Heinrich, 'Ethnobotany and Natural Products: The Search for New Molecules, New Treatments of Old Diseases or a Better Understanding of Indigenous Cultures?' (2003) 3(2) *Current Topics in Medicinal Chemistry* 141.

[82] Roht-Arriaza, above n 71, 929. See also generally, Shahid Alikhan and Raghunath Mashelkar, *Intellectual Property and Competitive Strategies in the 21st Century* (2004) Chapter 4.

[83] *Agenda 21*, UN Conference on Environment and Development, UN Doc.A/CONF.151/26/Rev.1 (1992).

practices, more efficient industrial processes and the means for environmental protection. It also views biotechnology as offering new opportunities for global partnerships between the technologically rich developed countries and the biodiversity rich developing countries in order to promote sustainable development.[84] The question is whether these aspirations can be realized under the current international legal regime.

The uses of biotechnology are not beneficial per se or detrimental to people and the environment, and its impacts on both would depend largely on the way it is managed. If used prudently and equitably, it can be beneficial to both. The implications of agricultural biotechnology for developing countries, particularly the adoption of industrial agricultural practices with their attendant implications, must be carefully considered and the costs and the benefits assessed. Undeniably, the potential benefits of this technology can be used to develop agricultural systems in the global south and ensure food security for the people of these countries as the Green Revolution did decades ago. However, in the light of lessons learnt from the Green Revolution, its adverse impacts should not be ignored.

One ramification of agricultural biotechnology is the potential loss of the agrobiodiversity which has evolved over thousands of years and which is critical to sustainable agriculture, together with the potential risks to biosafety. The Green Revolution has demonstrated that wholesale adoption of industrial agricultural practices do not necessarily benefit small farmers and will lessen incentives to develop more sustainable farming practices appropriate for safeguarding their livelihoods. In any event, the benefits of such agricultural systems for food security are debatable, as increased agricultural production alone does not reduce poverty or facilitate access to food.[85]

Another contentious issue is the free access of farmers to the Gene Revolution varieties. The development of agricultural biotechnology has resulted in the exponential enhancement of the value of PGRFA. Thus PGRFA have now become a source of potential profits to those who can acquire them and control their access and use. There are two dimensions to this issue.

The first is the fact that the natural resources which form the raw material of the technology were initially found largely in the countries of the global South. As discussed in Chapter 2, much of these resources are now stored in *ex situ* collections located in developed countries. The fact that these

---

[84] See also *Global Biodiversity Assessment*, above n 3, Chapter 10.

[85] Stone cites the example of India which has a situation of farm overproduction but where a quarter of a billion people are malnourished and 1.5 million children die each year from diseases linked to malnutrition – Stone, above n 43, 614.

resources were collected without the informed consent of these countries and are now being used for further development of plant varieties without recompense to them, raises questions of equity. These include bioprospecting and biopiracy, including the use of traditional knowledge, which were discussed above.

The second dimension is that the newly developed varieties are not freely available as the original resources or the Green Revolution varieties were. Notwithstanding the differences of opinion in regard to the Green Revolution, its plant varieties were developed by public sector institutions and made accessible to developing countries. While the new generation of Gene Revolution varieties are also being touted as the answer to enhancing agricultural productivity and combating world hunger, they are developed by corporate entities for commercial purposes. These corporations therefore have a stake in restricting access to them and marketing them, rather than making them freely available. Consequently, increased dependence upon necessary agricultural inputs including seeds and plant varieties will make developing countries vulnerable to corporate control of their food systems. Further, the development of new varieties will be guided by what will be most profitable and marketable rather than what will be most beneficial, and the advantages of these varieties to developing countries are debatable.

Biotechnology corporations have over a period of time, been canvassing for legal and institutional frameworks to be put in place in both the national and international spheres to create property rights over new varieties of PGRFA in order to ensure that their rights over their new plant varieties are protected. The negotiation of these regimes has been ongoing for decades. Depending on how these international systems are devised, they can either result in further entrenching the economic and political control of southern countries by corporate interests, or they can be used to achieve food security and sustainable agriculture in the former. Past historical events such as the Green Revolution presage that the likelihood of the first scenario is very high. Current developments in international law indicate that a legal structure is being constructed to create property rights over new plant varieties in order to facilitate control over them by corporate entities. The following chapters will explore this process further.

4. Property regimes over biological resources

INTRODUCTION

The previous chapter considered the appropriation and use of plant genetic resources and noted that those engaged in developing new plant varieties must ensure property rights over them. This chapter will consider the specific institutional arrangements or property regimes which may be applicable to biological resources including crop plants. The three regimes which will be discussed are of particular relevance since they each form the basis of the international agreements which impact on plant genetic resources for food and agriculture (PGRFA). The current international debate over rights to PGRFA by and large revolves around the question of whether these resources should be considered to be common property and governed by an open access regime as set out in the International Treaty on Plant Genetic Resources for Food and Agriculture of the Food and Agriculture Organization of 2001 (FAO Treaty), be subject to state sovereignty as set out in the Convention on Biological Diversity of 1992 (CBD), or be subject to private property rights as set out in the international property rights regime under the International Convention for the Protection of New Varieties of Plants (UPOV Conventions 1978 and 1991) (UPOV), the Agreement on Trade Related Aspects of Intellectual Property Rights (1994) (TRIPS Agreement) and the various agreements of the World Intellectual Property Organization (WIPO).

COMMON PROPERTY RESOURCES

John Locke acknowledged that natural resources 'belong to mankind in common, as they are produced by the spontaneous hand of nature.'[1] It can

[1] John Locke, *Two Treatises of Government and a Letter Concerning Toleration* (first published 1690, Ian Shapiro (ed) 2003), 'The Second Treatise: An Essay Concerning the True Original, Extent, and End of Civil Government', Chapter V, 'Of Property.'

be assumed that most resources were originally used in common, but as communities evolved, regulatory mechanisms for governing common-pool or common property resources (CPRs)[2] necessarily became more formalized. Appropriate management of CPRs has been cited as including two elements. These are restrictions on access on the one hand, and on the other, incentives or regulations for users to invest in the conservation and improvement of the resources, as opposed to merely over-exploiting them.[3]

It has been asserted that CPRs will continue as a core type of resource which has major theoretical and policy significance as long as humans depend on ecosystem services ranging from individual biodiversity components through to the oceans and the atmosphere.[4] Thus they exist at the community, national, regional, and international level, and CPRs as institutions continue to evolve in various forms.[5]

It has been suggested that there are four broad systems for the management of CPRs:[6] open access systems,[7] group property systems,[8] individual

---

[2] The terminology in relation to such resources, includes 'common pool resources', 'common-property institutions', 'the commons' and 'commoners' – Nives Dolsak and Elinor Ostrom, 'The Challenges of the Commons' in Nives Dolsak and Elinor Ostrom (eds), *The commons in the new millennium: challenges and adaptations* (2003) 3, 7.

[3] Elinor Ostrom, Joanna Burger, Christopher B Field, Richard B Norgaard and David Policansky, 'Revisiting the Commons – Local Lessons, Global Challenges' (1999) 284 (No 5412) *Science New Series* 278, 279.

[4] Dolsak and Ostrom, above n 2. In addition to natural resources, CPRs include such human constructed resources as irrigation systems, the Internet and space for air traffic – Ibid at 279.

[5] Dolsak and Ostrom, above n 2. The authors point out that in addition to the already existing forms of CPRs new forms are continuously being created. For example, although the modern corporation is often thought of as the embodiment of private property, a public corporation is in fact more representative of common property. A relatively recent example of a common property institution is the urban condominium which is a combination of private and common property. Bromley observes that a private club is a common property regime, being joint management regimes which control assets and allocate use rights among co-owners or members – Daniel W Bromley, *Environment and economy: property rights and public policy* (1991) Chapter 1, note 1 at 13.

[6] Ostrom et al, above n 3. See also James A Swaney, 'Are Democracy and Common Property Possible on Our Small Earth?' (2003) 37(2) *Journal of Economic Issues* 261, 278 and Bromley, above n 5.

[7] That is, systems with no property rights.

[8] That is, resource rights held by a group of users who can exclude others.

property systems,[9] and government property systems.[10] Of these, open access systems are in fact unregulated, while the latter three are regulatory systems. These four systems will be taken as the basis on which to develop the present analysis of international property regimes over PGRFA.

OPEN ACCESS OR UNREGULATED SYSTEMS

It has been suggested that open access constitutes the initial status of biological resources. In such a system there are no constraints to using and exploiting the resource so long as the supply is greater than the demand. Consequently, there is also no gain in conserving or improving it.[11] Even when the supply becomes scarce, the users have little incentive to conserve it as they will not get the benefit of doing so as long as others do not practice conservation. Therefore the likely consequences are that exploitation will increase and intensify until the resource is exhausted. Thus unrestricted open access will typically result in resource depletion.[12] On the demand side, open access invites excessive withdrawal of the resource as a result of competing interests to extract as much as possible, as quickly as possible, before others do.[13] The elements of the environment affected by such open access include freshwater and marine resources, land, and the atmosphere.

Therefore if the resource is to be conserved, access must be regulated and regimes for this purpose have now emerged at both national and international levels. At national level an appropriate regime would depend on many factors, including social, cultural, economic and political. At international level such factors would include international trade and market forces.

---

[9] That is, resource rights held by individuals or firms who can exclude others.

[10] That is, resource rights held by a government that can regulate or subsidize use.

[11] Louis De Alessi, 'Gains from Private Property: The Empirical Evidence' in Terry L Anderson and Fred S McChesney (eds), *Property rights: cooperation, conflict, and law* (2003), Chapter 4; Magnus Wijkman, 'Managing the Global Commons' (1982) 36(3) *International Organization* 511.

[12] Examples of the exhaustion of open access resources have been cited as the extinction of animal species by Paleoindian hunters in the Pleistocene period and by early Polynesian settlers in Hawaii and New Zealand – De Alessi, above n 11, Chapter 4. The near extinction of the American bison has been cited as another example – Terry L Anderson and Fred S McChesney (eds), *Property rights: cooperation, conflict, and law* (2003) Part II, Introduction 59, 61.

[13] Anderson and McChesney, above n 12, Part II, Introduction 59, 69.

The Public Domain and Public Goods

A concept that is related to unregulated or open access systems is that of the public domain. The public domain contains public goods which include 'the non-tradable social goods sector that exists in every society,' and which has socially binding importance, existing in all spheres of a community.[14] Although several characteristics have been attributed to public goods,[15] the term is understood as meaning a good 'that can be shared non-rivalrously by many, and from whose use non-payers are not easily physically excluded.'[16]

It can be argued that PGRFA is a resource that can in fact be maintained within an open access system or within the public domain without the threat of resource depletion. It is a resource which being renewable is intrinsically non-rivalrous, i.e. its free use by some will not inhibit its use by others. In the case of PGRFA its unrestricted availability will result rather in resource multiplication than in depletion, since it is subject to a continuous process of evolution and development, which in turn contributes to maintaining food security and genetic diversity for the benefit of all peoples. On the other hand, a property regime which makes it rivalrous would potentially result in the decrease of crop diversity and increased scarcity and this is the primary concern in regard to claims of intellectual property rights over PGRFA.

---

[14] Daniel Drache 'The return of the public domain after the triumph of markets – Revisiting the most basic of fundamentals' in Daniel Drache (ed), *The Market or the Public Domain? Global Governance and the Asymmetry of Power* (2001) Chapter 1.

[15] W Ver Eecke, 'Public goods: An ideal concept' (1999) 28(2) *Journal of Socio-Economics* 139.

[16] Wendy J Gordon, 'Authors, Publishers, and Public Goods: Trading Gold for Dross' (2002) 36 *Loyola of Los Angeles Law Review* 159, 164. Stone analyzes the difference between public goods and private goods with regard to a metaphor of a tropical forest. The berries produced by a tropical forest are potentially private goods since their consumption is rival. On the other hand the atmosphere enhancing attributes of a forest are a public good since they are non-rivalrous – Christopher D Stone, 'What to do about Biodiversity: Property Rights, Public Goods, and the Earth's Biological Riches' (1995) 68 *Southern California Law Review* 577.· Drache also notes that the constitutive elements of the public domain include 'social goods that benefit everyone and cannot be considered like private property belonging to the individual,' Drache above n 14, 44.

GROUP OR COMMON PROPERTY SYSTEMS

Common property which has been equated to the *res communes* of Roman law refers to a system whereby a group of people share rights of ownership and use of a resource.[17] There are several specific characteristics of this system.[18] Common property is a variation of private property since it is the property of a group of co-owners. It can potentially come into existence at various points of the socio-political scale, for example, the household, the village or the nation state,[19] and also internationally. There can be extensive variation between and among the groups in relation to their nature, size and internal structure, but they are social units with definite membership and boundaries, certain common interests, at least some interaction among members, some common cultural norms, and often their own authority systems.[20]

A second characteristic of common property is that individuals within the group have rights and duties in regard to the resource. The rights of use and of exclusion of non-members have been particularly emphasized. However, the members of the group may not transfer the use or ownership of the resource to any other person.[21] Effective common property regimes also have regulatory mechanisms by which the extraction and use of the resource are controlled.[22]

---

17 See James A Swaney, 'Common property, reciprocity, and community' (1990) 24(2) *Journal of Economic Issues* 451, 452.

18 Common property regimes have been organized on the basis of rules of access, withdrawal, management, exclusion and alienation – Craig Johnson, 'Uncommon Ground: The "Poverty of History" in Common Property Discourse' (2004) 35(3) *Development & Change* 407.

19 Mark Giordano, 'The Geography of the Commons: The Role of Scale and Space' (2003) 93(2) *Annals of the Association of American Geographers* 365.

20 Bromley, above n 5, 26. He goes on to cite tribal groups, or subgroups, or sub-villages, neighbourhoods, small transhumant groups, kin systems, or extended families as possible examples. See also Thomas Dietz, Nives Dolsak, Elinor Ostrom and Paul C Stern, 'The Drama of the Commons' in Elinor Ostrom et al (eds) *The drama of the commons / Committee on the Human Dimensions of Global Change* (2002) Chapter 1 at 12 where the authors note that research has stressed that most users of a common-pool resource in developing countries live in the same village where their families have lived for generations. This chapter also provides an account of the development of the literature on the commons.

21 Bromley, above n 5, Chapter 2.

22 Swaney, above n 17, 452; Bromley, above n 5, Chapter 1; Jules Pretty, 'Social Capital and the Collective Management of Resources' (2003) 302 (5652) *Science* 1912; Elinor Ostrom, 'Constituting Social Capital and Collective Action' in

Although common property regimes are vulnerable to breaking down due to various factors (as discussed below), it is important to note the distinction between these regimes and open access systems. The confusion in this regard is largely due to a misleading metaphor in the seminal article by Garrett Hardin.[23] In this article Hardin described the workings of common property by using the metaphor of a pasture open to all. He argued that it is to be expected that each herdsman will seek to keep as many cattle on the land as possible in order to maximize his personal gain. The negative impacts of overgrazing on the other hand are not borne by him alone but are shared among all. This situation continues until the commons breaks down.

Hardin's theory has been refuted by writers who point out that 'common property resources are often taken to be those for which markets are absent or poorly developed,' but in fact in the past these resources have been effectively managed by communities.[24] However, these regimes can be susceptible to external pressures and competing philosophical and political views on alternative uses of property.[25] The problems described by Hardin would rather tend to arise due to increased intensity of use or when these traditional management systems have been weakened by modernization.[26] If the modern state is indifferent or opposed to the system, it will not protect or uphold it. The willingness of the State to uphold these systems depends on its political ideologies and the perceptions of the group involved, which may be farmers, indigenous and local communities or others. Technological change may also pose challenges to common property, as it may lead to greater pressure to exploit common resources or commercialize their benefits,[27] and cause the common property system to disintegrate or to become

---

Robert O Keohane and Elinor Ostrom (eds), *Local commons and global interdependence: heterogeneity and cooperation in two domains*, (1995) Chapter 6; Regina Birner and Heidi Wittmer, 'Using Social Capital to Create Political Capital: How Do Local Communities Gain Political Influence? A Theoretical Approach and Empirical Evidence from Thailand' in Nives Dolsak and Elinor Ostrom (eds), *The commons in the new millennium: Challenges and Adaptations* (2003) Chapter 10.

[23] Garrett Hardin, 'The Tragedy of the Commons' (1968) 162 (No 3859) *Science, New Series* 1243.

[24] Gillespie notes that western definitions of common property generally equate it to open access rather than communal property – Alexander Gillespie, *The Illusion of Progress – Unsustainable Development in International Law and Policy* (2001), 57.

[25] Bromley, above n 5, Chapter 6.

[26] Ibid; Ronald E Lee, 'The Second Tragedy of the Commons' (1990) 16 *Population and Development Review* 315, 316; Swaney, above n 17.

[27] S V Ciriacy-Wantrup and Richard C Bishop, '"Common Property" as a Concept in Natural Resources Policy' (1975) 15(4) *Natural Resources Journal* 713

dysfunctional. When this takes place, common property can effectively revert to open access or no property, thus also permitting other property regimes to be established over the resources. It can also be pushed towards privatization.[28]

Some scholars have argued that it is in the developing countries of the tropics that one sees property regimes which most closely resemble the commons. They argue that the real tragedy of the commons is the process by which indigenous property systems were undermined and delegitimized, first by colonialism and then by the new nation states. They are pessimistic about the will or the ability of national governments in developing countries to effectively manage their natural resources for the greater good, and cite the failure of post-colonial nations to establish 'the implicit and explicit legal foundations of an economy and society that will guide individual actions toward social betterment.'[29] This in turn leads to a situation of fluidity and uncertainty, where social sanctions and conventions regarding land and natural resource use break down, leading to the destruction of the common property and threatening the communities that depend on it.

The importance of applying (or rather maintaining) a common property regime in regard to PGRFA is indisputable in view of global interdependence on these resources. It has already been argued that PGRFA is sustainable even in an open access regime. It can be asserted that PGRFA was, in fact, an open access regime and not subject to even the ownership found in common property systems. Communities and traditional farmers did not restrict the free flow of plants and, before the advent of modern biotechnology, it would have been practically impossible to do so.

The question whether PGRFA is found within an open access or common property regime is however, of less importance than the fact that it is now being removed from both.[30] While the FAO Treaty is based upon free access to these resources, its workings are being challenged by restrictions being imposed at both national and international levels. This is being done by state property, as well as private property, systems.

---

and Thrainn Eggertsson, 'Open Access versus Common Property' in Terry L Anderson and Fred S McChesney (eds), *Property rights: cooperation, conflict, and law* (2003) Chapter 3.

[28] Eggertsson, above n 27, Chapter 3.

[29] Bromley, above n 5, Chapter 6.

[30] W P Falcon and C Fowler, 'Carving up the commons – emergence of a new international regime for germplasm development and transfer' (2002) 27(3) *Food Policy* 197.

STATE PROPERTY SYSTEMS

State property has been likened to the *res publicae* of Roman law and constitutes another form of public property, that which is owned and controlled by the state.[31] In Roman times it included public structures, particularly the city walls and fortifications, which were essential to maintaining the security and integrity of the community. Under the circumstances they could neither be treated as open commons nor given over to private ownership, but had to be placed under the control of the central authority for the benefit of all. The same rationale would apply to resources under the control of modern States, including natural resources.

State property has been defined as a property regime in which:

> in principle, material resources are answerable to the needs and purposes of society as a whole, whatever they are and however they are determined, rather than to the needs and purposes of particular individuals considered on their own. No individual has such an intimate association with any object that he can make decisions about its use without reference to the interests of the collective.[32]

Therefore, as under Roman law, in the case of state property in the present context, the ownership and control over the resources in question rests with the state, whatever its form and structure.[33] The important rights exercised by the state include that of controlled inclusion and exclusion of its own citizens in the overall public interest. In regard to natural resources, protected areas are perhaps the archetypal example of this right.

State control over property may be exercised in two ways. First, as discussed above, property may be vested in the state. A feature of the colonial era of many countries was the conversion of common property regimes including communally held lands and village forests into state property.[34] Consequently, in some countries a large proportion of land is,

---

[31] Richard A Epstein, 'On the Optimal Mix of Private and Common Property' in Ellen Frankel Paul, Fred D Miller and Jeffrey Paul (eds), *Property rights* (1994) 17.

[32] Jeremy Waldron, *The Right to Private Property* (1988) 40.

[33] These resources of course would not be limited to natural resources and include other economic resources owned by the State, including harbours, airports, railways, highways and public corporate entities. Depending on the distribution of authority in the particular State, ownership can also vest in different levels of the state, i.e. central, regional, municipal, etc.

[34] Gregory Barton, 'Keepers of the Jungle: Environmental Management in British India, 1855–1900' (2000) 62(3) *Historian* 557. This was a repetition of the enclosure movement which took place in Europe from the 15th to the 19th century –

even now, state owned.[35] The second aspect of state control of property is the power vested in the state to regulate the types of ownership which may prevail within its jurisdiction, including the ownership rights of those holding individual and common property.

There are diverse implications of state property systems. To begin with, if the people of a country are equated with their government, it can be argued that theoretically, state property is in fact a common property regime in a larger dimension, with the state apparatus holding the reins of management and regulation.[36] Perhaps the quintessential state property system as a form of common property is that expounded by Karl Marx. He argued against property relations 'that are the conditions for the existence of the bourgeoisie and of its rule' and called for the abolition of private property which represents the exploitative system of production and appropriation of products. In direct opposition to Locke[37] he rejected the notion of the right to personally acquire property as the fruit of a person's own labour, arguing that wage labour does not create any property for the labourer, but creates capital which is a means of exploiting wage labour. Since bourgeois private property is the final and most complete expression of doing so, he called for its abolition. He also advocated that all instruments of production should be centralized in the hands of the state which he defined as 'the proletariat organised as the ruling class.'[38]

However, problems would arise where the people do not identify with the state regime and its policies, and may in fact be potentially at odds with it in regard to the resources in question, including PGRFA. Nonetheless, in a political institution where the state is at least theoretically accountable to the people and reflects the view of the majority, certain rules of management may be applicable, particularly where it acquires property, or divests itself of it. There is however, no guarantee that those who have acquired

---

James Boyle, 'The Second Enclosure Movement and the Construction of the Public Domain' (2003) 66 *Law and Contemporary Problems* 33.

[35] For example more than 60 years after independence over 80 per cent of land in Sri Lanka is still under some form of State control – Ministry of Forestry and Environment, Sri Lanka, *Biodiversity Conservation in Sri Lanka, A Framework for Action* (1998) 10. The situation has not changed since this report was written.

[36] Carol Rose takes the view that this would be merely a variant on private property where an organized body takes exclusive control over property – Carol M Rose, 'The Comedy of the Commons: Custom, Commerce, and Inherently Public Property' (1986) 53 *University of Chicago Law Review* 711, 730.

[37] See the section on Individual or Private Property Systems below.

[38] Karl Marx and Friedrich Engels, *The Communist Manifesto* (A J P Taylor trans. first published 1848, 1967 ed).

political power will act according to the wishes of their constituents.[39] The position becomes further complicated when the interests of various segments of the people are at variance with each other and specific groups are excluded or exploited. Such situations may arise, for example, in the case of indigenous and farming communities in relation to PGRFA.

Nevertheless, the State, as an owner and regulator of property, is a factor which now has to be contended with in the present debate on access to natural resources including PGRFA, and the equitable sharing of their benefits. This position has been reinforced by the CBD which clearly recognizes that sovereignty over natural resources rests with the state.[40] Therefore it is the state property regime which has been given explicit recognition in the international sphere, and in the debate on these resources. Writers have argued that state sovereignty over PGRFA amounts to closing off the commons of the global spread of these resources.[41] In doing so, states may also threaten the common property regimes within their jurisdiction, thus impacting adversely on farmers and other communities.[42]

INDIVIDUAL OR PRIVATE PROPERTY SYSTEMS

The discourse on private property must necessarily begin with a question regarding original ownership, namely why a particular object or thing, including something intangible, should belong to a particular individual, and how that individual acquired that object or thing in the first place. This question is usually answered with reference to Locke's labour theory of property.

Locke started from the position that all the resources of the earth are produced spontaneously by nature and that nobody has an original private and exclusive dominion over them in their natural state.[43] He maintained that there must necessarily be some means of appropriating them before they could be of use to any individual. The means of doing so are by using the labour of one's own body to remove it out of the state of nature, thereby

---

39 Boudewijn Bouckaert 'What is property?' (1990) 13(3) *Harvard Journal of Law & Public Policy* 775.

40 CBD, Article 3.

41 Falcon and Fowler, above n 30.

42 For a discussion of the legal status of genetic resources in national law in some countries see UNEP/CBD/WG-ABS/5/5 – Ad Hoc Open-Ended Working Group on Access and Benefit-Sharing, Fifth meeting, 8–12 October 2007, *Report on the Legal Status of Genetic Resources in National Law, Including Property Law, Where Applicable, in a Selection of Countries*, 30 August 2007.

43 Locke, above n 1, Book II Second Treatise, Chapter V, paragraph 26.

making it one's own property. This position is justified on the basis that every man owns his own person, and therefore 'the labour of his body, and the *work* of his hands ... are properly his.'[44] Therefore if he removes something out of the state of nature by means of the labour of his own body, that thing becomes a part of his body and exclusively his own. The consent of 'all mankind' is not a pre-requisite for this acquisition, the labour that was expended in doing so being sufficient. Locke also held that a person can assert property claims over resources only 'where there is enough, and as good, left in common for others,' and that the fair share of an individual is limited to whatever he or she can make use of and enjoy before it spoils, anything beyond this belonging to others.

The question of whether the resources of the earth to which Locke was referring indicate communal property or open access regimes is ambiguous. Locke's initial theory of acquisition of resources seems to be analogous to the Roman law concept of *res nullius*, by which some things were unowned, but could become the private property of any person who acquired actual control over them, by whatever means. Similarly, in open access or no property regimes, any person who acquired a component of the resource could establish a property claim over it.[45]

Locke's hypothesis of private property is that it is a natural phenomenon which exists prior to, and distinct from, the state and civil society. The latter in fact have the primary roles of protecting these pre-existing rights. Contrary to this hypothesis however, it has also been argued that private property rights over natural resources are fundamentally a political and social construct which can simply be justified on pragmatic and utilitarian grounds, rather than grounds of natural rights or of efficient utilization of resources.[46] This construct has been extended from the regimes which permitted the propertization of physical resources, from land to genetic resources, and subsequently to the more intangible resources of knowledge and information.

---

[44] Ibid, paragraph 27.

[45] Some scholars take the view that Locke was in fact referring to common property rather than open access systems – Kristin Shrader-Frechette, 'Locke and Limits on Land Ownership' (1993) 54(2) *Journal of the History of Ideas* 201; Rebecca P Judge, 'Restoring the Commons: Toward a New Interpretation of Locke's Theory of Property' (2002) 78(3) *Land Economics* 331. However, his reference to America seems to categorize it as *terra nullius* rather than as the communal property of the peoples who inhabited it.

[46] See for example, Bradley Bryan, 'Property as Ontology: On Aboriginal and English Understandings of Ownership' (2000) 13 *Canadian Journal of Law & Jurisprudence* 3, 6. Intellectual property rights are an appropriate example of this.

Intellectual Property

Intellectual property is a form of private property which gives individuals or specific groups exclusive rights over intangible and incorporeal objects such as knowledge, ideas, and processes. It has also been described as representing 'the commodification of creativity or innovation,'[47] and the commodification of information and knowledge, which is often the principal source of wealth generation.[48]

Intellectual property has been defined as 'nonphysical property which stems from, is identified as, and whose value is based upon some idea or ideas.'[49] Within this value there must be some element of novelty, which though not absolute, requires that the object of the idea must have been generally unknown at the time of the claim. Thus the object or *res* of intellectual property is 'a product of cognitive processes and can exist privately, known only to its creator.'[50] This is what differentiates the objects of intellectual property from other forms of intangible property such as stocks and bonds. The second aspect of intellectual property is that it is not the idea per se which is granted protection, but rather the use and value to be derived from it. Therefore although the idea is intangible, what is in fact protected is the tangible manifestation of it.[51] This could range from machinery or medicinal drugs to computer programmes or biotechnological processes. Intellectual property thus draws an analogy between intangible assets and corporeal property in order to provide the former with the protection given to the latter. It is therefore essentially a private property regime which grants certain economic rights to the property holder, and like other forms of private property it also encompasses the notion of exclusion.[52]

---

[47] Renée Marlin-Bennett, *Knowledge Power: Intellectual Property, Information, and Privacy* (2004) 5.

[48] Shahid Alikhan and Raghunath Mashelkar, *Intellectual Property and Competitive Strategies in the 21st Century* (2004), Chapter 1.

[49] Justin Hughes, 'The Philosophy of Intellectual Property' (1988) 77 *Georgetown Law Journal* 287, 294.

[50] Ibid at 294.

[51] Ibid. Intellectual property systems provide exclusive protection for the subject matter of the property for a specific period of time, usually 15–20 years.

[52] For a discussion of some economic and non-economic rights see Adam D Moore, 'Intellectual Property: Theory, Privilege, and Pragmatism,' (2003) 16 *Canadian Journal of Law & Jurisprudence* 191, 201. A significant change, which has emerged in the last few decades, is that much of the protection is being claimed by corporations rather than individuals.

Intellectual property is relatively recent in origin and in its present form is generally concentrated in the western legal tradition. It is now also the property regime which has the most widespread global impacts, and in a contemporary context is probably the most contentious. It has rightly been said that the 21st century is often called the 'century of knowledge', and leadership will be in the hands of those who create and harness it. Knowledge can also potentially be converted into wealth, and a country's ability to do so will determine its future in the comity of nations.[53]

The Lockean/labour theory of property fits well with intellectual property rights as it can be argued that a novel and original product emerged out of the labour of the creator.[54] However, directly opposing views have been taken by writers. For example, Richards points out that the Lockean theory of property as applied to intellectual property does not hold water as it is based on the assumption that ideas and inventions are the products of isolated individuals.[55] He argues that ideas are the result of social creations rather than individual ones and must work on an accumulation of existing ideas which are the result of social processes.[56] Thus claims of novelty are over rated. This argument would apply to modern varieties of plants which have been developed out of traditional varieties bred by farmers over centuries, and over which intellectual property rights are now being claimed on the grounds that the new versions fulfil the element of novelty.

This perception is also consistent with that held by many non-western cultures. It has been pointed out that intellectual property rights are 'fundamentally Western rules, emerging from medieval Europe and, later from

---

[53] Alikhan and Mashelkar, above n 48. The authors note that trade and industry are becoming more knowledge driven as can be seen in international trade. This has changed from an emphasis on commodities to high technology goods which have doubled their share of world merchandize exports.

[54] See for example Hughes, above n 49.

[55] Donald G Richards, *Intellectual Property Rights and Global Capitalism – The Political Economy of the TRIPS Agreement* (2004) 41. This notion has been termed the idea of the 'romantic author' or individual creative genius. It has also been argued that scholars show that 'the romantic ideal ignores the actual process of creation, where individuals often work within corporate settings, an audience collaborates with authors to infuse work with meanings, and authors draw upon earlier creations. Despite its flawed premise, the trope of the romantic author helps justify broad intellectual property rights.' – see Anupam Chander and Madhavi Sunder, 'The Romance of the Public Domain' (2004) 92 *California Law Review* 1331, 1339.

[56] Given the fact that in the present day those who produce new technology are employed by large corporations, intellectual property does not necessarily benefit those who laboured over it, but the corporate interests for whom they work.

Industrial Age Europe and North America,' and may be inconsistent with traditional non-western social and philosophical systems.[57]

The justification of intellectual property must also be viewed in the light of the notion of 'distributive scarcity.' The notion of scarcity has been cited by law and economics scholars as the primary rationale for property rights regimes.[58] When resources are abundant and sufficient for all, there would be no need of property. However, when two or more people require the same good for their needs, their use of the good becomes rivalrous. This results in 'distributive scarcity' and three potential outcomes are possible, namely, violence, withdrawal from the resource, or rules by which rights over the resource are allocated to individuals or groups.[59] A property rights regime is essentially the third option. It ensures the optimal efficient use of the resource and its conservation on the one hand, and also enables the maintenance of social stability on the other. However, a distinction has been made between natural and artificial scarcity. Natural scarcity occurs without any human, institutional or contractual arrangements and follows from the relationship between people and nature. Artificial scarcity on the other hand, is the deliberate outcome of such arrangements and may be caused by the legal regime which also justifies it.[60]

It can be argued that creating private property rights over PGRFA which was by and large freely accessible to all would amount to the deliberate creation of artificial scarcity. The monopolistic control over such resources granted to some individuals or groups would cause the resources to become rivalrous where they were previously not so. Their scarcity would also increase their value, thus making them a source of wealth to those who control them. Thus it can be asserted that the sanction of intellectual property rights over PGRFA amounts to an allocation of social wealth since those who own such resources have the power to dictate their use by others.[61] This sanction is rooted in the justification of private property in western jurisprudence which asserts that private property rights have social

---

[57] Marlin-Bennett, above n 47, Chapter 2.

[58] Carol M Rose, 'The Several Futures of Property: Of Cyberspace and Folk Tales, Emission Trades and Ecosystems' (1998) 83 *Minnesota Law Review* 129.

[59] Bouckaert, above n 39; Giordano, above n 19; Terry L Anderson and Peter J Hill, 'The Evolution of Property Rights' in Terry L Anderson and Fred S McChesney (eds), *Property rights: cooperation, conflict, and law* (2003) Chapter 5.

[60] Bouckaert, above n 39.

[61] The economic value of PGRFA has increased to immeasurable levels and it is now a source of extreme wealth – Chetan Gulati, 'The "Tragedy of the Commons" in Plant Genetic Resources: The Need for a New International Regime Centered around an International Biotechnology Patent Office' (2001) 4 *Yale Human Rights & Development Law Journal* 63.

benefits since they add value to the objects of property. It has been contended that value, as synonymous with utility or welfare, is the central concept uniting the law of property. Therefore a property system benefits both individuals and society at large, since protecting the property of individuals will contribute towards the overall strengthening of property value.[62] Consequently, property rights over modern varieties of PGRFA would be justified on the basis that protecting the entrepreneurial enterprise which creates them (and which also acquires wealth) ultimately benefits humanity as a whole by enabling the development of new plant varieties required for human nutrition and food security. Whether this justification has validity remains to be seen.

Bouckaert argues that the rights assigned to holders of intellectual property must necessarily differ from those assigned to holders of corporeal property. The latter rights pertain to resolving problems of natural distributive scarcity and give the holders exclusive rights over a specific good as a solution. Intellectual property on the other hand, does not address problems of natural scarcity and in fact serves to artificially create it. Bouckaert points out that if the holder of the idea does not disclose it, he/she remains the sole owner and no question of property arises. If he/she does disclose it, it gives rise to an obligation on the part of third persons to refrain from using it except under the specified conditions. As he notes:

> [t]hese obligations do not have any relationship with a physical control over something, as is the case with real rights on corporeal goods. They are merely intended to create an artificial scarcity to the advantage of the author and of the persons to whom he alienates his monopoly.[63]

The argument of artificial scarcity extends into the idea of the 'anticommons' put forward by Heller and Eisenberg.[64] Heller defines the anticommons as a situation where several owners each possess the right to exclude others from a scarce resource, in direct contrast to Hardin's commons where there were no owners and no rights of exclusion at all. Too much ownership

---

62 Bell and Parchomovsky compare a property system to a communications network 'whose value increases with each additional subscriber while the corresponding value each subscriber derives from the network also increases' – Abraham Bell and Gideon Parchomovsky, 'A Theory of Property' (2005) 90 *Cornell Law Review* 531, 559.

63 Bouckaert, above n 39. See also Richards, above n 55 Chapter 2. See also Christopher May, *The World Intellectual Property Organization: resurgence and the development agenda* (2007), Chapter 1.

64 See Michael A Heller, 'The Tragedy of the Anticommons: Property in the Transition from Marx to Markets' (1998) 111 *Harvard Law Review* 621.

in a resource therefore results in no one having an effective privilege of use. The resource is subject to under utilization, which he calls the 'tragedy of the anticommons' and he notes that it can appear whenever governments create new property rights.[65] Heller and Eisenberg analyze recent developments in biomedical research on the basis of this theory, and point to the fact that excessive propertization in the form of intellectual property rights of this field has resulted in under use and a tragedy of the commons in research which was once available in the public domain.[66]

Propertization of PGRFA is now taking place by way of intellectual property rights under the aegis of the TRIPS Agreement and UPOV. The question which arises is whether these resources too will be subject to a tragedy of the anticommons. When exclusion from plant varieties takes place, the further development of these resources and the enhancement of their diversity would be restricted. Restrictions on access to crop varieties critical for food security would also have negative impacts on farmers and developing countries. These concerns underly the international debate on PGRFA which will be discussed further in this book.

INTERNATIONAL PROPERTY REGIMES OVER BIOLOGICAL RESOURCES

Several principles of international law have evolved in relation to natural resources over the last few decades. These principles and their applicability have been re-assessed in the light of de-colonization and the assertion of sovereign rights by countries which were previously under colonial rule. They relate both to resources within the boundaries of nations as well as those beyond their jurisdiction. The principles applicable in international law are analogous to those discussed at national level. In this section I will examine the concepts of the global commons and the common heritage of humankind, which are essentially international common property regimes, and the principle of state sovereignty as a form of private property rights in the international sphere, and discuss their applicability to PGRFA and traditional knowledge.

---

[65] Ibid.

[66] Michael A Heller and Rebecca S Eisenberg, 'Can patents deter innovation? The anticommons in biomedical research' (1998) 280(5364) *Science* 698; Jonathan Michael Berger, 'Tripping over Patents: AIDS, Access to Treatment and the Manufacturing of Scarcity' (2002) 17 *Connecticut Journal of International Law* 157.

The Global Commons

International common property resources are the territories over which no one nation has exclusive jurisdiction. They traditionally include the atmosphere, the oceans beyond territorial seas and the marine resources contained in them, Antarctica and outer space.[67] Until a few decades ago these territories and their resources were unregulated and free for use and exploitation.[68] As in the case with other common property resources, this exploitation had two primary aspects, namely, the extraction of resources from the environment and the addition of wastes and pollutants into it.[69] Now termed the global commons, these resources were, until regulation took place, the archetypal open access regimes which best represented the analogy of the tragedy of the commons. On the one hand resources such as marine fish stocks were open to excessive exploitation,[70] and on the other, the atmosphere[71] and oceans[72] were free dumping grounds for discommodities such as wastes and pollution.

Genetic resources and traditional knowledge were also originally considered as falling within the global commons. Many of the countries and

---

[67] Christopher C Joyner, 'Global Commons: The Oceans, Antarctica, the Atmosphere, and Outer Space' in P J Simmons and Chantal de Jonge Oudraat (eds) *Managing global issues: lessons learned* (2001) Chapter 9. The term 'common space areas' and 'global common spaces' has also been used by Joyner – Christopher C Joyner, 'Legal Implications of the Concept of the Common Heritage of Mankind' (1986) 35(1) *International and Comparative Law Quarterly* 190.

[68] Historically, spaces outside the political boundaries of sovereign States in Europe were also considered *terra nullius* and available for expropriation – M Chemillier-Gendreau, 'The Idea of the Common Heritage of Humankind and its Political Uses' (2002) 9(3) *Constellations: An International Journal of Critical & Democratic Theory* 375.

[69] William M Ross, 'The Management of International Common Property Resources' (1971) 61(3) *Geographical Reviews* 325.

[70] Now regulated by the *Agreement for the Implementation of the Provisions of the United Nations Convention of the Law of the Sea of 10 December 1982, Relating to the Conservation and Management of Straddling Fish Stocks and Highly Migratory Fish Stocks*, UN Document A/CONF.164/37, 8 September 1995; 34 ILM 1542 (entered into force 11 December 2001).

[71] Now regulated by the *Vienna Convention for the Protection of the Ozone Layer* (1987) 26 ILM 1516 (entered into force 22 September 1988) and the *Framework Convention on Climate Change* (1992) 31 ILM 849 (entered into force 21 March 1994) and their Protocols.

[72] Now regulated by the *United Nations Convention on the Law of the Sea* 1833 UNTS 3, 397, 21 ILM 1261 (entered into force 10 December 1982) (hereinafter UNCLOS).

communities which possessed these resources had not staked formal proprietary claims to them, and in the absence of such claims of ownership they were assumed to be free for the taking. In the period in which many of these countries were under colonial domination such claims would, in any event, have been irrelevant. However, in the post-colonial period countries which were now sovereign entities began asserting their own claims over the resources within their jurisdiction and mounting a challenge to the assumption that these were common property available to all. In relation to biological resources these claims were concretized in the CBD with the acknowledgement that states have sovereign rights over the biological diversity within their jurisdiction.[73]

Thus, international common property systems in regard to natural resources including PGRFA, would be generally premised on two opposing principles, namely the common heritage of humankind and state sovereignty over natural resources.

The Common Heritage of Humankind

The primary concept upon which the regulation of international common property resources is based is that of the common heritage of humankind (CHH). A CHH regime repudiates the notion of State sovereignty over these resources in favour of allocating them equitably to all of humanity.[74] It would not assign ownership rights over them, but would rather allot rights of access and management[75] and also rights of common regulation, to all states.[76]

Although international common property resources have generally been designated the common heritage of humankind,[77] it has also been argued

---

[73] CBD, Article 3.

[74] J M Spectar, 'Elephants, Donkeys, or Other Creatures? Presidential Election Cycles & International Law of the Global Commons' (2000) 15 *American University International Law Review* 975.

[75] Joyner, 'Legal Implications' above n 67.

[76] It has been argued that because the principle is susceptible to varying interpretations this prevents it from becoming a principle of customary international law. Further, it is only binding on the countries that have signed the treaties in which it is incorporated. Therefore it is based on an unstable premise – Jennifer Frakes, 'The Common Heritage of Mankind Principle and the Deep Seabed, Outer Space, and Antarctica: Will Developed and Developing Nations reach a Compromise?' (2003) 21 *Wisconsin International Law Journal* 409. For a historical analysis of the principle see Chemillier-Gendreau, above n 68.

[77] See for example the UNCLOS, above n 72, Preamble and Part I Article 1 read with Article 136. See also *Agreement Governing the Activities of States on the*

that this concept has less to do with the conservation of these resources, than in ensuring access by states to their beneficial uses.[78] Baslar cites two important factors that have determined the motivation to formulate such a regime.[79] These are the technology parameter and the scarcity parameter. As some nations became technologically powerful, their ability to exploit and appropriate resources (for example marine resources) in common spaces increased, to the exclusion of other countries. The technology parameter relevant to this discussion would be the development of biotechnology, which enables such nations to exploit genetic resources. Further, expanding global populations and increased exploitation consequent to technological development resulted in increasing scarcity of once abundant resources. These factors resulted in new demands for an international regime to govern them.

Therefore the evolution of the concept was essentially grounded in political negotiations regarding the global commons, based on the differing positions of various blocs of countries. These were mainly divided between those in the northern and southern hemispheres, the latter including, in earlier decades, the communist states. The positions of these blocs on the concept of the CHH were based in large part on their perceptions as to how it could be interpreted to best protect their strategic interests.[80] To the countries of the global south the CHH principle was intrinsically tied up with the establishment of a new international economic order and 'served as a means of allocating global wealth through non-market mechanisms.'[81] As it has been pointed out, the South was trying to achieve through law what it had failed to achieve in the market place, and these countries interpreted the principle to mean common ownership of common property with an equal voice in its use and exploitation.[82]

Moon and Other Celestial Bodies, Resolution 34/68, annex – adopted on 5 December 1979, opened for signature on 18 December 1979, (entered into force 11 July 1984) (hereinafter Moon Treaty).

[78] Erin A Clancy, 'The Tragedy of the Global Commons' (1998) 5 *Indiana Journal of Global Legal Studies* 601; J M Spectar, 'Saving the Ice Princess: NGOs, Antarctica & International Law in the New Millennium' (1999) 23 *Suffolk Transnational Law Review* 57.

[79] Kemal Baslar, *The Concept of the Common Heritage of Mankind in International Law* (1998) Chapter 2.

[80] The north south divisions at these negotiations reflected to a large extent the negotiations of the CBD including the demands of southern countries for technology transfers in return for acceptance of northern positions – Spectar, above n 74.

[81] Spectar, above n 78, 62.

[82] Ibid at 61.

The North by contrast viewed the CHH principle as constituting a free and open access regime which facilitated commercial exploitation of the resources to which it applied, within a free enterprise system.[83] The development of CHH regimes was therefore perceived in large part by technology rich countries as a context within which they could exploit these resources within a structured system, while avoiding conflicts.[84] The United Nations Convention on the Law of the Sea (UNCLOS), the Antarctic Treaty and the Moon Treaty have been cited as examples of this position.[85]

As new resources originate or the value of existing resources increases, the issue of whether they should come within the purview of the CHH principle has given rise to considerable international polemics. While the original global commons were geographical spaces outside the territorial jurisdiction of states, the new contents consist of resources, natural or created, which exist within national boundaries and which are under the control of States and other entities within them. The disputes are usually triggered by the development of new technologies which create new resources or which enhance the potential to exploit existing ones. As in the earlier debates, these disputes also reflect the north/south disconnection in relation to such issues as equity, philosophy, and social and legal contexts. The debates on the human genome[86] and digitized information[87] have arisen relatively recently, while that over plant genetic resources has intensified in the last two decades.

---

[83] Ibid; Frakes, above n 76.

[84] Joyner, above n 67, Chapter 9; Spectar, above n 74.

[85] The Preamble to the UNCLOS does refer to promoting 'the peaceful uses of the seas and oceans, the equitable and efficient utilization of their resources, the conservation of their living resources, and the study, protection and preservation of the marine environment.' The Preamble to the Moon Treaty states that the States Parties desire 'to prevent the moon from becoming an area of international conflict.' Similarly the Preamble to the Antarctic Treaty 402 UNTS 71 (entered into force June 23, 1961) states that the Parties recognize 'that it is in the interest of all mankind that Antarctica shall continue for ever to be used exclusively for peaceful purposes and shall not become the scene or object of international discord.'

[86] See for example J M Spectar, 'Fruit of the Human Genome Tree: Cautionary Tales about Technology, Investment, and the Heritage of Humankind' (2001) 23 *Loyola of Los Angeles International & Comparative Law Review* 1; Richard B Smith, Halla Thorsteinsdottir, Abdallah S Daar, E Richard Gold and Peter A Singer, 'Genomics Knowledge and Equity: A Global Public Goods Perspective of the Patent System' (2004) 82(5) *Bulletin of the World Health Organization* 385.

[87] Pamela Samuelson, 'The Public Domain: Mapping the Digital Public Domain: Threats and Opportunities' (2003) 66 *Law and Contemporary Problems* 147.

The notion of common heritage was originally applied to PGRFA as these resources were considered as being in the public domain.[88] The debate on PGRFA as part of the global commons has been played out primarily in the FAO. While the FAO International Undertaking on Plant Genetic Resources initially designated these resources as the common heritage of humankind, opposition to this arose both from plant breeders on the one hand and developing country governments on behalf of their traditional farmers, on the other. Consequently the International Undertaking was re-negotiated, resulting in the FAO Treaty which has now provided for the inclusion of specific and designated plant varieties within the public domain.

State Sovereignty over Natural Resources

It has been commented that the term 'sovereignty' in international law has a long and troubled history and a variety of meanings. 'In its most common modern usage, sovereignty is the term for the "totality of international rights and duties recognized by international law" as residing in an independent territorial unit – the State.'[89] A comprehensive analysis of State sovereignty is beyond the scope of this book which will be confined to an examination of the principle in relation to natural resources.

The development of state sovereignty in regard to environment and natural resources has a long and complex history. The principle was premised on the rather obvious fact that the natural wealth and resources of a country belonged to its people. The period of de-colonization involved restructuring the legal arrangements by which natural resources had been exploited by colonial powers and foreign investors. The concept was initially linked to the human rights of the people of the former colonies, and was expressed in one of the early UN General Assembly resolutions on the subject, which recognized that 'the right of peoples to use and exploit their natural wealth and resources is inherent in their sovereignty.'[90] The notion was subsequently incorporated in both the human rights Covenants with

---

[88] Stephen B Brush, 'The Demise of "Common Heritage" and Protection for Traditional Agricultural Knowledge' in Charles McManis (ed), *Biodiversity and the law: intellectual property, biotechnology and traditional knowledge*, (2007) Chapter 20.

[89] James Crawford, *The Creation of States in International Law* (2006), 32.

[90] Resolution 626 (VII) of 21 December 1952. See also Subrata Roy Chowdhury, 'Permanent sovereignty over natural resources' in Kamal Hossain and Subrata Roy Chowdhury, *Permanent sovereignty over natural resources in international law: principle and practice* (1984) Chapter 1.

identical wording in Article 1.[91] The principle was also linked to the right of self-determination on the basis that the right to the natural resources within one's country constituted an important component of that right.[92]

The economic dimensions of the principle are reflected in the multitude of documents which incorporated it, beginning with the General Assembly Resolution of 1962 on Permanent Sovereignty over Natural Resources.[93] Subsequently, it became part of resolutions adopted by the United Nations Conference on Trade and Development (UNCTAD) in 1973,[94] the Declaration on the Establishment of a New International Economic Order,[95] the Programme of Action on the Establishment of a New International Economic Order[96] and in Article 2 of the Charter of Economic Rights and Duties of States adopted by the General Assembly in 1974.[97]

Several factors are noteworthy in the early formulation of the concept. In the first place it referred to the extraction of non-renewable resources, most importantly petroleum and other minerals.[98] The inequitable terms under which such extraction was being carried out at the time were inherently disadvantageous to the newly independent countries. The many UN Resolutions on the topic provided several criteria by which to test the compatibility of the contractual agreements with the principle, including that they must

---

[91] See Articles 1 of both the *International Covenant on Economic, Social and Cultural Rights* GA res. 2200A (XXI), 21 UN GAOR Supp. (No. 16) at 52, UN Doc. A/6316 (1966); 999 UNTS 171; 6 ILM 368 (1967) (entered into force 3 January 1976) and the *International Covenant on Economic, Social and Cultural Rights* GA res. 2200A (XXI), 21 UN GAOR Supp. (No. 16) at 52, UN Doc. A/6316 (1966); 999 UNTS 171; 6 ILM 368 (1967) (entered into force 3 January 1976) which read 'All peoples may, for their own ends, freely dispose of their natural wealth and resources without prejudice to any obligations arising out of international economic co-operation, based upon the principle of mutual benefit, and international law. In no case may a people be deprived of its own means of subsistence.'

[92] Chowdhury, above n 90. This chapter also contains a list of the original documents which contain references to this principle.

[93] *Permanent Sovereignty over Natural Resources*, G.A. Resolution 1803 (XVII), 17 U.N. GAOR Supp. (No.17) at 15, U.N. Doc. A/5217 (1962).

[94] 88 (XII) of 19 October 1973 of the Trade and Development Board of UNCTAD.

[95] 3021 (S-VI) of 1 May 1974.

[96] 3202 (S-VI) of 1 May 1974.

[97] Resolution 3281 (XXIX) of 12 December 1974.

[98] After the 1974 Declaration on the New International Economic Order and the Charter of Economic Rights and Duties the principles covers all foreign economic activities – Kamal Hossain, 'Introduction' in Kamal Hossain and Subrata Roy Chowdhury, above n 90.

(1) be in the interests of national development and well-being of the state concerned; (2) be in accordance with the national legislation in force; and (3) be freely entered into.[99] In succeeding years several contracts were re-negotiated and new types of agreements formulated to ensure that the developing countries maximized the benefits derived from their natural resources.

Up to this stage in the history of the principle, the resources in question were non-renewable and therefore necessarily rivalrous in use. However, the need to access natural resources has now been extended to renewable resources such as genetic resources. These are by nature both renewable and non-rivalrous. Unlike mineral resources, large quantities do not have to be extracted in order to obtain the economic benefits to be derived from them, since their importance is contained in the information within them. Consequently, since very small amounts of original sources are usually required for further development, it was more difficult for countries in possession of these resources to practically prevent them from being removed from their territories. As noted earlier, before recent biotechnological developments, PGRFA by their very nature were freely accessible, and traditional varieties are still open for the taking.

It has been noted that these factors 'blinded both germplasm collectors and bio-diversity rich countries to the possibility that these resources might also be considered subject to national sovereignty.'[100] In fact as noted above, the International Undertaking of 1983 held that genetic resources were the common heritage of humankind. It was with the advent of the 'seed wars' of the 1980s that this position was challenged.[101] The principle of sovereignty was subsequently applied to plant genetic resources and this subject was brought within the ambit of international law and politics.[102] The concept as it relates to these resources is now embodied in both the CBD[103] and the FAO Treaty.[104]

---

[99] Ibid.

[100] Anthony J Stenson and Tim S Gray, *The Politics of Genetic Resource Control* (1999) 120.

[101] Keith Aoki, 'Weeds, Seeds & Deeds: Recent Skirmishes in the Seed Wars' (2003) 11 *Cardozo Journal of International and Comparative Law* 247.

[102] Stenson and Gray, above n 100, Chapter 5.

[103] See the Preamble which states that 'States have sovereign rights over their own biological resources' and more importantly Article 15.

[104] International Treaty on Plant Genetic Resources for Food and Agriculture, adopted at the 31st Session of the FAO Conference on 3 November 2001 available at http://www.fao.org/AG/cgrfa/itpgr.htm and the website of the Treaty at http://www.planttreaty.org/ (hereinafter FAO Treaty) (both last accessed 30 June 2012), Preamble and Article 10.

CONCLUSION

Natural resources 'produced by the spontaneous hand of nature' can therefore be acknowledged as common property resources and four broad management regimes have been identified in relation to them. Of these, three are based on the premise that these resources constitute common property in varying forms and degrees. They range from open access or unregulated systems to those regulated at the community, state, and international spheres. In direct opposition to these are the individual or private property systems.

The question which arises is which of these systems is most conducive to the sustainable use of natural resources and PGRFA in particular, and to the equitable sharing of the benefits to be derived from them. It has been argued that until recently PGRFA by its very non-rivalrous nature could not in fact be propertized and access to it could not be controlled. Therefore it necessarily fell within an open access regime. This did not result in resource depletion, but rather facilitated its enhancement and increased its diversity. PGRFA is therefore a natural resource which is perhaps most conducive to widespread use and sharing.

Modern technology has now provided the means by which the use and development of germplasm can be physically controlled and therefore converted into private property by those who possess it. This is being done in the context of both private property rights, specifically intellectual property, and State sovereignty. There are several ramifications of this development. First, the control of germplasm by a few raises issues of equity, particularly in regard to those who conserved and developed it for centuries. It also raises issues of food security and agricultural development for the world at large, but particularly for developing countries. Second, such control may have impacts on genetic diversity. Where unimpeded access to PGRFA is restricted, continuing development of new plant varieties will necessarily be hindered. The marketing and use of modern varieties to the exclusion of traditional landraces will also reduce crop diversity in the field. This may result in a 'tragedy of the anticommons' in which over propertization of a resource results in its depletion.

The current debate over PGRFA revolves around which property regime should be applied to these resources. The application of private property rights to PGRFA, by way of the TRIPS Agreement and the UPOV Conventions, is of especial concern to developing countries, which would be particularly affected by both impacts noted above. The response of these countries to this process has been to impose their own claims by asserting State sovereignty over the germplasm within their jurisdiction and this position has been validated by the CBD. However, the end result of both these systems is to remove PGRFA from the public domain and to restrict access to vital resources. The FAO Treaty offers a possible compromise by creating an open access system in regard to specific plant varieties selected for their significance to agriculture and food security. The international agreements which reflect these three property regimes, and the negotiations on their applicability to PGRFA and traditional knowledge will be further explored in this book.

5. The international environmental regime on plant genetic resources and traditional knowledge

INTRODUCTION

This book will analyze two international legal regimes which deal with issues of access to plant genetic resources for food and agriculture (PGRFA) and traditional knowledge. These are the environmental/conservation regime and the trade and intellectual property rights regime. In this chapter I will examine the former regime consisting of the Convention on Biological Diversity of 1992 (CBD) and the FAO Treaty on Plant Genetic Resources for Food and Agriculture of 2001 (FAO Treaty), and the institutions relating to them. The primary objective of these agreements is universal access to genetic resources and the equitable sharing of the benefits arising out of them. Both have devised systems to achieve this objective, and to some extent they serve as a foil to the intellectual property regime whose aim is the imposition of private property rights over these resources. Consequently, they are perceived by developing countries as the preferred fora in which to further their goal of achieving equity in the use and benefits of PGRFA.

The purpose of this chapter is to provide an introductory overview of the two treaties, their evolution, conceptual framework, scope and structure. This will help to put in context the processes which have taken place within them in relation to PGRFA, and the way in which their respective fora have addressed the issue. This chapter will also consider their provisions on the conservation and use of PGRFA both *in situ* and *ex situ*.

THE CONVENTION ON BIOLOGICAL DIVERSITY

The Conceptual Framework and Structure of the Convention on Biological Diversity

The CBD is unusual among international environmental treaties and there are many different objectives in the conceptual framework underlying it. It is first, a compromise between the widely divergent positions of developing and developed countries in regard to biodiversity. The text of the convention essentially reflects the economic and political divisions between the North and the South. Northern interests were primarily in the conservation of biological resources and access to their uses and benefits. The South alternatively saw these resources, particularly those within their jurisdiction, as a tool by which to forge a more equitable international political and economic order in which economic capacity and technology would be more equitably distributed.[1] Second, it is a framework convention with little enforceability. It merely sets out guidelines for the conservation of biodiversity rather than imposing clearly defined and binding obligations on states parties. The articles setting out the duties and obligations of states are preceded by the words 'as far as possible and as appropriate,'[2] or 'in accordance with its particular conditions and capabilities.'[3] As a result of this terminology there is a lack of consistent and clearly defined standards by which to measure the extent to which its goals have been achieved, or to facilitate enforcement of its provisions.

The North/South divisions on the CBD were primarily manifested by the refusal of the US to sign the treaty. Notwithstanding the fact that the US had supported the original suggestion for a framework biodiversity convention, the main opposition to it also came from this direction. It is to date the only country which has not ratified it. It has been noted that throughout the initial negotiations, while the US endorsed the idea of such a convention, it remained opposed to proposals to include issues of biotechnology in it.[4] Developing countries on the other hand refused to support a convention

---

[1] Kal Raustiala and David G Victor, 'The Future of the Convention on Biological Diversity' (1996) 38(4) *Environment* 16.

[2] *Convention on Biological Diversity* (1992) 31 ILM 818 – Articles 5 to 11 (hereinafter CBD).

[3] CBD, Article 6.

[4] Declaration of the United States of America reproduced in the *Handbook on the Convention on Biological Diversity* (3rd ed 2005), 394 (hereinafter *CBD Handbook*).

which did not include this subject.[5] While there was considerable difference of opinion within the US as to whether the CBD should be signed or not, the main points of opposition related to the transfer of technology, intellectual property rights and the financing of conservation efforts.[6]

While previous 'environmental' conventions were typically sectoral in nature,[7] the CBD for the first time took a holistic overview of biodiversity and its management. This is reflected in the definition of biological diversity contained in Article 2.[8] The CBD is concerned with natural resources

---

[5] Fiona McConnell, *The Biodiversity Convention: A Negotiating History* (1996), 11.

[6] For a detailed account of the debate within the US in regard to the CBD, see Robert F Blomquist, 'Ratification Resisted: Understanding America's Response to the Convention on Biological Diversity, 1989–2002' (2002) 32 *Golden Gate University Law Review* 493. See also Valentina Tejera, 'Tripping over Property Rights: Is it Possible to Reconcile the Convention on Biological Diversity with Article 27 of the TRIPS Agreement?' (1999) 33 *New England Law Review* 967, 982; Raustiala and Victor, above n 1; Daniel T Jenks, 'The Convention on Biological Diversity – An Efficient Framework for the Preservation of Life on Earth?' (1995) 15 *Northwestern School of Law Journal of International Law & Business* 636, 637.

[7] Up to that time global conservation agreements had focused on for example, the conservation of particular species (*International Convention for the Regulation of Whaling*, 62 Stat. 1716; 161 UNTS 72 (entered into force 10 November 1948); *Bonn Convention on the Conservation of Migratory Species of Wild Animals*, 23 June 1979, 19 ILM 15 (1980) (entered into force 1 November 1983)); or on particular types of ecosystems or identified sites (*Convention on Wetlands of International Importance especially as Waterfowl Habitat (Ramsar Convention)* 996 UNTS 245; TIAS 11084; 11 ILM 963 (1972) (entered into force 21 December 1975); *Convention Concerning the Protection of the World Cultural and Natural Heritage (World Heritage Convention)* 1037 UNTS 151; 27 UST 37; 11 ILM 1358 (1972) (entered into force 17 December 1975)); or on a particular form of protective action (*Convention on International Trade in Endangered Species of Wild Fauna and Flora (CITES)* 27 UST 1087; TIAS 8249; 993 UNTS 243 (entered into force 1 July 1975)). At the regional level there are some treaties which take a more holistic view of biodiversity protection, for example the *African Convention on the Conservation of Nature and Natural Resources* (1968) (entered into force 16 June 1969, revised 2003), *Convention for the Conservation of Biological Diversity and the Protection of Priority Wild Areas in Central America*, 5 June 1992 and the *ASEAN Agreement on the Conservation of Nature and Natural Resources*, opened for signature 9 July 1985, (not yet entered into force). For a general discussion of these conventions see Cyrille de Klemm, *Biological diversity conservation and the law: legal mechanisms for conserving species and ecosystems* (1993).

[8] Article 2 states that '"Biological diversity" means the variability among living organisms from all sources including, inter alia, terrestrial, marine and other aquatic ecosystems and the ecological complexes of which they are part; this includes diversity within species, between species and of ecosystems.'

which are exclusively within the jurisdiction of states parties, and the sovereignty of states over them was explicitly recognized for the first time.[9] Its scope is also limited to *in situ* resources and it does not address *ex situ* collections that were not acquired in accordance with its provisions, or in other words those which were acquired before it came into force.[10] This has been a significant point of contention in the debate on access to genetic resources. Further, although the CBD is ostensibly a conservation based agreement, its provisions also potentially impact upon international trade and commerce.

The CBD is in fact rooted in an array of conflicting interests and its Preamble reflects this. To begin with, it acknowledges that biodiversity has both intrinsic and instrumental value. However, it is the instrumental value which is of greater concern and which pervades the document.[11] This value relates most importantly to maintaining the life sustaining systems of the biosphere and for meeting the food, health and other essential needs of the global population. The various interests involved are also reflected in the range and construction of acknowledged actors in relation to biodiversity which are referred to in the Convention. A unique feature is its recognition that the actors in this process are not only nation States, and there are explicit references to non-state actors which include local and indigenous communities, women, and the non-governmental sector.[12]

The Scope and Content of the CBD

The stated objectives of the CBD are the conservation of biological diversity, the sustainable use of its components and the fair and equitable sharing of the benefits arising out of the utilization of genetic resources.[13] While the first two objectives are generally desirable and uncontroversial, the uncertainty and contention surrounding the Convention revolves around the third.

---

[9] Article 3 states that 'States have, in accordance with the Charter of the United Nations and the principles of international law, the sovereign right to exploit their own resources pursuant to their own environmental policies, and the responsibility to ensure that activities within their jurisdiction or control do not cause damage to the environment of other States or of areas beyond the limits of national jurisdiction.'

[10] CBD, Article 15 read with Article 2.

[11] CBD, Preamble.

[12] CBD, Preamble, Paragraphs 12 and 13. The Preamble also notes the necessity for co-operation between States, inter-governmental and non-governmental organizations in the conservation and sustainable use of biodiversity – Preamble, Paragraph 14.

[13] CBD, Article 1.

It could also be argued that it is the third objective that really pervades the Convention and which was the driving force behind its negotiation. Therefore it is not so much an agreement on biodiversity conservation, as one which seeks to regulate access to the resources necessary for development, and their attendant political and economic implications.[14] Perhaps the most important of these resources are agricultural biodiversity including PGRFA, which sustain the agricultural productivity and nutrition security of nations.

Another notable feature of the CBD is that it recognizes the importance of human cultural diversity, more specifically the 'knowledge, innovations and practices' of indigenous peoples, at least, insofar as they relate to the conservation of biological diversity. This aspect will be discussed in depth in Chapter 6.

The institutions of the CBD have been instrumental in giving practical effect to its provisions in regard to both PGRFA and traditional knowledge. While the CBD is concerned with biodiversity as a whole, the Conference of the Parties (CoP) has addressed agricultural biodiversity as one of its thematic areas.[15] In its work on this area the CoP has taken up such issues as an international initiative for the conservation and sustainable use of pollinators, soil biodiversity, animal genetic resources, the impacts of trade liberalization on agricultural biodiversity, the impacts of genetic use restriction technologies on smallholder farmers, indigenous and local communities and farmers' rights.[16] Most recently the CoP noted that the CBD is the key international instrument for the integration of biodiversity related issues into the Millennium Development Agenda. It also noted the linkage between biodiversity, food and nutrition and the need to enhance the sustainable use of biodiversity to combat hunger and malnutrition and thereby contribute to achieving the targets of the Millennium Development Goals. It has therefore decided to bring forward options for a cross cutting

14 For an analysis of the CBD see Catherine Tinker, 'A "New Breed" of Treaty: The United Nations Convention on Biological Diversity' (1995) 13 *Pace Environmental Law Review* 191.

15 The other areas include marine and coastal biodiversity, forest biodiversity, biodiversity of inland waters and dry and sub-humid lands, mountain biodiversity and island biodiversity – CBD *Handbook*, above n 4, page xxx. The CoP Decisions on agricultural biodiversity are III/11, IV/6, V/5, VI/5, VII/3 and VIII/23.

16 *CBD Handbook,* above n 4, Decision VI/5 'Agricultural biological diversity,' 703.

initiative on biodiversity for food and nutrition within its programme of work on agricultural biodiversity.[17]

The CoP has also taken steps to address issues of equity in the uses of PGRFA and traditional knowledge, dealing with the topic in several fora. Most importantly, it established two *ad hoc* working groups in this regard. The Working Group on Article 8(j) and Related Provisions was established by Decision IV/9 entitled 'Implementation of Article 8(j) and related provisions' and the Working Group on Access and Benefit-sharing was established by Decision V/26 entitled 'Access to genetic resources.' The latter group would supplement the work of the Panel of Experts on Access and Benefit Sharing which had been established earlier by Decision IV/8. As will be further explored, these fora have made important contributions to the debate on PGRFA.

The Nagoya Protocol

The Nagoya Protocol on Access to Genetic Resources and the Fair and Equitable Sharing of the Benefits arising from their Utilization to the Convention on Biological Diversity was adopted at the Tenth Session of the CBD CoP in October 2010. The negotiation of the Protocol arose out of a Resolution of the Plan of Implementation of the World Summit on Sustainable Development in Johannesburg in 2002 to 'Negotiate within the framework of the Convention on Biological Diversity, bearing in mind the Bonn Guidelines, an international regime to promote and safeguard the fair and equitable sharing of benefits arising out of the utilization of genetic resources.'[18] The Resolution was followed up at the Seventh CoP in 2004 by Decision VII/19D, which also recalled Resolution 57/260 of 20 December 2002, adopted by the United Nations General Assembly at its fifty-seventh session. This latter Resolution also invited the CBD CoP to take steps to fulfil this commitment.[19] The CoP 7 decision was brought about by lobbying by developing countries, who were concerned that, since the entry

---

[17] Decision VII/32 'The programme of work of the Convention and the Millennium Development Goals' and Decision VIII/23 'Cross cutting initiative on biodiversity for food and nutrition.' See also UNEP/CBD/COP/8/26/Add.2 – CBD CoP, Eighth meeting, 20–31 March 2006, *Programme of Work on Agricultural Biodiversity, Options for a Cross-Cutting Initiative on Biodiversity for Food and Nutrition*, 20 January 2006.

[18] A/CONF.199/20, Chapter IV, paragraph 44 (o).

[19] UNEP/CBD/COP/DEC/VII/19 – CBD CoP Seventh meeting, 9–20 and 27 February 2004, *Decision Adopted by the Conference of the Parties to the Convention on Biological Diversity at its Seventh Meeting, VII/19. Access and benefit-sharing as related to genetic resources (Article 15)*, 13 April 2004.

into force of the CBD, user countries had not met their obligations for fair and equitable benefit sharing of genetic resources and traditional knowledge.

Writers have documented the long road to the conclusion of the Nagoya Protocol.[20] The Working Group on Access and Benefit Sharing was given the task of negotiating this regime and the process took over six years. It culminated at the Tenth CoP where the final text was adopted amidst allegations of secret negotiations and dealings, with Brazil, the EU and Japan being the key players.

As noted earlier, the basis of the Protocol was the concern of developing countries regarding the piracy of their genetic resources and the lack of an effective mechanism to ensure benefit sharing. However, an examination of several provisions in the Protocol demonstrates that the final outcome has not in fact met these concerns and it is heavily weighted in favour of developed countries, which by and large constitute the users of such resources.

The Preamble to the Protocol specifically refers to plant genetic resources for food and agriculture. It recognizes the:

> interdependence of all countries with regard to genetic resources for food and agriculture as well as their special nature and importance for achieving food security worldwide and for sustainable development of agriculture in the context of poverty alleviation and climate change and acknowledging the fundamental role of the International Treaty on Plant Genetic Resources for Food and Agriculture and the FAO Commission on Genetic Resources for Food and Agriculture in this regard.

The Preamble also refers to 'the importance of genetic resources to food security, public health, biodiversity conservation and the mitigation of and adaptation to climate change.' The importance of PGRFA for food security is reiterated in Article 8(c).

The Preamble notes the Multilateral System of Access and Benefit Sharing under the FAO Treaty and recognizes that international treaties

---

[20] Matthias Buck and Clare Hamilton, 'The Nagoya Protocol on Access to Genetic Resources and the Fair and Equitable Sharing of Benefits Arising from their Utilisation to the Convention on Biological Diversity' (2011) 20(2) *Review of European Community and International Environmental Law* 47; Kabir Bavikatte and Daniel F Robinson, 'Towards a People's History of the Law: Biocultural Jurisprudence and the Nagoya Protocol on Access and Benefit Sharing' (2011) 7/1 *Law, Environment and Development Journal* 35; Third World Network, *The Road to an Anti-Biopiracy Agreement – The Negotiations under the United Nations Convention on Biological Diversity* (2nd ed 2011).

related to ABS should be mutually supportive with a view to achieving the objectives of the Convention. It also refers to Article 8(j) of the CBD and notes the inter-relationship between genetic resources and traditional knowledge.

The sole objective of the Nagoya Protocol is to implement the third objective of the CBD, i.e. 'the fair and equitable sharing of the benefits arising out of the utilization of genetic resources.'[21] Regarding the temporal scope of the Protocol, Article 3 states that it shall apply to genetic resources within the scope of Article 15 of the CBD, and therefore *ex situ* collections which pre-date the CBD continue to remain outside its scope. Where *in situ* resources are concerned, developing countries lobbied for retroactive application of the Protocol. Writers have identified the issues regarding the ambit of the Protocol, and the questions were whether the Protocol should apply (a) to genetic resources accessed before the CBD; (b) to genetic resources accessed before the Protocol if there was no existing CBD compliant benefit sharing agreement at that point of time, (c) to continuing and new uses of such resources and traditional knowledge accessed before the CBD, and (d) to traditional knowledge accessed before the Protocol. Provider countries took the view that the scope of the Protocol should extend to all these situations, but they failed to establish their position in regard to any of them. While these provisions were present at the draft stages of the document they were dropped from the final version of the Protocol.[22]

The Protocol makes it clear that its provisions shall not affect the rights and obligations of any Party deriving from any international agreement except where it would cause a serious threat of damage to biodiversity.[23] This provision is identical to Article 22 of the CBD. Therefore it would not override the TRIPS Agreement or any other international agreement involving patenting of genetic resources or traditional knowledge. On the other hand, the Protocol permits parties to enter into specialized ABS instruments which are consistent with its provisions, and such instrument will take precedence over the Protocol. This permits parties to enter into bilateral agreements on ABS and reinforces the bilateral approach of the CBD to access and benefit sharing.

The Nagoya Protocol is a significant step in the evolution of a global system to ensure access and benefit sharing of genetic resources including

---

21 CBD Article 1.

22 Evanson Chege Kamau, Bevis Fedder and Gerd Winter, 'The Nagoya Protocol on Access to Genetic Resources and Benefit Sharing: What is New and what are the Implications for Provider and User Countries and the Scientific Community?' (2010) 6/3 *Law, Environment and Development Journal* 246 at 253.

23 Article 4.

PGRFA. It has not yet entered into force but the rate of signatories has been impressive. A preliminary appraisal indicates that the method by which it was brought to fruition was less than satisfactory, and the final document has clearly been watered down from the drafts which preceded it. Like the CBD, its language is largely exhortatory, and obligations of States Parties under it are qualified by phrases such as 'as appropriate,' 'shall endeavour,' 'shall encourage,' and 'as far as possible.' The Protocol is open to interpretation and the verdict of many has been to reserve judgement until its actual implementation can be observed. The observation of one commentator is that:

> ... the Nagoya Protocol was rushed through in the final hours of COP10 in an attempt to secure a binding instrument on ABS. As a result the Protocol represents, at best, a partially negotiated instrument. In the process, transparency, legal certainty and balance seem to have been sacrificed. The silver lining, however, is that the generalised provisions, crafted in an attempt to accommodate seemingly polarised positions, provide considerable flexibility.[24]

It remains to be seen how developing countries will use the Protocol to ensure that the objectives of the CBD on genetic resources are fulfilled. An analysis of specific provisions of the Protocol in the succeeding chapters will provide some indication as to whether these objectives will potentially be realized.

THE FAO GLOBAL SYSTEM ON PLANT GENETIC RESOURCES FOR FOOD AND AGRICULTURE

While the early work of the FAO on the conservation of PGRFA has already been discussed,[25] the turning point in its work came in 1983 when the FAO Global System on Plant Genetic Resources was established. The Global System is based on several principles including that nations have sovereign rights over the plant genetic resources in their territories, that genetic resources should be available without restriction on agreed terms for plant

---

[24] Gurdial Singh Nijar, The Nagoya Protocol on Access and Benefit Sharing of Genetic Resources: Analysis and Implementation Options for Developing Countries (South Centre, March 2011) at 37.

[25] See Chapter 2.

breeding and other scientific purposes of human benefit, and that all nations are potential donors and users of plant genetic resources.[26]

The Global System comprises the following components:[27] (a) International Agreements (which are discussed below);[28] (b) Codes of Conduct and International Standards;[29] (c) Global Mechanisms;[30] and (d) Global Instruments.[31] Some of these components constitute the supporting components of Part V of the FAO Treaty now in force.[32]

The International Undertaking on Plant Genetic Resources for Food and Agriculture of 1983 (International Undertaking)

The International Undertaking is no longer in force but will be discussed at this point in order to provide a historical perspective on the work of FAO in regard to the uses of PGRFA. As the precursor to the FAO Treaty, it is also important to put in context the issues which were raised in regard to its

---

[26] CGRFA-8/99/5 – Report of the Fifth Regular Session of the Commission on Genetic Resources for Food and Agriculture 19–23 April 1993, *Progress Report on the Global System for the Conservation and Utilization of Plant Genetic Resources.*

[27] See Commission on Plant Genetic Resources for Food and Agriculture, 'Plant Genetic Resources' available at http://www.fao.org/AG/cgrfa/PGR.htm#diagram (last accessed 30 June 2012).

[28] The FAO has identified the International Undertaking under this component. However, the FAO Treaty now supersedes the Undertaking.

[29] These comprise the Code of Conduct for Germplasm Collecting and Transfer, Gene Bank Standards and Guidelines and the Code of Conduct on Biotechnology – CGRFA-10/04/13, CGRFA, Tenth Regular Session, 8–12 November 2004, *Progress on the Draft Code of Conduct on Biotechnology as it Relates to Genetic Resources for Food and Agriculture: Policy Issues, Gaps and Duplications.*

[30] These comprise Crop and Thematic Networks, the International Network of *Ex situ* Collections and the World Information and Early Warning System.

[31] These comprise the Report on the State of the World's Plant Genetic Resources and the Global Plan of Action on Plant Genetic Resources. For information on these components see CGRFA-11/07/12 – CGRFA, Eleventh Regular Session, 11–15 June 2007, *Progress in the Preparation of the Second State of the World's Plant Genetic Resources for Food and Agriculture: A Basis to Update the Rolling Global Plan of Action*; CGRFA-11/07/11 – CGRFA, Eleventh Regular Session, 11–15 June 2007, *Follow Up to Recommendations of the Commission on Genetic Resources for Food and Agriculture Regarding Plant Genetic Resources for Food and Agriculture.*

[32] CGRFA-10/04/3 – CGRFA, Tenth Regular Session, 8–12 November 2004, *Overview of the FAO Global System for the Conservation and Sustainable Utilization of Plant Genetic Resources for Food and Agriculture and its Potential Contribution to the Implementation of the International Treaty on Plant Genetic Resources for Food and Agriculture*, 2.

provisions, and the processes by which these debates contributed to the negotiations of the latter agreement.

The International Undertaking was adopted at the Twenty-second Session of the FAO Conference in 1983 by Resolution 8/83. Although non-binding, it was the first international agreement to focus specifically on PGRFA.[33] It was based on the 'universally accepted principle that plant genetic resources are a heritage of mankind and consequently should be available without restriction,' and its objective was 'to ensure that plant genetic resources of economic and/or social interest, particularly for agriculture, will be explored, preserved, evaluated and made available for plant breeding and scientific purposes.'[34] Since the International Undertaking focused on plant genetic resources found *ex situ,* it theoretically covered all *ex situ* collections of PGRFA whether national or international, public or private.

Perhaps due to its rather idealistic objectives, the International Undertaking was fraught with controversy from the beginning, and like the CBD became bisected along the divergent positions of developed and developing countries on the issue of natural resources.[35] At the time of adoption several developed countries reserved their positions in regard to both the Resolution and the International Undertaking.[36] Their concerns centred on the effect that the Undertaking may have on the rights of plant breeders who were using biotechnology to develop commercial varieties of plants, i.e. formal innovators. The developing countries on the other hand sought recognition for informal innovators, i.e. farmers, who were also engaged in breeding new varieties of plants, although in an unstructured way. These disputes were resolved by a series of three agreed interpretations which

---

[33] Kerry ten Kate, and Carolina Lasén Diaz, 'The Undertaking revisited: A commentary on the revision of the International Undertaking on Plant Genetic Resources for Food and Agriculture' (1997) 6(3) *Review of European Community and International Environmental Law* 284. For an analysis of the Undertaking see David Cooper, 'The International Undertaking on Plant Genetic Resources' (1993) 2(2) *Review of European Community and International Environmental Law* 158.

[34] *International Undertaking on Plant Genetic Resources*, Resolution 8/83, Twenty-second Session of the FAO Conference, 5–23 November 1983, Article 1.

[35] Gregory Rose, 'International Law of Sustainable Agriculture in the 21st Century: The International Treaty on Plant Genetic Resources for Food and Agriculture' (2003) 15 *Georgetown International Environmental Law Review* 583, 600.

[36] These countries were Canada, France, Federal Republic of Germany, Japan, Switzerland, United Kingdom and the United States of America – Resolution 8/83, Twenty-second Session of the FAO Conference, Rome, 1983, International Undertaking on Plant Genetic Resources.

effectively amended the Undertaking. The first two interpretations which followed very quickly upon each other respectively recognized the rights of plant breeders as provided for in UPOV[37] on the one hand,[38] and on the other, conceptualized and recognized farmers' rights.[39] The first interpretation, while reiterating the principle that plant genetic resources are the common heritage of humankind, in effect went on to restrict it. The third interpretation restricted the principle still further by endorsing the position that states have sovereignty over their plant genetic resources.[40] The cumulative effect of the three interpretations was to drastically curtail the original objectives of the International Undertaking as set out in Article 1, and was in effect a retreat from the position that plant genetic resources constitute the heritage of humankind. Thus these resources would no longer be freely available in an open access system.

Global developments also contributed to the need for continuous revision of the International Undertaking.[41] In 1992, Agenda 21 in Chapter 14 identified the conservation and sustainable utilization of PGRFA as a component of promoting sustainable agriculture and rural development.[42] The objectives of the programme area in this regard included taking 'appropriate measures for the fair and equitable sharing of benefits and results of research and development in plant breeding between the sources and users of plant genetic resources.' The activities to implement the objectives were to be carried out at national, regional and international levels. At international level, the appropriate UN agencies were called upon to strengthen the Global System including realizing farmers' rights, and also to adjust it in line with the outcome of the negotiations of a convention on biological diversity.

The almost simultaneous negotiation and coming into force of the CBD gave the FAO Global System a new impetus. The interaction between the two was made clear by Resolution 3 of the Nairobi Final Act entitled 'The Interrelationship between the Convention on Biological Diversity and

---

[37] The International Union for the Protection of New Varieties of Plants, discussed in Chapter 7.

[38] Resolution 4/89 – *Agreed Interpretation of the International Undertaking*, adopted on 29 November 1989.

[39] Resolution 5/89 – *Farmers' Rights*, adopted on 29 November 1989.

[40] Resolution 3/91 – adopted on 25 November 1991.

[41] CPGR/93/REP – Report of the Commission on Plant Genetic Resources, Fifth Session, 19–23 April, 1993 – Appendix A *Resolution 93/1 Revision of the International Undertaking on Plant Genetic Resources*, paragraphs 1–4.

[42] *Agenda 21*, UN Conference on Environment and Development, UN Doc.A/CONF.151/26/Rev.1 (1992).

the Promotion of Sustainable Agriculture.'[43] The Resolution, referring to the importance of the conservation and sustainable use of PGRFA, also noted that the Preparatory Committee for the United Nations Conference on Environment and Development (UNCED) had recommended the strengthening of the Global System and its adjustment in line with the negotiations of the CBD. It further urged that ways and means should be explored to develop complementarity and co-operation between the CBD and the FAO Global System. The Resolution also recognized the need to seek solutions to outstanding matters concerning plant genetic resources with the Global System, particularly in regard to (a) access to *ex situ* collections not acquired in accordance with the Convention; and (b) the question of farmers' rights. This was therefore an implied acknowledgement that the draft Convention had an omission in this respect.

Consequently in 1993, the FAO conference passed Resolution 7/93 entitled 'Revision of the International Undertaking on Plant Genetic Resources' in which it referred to both Agenda 21 and the Nairobi Resolution.[44] It agreed that the International Undertaking should be revised in harmony with the CBD, and noted in particular the need to ensure the fair and equitable sharing of benefits with the countries providing plant genetic resources and the need to address the two issues raised in the Nairobi Resolution. The revision resulted in the FAO International Treaty on Plant Genetic Resources for Food and Agriculture of 2001.[45]

The FAO International Treaty on Plant Genetic Resources for Food and Agriculture (the FAO Treaty)

As the records of the FAO Commission on Genetic Resources for Food and Agriculture (CGRFA) show, the fusion of the FAO and CBD processes began with the revision of the International Undertaking.[46] The process required both making the revised document compatible with the CBD as

---

[43] On 22 May 1992, the agreed text of the CBD was adopted through the Nairobi Final Act of the Conference for the Adoption of the Agreed Text of the Convention on Biological Diversity. See *CBD Handbook*, above n 4, Section IX for the text of the Act.

[44] Resolution 7/93, Twenty-seventh Session of the FAO Conference, 1993, 'Revision of the International Undertaking on Plant Genetic Resources.'

[45] Rose is of the view that the status of the Undertaking is unclear after the adoption of the FAO Treaty. He observes that the CGRFA has not repealed it nor has the Treaty negated it. The Undertaking is therefore 'technically operative but functionally defunct' – Rose, above n 35, 600.

[46] CPGR-Ex1/94/REP – Report of the Commission on Plant Genetics Resources First Extraordinary Session, 7–11 November 1994.

well as filling in the gaps contained in the latter. At the Fifth Regular Session of the CGRFA in 1993, it was agreed that such revision should address several questions. These included the consolidation of the annexes into the International Undertaking and its harmonization with the CBD, access to PGRFA, especially those in *ex situ* collections not acquired in accordance with the CBD, farmers' rights, and funding of activities related to the conservation and sustainable use of plant genetic resources. Participants also agreed that the wording of the revised Undertaking must be aligned with that of the CBD as far as possible.[47] They further noted that the revised International Undertaking should take account of other international agreements such as Agenda 21 and the WTO Uruguay Round, particularly the provisions on *sui generis* intellectual property systems for plant varieties within the context of TRIPS, and that it should be a legally binding document.[48] Thus the strategy of synthesizing the CBD with the Undertaking formed the basis of the FAO Treaty[49] which was adopted in November 2001 at the Thirty-first Session of the Conference of FAO. It entered into force on 29 June 2004 after the required ratification by 40 states. A brief overview of the Treaty will be provided here, while specific issues will be discussed later in this book.

Unlike the International Undertaking, the Treaty is a legally binding document. As in the case of the other international agreements on biological resources, its negotiations were characterized by the North/South divide on access and benefit sharing of genetic resources. While 20 years previously the International Undertaking had been formulated on the basis of universal, unrestricted and free access to PGRFA, the Treaty proceeded on the premise that this was no longer tenable. Therefore, while it grew out of the International Undertaking, it has been heavily influenced by developments in the ensuing years, particularly the nature and scope of the CBD.

Unlike the CBD which addresses biological resources in general, as its name indicates, the Treaty deals very specifically with PGRFA. The Preamble reiterates the mutual interdependence of countries in regard to PGRFA and notes its importance to world food security and sustainable agricultural development.[50] It also acknowledges the past, present and future contribution of farmers in conserving and developing PGRFA, and affirms the need to realize such rights at both national and international

---

[47] Ibid, Appendix C, Report by the Chairman of the Working Group on the Group's Ninth Meeting, paragraph 10.

[48] Ibid, Appendix C, Report by the Chairman of the Working Group on the Group's Ninth Meeting, paragraph 10. This will be discussed in Chapter 8.

[49] Rose, above n 35.

[50] FAO Treaty – Preamble, Paragraphs 4 and 9.

levels.[51] The very specific and deliberate omission in the CBD is also addressed in the Treaty, namely that of *ex situ* collections of PGRFA acquired before the former came into force.[52]

Both the CBD and the FAO Treaty recognize the sovereign rights of nations over their biodiversity and PGRFA respectively, and acknowledge that the authority to determine access to such resources rests with national governments and is subject to national legislation.[53] This brings the latter in line with the CBD and consolidates the principle which was first enunciated in Resolution 3/91 of the International Undertaking. While both call upon national governments to facilitate access to these resources and to share in a fair and equitable way the benefits arising from their utilization, an important point of difference between the CBD and FAO Treaty is the system of access and benefit sharing. The CBD proposes a bilateral system for biodiversity in general founded on a system of property rights over the resources. The FAO Treaty advocates a multilateral one for a select group of PGRFA, in effect placing the resources into an open access system.[54] Thus while recognizing state sovereignty over PGRFA, the FAO Treaty has reverted to the original basis of the International Undertaking in the implementation of its objectives.

The objectives of the Treaty are the same as those of the CBD and these are to be attained by linking it to FAO and the CBD Secretariat.[55] Article 4 imposes a general obligation on states parties to ensure that their laws, regulations and procedures conform to their obligations as provided in this Treaty. Article 5 requires states parties to ensure the *in situ* and *ex situ* conservation of PGRFA and in doing so, to support the efforts of farmers and indigenous and local communities in this regard. Article 9 deals specifically with farmers' rights and will be discussed in Chapter 6. However, an inconsistency in the Treaty is seen in that while it follows the CBD in mentioning both farmers and indigenous and local communities in Article 9(1), the Article then goes on to analyze only the rights of farmers. In the CBD on the other hand, farmers are not mentioned at all and Article 8

---

51 FAO Treaty – Preamble, Paragraphs 7 and 8.

52 FAO Treaty – Article 15.

53 CBD – Preamble, Paragraph 4 and Article 3; FAO Treaty – Preamble, Paragraph 14 and Article 10.

54 See FAO Treaty – Part IV; CBD, Article 15.

55 Article 1. See also CGRFA-11/07/Inf.11 – CGRFA, Eleventh Regular Session, 11–15 June 2007, *Memorandum of Cooperation between the Food and Agriculture Organization of the United Nations and the Secretariat of the Convention on Biological Diversity*.

of the CBD dealing with *in situ* conservation refers only to indigenous communities in the context of conserving biodiversity in general.

PGRFA IN THE CONTEXT OF THE INTERNATIONAL ENVIRONMENTAL REGIME

As noted earlier, a significant omission in the CBD is that it deals only with PGRFA *in situ* and not *ex situ*. Since the CBD places the onus on the countries which already have access to genetic resources (i.e. providing countries), to share them with those that do not, it is important to be clear on these two categories. Articles 2 and 15 together explain what providing countries are. Article 15 (3) specifies that:

> [f]or the purpose of this Convention, the genetic resources being provided by a Contracting Party, ... are only those that are provided by Contracting Parties that are *countries of origin of such resources* or by the Parties that have *acquired the genetic resources in accordance with this Convention* [emphasis added].

Therefore providing countries fall into two categories, i.e. (a) countries of origin of genetic resources, or (b) those that have acquired genetic resources in accordance with the Convention.

Category (a) is defined in Article 2 which states that '*country of origin of genetic resources*' means the country which possesses those genetic resources in *in situ* conditions.' Article 2 also specifies that:

> "country *providing genetic resources*" means the country supplying genetic resources collected from *in situ* sources, or taken from *ex situ* sources, which may or may not have originated in that country [emphasis added].

Read together with Article 15(3) this means that if genetic resources contained in *ex situ* collections did not originate in that country, they should have been acquired in accordance with the provisions of the CBD. However, most *ex situ* collections pre-date the CBD. This therefore means that if a country possesses *ex situ* collections of germplasm which were acquired in a manner *not* in accordance with the CBD (in other words the collection of which pre-dated the CBD), it does not fall within the provisions of Article 15. Such a country is therefore not bound to facilitate access to these resources by others. As noted in Chapter 2 there are large collections of PGRFA in developed countries which pre-date the CBD and therefore fall outside its purview. These collections (or pre-CBD material) must therefore necessarily be addressed by the FAO system.

As discussed earlier perhaps the most significant *ex situ* collections of germplasm are those of the International Agricultural Research Centres (IARCs) maintained by the Consultative Group on International Agricultural Research (CGIAR) which are now part of the FAO International Network and therefore under the jurisdiction of the international community. It has been noted that in the light of the CBD and the agreements signed between FAO and the Centres, the germplasm maintained by the CGIAR Centres can be categorized as follows:

[1.] germplasm acquired prior to the entry into force of the CBD;
[2.] material developed by a Centre from germplasm acquired prior to the entry into force of the CBD;
[3.] germplasm acquired after the entry into force of the CBD but obtained with the agreement of the country of origin that such material will be conserved and utilized in accordance with mutually agreed terms; and,
[4.] material developed by a Centre from germplasm acquired wholly or in part after the entry into force of the CBD.[56]

The germplasm designated by the Centres to be placed under the auspices of FAO under the agreements fall into categories (1) and (2) which are those that have been specifically excluded from the ambit of the CBD by virtue of Article 15(3). Germplasm in the latter two categories may also be designated if the country of origin has given written consent to do so. The CPGR noted that '[s]uch consent might be granted conditional on new arrangements for distribution and use coming into effect once international agreement has been reached on the issues of terms of access and the fair and equitable sharing of benefits.'[57]

The status of the collections brought within the FAO International Network was initially determined by the agreements signed between the FAO and the IARCs.[58] These agreements were signed in 1994 and renewed twice, on 26 October 1998 and 26 October 2002, and were to be operative

---

[56] CPGR-6/95/12 ADD.1 – Commission on Plant Genetic Resources, Sixth Session, 19–30 June 1995, *The International Network of Ex Situ Collections, and the CGIAR Centres. Joint Report by FAO and the International Plant Genetic Resources Institute (on behalf of the CGIAR Centres) on the Implementation of the Agreement signed between FAO and the CGIAR Centres on 26 October 1994*, paragraph 2.

[57] Ibid, paragraph 3.

[58] *Agreement between [Name of Centre] and the Food and Agriculture Organization of the United Nations (FAO) Placing Collections of Plant Germplasm under*

until 26 October 2006. Several countries had also expressed their willingness to join the network and place their collections within it.[59]

Upon the coming into force of the FAO Treaty, on 16 October 2006 11 CGIAR Centres entered into agreements with the Governing Body of the Treaty placing their in-trust collections within the purview of the Treaty.[60] According to the terms of the Treaty, PGRFA listed in Annex 1 and held by

---

the Auspices of FAO signed in October 1994, available at archive.irri.org/GRC/GRChome/FAO-Centre%20agreement.pdf (last accessed 30 June 2012).

[59] CGRFA-8/99/7 – CGRFA, Eighth Regular Session, 19–23 April 1999, *Progress Report on the International Network of Ex Situ Collections under the Auspices of FAO*, paragraphs 3–4; CGRFA-9/02/11 – CGRFA, Ninth Regular Session, 14–18 October 2002, *Report on the International Network of Ex situ Collections Under the Auspices of FAO*, paragraphs 4–6; CGRFA-10/04/6 – CGRFA, Tenth Regular Session, 8–12 November 2004, *Report on the International Network of Ex situ Collections under the Auspices of FAO*, paragraphs 26–33. See also IT/GB-1/06/Report – *Report of the Governing Body of the International Treaty on Plant Genetic Resources for Food and Agriculture*, First Session, 12–16 June 2006, paragraphs 30–34.

[60] *Agreement between [Name Of Centre] and the Food and Agriculture Organization of the United Nations (FAO), Acting on Behalf of the Governing Body of the International Treaty on Plant Genetic Resources for Food And Agriculture* available at http://www.cgiar.org/pdf/model_agreement_centers_2007.pdf (last accessed 30 June 2012), (hereinafter FAO Treaty/CGIAR Agreement). Article 15 of the Treaty calls upon the IARCs to sign agreements with the Governing Body with regard to such collections in accordance with the terms and conditions contained in it. The Ministerial Declaration of the First Session of the Governing Body also called upon the IARCs to sign these agreements in accordance with the Treaty. See IT/GB-1/06/Report above n 59 page viii. See also IT/GB-1/06/9 – International Treaty on Plant Genetic Resources for Food and Agriculture, First Session of the Governing Body, 12–16 June 2006, *Draft Agreements Between the Governing Body and the IARCS of the CGIAR and Other Relevant International Institutions,* March 2006; CGRFA-11/07/19.2 – CGRFA, Eleventh Regular Session, 11–15 June 2007, *Reports from International Organizations on their Policies, Programmes, and Activities on Agricultural Biological Diversity: (2) International Agricultural Research Centres of the Consultative Group on International Agricultural Research (CGIAR)*, paragraph 12; IT/GB-2/07/17 – International Treaty On Plant Genetic Resources For Food And Agriculture, Second Session Of The Governing Body, 29 October – 2 November 2007, *Report on the Status of Cooperation with Other International Organizations, including Agreements between the Governing Body and the International Agricultural Research Centers of the Consultative Group on International Agricultural Research and Other Relevant International Institutions*, paragraphs 8–12. See also Statement of the CGIAR Centres Regarding Implementation of the Agreements between the Centres and the Governing Body of the International Treaty on Plant Genetic Resources for Food and Agriculture, available at http://library.cgiar.org/handle/10947/5152 (last accessed 30 June 2012).

the IARCs will be made available under the provisions of Part IV of the Treaty relating to the multilateral system of access and benefit sharing.[61] PGRFA which have not been listed in Annex 1 and which were acquired before the entry into force of the Treaty shall be made available in accordance with the provisions of the Standard Material Transfer Agreement (SMTA) currently in use pursuant to the agreements between the IARCs and the FAO.[62] Non-Annex 1 PGRFA received by Centres after the coming into force of the Treaty, shall be made available for access on terms consistent with those mutually agreed upon between the Centre and the country of origin.[63] Further, the contracting parties which are countries of origin of the PGRFA have the right to receive samples on demand without a Material Transfer Agreement (MTA).[64] These provisions are reflected in the agreement with the governing body. The revised agreement states that it is the intention of the parties that this Agreement should remain in force in perpetuity, although there are provisions to terminate it under specified circumstances.[65]

CONCLUSION

As will be further demonstrated in this book, the negotiating history and structure of the CBD had initially made it a rather ambivalent forum for resolving questions of equity in the uses of biological resources including PGRFA. The inclusion of provisions on access and benefit sharing of *in situ* biological resources, while excluding *ex situ* collections from its ambit, was a setback for developing countries. However, the reality is that the Convention would not have been signed by countries possessing *ex situ* collections if these had been included within it.

Notwithstanding this omission, as will be shown, since its entry into force, the implementing mechanisms of the Convention have been instrumental in the efforts to negotiate equitable procedures by which benefit sharing of *in situ* resources should take place. Developing countries have largely opted for the CBD as the preferred institution by which to ensure that their interests in *in situ* genetic resources as well as traditional knowledge are safeguarded. Whether the processes of the CBD have helped to fulfil their objectives remains to be seen.

---

[61] FAO Treaty – Article 15.1(a).
[62] FAO Treaty – Article 15.1(b).
[63] FAO Treaty – Article 15.3.
[64] FAO Treaty/CGIAR Agreement – Article 2 (b) (ii).
[65] FAO Treaty/CGIAR Agreement – Article 6.

The FAO Treaty in its provisions subsequently addressed the omissions in the CBD in regard to benefit sharing of *ex situ* collections of PGRFA. The entry into force of the Treaty and the placing of Annex I germplasm in the public domain is expected to facilitate the flow of such germplasm to developing countries and ensure equitable sharing of their benefits. The FAO International Networks and the voluntary placing of accessions in the public domain have also ensured accessibility to these collections, including by developing countries. In fact it has been pointed out that these countries have received more genetic materials than they have contributed to the Centres and an open access system of germplasm flows will materially benefit them.[66] Nevertheless, some concerns have been expressed as to whether the structure and processes of the Treaty are, while achieving this purpose, also facilitating the acquisition and propertization of germplasm. These concerns will be examined in Chapter 9.

[66] Cary Fowler, Melinda Smale and Samy Gaiji, 'Unequal Exchange? Recent Transfers of Agricultural Resources and their Implications for Developing Countries' (2001) 19(2) *Development Policy Review* 181.

6. Farmers, indigenous and local communities and traditional knowledge

INTRODUCTION

The propertization of plant genetic resources for food and agriculture (PGRFA) has potential negative implications for national agricultural systems and food security of all peoples, particularly in developing countries. However, the CBD and the FAO Treaty have focused their concerns on two particular groups of people. These groups are farmers and indigenous peoples, particularly those in developing countries, whose livelihoods and way of life may be threatened by these developments.

The concept of farmers' rights entered the international discourse on PGRFA by way of the FAO, initially in its International Undertaking on Plant Genetic Resources. The issue is now embedded in the FAO Treaty. Similarly, Article 8(j) of the CBD calls upon States Parties to respect, preserve and maintain the knowledge, innovations and practices of indigenous and local communities, and the Conference of the Parties has taken up the topic as a distinct issue.

The questions which arise in this context are, firstly why the rights of these two groups were identified in the international discourse on PGRFA as requiring particular concern, and how they were conceptualized. A further question is whether such conceptualization has contributed to ensuring equitable access to PGRFA, and safeguarding the agricultural systems and food security of nations.

In this chapter I will argue that while the rights of farmers and indigenous and local communities have become one of the principal elements on which the debate on PGRFA is based, to date their nature, scope and content have still not been clearly elucidated, and it is a concept which is unclear and uncertain. It is not disputed that particular rights can and should be attributed to these groups as distinct categories of peoples. However, the question that arises is whether attributing rights over PGRFA to these groups in particular would also contribute to sustainable agricultural development and conservation of these resources for the benefit of everybody.

Since the discourse on the rights of farmers and indigenous peoples has taken two distinct paths, I will discuss the two groups separately. I will then discuss the related issue of traditional knowledge relevant to PGRFA.

FARMERS' RIGHTS

The development of farmers' rights in international law is a reaction to the propertization of PGRFA. Until relatively recently the role of farmers in plant breeding and agricultural production was not enclosed in a framework of rights but was simply a part of the process of conserving, developing and using PGRFA.[1] For generations and until recently, seed varieties developed by traditional farmers were viewed as a public good to be freely used, saved and exchanged. As has been discussed above, with the development of modern technology plant breeding became more amenable to technological manipulation, which has resulted in faster adaptations of plant varieties. Consequently the process has come to be dominated by institutional plant breeders who began producing what were designated as 'modern,' 'elite' and 'high yielding' varieties of seeds, which were bred in a relatively short space of time and contained specific and identifiable characteristics. Plant breeding was analogized to inventions rather than to natural processes of evolution, and on the basis of the analogy, claims of intellectual property rights were extended to the end results. These were justified on the premise that it was necessary to recognize the plant breeders' role in developing 'modern varieties' of seeds and to ensure monetary compensation for their products.[2]

This position was advantageous to institutional plant breeders but worked to the detriment of traditional farmers working informally, whose efforts in plant breeding, spanning generations, for the most part went unacknowledged. Western technology and legal concepts have essentially reconstructed their role in food production. It has trivialized their contribution to the development and improvement of PGRFA and the maintenance of

---

[1] For a history of the development of farmers' rights see Regine Andersen, *The History of Farmers' Rights, A Guide to Central Documents and Literature* (2005) The Fridtjof Nansen Institute, The Farmers' Rights Project, Background Study 1, available at http://www.fni.no/doc&pdf/FNI-R0805.pdf (last accessed 30 June 2012). See also generally Martin A Girsberger, *Biodiversity and the Concept of Farmers' Rights in International Law: Factual Background and Legal Analysis* (1999).

[2] C S Srinivasan, 'Exploring the Feasibility of Farmers' Rights' (2003) 21(4) *Development Policy Review* 419.

agricultural biodiversity and food security. Further, the property rights awarded to the latter have threatened to displace their own rights to save and re-use seed, endangering their traditional livelihoods and farming practices including that of breeding.[3] Another cause of concern was the potential loss of genetic diversity as a result of the replacement of farmers' landraces with these 'modern' varieties.

The campaign for farmers' rights was triggered by the inequity caused by granting legal recognition to plant breeders' rights over their plant varieties, while the contributions made by farmers to this process went unrewarded. An analogy was drawn with intellectual property rights claimed by plant breeders and extended to this new debate, and the former claims were countered by parallel claims to the rights of farmers. As Borowiak observes:

> [i]f 'breeders' rights' was the pivot upon which agribusinesses lobbied for changes in commercial law, 'farmers' rights,' 'indigenous rights,' and, more recently, 'human rights' provide the ground upon which resistance to plant variety IPRs is being waged.[4]

The subject was raised in fora including the FAO and the CBD, but the mandate to develop the concept has been taken up by the former.[5] However, the formulation of the concept is not articulated in the usual vocabulary of human rights and there is uncertainty as to what they are, who holds them, and whether they are in any way justiciable.

The Conceptualization of Farmers' Rights as Human Rights

It is unclear whether farmers' rights as a response to plant breeders' rights should be analogized to human rights or property rights. Human rights are grounded on principles of justice, equity, and human dignity, while property rights are premised on principles of possession and ownership. In articulating the concept as a response to plant breeders' rights, writers have identified three interrelated rationales for farmers' rights: conservation,

---

[3] Craig Borowiak, 'Farmers' Rights: Intellectual Property Regimes and the Struggle over Seeds' (2004) 32 *Politics Society* 511.

[4] Ibid at 512.

[5] Resolution 3 of the Nairobi Final Act entitled 'The Interrelationship between the Convention on Biological Diversity and the Promotion of Sustainable Agriculture' noted that the question of farmers' rights was one of the outstanding matters concerning PGR for which solutions should be sought within the Global System – CBD/UNEP – *Handbook on the Convention on Biological Diversity* (3rd ed 2005), 406.

equity, and the preservation of farming practices.[6] These three aspects will be examined in turn to determine whether and how they provide a basis to conceptualize the human rights of farmers, and to what extent they also further the objective of equitable access to PGRFA for all peoples.

Equity

The equity rationale of farmers' rights revolves around the current international dimensions in agricultural production and trade, including property rights over seed varieties.[7] As noted earlier, farmers practising traditional agriculture in developing countries have not been compensated for developing the germplasm on which modern high yielding varieties are based. Further, when farmers in these countries adopt modern agricultural processes including high yielding seed varieties commercialized by plant breeders, they are charged market prices by the latter.[8] These factors have not been addressed by the international regime which has failed to take a holistic overview of the issue.

The equity rationale is problematic as these issues, including the asymmetry in assigning value to seed varieties produced by farmers on the one hand and by plant breeders on the other, do not impact upon farmers alone. In the context of domestic food production, the interests of farmers are intrinsically linked to the interests of the country in which they are located. The inequity directly impacts upon farmers to the extent that it affects their livelihoods. However, there is also a wider dimension to the issue of propertizing and marketing modern plant varieties including its impacts on sustainable development and food availability in developing countries.

It would not be in the interests of a nation's economy and food security if its means of food production were under the monopolistic control of agribusinesses which are outside its jurisdiction, particularly where the latter's operations are facilitated by the current trends in intellectual property rights and the global trade in agriculture and agricultural products. Consequently, the interests of the wider population would also be threatened, and the matter would have to be addressed in a different context and dimension, rather than by international agreements on natural resources conservation or human rights. Therefore while the equity rationale includes the interests of farmers, it cannot be articulated in that context alone.

---

6 Borowiak, above n 3, 524.

7 Ibid; Timothy Swanson, 'Why is there a Biodiversity Convention – The International Interest in Centralised Development Planning' (1999) 75(2) *International Affairs* 307.

8 Swanson, above n 7, 327.

Conservation

The conservation aspect addresses the problem of the global loss of biodiversity including diversity in PGRFA. Its continuing conservation and enhancement, particularly *in situ*, is to a large extent dependent on the traditional agricultural practices of local farmers, including plant breeding. However, while these practices are important in the long term, they are not rewarded in the short term under the existing proprietary system. Farmers are not compensated for their conservation practices or for the continued use of traditional plant varieties and may in fact be at a competitive disadvantage vis-à-vis those who use high yielding varieties or genetically engineered crops.[9] Borowiak argues that:

> [f]rom this perspective and for the sake of future innovation in agriculture, as well as in other bioindustries, farmers' rights are seen as a way to materially support (and thereby offer incentives to) farmers who conserve biodiversity.[10]

It again appears that if farmers' rights are based on the necessity to compensate them for conserving biodiversity, it is not founded solely on the interests of farmers per se. It seems rather that the conservation rationale of farmers' rights views them as the custodians of agricultural diversity and as the means by which to preserve such diversity for the greater good. The wording of both the CBD and the early FAO documents clearly reflect this linkage. For example, Annex 2 of the International Undertaking declares that 'plant genetic resources are a common heritage of mankind to be preserved and to be freely available for use, for the benefit of present and future generations.' It then goes on to endorse the concept of farmers' rights in order to, *inter alia*, ensure that the need for conservation is globally recognized, and to assist farmers and farming communities, in all regions of the world, but especially in the areas of origin/diversity of PGRFA, in the protection and conservation of such resources. While this is necessary for farmers' livelihoods, it is also crucial for the survival of the global population. Such diversity is also by and large located in the developing world in the custody of those who are among the poorest, and on whom the burden falls to conserve it. Therefore the conservation rationale clearly does not prioritize the interests of farmers, but rather focuses on their capacity to conserve biodiversity as a public good.

---

9 Kathleen McAfee, 'Corn Culture and Dangerous DNA: Real and Imagined Consequences of Maize Transgene Flow in Oaxaca' (2003) 2 (1) *Journal of Latin American Geography* 18.

10 Borowiak, above n 3, 524.

The preservation of farming practices

The preservation of farming practices is perhaps the aspect of farmers' rights that can be most appropriately brought within the framework of farmers' human rights. This is the aspect that directly concerns the interests of farmers as a distinct category, irrespective of the rights of others. The rights articulated in the FAO Treaty, include the protection of traditional knowledge relevant to PGRFA, the right to equitably participate in the sharing of benefits arising from the use of PGRFA, and the right to participate in making decisions at the national level on matters relating to the conservation and sustainable use of PGRFA. These rights as well as the others specified, i.e. the rights to save, use, exchange, and sell farm-saved seed/propagating material, are aspects of the right to their livelihood, and clearly fall within the dimensions of farmers' human rights.[11] The rights are also expressed in a vocabulary which is consistent with the language of human rights and which is possibly enforceable at national if not at international level.

However, even in this respect, the rationale for farmers' rights in the FAO Treaty is prioritized by the need for conservation of PGRFA rather than the protection of a category of people who are essentially disadvantaged and voiceless in many respects. The Preamble to the Treaty affirms:

> that the past, present and future contributions of farmers in all regions of the world, particularly those in centres of origin and diversity, in conserving, improving and making available these resources, is the basis of Farmers' Rights.[12]

Therefore once again the rights of farmers have been subsumed to the wider interests of conserving and developing PGRFA for the benefit of humankind.

The Conceptualization of Farmers' Rights as Property Rights

Having argued that farmers' rights as they are presently articulated cannot be clearly sited within the human rights agenda, the next question is whether they can be located within the boundaries of property rights. This

---

[11] *International Treaty on Plant Genetic Resources for Food and Agriculture*, adopted at the 31st Session of the FAO Conference on 3 November 2001 available at http://www.fao.org/AG/cgrfa/itpgr.htm and the website of the Treaty at http://www.planttreaty.org/ (hereinafter FAO Treaty) (both last accessed 30 June 2012), Article 9 entitled 'Farmers' Rights.'

[12] FAO Treaty – Preamble, paragraph 7.

question also does not have a clear answer. Although farmers have historically been the custodians and developers of PGRFA they have not asserted property rights over them, such resources being in the public domain with open access to all. In international law, rights over PGRFA have now shifted from the sphere of common heritage to that of state sovereignty.[13] Therefore property in PGRFA is now clearly within the jurisdiction of national governments. This is inevitable since it would not be feasible for governments to accord farmers such exclusive rights over plant varieties vis-à-vis the rest of a country's population.

As noted before, the idea of farmers' rights emerged as a strategic response to the exclusive intellectual property rights accorded to plant breeders. However, the practical objective was to prevent these rights from disadvantaging farmers or from dislodging them from their traditional role and functions. The need was to ensure that their role in agriculture received equal recognition as that of plant breeders, and that they received compensation for their part in the conservation and management of those resources, and an equitable share of the benefits derived from them. It was not envisaged that they would be assigned property rights over them.

Even advocacy groups have stopped short of suggesting that plant breeders' property rights over PGRFA should be duplicated with farmers' property rights. Borowiak cites one farmer advocacy group, Via Campesina, as campaigning for farmers' rights to be interpreted to include the following:[14]

- the right to conserve biodiversity;
- the right to achieve food security;
- the right to land, water, and air;
- the right to participate in policies linked to genetic resources;
- the right to appropriate technology;

---

[13] *International Undertaking on Plant Genetic Resources*, Resolution 8/83, Twenty-Second Session of the FAO Conference, 5–23 November 1983 (hereinafter IUPGR) – Annex 3; *Convention on Biological Diversity* (1992) 31 ILM 818, Preamble, and Article 3; FAO Treaty – Article 10.

[14] Borowiak, above n 3, 529. The website of Via Campesina is available at http://viacampesina.org. See also the *Bamako Declaration – Declaration of the Farmer Exchange on the Privatisation of Seeds*, organized by the CNOP, BEDE and IIED, Preparatory process for the International Forum on Food Sovereignty of Nyeléni, Mali, Bamako, 21 February 2007, available at http://www.iied.org/international-farmers-exchange-for-mutual-learning-privatisation-knowledge-seeds (both last accessed 30 June 2012).

- the right to define the control and handling of benefits derived from the use of genetic resources;
- the right to develop models of sustainable agriculture; and
- the right to use, choose, store, and freely exchange, genetic resources.[15]

Notably this list does not include property rights over PGRFA. In any case it would be practically impossible to enforce such rights. While scientifically bred varieties can be identified and assigned to their respective owners, the very nature of farmer bred seeds and the processes by which they are freely exchanged, shared and developed in common, preclude this.[16] Thus the concept of farmers' rights is clearly not intended to assign property rights over seed varieties to farmers, and at most is a defensive strategy to ward off the propertization of what was historically in the public domain.

The Scope and Content of Farmers' Rights in International Documents

International documents do not throw much light on the concept of farmers' rights. The scope and content of these rights was not enunciated in precise terms in the early documents. Annex 2 of the International Undertaking which was the first document to give expression to them states that farmers' rights are those rights:

> arising from the past, present and future contributions of farmers in conserving, improving, and making available plant genetic resources, particularly those in the centres of origin/diversity.[17]

This statement merely offers an explanation of the origins of such rights and does not articulate their scope or content. The Annex had earlier noted that 'farmers, especially those in developing countries, should benefit fully from the improved and increased use of the natural resources they have preserved.' However, here too it did not indicate in what ways they should benefit.

---

[15] See also the rights noted by the CGRFA – CPGR-6/95/REP – Report of the Commission on Plant Genetic Resources Sixth Session, 19–30 June 1995, Appendix C, Report by the Chairman of the Tenth Session of the Working Group of the Commission on Plant Genetic Resources, paragraph 24.

[16] Borowiak, above n 3.

[17] Annex 2, Resolution 5/89 to the International Undertaking entitled 'Farmers' Rights.' The wording is reproduced in Article 2 of the *FAO International Code of Conduct for Plant Germplasm Collecting and Transfer* of 1993 and in the *FAO Draft Code of Conduct on Biotechnology* of 1991.

Annex 1 of the International Undertaking stated that:

> the adhering states consider that the best way to implement the concept of Farmers' Rights is to ensure the conservation, management and use of plant genetic resources, for the benefit of present and future generations of farmers.

This provision thus calls for the implementation of rights without specifying what they are. Further, interests in PGRFA while necessary for their livelihood, are not confined to farmers, and are a matter of national and global concern. Therefore, it is unclear how conserving these resources would uniquely promote the rights and interests of farmers.

The indeterminate wording of the expressions in the International Undertaking on farmers' rights reflects early attempts to conceptualize them, which fall short of giving them concrete expression. While the range of rights to which farmers *as farmers* are entitled may be extensive and diverse, it is generally accepted that at a minimum they include the right to use, save, sell and exchange seed,[18] but these have not been articulated in the International Undertaking.

Some references to these specific rights can be found in international documents of the 1990s. One (though indirect) is contained in Paragraph 9 of the FAO Global Plan of Action of 1996,[19] which refers to:

> the needs and individual rights of farmers and, collectively, where recognized by national law, to have non-discriminatory access to germplasm, information, technologies, financial resources and research and marketing systems necessary for them to continue to manage and improve genetic resources.

However, while the Plan spoke at length of the need to enhance the knowledge, capacity and livelihoods of farmers, to include them in decision making and to promote the conservation and development of plant genetic resources for their benefit, it did not elaborate further on how this should be achieved or how the rights should be enforced.[20]

---

[18] John E Haapala, 'Farmers' Rights' (2004) *Journal of Environmental Law and Litigation* 467.

[19] *Global Plan of Action for the Conservation and Sustainable Utilization of Plant Genetic Resources for Food and Agriculture*, 1996 (hereinafter Global Plan of Action).

[20] Another reference, again indirectly, is contained in Decision V/5 of CoP 5. Section 3 of the Decision on Genetic Use Restriction Technologies refers to the rights of farmers to keep, use, exchange and sell seed or propagating material which may be obstructed by the use of GURTS. References to farmers' rights are also found in Agenda 21, Chapter 14.59. Chapter 14 deals with 'Promoting Sustainable Agriculture and Rural Development' and calls upon the Global System to, inter alia,

The FAO Treaty attempted to explicate the concept to some degree but its provisions are tentative at best.[21] According to Article 9.2 the contracting parties agree that the realization of the rights rests with national governments, but again the provision refers to the rights of farmers only 'as they relate to plant genetic resources for food and agriculture.' The Article states that farmers' rights include:

- protection of traditional knowledge relevant to PGRFA;
- the right to equitably participate in sharing benefits arising from the utilization of PGRFA; and
- the right to participate in making decisions, at the national level, on matters related to the conservation and sustainable use of PGRFA.

Therefore the definition and ambit of farmers' rights for the purposes of the Treaty are limited to those directly related to PGRFA, and other rights whether civil, political, or socioeconomic, would not come within the ambit of the Treaty.[22]

Article 9.3 specifies that Article 9.2 shall not be interpreted to limit any rights that farmers have to save, use, exchange and sell farm-saved seed/ propagating material. However, unlike the general discourse of human rights, all these rights are subject to the discretion of national governments and thus it is clear that the rights of farmers even in regard to PGRFA are subsumed to the national interest.

The Justiciability of Farmers' Rights

Having determined at least in a limited way what the substantive rights of farmers are, the next question to assess is the extent to which they are justiciable. The justiciability of farmers' rights is constrained by several factors. A notable drawback in the original formulation of farmers' rights in

take further steps to realise farmers' rights. Article 16.7 which deals with Environmentally Sound Management of Biotechnology calls upon governments to promote specified activities in conformity with international agreements or arrangements on biological diversity, as appropriate, including rights associated with intellectual property and informal innovations, including farmers' and breeders' rights. Chapter 32 entitled 'Strengthening the role of farmers' also provides some indication of what farmers' rights may entail.

21 See above n 11 and accompanying text.

22 See also for example, the *African Model Legislation for the Protection of the Rights of Local Communities, Farmers and Breeders, and for the Regulation of Access to Biological Resources*, (2000), Article 26 of which sets out farmers' rights that are limited to those relating to PGRFA.

the International Undertaking was that neither the rights holders nor those who were obliged to uphold or implement the rights, were precisely identifiable. Farmers' rights are held by 'farmers' and 'farming communities.' These categories encompass a large proportion of populations in developing (and other) countries, which comprise heterogeneous, continuously fluctuating, and socially and politically undefinable groups. As Borowiak notes:

> it is not even clear who should count as a farmer. There is no clear reason why, for instance, farmers' rights should not extend beyond cultivators of field crops to include fisher folk, hunters, pastoralists, nomads, and gatherers, all of whom contribute to the conservation of biodiversity.[23]

In many countries a high proportion of the workforce is in any case, involved directly or indirectly in agriculture and it would be difficult to demarcate this group and its interests from the rest of the population. None of the international documents dealing with farmers' rights attempt to define or construct what is meant by 'farmer' in the context of the rights, probably because this is not possible. The Global Plan of Action describes farmers as 'a large, economically disadvantaged population.'[24] Chapter 32 of Agenda 21 is a little more specific, stating that:

> in this chapter, all references to 'farmers' include all rural people who derive their livelihood from activities such as farming, fishing and forest harvesting. The term 'farming' also includes fishing and forest harvesting.[25]

However, it is doubtful whether even this definition is a basis on which to precisely identify members of a particular social, political or economic group.[26] Most notably, the FAO Treaty which is now the definitive document dealing with these rights, does not provide any definition of the term. It has been left to national legislation to spell it out so as to make such groups identifiable in the relevant context.

In order for a right to be justiciable it must necessarily vest in the rights holders who should have the capacity to enforce it as against an identifiable entity. International human rights documents confer rights upon individuals

---

23 Borowiak, above n 3, 530.

24 *Global Plan of Action*, above n 19, paragraph 30.

25 *Agenda 21*, UN Conference on Environment and Development, UN Doc.A/CONF.151/26/Rev.1 (1992) – Chapter 32.

26 For a discussion on this issue see Martin A Girsberger, *Biodiversity and the Concept of Farmers' Rights in International Law: Factual Background and Legal Analysis* (1999) 221.

vis-à-vis their national governments. The International Undertaking took the unusual step of vesting farmers' rights not in farmers, but rather in the international community as trustee for present and future generations of farmers. Since the 'international community' is as nebulous an entity as the global population of farmers this does not help to either clarify or enforce the concept.

The International Undertaking envisaged that farmers' rights would be implemented by way of an international fund which would support the conservation and utilization of PGRFA, particularly but not exclusively, in developing countries.[27] Reference to the International Fund for Plant Genetic Resources already established by the FAO had earlier been made in Annex 1 to the International Undertaking.[28] Contributions to the Fund were proposed on the basis of differential responsibilities of States, it being pointed out that the countries which have benefited most from the use of germplasm should supplement it. However, the beneficiaries of the Fund are not limited to farmers, and its objectives include educational programmes for biotechnology specialists and strengthening the capabilities of developing countries in general.

The FAO Treaty took the more practical step of vesting the responsibility of realizing farmers' rights in national governments of the Contracting Parties, reflecting the structure of international human rights documents. This serves two purposes. National governments are identifiable political entities that operate within specific geographical and political boundaries. Therefore this also enables the farmers as rights holders to be more easily delineated as national groups within those boundaries, rather than as an indeterminate part of the global population. However, the Treaty stops short of imposing definitive obligations on national governments and the contracting parties are required to protect and promote farmers' rights only 'as appropriate and subject to its national legislation.'[29] These obligations are merely exhortatory and the Treaty gives states wide leeway in determining the means and extent to which they could or should fulfil them.[30]

---

[27] FAO International Undertaking on Plant Genetic Resources – Annex II, Resolution 5/89, 'Farmers' Rights.'

[28] *FAO International Undertaking on Plant Genetic Resources* – Annex I, Resolution 4/89, 'Agreed Interpretation of the International Undertaking,' paragraph 4.

[29] Article 9.2.

[30] Several countries have enacted legislation addressing issues of farmers' rights, see Stephen B Brush 'Protecting Traditional Agricultural Knowledge' (2005) 17 *Washington University Journal of Law & Policy* 59, see also http://www.farmersrights.org/database/index.html (last accessed 30 June 2012).

Conclusion

It can be argued that the concept of farmers' rights has two dimensions. Firstly, farmers, as a community, possess characteristics based upon their way of life and livelihood which is unique to them and which give rise to certain rights. These rights are difficult to define precisely, but at a minimum may be articulated in the context of human rights, including political and socio-economic rights. Those defined by Via Campesina are appropriate examples. The international human rights agenda has recognized that the rights of certain groups – women,[31] children,[32] minorities[33] – require specific action beyond the general discourse of rights. Therefore farmers could also be identified as a group whose needs are sufficiently distinctive so as to necessitate such specific action, although problems of identification of the group and of justiciability would have to be addressed.

The role of farmers in agricultural production also gives rise to certain other rights peculiar to them, as custodians of plant diversity and producers of food, including the right to save, use and freely exchange genetic resources. The articulation and recognition of these rights was initiated as a strategy of resistance to the propertization of seeds by commercial plant breeders which threatened the ability of farmers to maintain this role. However, the threat posed by the control over seeds by plant breeders and corporations does not concern farmers alone and must be considered in the context of the interests of countries and peoples. These wider national interests include the right to political and economic autonomy, and the need to maintain sustainable agricultural systems and national food security, and farmers are also actors in this process. The Farmers' Rights website notes 'As farmers are custodians and developers of crop genetic resources, their rights in this regard are crucial for enabling them to maintain this vital role for local and global food security, and they are a central means in the fight

---

[31] *Convention on the Elimination of All Forms of Discrimination against Women*, GA res. 34/180, 34 UN GAOR Supp. (No. 46) at 193, UN Doc. A/34/46; 1249 UNTS 13; 19 ILM 33 (1980) (entered into force 3 September 1981).

[32] *Convention on the Rights of the Child*, GA res. 44/25, annex, 44 UN GAOR Supp. (No. 49) at 167, UN Doc. A/44/49 (1989); 1577 UNTS 3; 28 ILM 1448 (1989) (entered into force 2 September 1990).

[33] *International Convention on the Elimination of All Forms of Racial Discrimination*, GA res. 2106 (XX), Annex, 20 UN GAOR Supp. (No. 14) at 47, UN Doc. A/6014 (1966), 660 UNTS 195, (entered into force 4 January 1969); *Declaration on the Rights of Persons Belonging to National or Ethnic, Religious and Linguistic Minorities*, Adopted by General Assembly Resolution 47/135 of 18 December 1992.

against poverty.'[34] The Special Rapporteur on the Right to Food, referring to the global food crisis of 2007–2008, has stated that:

> States therefore face two separate challenges. They must ensure that the commercial seed systems not only raise aggregate yields, but also that they work for the benefit of the farmers most in need to have their incomes raised – smallholders in developing countries. And they must support farmers' seed systems, on which not only these farmers depend, but the enhancement of which is vital, in addition, for our long-term food security.

This wider dimension of the problem has not been acknowledged in international documents such as the CBD, the FAO International Undertaking, or the FAO Treaty, which have merely attempted to confer unenforceable rights on an undefinable category of people.

It is debatable whether the threat posed to food security by the application of intellectual property rights to PGRFA should be countered by a construction of farmers' rights to these resources. It is also unclear whether this strategy has proved to be effective. It has been noted above that the discourse on farmers' rights has stopped short of recognizing rights over PGRFA, as a response to breeders' rights. Further, as Borowiak points out farmers' rights do not contest breeders' rights and therefore implicitly concede their legitimacy.[35] The Special Rapporteur on the Right to Food has also stated that 'The protection against the misappropriation of genetic resources should not result in new enclosures preventing access to genetic resources as a common heritage.'[36]

A more appropriate response to property rights over PGRFA would be to locate the issue within the discourse of the human right to food and the right to life of all peoples. The right to food and food security is a universal human right which encompasses both farmers and the wider community. This right cannot be fulfilled without unrestricted access to seed varieties. It can also be argued that the appropriation of plant varieties is in conflict with the need to conserve genetic resources and agrobiodiversitiy. Therefore rather than engaging in a retaliatory strategy of countering enclosures of these resources with further enclosures, the international community should rather resist their privatization and maintain the stance that plant varieties

---

[34] See http://www.farmersrights.org/about/why_fr_matters.html (last accessed 30 June 2012).

[35] Borowiak, above n 3, 532.

[36] United Nations General Assembly, A/64/170 (23 July 2009), 'The right to food: Seed policies and the right to food: enhancing agrobiodiversity and encouraging innovation', Report of the Special Rapporteur on the right to food at 16.

constitute the common heritage of humankind and must be kept in the public domain.

INDIGENOUS AND LOCAL COMMUNITIES

The second category of peoples singled out in the context of the debate on plant genetic resources for food and agriculture (PGRFA) is that of indigenous and local communities. As in the case of farmers, the issue of indigenous peoples is one that has entered the international law discourse relatively recently, and within the context of rights. The past decades witnessed a growing recognition that indigenous peoples have, for centuries, been systematically victimized by the invasion and colonization of their homelands, the destruction of their political, social and cultural institutions and the plundering of their resources. Even after the end of the colonial era, these groups continue to be, by and large, politically and economically marginalized within the wider political milieu of the countries they live in. The acknowledgement of these grievances has been translated into efforts in international law to ensure that redress for past injustices and the prevention of further exploitation is carried out effectively. Thus the rights of indigenous peoples originated in a somewhat different context from that of farmers.

The topic of indigenous rights obviously covers the gamut of human rights, but the discussion in this book will be confined to those relating to PGRFA and traditional knowledge. Indigenous rights in regard to these issues have generally been addressed as a subject distinct from that of farmers and local communities, largely due to the fact that the Conference of the Parties to the Convention on Biological Diversity (CBD CoP) has taken it up as a specific matter.

It is necessary to identify what specific rights indigenous communities possess vis-à-vis genetic resources, management of biodiversity, sustainable development and traditional knowledge. While many of these rights are clear and undisputed, there are others which again are controversial both in regard to their content and those against whom they are claimed. Also, since there are several areas of similarity in regard to the rights of indigenous peoples, farmers and local communities in relation to biological resources, the issues discussed here will also be relevant to the latter two categories. This discussion will demonstrate that while questions of indigenous rights to PGRFA are important to the debate on the topic, they are also imprecise, and difficult to conceptualize and enforce.[37]

The Rights of Indigenous Peoples

Indigenous peoples as a group differ significantly from farmers in that unlike the latter who are viewed as a disadvantaged category within mainstream social and political groups, the former claim distinctiveness and often political autonomy from the mainstream. Under the circumstances, while some rights attributed to both groups may overlap, the rights of indigenous peoples are often distinct and may also encompass a wider range.

Indigenous peoples' rights cover the general gamut of human rights, civil and political as well as economic, social and cultural. Internationally recognized human rights of ethnic, linguistic and other minorities are also applicable to them.[38] However, there is a significant dimension in indigenous rights which sets them apart from the general discourse of human rights, i.e. that they are collective in nature. Human rights, as articulated in the main international documents,[39] are essentially individual rights held

---

37 Although the CBD refers to 'indigenous and local communities' as a single phrase, (see *Convention on Biological Diversity* (1992) 31 ILM 818, Preamble, Articles 8 and 26), (hereinafter CBD), it does not define either term. Given the international law developments in regard to indigenous communities, this group will be discussed as a separate issue. The term 'local communities' appears to be more easily combined with that of farmers. A paper submitted by the Permanent Forum on Indigenous Issues has attempted to explain the term 'local communities' as opposed to indigenous communities – see PFII/2004/WS.1/3/Add.1 – United Nations Department of Economic and Social Affairs, Secretariat of the Permanent Forum on Indigenous Issues, *The Concept of Local Communities, Background paper prepared by the Secretariat of the Permanent Forum on Indigenous Issues for the Expert Workshop on the Disaggregation of Data*, 19–21 January 2004.

38 See for instance, *United Nations Declaration on the Elimination of All Forms of Racial Discrimination* Proclaimed by General Assembly Resolution 1904 (XVIII) of 20 November 1963; *International Convention on the Elimination of All Forms of Racial Discrimination*, above n 33; *Declaration on Race and Racial Prejudice*, adopted and proclaimed by the General Conference of the United Nations Educational, Scientific and Cultural Organization at its twentieth session, on 27 November 1978; *Declaration on the Rights of Persons Belonging to National or Ethnic, Religious and Linguistic Minorities*, above n 33.

39 *Charter of the United Nations* 59 Stat. 1031; TS 993; 3 Bevans 1153 (entered into force 24 October 1945); *International Covenant on Civil and Political Rights* GA res. 2200A (XXI), 21 UN GAOR Supp. (No. 16) at 49, UN Doc. A/6316 (1966); 993 UNTS 3; 6 ILM 368 (1967) (entered into force 23 March 1976) (hereinafter

vis-à-vis the state.[40] It has been pointed out that indigenous peoples entered the sphere of international human rights as the subjects of collective rights (or group rights) which had not up to then been conferred on any other category of people.[41] The collective nature of indigenous rights is also relevant when addressing issues of genetic resources and traditional knowledge, and, as will be seen in the further discussion, it is this very factor which often makes it difficult to find solutions to the problems.

The point of reference of indigenous rights in the context of the debate on genetic resources is the misappropriation of these resources, as well as in some instances, the traditional knowledge relating to them. Therefore it would be pertinent to examine the nature and scope of these rights and the basis from which they arise.

The Right to Self-Determination

The collective rights of indigenous peoples emanate from the most fundamental of such rights – that of self-determination. Self-determination has been defined as:

> The idea of a community's rights to control its own future, and thus physically to survive and prosper to the fullest extent possible. A community's powers of 'self-determination' are perceived as a crucial aspect of its identity, and so also, in holistic terms of its health and survival.[42]

ICCPR); *International Covenant on Economic, Social and Cultural Rights* GA res. 2200A (XXI), 21 UN GAOR Supp. (No. 16) at 52, UN Doc. A/6316 (1966); 999 UNTS 171; 6 ILM 360 (1967) (entered into force 3 January 1976) (hereinafter ICESCR).

[40] This is so even in the case of minority rights, since they relate to the rights of individuals belonging to minority groups rather than to the group as a whole. For example the *International Convention on the Elimination of All Forms of Racial Discrimination* above n 33 refers to groups or individuals belonging to them. Article 5 of the Convention lists the rights which States are required to uphold, which are rights of individuals belonging to certain groups rather than to the group as a whole.

[41] Marcus Colchester, 'Indigenous rights and the collective conscious' (2002) 18(1) *Anthropology Today* 1, 1. See also Russel Lawrence Barsh, 'Indigenous Peoples in the 1990s: From Object to Subject of International Law?' (1994) 7 *Harvard Human Rights Journal* 33. Barsh observes that indigenous peoples have achieved greater recognition of collective rights than minorities and other social groups.

[42] C E Foster, 'Articulating self-determination in the Draft Declaration on the Rights of Indigenous Peoples' (2001) 12(1) *European Journal of International Law* 141, 142. Self-determination may be either external or internal and therefore is not confined to a colonial context and is potentially applicable to a group of peoples

Self-determination is an inherent aspect of minority rights as spelt out in international human rights documents. Article 3 of the UN Declaration on the Rights of Indigenous Peoples states that:[43]

> [i]ndigenous peoples have the right of self-determination. By virtue of that right they freely determine their political status and freely pursue their economic, social and cultural development.

This Article is identical to those contained in the two human rights Covenants which refer to 'all peoples.'[44] Barsh notes that based on the argument that they are 'peoples' under the UN Charter, indigenous peoples have been claiming the right to self-determination and the right to be recognized as subjects of international law rather than objects of international concern.[45] In exercising the right to self-determination they have the right to 'autonomy or self-government in matters relating to their internal and local affairs, as well as ways and means for financing their autonomous functions.'[46]

The right to self-determination also provides the basis for other civil and political, as well as economic, social and cultural rights.[47] In relation to indigenous groups, the Declaration is the only document which has attempted to articulate the specific elements of this right.[48] While the

---

within any state – Robert McCorquodale, 'Self Determination: A Human Rights Approach' (1994) 43(4) *International and Comparative Law Quarterly* 857; Patrick Thornberry, 'Self Determination, Minorities and Human Rights' (1989) 38(4) *International and Comparative Law Quarterly* 867.

[43] United Nations Declaration on the Rights of Indigenous Peoples, A/RES/61/295, 2 October 2007.

[44] International Covenant on Civil and Political Rights (ICCPR), Article 1 and International Covenant on Economic, Social and Cultural Rights (ICESCR), Article 1 – 'All peoples have the right of self-determination. By virtue of that right they freely determine their political status and freely pursue their economic, social and cultural development.'

[45] Barsh, above n 41, 35. This is probably one aspect that differentiates indigenous peoples from 'farmers' in international law since farmers as a social group cannot be categorized as peoples.

[46] Declaration, above n 43, Article 4.

[47] ICPPR, Article 1 and ICESR Article 1, above n 44; Declaration, above n 43, Article 3.

[48] The ILO Convention 169, while enumerating a range of indigenous rights is silent on the issue of self-determination. However, Richardson argues that these rights are based on this principle – Benjamin J Richardson, 'Indigenous Peoples, International Law and Sustainability' (2001) 10(1) *Review of European Community and International Environmental Law* 1, 5.

generally accepted rights will not be discussed here, those more specific to these groups and which relate directly or indirectly to natural resources will be explored further.

Even where the rights articulated in the Declaration and the ILO Convention fall within the general discourse of human rights, in the context of indigenous peoples they may take on particular implications. For example, several rights are defined in the context of land and territories and the natural resources which are part of them, and these may have political, economic and cultural connotations.[49] The implementation of these rights requires at a minimum the recognition of historical indigenous rights to land prior to colonization, and also the recognition of indigenous land tenure systems which may differ from that of the political mainstream.[50]

The Right to Natural Resources

It is important at this point to determine the rights of indigenous peoples vis-à-vis biological resources, including the extent and scope of such rights. Indigenous peoples' rights to biological resources have been approached from two spheres of international law, namely, human rights law and environmental law.[51]

The human rights approach

The human rights approach was founded on the need to address the historical injustices committed against indigenous peoples, including the appropriation and colonization of their traditional homelands, the exploitation of the natural resources within these territories, and the disruption of their traditional lifestyles. Given the close relationships between land and

---

[49] UN Declaration – Preamble, Articles 8, 10, 25–30 and 32. ILO Convention 169 – Preamble, Articles 13 and 14. Anaya observes that while there is diversity among indigenous groups a common characteristic tends to be strong ties to land and territory – S James Anaya, 'International Human Rights and Indigenous Peoples: The Move toward the Multicultural State' (2004) 21 *Arizona Journal of International and Comparative Law* 13. For a discussion on the international law relating to indigenous rights to land see Michael Holley, 'Recognizing the Rights of Indigenous People to their Traditional Lands: A Case Study of an Internally-Displaced Community in Guatemala' (1997) 15 *Berkeley Journal of International Law* 119.

[50] Anaya, above n 49.

[51] Richardson, above n 48; Lee P Breckenridge, 'Protection of Biological and Cultural Diversity: Emerging Recognition of Local Community Rights in Ecosystems under International Environmental Law' (1992) 59 *Tennessee Law Review* 735.

culture among them, these injustices impacted particularly strongly on their traditional lifestyles. Also, the destruction of natural resources would have a greater impact on communities that have a more direct dependence on them for sustenance and livelihoods. The human rights approach therefore views such destruction and exploitation as a violation of indigenous rights.

The main human rights documents do not provide any indication of specific rights in relation to biological resources.[52] The Conventions which refer to discrimination against ethnic, linguistic, social or cultural minorities[53] also focus primarily on civil and political rights, and do not throw any light on this question, which would rather fall within the category of economic and social rights. Rights in relation to biological resources would therefore have to be inferred as aspects of the right to self-determination as recognized in these latter documents. However, these documents do not explicate the scope of the rights either.

ILO Convention 169 in Part II entitled 'Land' is the only convention that specifically addresses the issue of rights over land and natural resources. Article 14(1) states that '[t]he rights of ownership and possession of the peoples concerned over the lands which they traditionally occupy shall be recognised.' Article 15(1) states:

> The rights of the peoples concerned to the natural resources pertaining to their lands shall be specially safeguarded. These rights include the right of these peoples to participate in the use, management and conservation of these resources.

The Convention does not acknowledge exclusive rights of ownership over natural resources on indigenous land whether renewable or non-renewable. On the contrary Article 15(2) refers to instances 'in which the State retains the ownership of mineral or sub-surface resources or rights to other resources pertaining to lands.' In such situations the state is only required to establish procedures of consultation before exploiting the resources, and wherever possible the peoples shall participate in the benefits of the resources and receive compensation for any damages which they may sustain. Therefore indigenous peoples' rights of ownership and possession over their lands, and the natural resources pertaining to them, are limited, and the Convention recognizes the overriding rights of the state.[54]

---

[52] See the *Universal Declaration of Human Rights*, G.A. res. 217A (III), UN Doc A/810 at 71 (1948); the ICCPR and the ICESCR.

[53] See the Conventions listed in n 38 above.

[54] The OAS Declaration also follows the approach of the ILO Convention – see Article XVIII of the Proposed American Declaration on the Rights of Indigenous

The UN Declaration on the Rights of Indigenous Peoples is perhaps the most explicit on the issue of rights to natural resources. Article 26 states that '[i]ndigenous peoples have the right to the lands, territories and resources which they have traditionally owned, occupied or otherwise used or acquired.' They derive this right 'by reason of traditional ownership or other traditional occupation or use, as well as those which they have otherwise acquired,' and states shall give legal recognition and protection to these lands. The Declaration therefore confers greater rights of ownership and control over natural resources as against the State in which these peoples are located. However, it must be noted that the Declaration constitutes only soft law and is not binding upon states.[55]

The human rights regime falls short of granting exclusive rights to indigenous peoples in regard to land and natural resources. While rights of ownership and possession over traditional lands including the total environment pertaining to it are recognized, it is limited to rights of occupation and the use of the land and its resources. There are no exclusive rights to the land vis-à-vis the state, since relocation of the peoples by the state is not prohibited.[56] Similarly, the state may exploit and use the resources on indigenous lands so long as it is in accordance with the specified conditions, including consultation with the people concerned, and ensuring that they participate in the benefits and receive just compensation. Such power of the state would also apply to PGRFA since no distinction has been made between renewable and non-renewable resources.

While international law has not recognized indigenous rights over PGRFA, some regional and national laws and agreements have taken more specific measures in this regard. For example the OAU Model Law of 2000 specifically provides that the state recognizes the rights of local and indigenous communities to their biological resources.[57] Similarly, the Biodiversity Law of Costa Rica has acknowledged the rights of local and

---

Peoples (Approved by the Inter-American Commission on Human Rights on February 26, 1997, at its 1333rd session, 95th Regular Session), OEA/Ser/L/V/.II.95 Doc.6 (1997).

[55] Other soft law instruments also refer to the link between indigenous peoples and their land. See for example Agenda 21, paragraph 26; the Programme of Action of the UN International Conference on Population and Development, paragraph 6; and the Programme of Action of the World Summit on Social Development, paragraph 32.

[56] See Article 16 of the ILO Convention 169 which permits relocation in accordance with the specified conditions.

[57] *African Model Legislation for the Protection of the Rights of Local Communities, Farmers and Breeders, and for the Regulation of Access to Biological Resources*, 2000 – Part IV.

indigenous communities to oppose any access rights to their resources.[58] The Philippines has also given wide recognition to indigenous rights, including rights of ownership over traditional domains and the natural resources pertaining to them.[59] It would therefore be left to national policy to determine the extent and scope of such rights.

The environmental law approach

The environmental law approach to indigenous peoples and biological resources has been even more complex and tentative, and is in effect the converse of the former approach. It is based upon the link between the cultural and biological diversity which is located within the purview of indigenous and local communities,[60] and essentially views such peoples as an enabling factor in the conservation of such diversity, which is a global resource. To begin with, the international environmental law discourse categorically places sovereign rights over biological diversity in the hands of nation states, rather than on specific groups within national populations such as indigenous peoples and local communities.[61] While holding sovereign rights, states also have international obligations to conserve these resources for the benefit of the global community. In order to fulfil these obligations they are required to enlist the co-operation of indigenous and local peoples and to draw upon their cultural diversity, knowledge, and practices in doing so. In return, they have an obligation towards these peoples to ensure that they, in turn, receive an equitable share of the benefits arising from these resources.

In essence, this approach is enviro-centric rather than human-centric since it views indigenous peoples only as a means to the conservation of a global natural resource. While the human rights approach does recognize the rights of indigenous peoples to ownership and possession over land and natural resources, and then qualifies it with the rights of the State, the environmental approach primarily emphasizes the sovereignty of states over biological resources with the obligation to have due regard to the rights of indigenous peoples.

---

[58] *Biodiversity Law* No. 7788 of Costa Rica – Article 66.

[59] *Indigenous Peoples Rights Act* of 1997 of the Philippines – Chapter III and Section 57.

[60] Breckenridge, above n 51. For a discussion on the environmental law approach to indigenous rights see Klaus Bosselmann, 'The Right to Self-determination and International Environmental Law: An Integrative Approach' (1997) 1(1) *New Zealand Journal of Environmental Law* 1.

[61] CBD, Article 3.

Several international environmental documents, including those which emerged from the United Nations Conference on Environment and Development (UNCED) in 1992, refer to the link between indigenous peoples and the environment, but with somewhat differing frames of reference. The Rio Declaration[62] and the Forest Principles[63] clearly take an environment focused rather than a rights focused approach to the link between the two. On the other hand, Chapter 26 of Agenda 21, although reiterating the importance of environmental conservation, appears more people focused in defining the relationship between indigenous peoples and biological resources, continually noting the rights of peoples rather than the objectives of environmental conservation. This resembles the perspective found in the UN Declaration and the ILO Convention 169.[64]

The CBD unequivocally views indigenous peoples as a resource for achieving its objectives of environmental conservation.[65] The Preamble recognizes the close and traditional dependence that such communities have on biological resources, and notes the desirability of equitably sharing the benefits arising from the use of traditional biodiversity related knowledge, innovations, and practices which are relevant to the conservation of biological diversity and the sustainable use of its components. The clause is ambiguous, since it is unclear whether the objective is to ensure that everyone benefits from the traditional biodiversity related knowledge of the peoples concerned, or, having appropriated such knowledge, to ensure that

---

[62] *Rio Declaration on Environment and Development*, 31 ILM 876 – Principle 22 – 'Indigenous people and their communities and other local communities have a vital role in environmental management and development because of their knowledge and traditional practices. States should recognize and duly support their identity, culture and interests and enable their effective participation in the achievement of sustainable development.'

[63] *Non-legally Binding Authoritative Statement of Principles for a Global Consensus on the Management, Conservation and Sustainable Development of all Types of Forests* 31 ILM 881(1992) – Principle 5(a) – 'National forest policies should recognize and duly support the identity, culture and the rights of indigenous people, their communities and other communities and forest dwellers. Appropriate conditions should be promoted for these groups to enable them to have an economic stake in forest use, perform economic activities, and achieve and maintain cultural identity and social organization, as well as adequate levels of livelihood and well-being, through, inter alia, those land tenure arrangements which serve as incentives for the sustainable management of forests.'

[64] See in particular Part VI of the UN Declaration.

[65] As does the FAO Treaty in relation to farmers.

the latter receive an equitable share of the resulting benefits.[66] This ambiguity is reinforced in Article 8(j) which requires states, as far as possible and as appropriate, to:

> subject to its national legislation, respect, preserve and maintain knowledge, innovations and practices of indigenous and local communities embodying traditional lifestyles relevant for the conservation and sustainable use of biological diversity and promote their wider application with the approval and involvement of the holders of such knowledge, innovations and practices and encourage the equitable sharing of the benefits arising from the utilization of such knowledge, innovations and practices.

In terms of the CBD, indigenous peoples and local communities are significant only if they embody *traditional lifestyles* that are relevant for the conservation and sustainable use of biological diversity. This begs the question as to how this issue would be defined and determined. Further, while referring to communities embodying traditional lifestyles, the CBD does not uphold the rights of the peoples to maintain such lifestyles. The reference to indigenous peoples is only as regards their *traditional knowledge, innovations and practices,* and it appears that States are required to protect these only insofar as they are relevant for the objectives of the Convention. Notably, the CBD does not recognize or make reference to the rights of indigenous peoples to their traditional lands and territories and the natural resources including PGRFA, since, as noted earlier, it categorically confers sovereign rights over such resources upon nation states.[67]

The approach of the CBD can be critiqued on several grounds. To begin with, the premise that indigenous peoples' traditional lifestyles make them uniquely suitable for resource conservation has been challenged by writers, who argue against overly romanticizing such groups of peoples in this regard.[68] It is also questionable in view of the pressures of modern life which may compel them to change that very lifestyle, possibly making it less environmentally sustainable. Writers also argue against stereotypical perceptions of indigenous peoples, noting that for example, traditional methods of resource exploitation may in fact, often be at odds with

---

66 The ambiguity is explained in documents of the CBD CoP which notes that the Convention 'recognizes that indigenous and local communities should share in the benefits derived from ideas and innovations they have developed that prove useful to others' – UNEP/CBD/COP/3/19 – CBD CoP, Third meeting, 4–15 November 1996, *Knowledge, Innovations and Practices of Indigenous and Local Communities: Implementation of Article 8(J)* 18 September 1996, paragraph 9.

67 CBD, Article 15(1).

68 Richardson, above n 48, 3.

objectives of species protection and resource conservation.[69] The premise is also based on the assumption that indigenous peoples are permanently entrenched in a particular lifestyle, which in addition to being unrealistic, would also negate their rights to make choices in development and social change. This position would be at odds with the human rights approach, which holds that such peoples have the right to decide their own priorities for the process of development.[70] Therefore whatever the justification or otherwise for making the link between indigenous peoples and biological resource conservation, it is fundamentally flawed from a human rights perspective.

A similar worldview is taken by the FAO Treaty in its reference to indigenous peoples. Article 5(1) requires Contracting Parties to 'promote *in situ* conservation of wild crop relatives and wild plants for food production, including in protected areas, by supporting, inter alia, the efforts of indigenous and local communities.' Article 9(1) acknowledges the enormous contribution that local and indigenous communities and farmers have made to the conservation and development of plant genetic resources. In this instance too, indigenous peoples are viewed in the context of their contribution to this end.

The Right to Culture

The second important right of indigenous peoples in the context of this book is that of the right to culture. The culture of indigenous peoples is also inherently linked to land and territory, as recognized in the UN Declaration. The Preamble to the Declaration recognizes the 'urgent need to respect and promote the inherent rights of indigenous peoples which derive from their political, economic and social structures and from their cultures, spiritual

---

[69] Ibid; William Bradford, '"Save the Whales" v Save the Makah: Finding Negotiated Solutions to Ethnodevelopmental Disputes in the New International Economic Order' (2000) 13 *St Thomas Law Review* 155. Some writers have also expressed scepticism at the 'ecological dimension to indigenous claims' – Rhiannon Morgan, 'Advancing Indigenous Rights at the United Nations: Strategic Framing and its Impact on the Normative Development of International Law' (2004) 13(4) *Social & Legal Studies* 481. However, other writers take the opposite view – Breckenridge, above n 51; Gregory F Maggio, 'Recognizing the Vital Role of Local Communities in International Legal Instruments for Conserving Biodiversity' (1997/1998) 16 *UCLA Journal of Environmental Law & Policy* 179.

[70] ILO Convention 169 – Article 7.

traditions, histories and philosophies, especially their rights to their lands, territories and resources.'[71]

Indigenous peoples' rights to culture take on particular importance in the light of the threats of destruction and misappropriation of cultural property which they have faced since colonization, and which has exponentially increased in a progressively globalized and commercially dominated world. The threats include the appropriation of such manifestations of culture as folklore, sacred songs, symbols, dances and art.[72] In the present context however, the element of indigenous culture which has become most economically valuable and politically contentious is that of traditional ecological knowledge, which has been often exploited over the years for commercial gain without their consent. Questions of rights regarding traditional knowledge have not been directly addressed by the international human rights regime, although they could be brought within the ambit of the right to culture.[73] It has however, been addressed by international environmental law, particularly the CBD.[74] Issues of traditional biodiversity related knowledge are discussed further below, and some contentious aspects of it will be explored in later chapters.

---

[71] UN Declaration – Preamble and Article 8. See also Benedict Kingsbury, 'Indigenous Peoples' in 'International Law: A Constructivist Approach to the Asian Controversy' (1998) 92 *American Journal of International Law* 414, 437.

[72] See for example Breckenridge, above n 51. See also UN Declaration, Article 31.

[73] The traditional knowledge and cultural expressions of indigenous peoples has been specifically cited in the *UNESCO Convention on the Protection and Promotion of the Diversity of Cultural Expressions*, CLT-2005/CONVENTION DIVERSITE-CULT REV, 20 October 2005 – Preamble. See also the Action Plan for the Implementation of the *UNESCO Universal Declaration on Cultural Diversity*, adopted by the Thirty-first Session of the General Conference of UNESCO, Paris, 2 November 2001, Article 14.

[74] Decision VI/10 entitled 'Article 8(j) and related provisions' of the CoP recognized that 'the Convention on Biological Diversity is the primary international instrument with the mandate to address issues regarding the respect, preservation and maintenance of knowledge, innovations and practices of indigenous and local communities embodying traditional lifestyles relevant to the conservation and sustainable use of biological diversity.' Although the FAO Treaty does not directly deal with traditional knowledge, the interface between the FAO Treaty and Article 8(j) of the CBD was discussed in UNEP/CBD/COP/7/INF/18 – CBD CoP, Seventh Meeting, 9–20 and 27 February 2004, *The Implications of the International Treaty on Plant Genetic Resources for Food and Agriculture on the Issues under Article 8(j) and Related Provisions*, 17 December 2003.

Conclusion

This review of international documents relating to indigenous peoples' rights reveals that while international law does recognize that they have certain rights in biological resources, such rights do not amount to exclusive rights of ownership and possession as against the states in which they are located. The general human rights instruments including the Universal Declaration of Human Rights of 1948 (UDHR) and the two human rights Covenants do not shed any light on this question. While the right to self-determination contained in these documents has many connotations, they do not extend to rights over biological resources. Although ILO Convention 169 contains the most specific references to such rights, it too stops short of absolute ownership, and in fact acknowledges that states may retain ownership of mineral or sub-surface resources, or rights to other resources pertaining to land. This position is reinforced by the CBD which unequivocally recognizes the sovereign rights of states over biological resources. Soft law instruments merely refer to the need to recognize the relationship of indigenous peoples to their land, including their direct dependence on renewable resources and ecosystems, ensure environmentally sustainable development and recognize their values, traditional knowledge and resource management practices.

There are admittedly difficulties in granting certain groups within nation states monopolistic property rights over natural resources found within specific areas of such states. The first difficulties relate to the people claiming such rights. As discussed earlier, international law has differentiated between indigenous peoples and other ethnic minorities, acknowledging a greater range of rights in the former. However, unless secession or federalism from the state takes place, even minority groups are seldom granted absolute control over vital natural resources. There would need to be strong justification for doing so in the case of indigenous peoples. While it could be argued that this justification could be applicable in countries where colonization, displacement and extreme exploitation of indigenous groups took place, it would be less so in countries where it did not. In the latter instance, the differential treatment of indigenous and other minorities would need to be substantiated to a greater degree. However, some countries have, in fact, granted broad rights to indigenous communities in this regard.

The nature of the resources would also pose certain problems in granting exclusive rights to specific categories of peoples. There could, for example, be justification for acknowledging indigenous rights to mineral resources found on their traditional lands on the basis that what is found on land accrues to the owner, though even the ILO Convention does not grant this.

There would however, be much less justification for granting specific groups private property rights over genetic resources which are vital for food, medicines and other uses for humanity. Further, unlike non-renewable resources, most PGRFA would not in any case be located exclusively within the jurisdiction of specific communities. As argued earlier in this book, historically these resources were in the public domain and removing them from an open access regime and putting them in the control of any group of people would be a questionable response to the privatization of such resources by corporate interests.

Traditional knowledge, on the other hand, as an aspect of culture, would have to be addressed differently and this is discussed below.

TRADITIONAL BIODIVERSITY RELATED KNOWLEDGE

Traditional knowledge as an aspect of human cultural diversity was discussed in Chapter 2, with a particular focus on traditional ecological knowledge. The knowledge of the uses and benefits of plant varieties held by indigenous and local communities, has gained increasing commercial value in situations where it can provide leads to the possible exploitation of plants. As noted in Chapter 3, the unauthorized appropriation of plants and the knowledge related to them, has given rise to allegations of biopiracy. Therefore problems of traditional knowledge are closely linked to those of genetic resources and both have been raised simultaneously in international fora. This section will expand on the topic of traditional knowledge and provide an introductory overview of the issues relating to it in this context, while specific aspects will be discussed in the following chapters.

Questions of traditional knowledge have not been directly addressed by the international human rights regime, although they could be brought within the ambit of the right to culture. It has however, been addressed by international environmental law, specifically the CBD.[75]

The first question to be considered is how the term 'indigenous or traditional knowledge' is defined in international instruments.[76] Despite the

---

[75] Decision VI/10 Ibid.

[76] A distinction has been made between traditional and indigenous knowledge. Brush notes that '[t]raditional knowledge is a broader category that includes indigenous knowledge as a type of traditional knowledge held by indigenous communities. While traditional knowledge has recently emerged in international discourse ... indigenous knowledge is a term long in use by anthropologists and other investigators of non-industrialised societies ... Nevertheless, apart from the

CBD being the only international document to deal with traditional/ indigenous knowledge it does not define the words indigenous, traditional or knowledge.[77] The phrase 'traditional' or 'indigenous' knowledge is usually described rather than defined. One writer does so in these terms:[78]

> Generally, IK is considered a body of knowledge associated with a fixed territorial space for a considerably long period of time. Such systems of knowledge are informal, experiential, and uncodified compared to the knowledge systems associated with the Western sciences.
>
> IK is unique to a community, culture, or society; is the basis for local-level decision making in agriculture, health, natural resource management, and other activities; is embedded in community practices, institutions, relationships, and rituals; and as such is a powerful tool to create sustainable change, particularly in resource-poor rural communities.

As can be seen, the definitions of traditional knowledge tend to be ostensive, merely describing what it comprises rather than providing an explanation of what it is.[79] The constituents of traditional knowledge therefore include knowledge, innovations and practices, as well as institutions, relationships and rituals. These are not limited to knowledge in relation to genetic resources but also encompass for example, such manifestations of knowledge as traditional medicine and its attendant practices.[80]

The appropriation of traditional or indigenous knowledge has been facilitated in large part by the construction of 'knowledge' and 'modern

---

designation of the type of holder, the definitions applied to indigenous knowledge also apply to traditional knowledge.' – Stephen B Brush, 'The Demise of "Common Heritage" and Protection for Traditional Agricultural Knowledge' in Charles McManis (ed), *Biodiversity and the law: intellectual property, biotechnology and traditional knowledge* (2007) 301. See also Chidi Oguamanam, 'Between Reality and Rhetoric: The Epistemic Schism in the Recognition of Traditional Medicine in International Law' (2003) 16 *St. Thomas Law Review* 59.

77 The terms occur in Article 17 – 'indigenous and traditional knowledge'; Article 18(2) – 'indigenous and traditional technologies.' Other references are to 'lifestyles' (Preamble, paragraph 12 and Article 8(j)) and 'cultural practices' (Article 10(c)).

78 Jude L Fernando, 'NGOs and Production of Indigenous Knowledge under the Condition of Postmodernity' (2003) 590 *Annals* 54, 57.

79 Bernard O'Connor, 'Protecting Traditional Knowledge. An Overview of a Developing Area of Intellectual Property Law' (2003) 6(5) *Journal of World Intellectual Property* 677, 678 where he merely describes traditional knowledge as 'as the knowledge, innovations and practices of indigenous peoples and local communities.'

80 See for example, Oguamanam, above n 76.

science' to exclude the informal knowledge systems of indigenous and local communities (or even nations as a larger community), deeming it valueless and therefore not worthy of propertization.[81] It has been further facilitated by the assumption that such knowledge is not owned and may be appropriated. Where this has taken place, the holders (whether communities or states) have not received either compensation or a share of the benefits of its commercial use.[82]

To some extent, though not invariably, traditional knowledge has been in the public domain, with natural resource centred knowledge being by and large freely shared, exchanged, and disseminated. Often, knowledge relating to particular plants may be widespread throughout countries or regions. For example, knowledge relating to the medicinal properties of turmeric, and the tree *Azadirachta indica* (neem in India and kohomba in Sri Lanka), is common to both countries.[83] Traditional agricultural knowledge would also be common knowledge, with PGRFA being in the public domain. However, as Dutfield has pointed out, while there is a strong, sharing ethos with regard to such knowledge, 'this does not mean that everything is shared with everybody.'[84] He goes on to note that proprietary systems do exist in many traditional societies, and all traditional knowledge is not in the public domain.[85] In any event, knowledge in the public domain can no more be privatized than the knowledge specific to communities, and where this has taken place, the process has been challenged. Examples of these instances will be noted in the continuing discussions. However, the discourse on the

---

[81] See Naomi Roht-Arriaza, 'Of Seeds and Shamans: The Appropriation of the Scientific and Technical Knowledge of Indigenous and Local Communities' (1996) 17 *Michigan Journal of International Law* 919.

[82] See for example Michael Woods, 'Food for Thought: The Biopiracy of Jasmine and Basmati Rice' (2002) 13 *Albany Law Journal of Science & Technology* 123; Sumathi Subbiah, 'Reaping What They Sow: The Basmati Rice Controversy and Strategies for Protecting Traditional Knowledge' (2004) 27 *Boston College International and Comparative Law Review* 529; Muriel Lightbourne, 'Of Rice and Men. An Attempt to Assess the Basmati Affair' (2003) 6(6) *Journal of World Intellectual Property* 875; Shayana Kadidal, 'Subject-Matter Imperialism? Biodiversity, Foreign Prior Art and the Neem Patent Controversy' (1997) 37 IDEA 371.

[83] See FAO Regional Office for Asia and the Pacific (RAPA), *Non-Wood Forest Products in Asia* (1994), available at http://www.fao.org/docrep/X5334e/x5334e00.htm#Contents (last accessed 30 June 2012).

[84] Graham Dutfield, 'The Public and Private Domains: Intellectual Property Rights in Traditional Knowledge' (2000) 21 *Science Communication* 274, 281.

[85] Ibid.

question of traditional knowledge has generally focused on that of indigenous and local communities and therefore this discussion will also maintain this perspective.

Rights to Traditional Biodiversity Related Knowledge

There is a strong human rights justification for protecting traditional knowledge in the interests of indigenous and other peoples, other than that of biodiversity conservation. Traditional knowledge, innovations and practices constitute an integral part of the cultural practices of a community. While the human rights discourse on indigenous peoples has stopped short of granting them exclusive ownership of biological resources, its provisions on cultural rights would clearly encompass knowledge, innovations and practices.[86]

Articles 1 of both the International Covenant on Civil and Political Rights (ICCPR) and the International Covenant on Economic, Social and Cultural Rights (ICESCR) which address the right of self-determination, note that the rights include the right to freely pursue economic, social and cultural development. Article 27 of the ICCPR declares that in states in which ethnic, religious or linguistic minorities exist, persons belonging to such minorities shall not be denied the right, in community with the other members of their group, to *inter alia*, enjoy their own culture. In its General Comment on this Article the Human Rights Committee has noted that 'culture manifests itself in many forms, including a particular way of life associated with the use of land resources, especially in the case of indigenous peoples.'[87] The General Comment also observes that although the rights in question are individual rights, they depend upon the ability of the minority group to maintain its culture, language, or religion. It therefore imposes positive obligations upon states to protect these rights.[88] ILO Convention 169 also links the cultural values and practices of these peoples

---

86 Several documents on cultural diversity also refer to traditional knowledge and knowledge systems including with regard to natural resources, but do not deal with rights in respect of it – *UNESCO Convention on the Protection and Promotion of the Diversity of Cultural Expressions*, above n 73; *UNESCO Universal Declaration on Cultural Diversity*, above n 73; *Convention for the Safeguarding of the Intangible Cultural Heritage*, Paris, 17 November 2003, UNESCO Doc.MISC/2003/CLT/CH/14.

87 *General Comment No. 23: The Rights of Minorities* (Art. 27): 08/04/94. CCPR/C/21/Rev.1/Add.5, paragraphs 7 and 3.2.

88 Ibid, paragraph 6.2.

to land and natural resources,[89] and the UN Declaration on the Rights of Indigenous Peoples clearly recognizes the protection of indigenous culture as a developmental right of indigenous peoples rather than as a means of resource conservation.[90]

Legal writers have argued that one basic justification for protecting traditional knowledge is on moral grounds. Amiott argues that:

> because traditional knowledge is crucial for the economic and cultural survival of knowledge-holders as distinct peoples, indigenous and local communities should be permitted to live how and where they presently live – and to maintain the cultural and economic systems and relationships with the land that they and their ancestors have developed over countless generations.

She further points out that holders of traditional knowledge are often among the world's poorest people and therefore protecting it is essential to sustain them.[91]

The question is whether the CBD is also based upon this moral imperative or on the wider interests of the commercial uses which can be derived from indigenous knowledge of biological resources and the sharing of the benefits accruing from them. This factor would be relevant when examining its stance in the international debate on the issue.

As argued earlier, the CBD is less concerned with the human rights of indigenous peoples than with the need to protect and preserve their traditional knowledge for its own objectives. The importance of traditional knowledge for the purposes of the CBD was expressed at the Third CoP meeting in these terms:

> Traditional knowledge has and will continue to give critical clues to scientists in the agricultural, medicinal and industrial fields. In addition, traditional knowledge provides important directions for natural resource use and ecosystem

---

89 ILO Convention 169 – Article 4(1), Article 13(1) and Article 23(1).

90 UN Declaration above n 43, Preamble, paragraphs 7 and 10. The Declaration also recognizes that 'respect for indigenous knowledge, cultures and traditional practices contributes to sustainable and equitable development and proper management of the environment' – Preamble, paragraph 11.

91 Jennifer Amiott, 'Investigating the Convention on Biological Diversity's Protections for Traditional Knowledge' (2003) 11 *Missouri Environmental Law & Policy Review* 3, 10–11. See also UNEP/CBD/TKBD/1/3 – *Report of the Workshop on Traditional Knowledge and Biological Diversity*, Madrid, 24–28 November 1997.

> management. Indigenous and local communities not only have extensive knowledge of their surrounding environment, but they also have an important role in implementing any conservation policy on the ground.[92]

This statement makes no mention of indigenous peoples' rights to maintain their traditional knowledge and practices that form an intrinsic aspect of their culture and way of life. Although the document notes that the CBD recognizes that 'indigenous and local communities should share in the benefits derived from ideas and innovations they have developed that prove useful to others,' this is more to provide them with incentives to conserve biodiversity than to further their own interests.[93]

The Nagoya Protocol addresses at length the issue of indigenous peoples' traditional knowledge as associated with genetic resources. The introduction to the Protocol states that 'the Protocol's provisions on access to traditional knowledge held by indigenous and local communities when it is associated with genetic resources will strengthen the ability of these communities to benefit from the use of their knowledge, innovations and practices.' However, this has been disputed by a joint submission of several indigenous groups made to the first meeting of the Open-Ended Ad Hoc Intergovernmental Committee for the Protocol in June 2011.[94]

The Preamble to the Protocol states that it is 'Mindful that it is the right of indigenous and local communities to identify the rightful holders of their traditional knowledge associated with genetic resources, within their communities,' notes the UN Declaration on the Rights of Indigenous Peoples, and affirms that 'nothing in this Protocol shall be construed as diminishing or extinguishing the existing rights of indigenous and local communities.' Nevertheless this commitment is not supported in its provisions.

The rights of indigenous peoples in regard to genetic resources and associated traditional knowledge are addressed in several Articles of the Protocol, including on fair and equitable benefit sharing, access to genetic resources and access to traditional knowledge associated with genetic resources.[95] According to these provisions states parties must take measures

---

92 UNEP/CBD/COP/3/19 – CBD CoP, Third meeting, 4–15 November 1996, *Knowledge, Innovations and Practices of Indigenous and Local Communities: Implementation of Article 8(J) (18 September 1996),* paragraph 8.

93 Ibid, paragraph 9.

94 Open-Ended Ad Hoc Intergovernmental Committee for the Nagoya Protocol on Access to Genetic Resources and the Fair and Equitable Sharing of Benefits Arising from their Utilization, First meeting, 6–10 June 2011, *Nagoya Protocol on Access and Benefit Sharing: Substantive and Procedural Injustices relating to Indigenous Peoples' Human Rights.*

95 Articles 5–7, See also Articles 11–14, and 16.

to ensure benefit sharing with indigenous peoples in regard to genetic resources and traditional knowledge held by them, and to ensure that their prior informed consent and approval is obtained before acquisition. However, this obligation is severely diluted by phrases which require the measures to be 'as appropriate' and 'in accordance with domestic legislation regarding the established rights' of such peoples, or 'where they have the established right to grant access to such resources.' Such wording is equivocal and does not specify what parties' obligations are in relation to indigenous peoples. The dominance of states over indigenous peoples within their jurisdiction is reinforced by provisions which require such parties to ensure that the prior informed consent of indigenous peoples is obtained for access to genetic resources and traditional knowledge only 'in accordance with domestic law.' This undermines the autonomy of these communities over such knowledge and makes them dependent on the discretion of states to uphold their rights.

The joint submission of indigenous groups drew attention to both procedural and substantive injustices towards these groups in the drafting of the Protocol. In regard to substantive injustices the submission noted that indigenous peoples continue to face dispossession and biopiracy of their land and natural resources and need urgent international and domestic safeguards for their human rights. However, this is not specifically referred to in the Protocol. Generally, indigenous peoples' human rights were largely disregarded in the Protocol and progressive international standards such as the UN Declaration on the Rights of Indigenous Peoples were not fully respected. The submission states that 'In relation to Indigenous peoples and local communities, the Protocol must be consistent with the principles of justice, democracy, equality, non-discrimination, respect for human rights and rule of law. The rights, security and well-being of present and future generations must be ensured.'[96]

The FAO International Treaty on Plant Genetic Resources for Food and Agriculture takes a similar stance on indigenous biodiversity knowledge in the context of farmers' rights, stating that Contracting Parties:

> … should, as appropriate, and subject to its national legislation, take measures to protect and promote Farmers' Rights, including:
>
> (a) protection of traditional knowledge relevant to plant genetic resources for food and agriculture.

---

[96] Above n 94, page 5.

In this instance too, the Treaty is specifically concerned only with the knowledge relevant for its purposes. Further, as in the CBD and the Nagoya Protocol, its indeterminate wording leaves it to the discretion of States Parties to determine what measures will be taken to protect this knowledge. These issues will be examined further in succeeding chapters.

7. The international property rights regime

INTRODUCTION

Chapter 5 dealt with the environmental/conservation regime on PGRFA. The second regime which impacts upon the use of these resources, is the international property rights regime. It is not concerned with the conservation and sustainable use of these resources or with the equitable sharing of their beneficial uses. Rather, its objective is to promote and enforce intellectual property protection globally, including in relation to PGRFA, and its functions have been directed towards this end. Consequently, it is at variance with the former regime, and the international debate on PGRFA has by and large focussed on efforts to resolve the conflicts which arise in the implementation of the two.

In this chapter I will provide an introduction to the three agreements which make up this system, and the international institutions which administer them. While these agreements and institutions deal with a broad range of issues, of which PGRFA is only one, it is necessary to understand their history, mandates and functions in order to analyze how they affect the use of these resources. The international property rights regime is intended and structured so as to enforce intellectual property rights (IPRs) globally, and this will necessarily remove PGRFA from the public domain and affect access to and benefit sharing of its uses. This chapter will provide an overview of the three agreements, while their specific provisions in relation to PGRFA will be examined in the following chapter.

The need to develop a global regime of intellectual property protection derives from the fact that IPRs are national in application, and a patent traditionally could not be recognized internationally. For example, a patent issued in the US or a European country will not necessarily be honoured in any other country. In order to safeguard such a patent the holder would need to apply for patent rights in all the countries where it may be needed and his/her ability to do so would depend on their laws. Since there is no legal concept of an 'international patent,' it would be in the interests of those who require some form of legal protection for their products to ensure that the national laws of all countries are harmonized to facilitate the recognition of patents or other forms of intellectual property protection. International agreements are therefore the means by which to develop a uniform global system of such protection, requiring of its signatories that they bring their domestic laws into conformity with international standards in this regard.[1] This process has been played out in the International Union for the Protection of New Varieties of Plants (UPOV), the World Intellectual Property Organization (WIPO) and the World Trade Organization (WTO) by way of the treaties administered by them. These will be discussed in turn.

THE INTERNATIONAL CONVENTION FOR THE PROTECTION OF NEW VARIETIES OF PLANTS (UPOV CONVENTION)

The International Convention for the Protection of New Varieties of Plants (UPOV Convention) was signed in 1961 and entered into force in 1968.[2] It is the agreement which deals solely and specifically with plant varieties and rights of ownership over them. The provisions of the UPOV Convention established a specific system of intellectual property tailored to protect plant breeders' rights (PBRs), also called plant variety protection (PVP).[3] These rights are similar to patents and copyrights, giving the breeder of a new plant variety exclusive rights of ownership over the product.[4] The

---

[1] Anne E Crocker, 'Will Plants Finally Grow Into Full Patent Protection on an International Level? A Look at the History of US and International Patent Law regarding Patent Protection for Plants and the Likely Changes after the US Supreme Court's Decision in JEM Ag Supply v Pioneer Hi-Bred' (2003) 8 *Drake Journal of Agricultural Law* 251.

[2] *International Convention for the Protection of New Varieties of Plants*, Act of 1961 adopted by the Diplomatic Conference on 2 December 1961, available at http://www.upov.int/en/publications/conventions/1961/act1961.htm (last accessed 30 June 2012).

[3] For a comprehensive discussion of UPOV see Rolf Jördens, 'Progress of plant variety protection based on the International Convention for the Protection of New Varieties of Plants (UPOV Convention)' (2005) 27(3) *World Patent Information* 232; Graham Dutfield, 'Turning Plant Varieties into Intellectual Property: The UPOV Convention' in Geoff Tansey and Tasmin Rajotte (eds), *The future control of food: a guide to international negotiations and rules on intellectual property, biodiversity, and food security* (2008).

[4] Max Thiele-Wittig and Paul Claus, 'Plant variety protection – A fascinating subject' (2003) 25(3) *World Patent Information* 243. The Article also sets out the differences between plant variety protection and patents at 247.

Convention established the International Union for the Protection of New Varieties of Plants (UPOV) which is an international organization endowed with legal personality.[5] The UPOV Convention and the creation of UPOV institutionalized the process by which these rights would be enforced, and the latter serves as the forum to achieve the objective of implementing the commercial rights of plant breeders.

The UPOV Convention was revised in 1972, 1978 and 1991.[6] After the 1978 Act entered into force states could no longer accede to the 1961 Convention. The Convention was again revised in 1991, creating the 1991 UPOV Act and after this came into force in 1998, the 1978 Act was closed for further accession. As of February 2012, 21 states are bound by the 1978 Act and 48 states are bound by the 1991 Act.[7]

The debate on PGRFA has not been significantly carried out in the fora of UPOV, but the provisions of the UPOV Convention are being upheld as the appropriate standard of *sui generis* plant variety protection, which should be adopted by all countries. This will be further examined in Chapter 10.

THE WORLD INTELLECTUAL PROPERTY ORGANIZATION

Introduction

The second institution whose treaties have a direct impact on the uses of PGRFA is the World Intellectual Property Organization (WIPO). WIPO was established in 1970 by the WIPO Convention,[8] and by 1974 it had

---

[5] International Convention for the Protection of New Varieties of Plants of 2 December 1961, as revised at Geneva on 10 November 1972, on 23 October 1978, and on 19 March 1991, Article 14, available at http://www.upov.int/en/publications/conventions/1991/act1991.htm (hereinafter UPOV Act 1991) Article 24. The website of UPOV is available at http://www.upov.int/index_en.html (both last accessed 30 June 2012).

[6] See UPOV Act 1991.

[7] See http://www.upov.int/members/en/ (last accessed 30 June 2012).

[8] The Convention establishing the World Intellectual Property Organization was signed at Stockholm on 14 July 1967 and amended on 28 September 1979, available at http://www.wipo.int/treaties/en/convention/trtdocs_wo029.html (hereinafter WIPO Convention) (last accessed 30 June 2012). See also Sisule F Musungu and Graham Dutfield, *Multilateral agreements and a TRIPS-plus world: The World Intellectual Property Organization (WIPO)* (2003) Quaker United Nations Office

become a specialized agency of the United Nations.[9] As its name indicates, its strategic goals are to promote the development and use of intellectual property rights internationally.[10] In furtherance of these goals WIPO's core tasks are developing international intellectual property laws and standards, delivering global IP protection services, encouraging the use of intellectual property for economic development, promoting better understanding of IP and providing a forum for debate.[11] WIPO administers 24 intellectual property related treaties[12] and currently has 185 member states.[13]

While WIPO's objective is to promote intellectual property rights globally, its role as a UN agency also requires it to pursue a development policy for the benefit of developing countries. The Agreement between the UN and WIPO states that the UN recognizes WIPO as:

> being responsible for taking appropriate action … *inter alia,* for promoting creative intellectual activity and for facilitating the transfer of technology related to industrial property to the developing countries in order to accelerate economic, social and cultural development.[14]

---

and Quaker International Affairs Programme, Chapter 2, available at http://www.iprsonline.org/ictsd/docs/WIPO_Musungu_Dutfield.pdf (last accessed 30 June 2012).

9 See *Agreement between the United Nations and the World Intellectual Property Organization* (entered into force 17 December 1974), available at http://www.wipo.int/treaties/en/agreement/pdf/un_wipo_agreement.pdf (hereinafter UN/WIPO Agreement) (last accessed 30 June 2012).

10 More specifically these goals are to promote an IP culture; to integrate IP into national development policies and programmes; to develop international IP laws and standards; to deliver quality services in global IP protection systems; and to increase the efficiency of WIPO's management and support processes, see http://www.wipo.int/about-wipo/en/what_is_wipo.html (last accessed 30 June 2012). See also *World Intellectual Property Organization Proposed Program and Budget* for 2006/07, presented by the Director General.

11 WIPO/IP/DEV/GE/11/2 – Evaluation Seminar Series, Learning from Existing Evaluation Practices on the Impacts and Effects of Intellectual Property on Development, Intellectual Property Facts, prepared by the Secretariat (October 2011).

12 See http://wipo.int/treaties/en/ (last accessed 30 June 2012). The WIPO Convention provides the framework for the organization and is only an administrative treaty. The various categories of IPRs are dealt with by separate treaties which WIPO administers, and they have different aims and objectives and different contracting parties. See also Musungu and Dutfield, above n 8, Chapter 2.

13 See http://www.wipo.int/members/en/ (last accessed 30 June 2012).

14 UN/WIPO Agreement, above n 9, Article 1.

WIPO is also required to follow any UN recommendations[15] and to render such assistance as the latter may request.[16] A further objective is to promote and facilitate the transfer of technology to developing countries so as to assist them in attaining their objectives in the fields of science and technology and trade and development, and to this end it is required to co-operate with the UN and its organs.[17] It is clear therefore, that its status as a specialized UN agency must necessarily be consistent with the latter's overall developmental focus.[18]

The inconsistency between WIPO's mandate to promote IPRs[19] and its development focus has caused some degree of tension between its developed and developing country members, and some ambivalence in their perceptions of the institution.[20] Its structure and functions have also contributed to this situation. To begin with, unlike many international institutions WIPO is predominantly funded by fees earned by the administration of the Patent Cooperation Treaty (PCT), and therefore not dependent on the contributions of its member countries. This has meant that the developed countries are less able to dominate its activities by controlling the budget.[21] The developed countries' dissatisfaction is further enhanced by the fact that being a subsidiary organization of the United Nations where they are outnumbered by developing countries, WIPO's 'allegiance' is seen as being towards the latter.[22] Further, WIPO does not have a dispute settlement mechanism through which its intellectual property standards can be

---

15 Ibid, Article 5.

16 Ibid, Article 8.

17 Ibid, Article 10.

18 Christopher May, *The World Intellectual Property Organization: resurgence and the development agenda* (2007) 25. It must be noted however, that WIPO's objectives do not include a development agenda – WIPO Convention – Articles 3 and 4.

19 WIPO Convention – Articles 3 and 4.

20 See generally Musungu and Dutfield, above n 8.

21 May, above n 18, 24–25. The revenue earned by administering the PCT provides about 80 per cent of WIPO's total income with expected increases in this figure – GRAIN, *One global patent system? WIPOs Substantive Patent Law Treaty* (2003), see http://www.grain.org/article/entries/109-one-global-patent-system-wipo-s-substantive-patent-law-treaty (last accessed 30 June 2012).

22 David G Scalise and Daniel Nugent, 'International Intellectual Property Protections for Living Matter: Biotechnology, Multinational Conventions and the Exception for Agriculture' (1995) 27 *Case Western Reserve Journal of International Law* 83, 107. See also *U.S. Vows to 'Fight' the Push for WIPO Reform* (2004) Intellectual Property Watch Vol. 1 No. 1, available at http://www.ip-watch.org/2004/11/04/us-vows-to-fight-the-push-for-wipo-reform/ (last accessed 30 June 2012).

enforced and conflicts can be resolved, which could also have worked to the advantage of developed countries.

Some scholars suggest that developing countries also view WIPO as being fundamentally hostile to issues of equity and development[23] and as being biased in favour of developed countries efforts to strengthen IP protection.[24] This perception has not been offset by the Development Agenda which WIPO launched in 2004 and which is designed to ensure that IPRs are used to further development. Suspicion has been further deepened by its simultaneous role in the international patent harmonization process and the negotiations of the Substantive Patent Law Treaty (SPLT)[25] which has raised the ire of some developing countries who view it as being detrimental to their interests.[26] WIPO is therefore placed in a unique position, as notwithstanding its Charter, it is simultaneously pursuing both a patent and a development agenda and it is not clear whether these two objectives are mutually compatible.

WIPO as an institution does not have a specific mandate in regard to either PGRFA or traditional knowledge. However, its mandate to promote intellectual property rights worldwide, and specifically its role in the patent harmonizaton process, would necessarily impact upon the application of such rights to both these resources. As will be shown, it has played a significant part in the debate on these two resources and to some extent it is perceived by developing countries as a more favourable forum in which to safeguard their interests than the World Trade Organization (WTO). It is pertinent therefore to consider its general functions in relation to its patent and development agendas.

---

[23] Ronan Kennedy, 'International Conflicts over Plant Genetic Resources: Future Developments?' (2006) *Tulane Environmental Law Journal* 1, 17. See also Crocker, above n 1.

[24] Sangeeta Shashikant, *Intellectual Property and the WIPO Development Agenda* (date not available), available at http://www.twnside.org.sg/title2/FTAs/Intellectual_Property/IP_and_Development/IPandtheWIPODevelopmentAgenda-SangeetaShashikantWSIS.pdf.

[25] SCP/10/4 – Standing Committee on the Law of Patents Tenth Session, 10–14 May 2004, *Draft Substantive Patent Law Treaty*, 30 September 2003 (hereinafter SLPT).

[26] James Boyle, 'A Manifesto on WIPO and the Future of Intellectual Property' (2004) *Duke Law & Technology Review* 9; Commission on Intellectual Property Rights, *Integrating Intellectual Property Rights and Development Policy* (2002), available at http://www.iprcommission.org/papers/pdfs/final_report/CIPRfullfinal.pdf (last accessed 30 June 2012).

WIPO's Patent Agenda

While WIPO's patent agenda is not directly related to the propertization of genetic resources or traditional knowledge, its development would facilitate this process. The purpose of the agenda which was launched in 2001 was to promote international patent law harmonization both substantively and procedurally.[27] The objective of patent law harmonization is the creation of an international unified patent system to which every country would adhere. This would replace the current territorial system whereby each country sets standards as it deems appropriate in regard to both the subject matter of patents, the degree of protection awarded and the procedures to process patent applications. Therefore, harmonization would impact upon property rights to PGRFA too, as once the system comes into force countries would lose the flexibility to decide which property regime it would apply to these resources.

The WIPO Patent Harmonization Treaties

The WIPO Patent Agenda is implemented by the Standing Committee on the Law of Patents (SCP) whose function is to promote international harmonization of patent law. This process is to be implemented by way of three treaties, namely, the PCT[28] which was last modified in 2001, the Patent Law Treaty (PLT) of 2005[29] and the draft SPLT which is currently suspended.

The first two treaties seek to harmonize the procedural aspects of patent applications. The PCT does so by providing a unified system for filing, searching and examining them. Under its provisions an applicant (who must be a national or resident of a Contracting Party) may seek patent protection simultaneously in each of several countries by filing an international patent

---

27 Carlos M Correa and Sisule F Musungu, *The WIPO Patent Agenda: The Risks for Developing Countries* (2002) South Centre, available at http://www.southcentre.org/index.php?option=com_content&task=view&id=76&Itemid=67 (last accessed 30 June 2012); WIPO Document A/36/14 – *Agenda for Development of the International Patent System – Memorandum of the Director General*, 6 August 2001; WIPO Publication No. 441(E) – *Annual Report 2005* states that 'One of WIPO's principal tasks is to promote and develop international harmonization of IP laws, standards and practices.'

28 *Patent Cooperation Treaty*, Done at Washington on 19 June 1970, amended on 28 September 1979, modified on 3 February 1984, and 3 October 2001 (as in force from 1 April 2002) (hereinafter PCT).

29 *Patent Law Treaty,* Adopted at Geneva on 1 June 2000, available at http://www.wipo.int/treaties/en/ip/plt/ (hereinafter PLT) (last accessed 30 June 2012).

application. It may be filed either in the national patent office of the State of his/her nationality/residency or with the International Bureau of WIPO. The application is then put through an 'international search' by a WIPO appointed International Searching Authority (ISA), which investigates all published documents that might affect the patentability of the subject matter, and which also prepares a written opinion on patentability. On the basis of this investigation the applicant would decide whether to continue with the process or not.[30]

The objectives of the PLT are also to harmonize the procedural aspects of applying for, obtaining, and maintaining patents. Its provisions relate to such issues as filing date, application, representation, communications, notifications, validity of patents and revocation, and relief in respect of time limits, reinstatement of rights, and correction or addition of priority claims and restoration of priority rights.[31] The Treaty thus obviates the necessity for patent applicants to deal with different laws in regard to these issues. This harmonization process would greatly facilitate IPR claims on plant varieties since an applicant could obtain such rights globally with a single application. Countries would no longer have the authority to process such applications according to their legal requirements.

While the PCT and PLT deal with procedural issues, the third pillar on which WIPO's patent agenda rests, the SPLT, deals with substantive issues. While discussions on the SPLT began in 2001 at the Fifth Session of the SCP, they have currently been suspended, reflecting developed/developing country divisions on these issues. The US, Japan and the European Patent Office put forward what was dubbed the Trilateral proposal, pushing to have an initial package of issues prioritized for discussion, namely, definition of prior art, grace period, novelty and inventive step/non obviousness.[32] Questions of prior art and novelty have direct impacts on genetic resources

---

[30] See http://www.wipo.int/pct/en/treaty/about.htm (last accessed 30 June 2012). The vast majority of PCT applications are filed by developed countries, mainly the US, European countries, Japan, Australia and Canada – WIPO Publication *The International Patent System in 2006 – PCT Yearly Review (2006).* See also WIPO Patent Report – *Statistics on Worldwide Patent Activities* (2007) for similar statistics. For a detailed account of the PCT reforms see Correa and Musungu, above n 27.

[31] PLT, Articles 5–13.

[32] WO/GA/31/9 – WIPO General Assembly Thirty-First (15th Extraordinary) Session 27 September – 5 October 2004, *Proposal by the United States of America, Japan and the European Patent Office for Establishing a New Work Plan For The Standing Committee on the Law of Patents (SCP)* 23 July 2004; WO/GA/31/10 – WIPO General Assembly Thirty-First (15th Extraordinary) Session 27 September – 5 October 2004, *Proposal by the United States of America and Japan*

and traditional knowledge and resolving these issues would make it easier to patent them.[33] This proposal met with resistance from developing countries who in turn raised concerns regarding issues such as patentable subject matter, the exceptions to patentability and disclosure of origin of genetic resources, and associated knowledge where the subject matter was based on them.[34] Nevertheless in 2005 it was agreed that the following issues would be prioritized within WIPO: prior art, grace period, novelty, inventive step, sufficiency of disclosure and genetic resources. The first four issues would be addressed by the SCP, and the last two by the Intergovernmental Committee on Intellectual Property and Genetic Resources, Traditional Knowledge and Folklore (IGC).[35] The meeting also agreed that work on issues of development and intellectual property should be pursued so that an

---

for Establishing a New Work Plan for the Standing Committee on the Law of Patents (SCP), 27 August 2004.

33 WO/GA/31/9, above n 32; WO/GA/31/10, above n 32.

34 WO/GA/31/15 – WIPO General Assembly Thirty-First (15th Extraordinary) Session, 27 September – 5 October 2004, *Report adopted by the Assembly,* 5 October 2004; Carlos M Correa, *An Agenda for Patent Reform and Harmonization for Developing Countries* (2005), available at http://www.iprsonline.org/unctadictsd/bellagio/Bellagio2005/CorreaPiece_REV.pdf (last accessed 30 June 2012); South Centre and Centre for International Environmental Law, *Intellectual Property and Development: Overview of Developments in Multilateral, Plurilateral, and Bilateral Fora* (2004) 15, available at http://www.ciel.org/Publications/IP_Update_3Q04.pdf (last accessed 30 June 2012).

35 After the Diplomatic Conference for the Adoption of the Patent Law Treaty in mid 2000 at which consultations on TK and genetic resources also took place, a proposal was submitted to the 2000 WIPO General Assembly to establish an Intergovernmental Committee on Intellectual Property and Genetic Resources, Traditional Knowledge and Folklore (IGC). The IGC would address three primary themes, namely, (i) access to genetic resources and benefit sharing; (ii) protection of traditional knowledge, whether or not associated with those resources; and (iii) the protection of expressions of folklore including handicrafts. This proposal was approved by the General Assembly at its Twenty-Sixth Session in 2000 – WO/GA/26/6 – WIPO General Assembly Twenty-Sixth (12th Extraordinary) Session, 25 September – 3 October 2000, *Matters Concerning Intellectual Property and Genetic Resources, Traditional Knowledge and Folklore,* 25 August 2000; WO/GA/26/9 – WIPO General Assembly Twenty-Sixth (12th Extraordinary) Session, 25 September – 3 October 2000, *Traditional Knowledge and the Need To Give It Adequate Intellectual Property Protection – WIPO Committee on the Relationship between Intellectual Property, Genetic Resources and Traditional Knowledge, Documents prepared by the Group of Countries of Latin America and the Caribbean* 14 September 2000; WO/GA/26/10 – WIPO General Assembly Twenty-Sixth (12th Extraordinary) Session, 25 September – 3 October 2000, *Report adopted by the Assembly*, 3 October 2000.

effective WIPO Development Agenda could emerge.[36] At the 2005 General Assembly, members decided to hold an Open Forum on the SPLT in 2006 and then convene an informal session of the SCP to agree on a work programme[37] after which the SCP would begin work.[38] The 2006 General Assembly subsequently decided to continue with consultations the following year, 2007, with a view to establishing a work plan for 2008/2009.[39] However, no further progress was made on the draft treaty.

The SPLT had provoked opposition from many developing countries on several fronts. A comprehensive analysis of all its provisions is beyond the scope of this book and the present discussion will be confined to its implications vis-à-vis the potential propertization of genetic resources and traditional knowledge.[40] At this point it could be argued that a global patent convention which overrides national intellectual property laws potentially erodes a country's sovereign rights to determine its own intellectual property policy and its development strategies.[41] Its application to resources

---

[36] SCP/11/3 – Standing Committee on the Law of Patents Eleventh Session, 1 and 2 June 2005, *Future Work Program for the Standing Committee on the Law of Patents* (2005).

[37] WO/GA/32/13 – WIPO General Assembly Thirty-Second (17th Ordinary) Session, 26 September – 5 October 2005, *Report adopted by the General Assembly*, 5 October 2005.

[38] SCP/IM/GE/06/2 – Standing Committee on the Law of Patents Informal Session, April 2006 *Future Work Program for the Standing Committee on the Law of Patents*, 7 March 2006.

[39] WO/GA/33/10 – WIPO General Assembly Thirty-Third (16th Extraordinary) Session, 25 September – 3 October 2006, *Report adopted by the Assembly*, 3 October 2006.

[40] For a detailed analysis of the SPLT provisions vis-à-vis developing countries see Carlos M Correa, *The WIPO draft Substantive Patent Law Treaty: a review of selected provisions* (2004) South Centre, available at http://www.southcentre.org/index.php?option=com_content&view=article&id=77%3Athe-wipo-draft-substantive-patent-law-treaty-a-review-of-selected-provisions&catid=41%3Ainnovation-technology-and-patent-policy&lang=en (last accessed 30 June 2012).

[41] Donald P Harris 'TRIPS' Rebound: An Historical Analysis of How the TRIPS Agreement Can Ricochet Back Against the United States' (2004) 25 *Northwestern Journal of International Law & Business* 99. See also Sisule F Musungu, Rethinking innovation, development and intellectual property in the UN: WIPO and beyond (2005) *Quaker International Affairs Programme* 9, available at www.quno.org/geneva/pdf/economic/Issues/TRIPS53.pdf (last accessed 30 June 2012); John Braithwaite and Peter Drahos, *Global Business Regulation* (2000) 75.

such as PGRFA, which are of critical importance to developing countries' agriculture and food security, would be of particular concern.[42]

To date developed countries have not succeeded in pushing the SPLT to a final conclusion and it remains in abeyance.[43] Some writers note that points of disagreement had arisen as developing countries became aware of the implications of patent harmonization.[44] Commentators have also expressed concern at the asymmetry in preparation and participation in the negotiations demonstrated by the latter in contrast to developed countries.[45] It remains to be seen whether developing countries will continue to prevent a process which is essentially disadvantageous to them.

WIPO's Development Agenda

WIPO's development agenda was initiated in 2004 by a group of 14 developing countries known as the Group of Friends of Development (FOD) as an attempt to counter the patent harmonization agenda that was being pushed forward by developed nations. The proposal submitted to the WIPO General Assembly argued that despite the scientific and technological advances of the recent past which are important sources of material progress and welfare, a significant gap exists between rich and poor nations in their ability to access these resources. In this context the role of intellectual property protection which is intended as an instrument to

---

[42] The UK IPR Commission has observed that developing countries have already had a foretaste of the possible outcomes of these negotiations, given their experiences in 1991 when a substantive patent law treaty was almost concluded. It notes that the final treaty 'was essentially a hybrid of the laws prevailing in a number of developed countries, in particular the US and the EU. As the delegate of one developing country noted, there was a paradox that through a harmonisation process, the majority of the countries were being asked to align their law with the provisions of a minority' – Commission on Intellectual Property Rights, above n 26, 132.

[43] WO/GA/33/6 – WIPO General Assembly, Thirty-Third (16th Extraordinary) Session, 25 September – 3 October 2006, *Report on the Progress of the Standing Committee of the Law of Patents in Respect of the Draft Substantive Patent Law Treaty and Consideration of a New Work Plan for 2007*, 30 June 2006.

[44] It must be noted that developing countries are not themselves in agreement on all aspects of the negotiations – Correa and Musungu, above n 27.

[45] Ibid. GRAIN also observes that the discussions on the SPLT are largely between the US and Europe and the developing countries hardly participate, with a few exceptions led by Brazil – GRAIN, *WIPO Moves Toward 'World' Patent System* (2002), available at http://www.grain.org/docs/wipo-patent-2002-en.pdf (last accessed 30 June 2012).

promote technological innovation and to transfer and disseminate technology has been widely debated. The proposal observes that '[i]ntellectual property protection cannot be seen as an end in itself, nor can the harmonization of intellectual property laws leading to higher protection standards in all countries, irrespective of their levels of development.'[46] Intellectual property protection has both costs and benefits which may vary according to a country's level of development and it must be ensured that the costs do not outweigh the benefits.

The proposal also raised specific concerns about the draft SPLT.[47] It pointed out that the proposed treaty would raise patent protection standards, creating new obligations which developing countries will be unable to implement. It noted that these countries had suggested amendments to make the draft more responsive to public interest concerns and their specific development needs, and urged that these be taken into account.

Finally the proposal set out eight specific measures by which its concerns could be addressed. These included the adoption of a high level declaration on intellectual property and development which should address the development concerns raised by a number of WIPO member states and the international community at large, and amendments to the WIPO Convention to explicitly incorporate the development dimension into WIPO's objectives and functions.[48] It also proposed the establishment of a Working Group on the Development Agenda to further discuss its implementation.[49]

---

[46] WO/GA/31/11 – WIPO General Assembly Thirty-First (15th Extraordinary) Session, 27 September – 5 October 2004, *Proposal by Argentina and Brazil for the Establishment of a Development Agenda for WIPO,* 27 August 2004, 1. See also PCDA/1/5 – Provisional Committee on Proposals Related to a WIPO Development Agenda, First Session, 20–24 February 2006, *Proposal for the Establishment of a Development Agenda for WIPO: A Framework for Achieving Concrete and Practical Results in the Near and Longer Terms,* 17 February 2006.

[47] Progress on the Development Agenda appears to be tied up with the negotiation of the SPLT. As noted earlier, the initial proposal of Brazil and Argentina expressed concern about the negotiations of this Treaty. At the 2005 General Assembly the FOD led by Brazil made further discussions on the SPLT conditional on progress on the Development Agenda – ICTSD, *WIPO Development Agenda Status Unclear* (2005) BRIDGES No. 9 (September – October 2005), available at www.iprsonline.org/ictsd/docs/BridgesMonthly9–9WIPODevAgenda.pdf (last accessed 30 June 2012).

[48] Note the concerns raised by the UK IPR Commission regarding the absence of such a provision in the WIPO Convention – Commission on Intellectual Property Rights, above n 26, Chapter 8.

[49] For a commentary of the proposal see South Centre, Analytical Note SC/TADP/AN/IP/3 – *Establishing a 'Development Agenda' for the World Intellectual Property Organization (WIPO): Commentary on Proposal by Argentina and*

The proposal received mixed responses and some cautious support from developed countries,[50] in contrast to the enthusiastic response from a number of civil society organizations.[51] However, the General Assembly agreed to convene inter-sessional intergovernmental meetings to examine it,[52] and subsequently established a Provisional Committee on Proposals related to a WIPO Development Agenda (PCDA) to carry forward the process.[53]

The PCDA process was carried forward into 2007. At the Fourth Session held in June 2007 the PCDA agreed that the General Assembly in September 2007 be requested to adopt the recommendations for action in the agreed proposals contained in Annex I of its report.[54] It also recommended that a Committee on Development and Intellectual Property (CDIP) be

---

Brazil (2004), available at http://www.wipo.int/patent-law/en/developments/economic.html (last accessed 30 June 2012).

[50] WO/GA/31/15, above n 34. See also *U.S. Vows to 'Fight' the Push for WIPO Reform*, above n 22; Sisule F Musungu, *The WIPO Assemblies 2004: A Review of the Outcomes* (2004) South Bulletin (15 October 2004) 89.

[51] Prior to the General Assembly, a consortium of non-profit organizations, scientists, academics and others had signed the 'Geneva Declaration on the Future of WIPO' available at http://www.cptech.org/ip/wipo/futureofwipodeclaration.pdf (last accessed 30 June 2012). This Declaration, inter alia, urged WIPO to work within the 1974 UN/WIPO agreement 'and take a more balanced and realistic view of the social benefits and costs of intellectual property rights as a tool, but not the only tool, for supporting creative intellectual activity.' It also declared that '[t]here must be a moratorium on new treaties and harmonization of standards that expand and strengthen monopolies and further restrict access to knowledge.'

[52] WO/GA/31/15, above n 34. In addition to these meetings several more were held with UN and international organizations as well as in other fora, revealing that 'the discussions on the establishment of a WIPO development agenda are no longer a simple WIPO issue but a global discussion' – PCDA/1/5, above n 46. For an account of the discussions which took place in the meetings see Shashikant, above n 24.

[53] It has been noted that the establishment of this Committee was a compromise since delegates to the General Assembly differed as to whether discussions should continue at high level meetings reporting to the General Assembly or should be confined to the Permanent Committee on Co-operation for Development Related to Intellectual Property (PCIPD), a relatively unimportant forum concerned with technical assistance – ICTSD, above n 47, 22.

[54] These proposal were contained in four clusters – Technical Assistance and Capacity Building; Norm-Setting, Flexibilities, Public Policy and Public Domain; Technology Transfer, Information and Communication; Technologies (ICT) and Access to Knowledge; Assessment, Evaluation and Impact Studies; Institutional Matters Including Mandate and Governance; and Other Issues – PCDA/4/3 – Provisional Committee on Proposals Related to a WIPO Development Agenda

immediately established to develop a work programme for implementing the adopted recommendations. The Committee would be composed of Member States of WIPO and would be open to all accredited intergovernmental and non-governmental organizations. The Committee will report and make recommendations annually to the General Assembly.[55] The Permanent Committee on Co-operation on Development Related to Intellectual Property (PCIPD) will cease to exist and the mandate of the PCDA will also not be renewed.[56] The work of the Committee is ongoing, including discussions on the misappropriation of genetic resources and traditional knowledge.

THE AGREEMENT ON TRADE RELATED ASPECTS OF INTELLECTUAL PROPERTY RIGHTS (THE TRIPS AGREEMENT)

Introduction

While UPOV is specifically concerned with plant variety protection, and WIPO's mandate is that of promoting intellectual property protection, much of the debate on patenting plant varieties has taken place in the Council for Trade Related Aspects of Intellectual Property Rights (the TRIPS Council) of the World Trade Organization. This is in large measure due to the structure and content of the TRIPS Agreement which contains, *inter alia*, provisions linking intellectual property rights to trade, sets minimum standards of such rights, and most importantly, contains effective measures to enforce its provisions. A discussion of the historical antecedents of TRIPS, the negotiations of its provisions and its scope and content will place in context the current debates which are taking place within it.

(PCDA), Fourth Session, 11–15 June 2007, *Report Adopted by the Meeting*, 4 September 2007, Annex 1.

[55] The First Session of the CDIP took place 3–7 March 2008, see http://www.wipo.int/meetings/en/details.jsp?meeting_id=15082 (last accessed 30 June 2012). This session, as approved by the WIPO General Assembly (September–October 2007), is to develop a work-programme for implementation of the adopted recommendations; monitor, assess, discuss and report on the implementation of all recommendations adopted; and to discuss intellectual property and development related issues as agreed by the Committee, as well as those decided by the General Assembly – WO/INF/10/78 Rev – *List of Selected WIPO Meetings from February to December 2008*, February 2008.

[56] PCDA/4/3, above n 54, 30.

History of the TRIPS Agreement

The origins of the TRIPS Agreement date back to the General Agreement on Tariffs and Trade (GATT). The GATT has been described as an offshoot of a wider project – the International Trade Organization (ITO). The latter was the institution to administer the Havana Charter for an International Trade Organization being negotiated at the time. The GATT provisionally entered into force on 1 January 1948 pending the conclusion and entry into force of the Havana Charter. It has been described as 'a legal instrument aimed at relaxing government-mandated trade protection.' Since the Havana Charter was never concluded, the GATT was applied for 47 years on a provisional basis.[57]

The Agreement establishing the World Trade Organization (WTO)[58] came into effect on 1 January 1995 emerging out of the Uruguay Round of Multilateral Trade Negotiations and became the successor to the GATT. The Agreement on Trade Related Aspects of Intellectual Property Rights (TRIPS) formed the Annex to the WTO Agreement.[59] The history of the TRIPS process originated with, inter alia, the concerns of multinational corporations (MNC) based in developed countries in regard to the counterfeiting and misappropriation of goods manufactured by them.[60] The purpose of this coalition was to encourage national governments to take action to prevent the trade in counterfeit goods. From about this time corporate interests including book publishers, agricultural chemical producers and others had also started taking action to combat the piracy of their products.[61]

---

[57] Petros C Mavroidis, *The General Agreement on Tariffs and Trade: A Commentary* (2005), Chapter 1.

[58] Uruguay Round Agreement, *Marrakesh Agreement Establishing the World Trade Organization*, 1867 UNTS 154; 33 ILM 1125 (1994); available at http://www.wto.org/english/docs_e/legal_e/04-wto_e.htm (last accessed 30 June 2012).

[59] *Agreement on Trade-Related Aspects of Intellectual Property Rights*, Annex 1C of the Marrakesh Agreement Establishing the World Trade Organization, signed in Marrakesh, Morocco on 15 April 1994, 1869 UNTS 299; 33 ILM 81 (1994) (hereinafter TRIPS Agreement).

[60] May, above n 18; Duncan Matthews, *Globalizing intellectual property rights: the TRIPs agreement* (2002). For a discussion of the role of US industries in the TRIPS negotiations see Susan K Sell, 'Industry Strategies for Intellectual Property and Trade: The Quest for TRIPS and Post-TRIPS Strategies' (2002) 10 *Cardozo Journal of International and Comparative Law* 79.

[61] Matthews notes that in lobbying on the issue US business interests used language that was 'emotive, portraying the "theft" being undertaken by developing countries and those copying U.S. products as "pirates." By using the language of incursion and theft, U.S. companies effectively changed the policy debate' –

As a result of effective lobbying, the 1980s saw the US government responding to the problem through a variety of ad hoc strategies, including bilateral negotiations, to persuade countries to protect the intellectual property of MNCs based within them. Within a short space of time both corporate interests and governments in the US, Europe, Canada and Japan had united to take up the question in global fora.

The issue was placed on the agenda at the Tokyo Round of the GATT negotiations which took place between 1973 and 1979, but proposals regarding measures to address it failed to gain support from other countries. Consensus was again absent at the Ministerial Meeting of GATT in 1982 where it met with opposition from developing countries.[62] Nevertheless it was agreed that further work on the matter of counterfeit goods should go ahead. In addition, despite the opposition of some developing countries, intellectual property rights (IPRs) were included in the list of subjects for negotiation in the Ministerial Declaration of 1986.[63] This Declaration which launched the Uruguay Round of trade negotiations included Trade Related Aspects of Intellectual Property Rights.

Negotiation of the TRIPS Agreement

The negotiations of the TRIPS Agreement were marked by several factors including the prominent role played by developed country corporate interests,[64] the alleged arm twisting tactics used by the US to overcome continuing developing country opposition to the negotiations[65] and the lack

---

Matthews, above n 60, 14. The same language is now used by developing countries to define the misappropriation and acquisition of their genetic resources by these same business interests.

[62] Ibid, Chapter 1.

[63] Developing countries were not unanimous in their opposition to the inclusion of IPRs in the GATT Ministerial meeting and the newly industrialized countries of South East Asia did acknowledge the need to provide more effective protection – Ibid, Chapter 1.

[64] For a discussion on corporate influence in international trade negotiations see ActionAid International, *Under the influence – Exposing Undue Corporate Influence over Policy-Making at the World Trade Organisation* (2006), available at http://www.actionaid.org.uk/doc_lib/174_6_under_the_influence_final.pdf (last accessed 30 June 2012).

[65] For a discussion of this aspect see Matthews, above n 60, Chapter 2. See also ActionAid International, *Divide and Rule – The EU and U.S. response to developing country alliances at the WTO* (2004), available at www.actionaid.org.uk/doc_lib/30_1_divide_rule.pdf (last accessed 30 June 2012).

of transparency in the negotiating process.[66] In general, developing countries were opposed to an all encompassing agreement, i.e. one that incorporated both the trade in counterfeit and pirated goods as well as the 'availability, use and scope' of intellectual property rights.[67] They also reiterated their position that WIPO was a more appropriate forum to address the latter issue rather than GATT.

The developing country concerns which were expressed throughout the negotiations centred generally on the impacts that the Agreement would have on their economies and development processes. More specifically they pointed to the likelihood that it could impede the transfer of technology and also increase the costs of agricultural and pharmaceutical products. They also took issue with the inclusion of trade secrets and pushed for compulsory licensing of patents[68] and exceptions to patentability on grounds of public interest, health and nutrition.[69]

Ultimately the impetus to reach a final conclusion came not from the negotiating process but rather from the threats of bilateral sanctions brought by the United States under Section 301 of the US Omnibus Trade and Tariff Act of 1988.[70] Action under Section 301 was taken against India, China and

---

[66] Peter Drahos, *Developing Countries and International Intellectual Property Standard Setting* (2002) Commission on Intellectual Property Rights Study Paper 8, available at http://www.iprcommission.org/papers/pdfs/study_papers/sp8_drahos_study.pdf (last accessed 30 June 2012).

[67] Daniel Gervais, *The TRIPS Agreement – Drafting History and Analysis* (2nd ed 2003) 18.

[68] Compulsory licensing is provided for under Article 31 of TRIPS which permits the subject matter of a patent to be used without the authorization of the patent holder under specified circumstances, including national emergency or other situations of urgency. The patent holder must be adequately compensated for such use.

[69] Gervais, above n 67, Part 1.

[70] Matthews, above n 60, 31. Matthews explains that initially the US had responded to complaints by businesses on an ad hoc and informal basis with its embassies abroad assisting in sorting out the problems. However, consequent to the failure to reform the WIPO conventions it adopted a bilateral approach to the issue and enacted new legislation to deal with it, specifically the Trade Act of 1984. Section 301 of this Act operated in three ways. Firstly, it permitted the US Trade Representative to investigate the appropriateness of another country's intellectual property regime without waiting for a complaint from US businesses. Secondly, it made the failure to protect intellectual property rights actionable with trade sanctions. Thirdly, it made intellectual property protection a criterion for eliminating tariff privileges for imports into the US of goods from developing countries under the Generalised System of Preferences (GSP).

Thailand in 1991 and later against South Korea and Brazil, effectively compelling them to change their stand on the negotiations. Matthew comments that:

> [b]y threatening trade sanctions against recalcitrant countries one by one, the United States could effectively be seen to have weakened opposition to a TRIPS Agreement while ensuring that negotiations could at least take place within the Uruguay Round and increasing the prospects of an acceptable TRIPS Agreement.[71]

After these countries, which were relatively more powerful among the developing nations capitulated, little resistance could be expected from others. Having effectively fragmented the opposition it was left to the US, Europe and Japan to determine the final text of the Agreement.[72]

However, Dutfield comments that coercion of the South by the North does not completely explain the complexities of the TRIPS negotiations. He points out that 'the developing world is extremely heterogeneous in terms of countries' levels of industrialization and social and political development.' While some least developed countries totally lacked a manufacturing sector and were extremely indebted and poor, Latin American countries were relatively industrialized but were heavily indebted too. Some Asian countries 'had extremely dynamic export-oriented industrial economies with firms beginning to develop their own IPR-protectable products and technologies.' Therefore the IPR related interests of these countries varied as did the interests of the different industrial sectors within them.[73]

The Nature, Scope and Content of the TRIPS Agreement

In relation to its content and scope, it is generally agreed that the TRIPS Agreement is the most comprehensive and far-reaching international legal regime on intellectual property rights. It crosses the traditional line that

---

[71] Ibid at 32.

[72] The fact that India, which was a particularly vociferous opponent of the negotiations, also surrendered its position is significant. Matthews notes that in 1992 the US suspended GSP tariff exceptions for Indian pharmaceutical products, imposing a cost on Indian exports of an estimated $60 million – Ibid, Chapter 2.

[73] Graham Dutfield, *Trade, Intellectual Property and Biogenetic Resources: A Guide to the International Regulatory Landscape* (2002) International Centre for Trade and Sustainable Development (ICTSD) and Centre for Policy Dialogue, Bangladesh, 11, available at http://www.cid.harvard.edu/cidtrade/issues/biotechnologypaper.html (last accessed 30 June 2012).

separates the two main categories of IPRs, i.e. copyright and industrial property.[74] It also establishes universal minimum standards of patent protection across these areas. Further, unlike previous international treaties it contains detailed provisions on enforcement.[75]

The Agreement consists of four main elements.[76] First, it provides a set of substantive standards regarding the availability, scope and use of IPRs in relation to the various areas covered by it. Second, its enforcement provisions permit action against acts of infringement, including remedies to prevent them and those that deter further infringements. Third, it provides a dispute settlement mechanism to resolve disputes involving intellectual property matters. The fourth element has been described as the 'general provisions for the agreement, which identify some basic rules and the general principles that preside over TRIPS obligations, as well as the norms on transitional arrangements.'[77]

It has been noted that '[t]he real novelty of the Uruguay Round Declaration on trade-related aspects of IPRs resided in its GATT-based approach.'[78] This link between IPRs and trade has been expressed in the Preamble to the Agreement which expresses its objective as:

> to reduce distortions and impediments to international trade, and taking into account the need to promote effective and adequate protection of intellectual property rights, and to ensure that measures and procedures to enforce intellectual property rights do not themselves become barriers to legitimate trade.[79]

The Preamble does not however, throw light on the question as to why the subject of intellectual property rights was brought within the ambit of multilateral trade negotiations rather than that of specialized organizations

---

[74] The latter encompasses trademarks, geographical indications, industrial designs, patents, layout designs of integrated circuits and undisclosed information – South Centre, *The TRIPS Agreement: A Guide for the South. The Uruguay Round Agreement on Trade-Related Intellectual Property Rights* (1997) 17, available at http://www.southcentre.org/index.php?option=com_content&task=view&id=87&Itemid=67 (last accessed 30 June 2012).

[75] Nuno Pires de Carvalho, *The TRIPS Regime of Patent Rights* (2005) 28.

[76] Ibid at 30.

[77] Ibid.

[78] Abdulqawi A Yusuf, 'TRIPS: Background, Principles and General Provisions' in Carlos M Correa and Abdulqawi A Yusuf (eds), *Intellectual property and international trade: the TRIPS Agreement* (2nd edn 2008) Chapter 1.

[79] TRIPS Agreement, Preamble.

dealing exclusively with this subject such as WIPO. The answer may have more to do with strategy than substance.

First, opening up markets for developing country exports was made conditional upon them accepting the provisions of TRIPS. Developing countries also agreed to liberalize trade by reducing or eliminating tariff and non-tariff trade barriers. This enabled developed countries to increase exports of products based upon technology protected by intellectual property rules, thus eliminating competition from domestic products in the importing country. Perhaps most importantly, merging issues of trade and intellectual property in an agreement which also includes effective enforcement mechanisms enables non-compliance in one area to be penalized with retaliatory measures in the other. Therefore countries breaching TRIPS patent provisions could be subject to retaliation in trade.[80] Thus unlike WIPO, compliance could be ensured.

The relevant provisions of the TRIPS Agreement for the purposes of this book are those concerning patents insofar as they impact on PGRFA and related traditional knowledge. The remainder of the discussion in this book will be confined to this issue.

BILATERAL TREATIES AND 'TRIPS-PLUS' MEASURES

While intellectual property (IP) standards and related issues are being discussed in a range of multilateral fora, negotiations are simultaneously taking place at the bilateral and regional level. These negotiations are often, though not invariably, between developed and developing countries, the former being usually the US and the EU. Bilateralism is being mainly driven by the US, although the EU[81] and the European Free Trade

---

[80] South Centre, above n 74, 6.

[81] Maximiliano Santa Cruz, Intellectual Property Provisions in European Union Trade Agreements: Implications for Developing Countries (2007), available at http://www.iprsonline.org/resources/docs/Santa-Cruz%20Blue20.pdf; GRAIN, *'TRIPS-Plus' Must Stop – The European Union caught in blatant contradictions* (2003), available at http://www.grain.org/briefings_files/trips-plus-eu-2003-en.pdf (both last accessed 30 June 2012).

Association (EFTA)[82] and to a somewhat lesser extent Japan, have played a significant role.[83]

Bilateral treaties have been described as 'direct, individual agreements between two or more countries on a range of topics such as trade, investment, scientific research, development cooperation/aid or intellectual property.'[84] These treaties can take the form of free trade agreements, bilateral investment treaties, development co-operation, aid and partnership or association agreements, bilateral science and technology (or research co-operation) agreements and bilateral IPR agreements.[85] For the sake of clarity the term 'bilateral treaty' will be used in this discussion to include the range of such bilateral, regional or sub-regional agreements.

Bilateral treaties can sometimes involve two blocs of countries, as in the case of the special partnership agreement between the EU and African, Caribbean and Pacific (ACP) countries, which are comprised of 15 and 78 nations respectively.[86] The US has also entered into agreements with blocs of countries.[87] Notwithstanding the number of parties actually involved in the agreements, and the structure of the treaties, their ultimate objective is to negotiate terms and conditions which are applicable only to them and which are outside the multilateral trading system.

---

[82] The EFTA is composed of four European States which are not members of the EU – Switzerland, Norway, Iceland and Liechtenstein. See also Berne Declaration, Switzerland – *'TRIPS – Plus' through EFTA's back door – How Free Trade Agreements concluded with EFTA-States impose much stronger rules on developing countries for IPRs on life than the WTO*, available at www.evb.ch/cm_data/Trips-plus_through_EFTAs_back_door_rev2.pdf (last accessed 30 June 2012).

[83] Drahos, above n 66, 43. GRAIN has noted that Japan is also increasingly turning to bilateral agreements to boost its corporations' market interests and to protect its food and energy security interests – GRAIN, *Japan digs its claws into biodiversity through FTAs* (2007), available at http://www.grain.org/article/entries/172-japan-digs-its-claws-into-biodiversity-through-ftas (last accessed 30 June 2012).

[84] GRAIN, *'TRIPS-plus' through the back door – How bilateral treaties impose much stronger rules for IPRs on life than the WTO* (2001), available at http://grain.org/briefings_files/trips-plus-en.pdf (last accessed 30 June 2012).

[85] Ibid.

[86] Ibid.

[87] For example the Andean Trade Preferences Act, 1991 and the Caribbean Basin Trade Partnership Act, 2000 – GRAIN, *Bilateral agreements imposing TRIPS-plus intellectual property rights on biodiversity in developing countries* (2008), available at www.grain.org/.../3645-bilateral-agreements-imposing-trips-plus-intellectual-property-rights-on-biodiversity-in-developing-countries.pdf (last accessed 30 June 2012).

Bilateral negotiations between developed and developing countries are intrinsically more disadvantageous to the latter than negotiations in multilateral fora where their numerical advantage and the mutual support among them operate as counterbalances to the power of developed countries. Bilateral negotiations are also often marked by a lack of transparency, even secrecy, where neither the legislature nor the public of the countries concerned are aware of the terms of the negotiations until the agreement has been signed, thus preventing any form of democratic control over them.[88]

'TRIPS-plus' Provisions in Bilateral Treaties

The most controversial feature of bilateral treaties is the provision which has been termed 'TRIPS-plus.' This term refers to provisions in these treaties which impose more stringent standards of intellectual property protection than that contained in the TRIPS Agreement. These TRIPS-plus standards are usually imposed by the developed country partners to the agreement in return for the trade concessions needed by the other partner/s, usually developing countries.[89]

TRIPS imposes only minimum standards of IP protection, reserving the freedom of member countries to impose higher levels so long as they respect the principles of national treatment[90] and most favoured nation treatment.[91] Therefore it does not totally serve developed country objectives in regard to raising the levels of such protection. TRIPS-plus provisions in bilateral treaties may include those that require a signatory State to implement a higher standard of IP protection than that required under TRIPS, and

---

88 Berne Declaration, above n 82, 6.

89 Pedro Roffe, *Intellectual Property, Bilateral Agreements and Sustainable Development: The Challenges of Implementation* (2007) Center for International Environmental Law, available at http://www.ciel.org/Publications/FTA_ImplementationPub_Jan07.pdf. However, such treaties entered into by and between southern countries are also increasing – GRAIN, *Sharing FTA experiences* (2006), available at http://www.grain.org/seedling_files/seed-06-10-4.pdf (both last accessed 30 June 2012).

90 Under Article 3 of the TRIPS Agreement a Member 'shall accord to the nationals of other Members treatment no less favourable than that it accords to its own nationals with regard to the protection of intellectual property.' This is subject to certain specified exceptions.

91 Article 4 of the TRIPS Agreement states that '[w]ith regard to the protection of intellectual property, any advantage, favour, privilege or immunity granted by a Member to the nationals of any other country shall be accorded immediately and unconditionally to the nationals of all other Members.' This is also subject to certain specified exceptions.

provisions that eliminate the flexibilities under TRIPS.[92] Some agreements also compel developing countries to begin implementation of their TRIPS obligations before the expiration of transition periods and to accede to other multilateral intellectual property agreements.[93] While these TRIPS-plus measures cover all aspects of intellectual property, they will also necessarily impact on the propertization of PGRFA.

The Development of TRIPS-plus Bilateralism

While the use of bilateral measures to impose higher standards of intellectual property protection has seen an upsurge in the past decade, it is not a new phenomenon. Rather, it forms part of a periodic cycle of multilateralism and bilateralism initiated by developed countries to attain the 'upward harmonization' of IP standards.[94] Bilateral IP agreements of the 1980s were, in fact, a precursor to TRIPS and as noted earlier, the US used the threat of bilateral trade sanctions to coerce countries into adopting higher intellectual property standards. It has been observed that '[t]he most fundamental U.S. strategy has been to act tough on bilateral negotiations to set frameworks for subsequent multilateral negotiation.'[95]

Developing countries agreed to TRIPS on the expectation that if they did so the US would desist from negotiating IP standards bilaterally.[96] Notwithstanding this expectation, since TRIPS was signed there has in fact been an

---

92 Peter Drahos, *Bilateralism in Intellectual Property* (2001), available at http://www.bilaterals.org/IMG/pdf/Drahos_study_2001.pdf (last accessed 30 June 2012).

93 Laurence R Helfer, 'Regime Shifting: The TRIPS Agreement and New Dynamics of International Intellectual Property Lawmaking' (2004) 29 *Yale Journal of International Law* 1, 24; Beatrice Lindstrom, 'Scaling back TRIPS-plus: An Analysis of Intellectual Property Provisions in Trade Agreements and Implications For Asia and the Pacific' (2010) 42 *International Law and Politics* 217.

94 Ruth Mayne *Regionalism, bilateralism, and TRIPS plus-provisions on public health: the threat to developing countries* (2005) Human Development Report Office Occasional Paper, available at http://hdr.undp.org/docs/publications/background_papers/2005/HDR2005_Mayne_Ruth_18.pdf (last accessed 30 June 2012).

95 Braithwaite and Drahos, above n 41, 198. See also Drahos, above n 66, 14.

96 David Vivas-Eugui, *Regional and bilateral agreements and a TRIPS-plus world: the Free Trade Area of the Americas (FTAA)* Quaker United Nations Office, Quaker International Affairs Programme and International Centre for Trade and Sustainable Development (2003), available at homepages.3-c.coop/tansey/pdfs/ftaa-a4.pdf (last accessed 30 June 2012).

increase in bilateral IP negotiations.[97] This increase particularly took off after the failed Seattle Ministerial Meeting in 1999.[98]

The reversion to a bilateral strategy can therefore be largely attributed to the failure of developed countries to advance their objectives of higher levels of intellectual property protection in multilateral fora such as WIPO and the TRIPS Council.[99] Developed countries led by the US forum shifted from WIPO to the WTO when they believed that the former was dominated by developing country interests. Having launched TRIPS, they faced similar opposition in the WTO when developing countries formed themselves into coalitions in both fora which successfully stalled moves to further enhance international intellectual property standards.[100]

Negotiation of bilateral treaties is a strategy by which to fragment these alliances and enter into agreements with individual members of the coalitions which undermine their common position. They may also bypass the constraints contained in the TRIPS Agreement. Bilateral treaties negotiated with a single country or a bloc of countries, constitute a new form of international intellectual property standard setting. Moving away from the multilateral into the bilateral sphere, has in fact enabled countries such as the US and those of the EU to impose on developing countries far higher standards of intellectual property protection than they would have achieved within TRIPS.[101]

The success of this strategy can be seen for example in the case of Peru which has consistently taken a strong position in the WTO Council on issues of genetic resources and traditional knowledge, but which nevertheless signed a Free Trade Agreement with the US with potential negative consequences on it in regard to these resources.[102] The negotiation of the

---

[97] Drahos, above n 66.

[98] Bryan Mercurio, *TRIPS-Plus Provisions in FTAs: Recent Trends (*date not available), available at http://papers.ssrn.com/sol3/papers.cfm?abstract_id=947767 (last accessed 30 June 2012).

[99] GRAIN, above n 89; Mayne, above n 94.

[100] Mayne, above n 94, 1.

[101] GRAIN, above n 89. See also UNCTAD/TDR/2007 – United Nations Conference on Trade and Development, *Trade and Development Report 2007,* for an analysis of the impacts of bilateral agreements on developing countries.

[102] BRIDGES, *IP Standards in the US-Peru FTA: Health and Environment* (2006) BRIDGES No. 1, January – February 2006, 17, available at www.iprsonline.org/resources/…/Pages%20from%20BRIDGES10–1%202.pdf; Susan K Sell, *Books, Drugs and Seeds: the Politics of Access* (2006) 45, available at http://www.iprsonline.org/resources/docs/Pages%20from%20BRIDGES10–1%202.pdf (both last accessed 30 June 2012).

agreement was conducted behind closed doors without the involvement of civil society or the Environment Ministry, though there was industry involvement. The IPR provisions in the Agreement allow genetic resources and traditional knowledge to be patented, and further does not require patent applicants to disclose the origin of the plants or obtain authorization before using traditional knowledge.[103] Developing country groups such as the G20[104] have also been targeted, with some Latin American countries leaving the coalition after the Cancun Ministerial when the US declared that it would not approve Free Trade Agreements with members.[105] On the other hand some countries such as Argentina and Brazil have resisted these attempts,[106] while in Ecuador FTA negotiations have stopped as a result of social mobilization, and in South Korea they have been delayed for the same reason.[107]

The question therefore is why developing countries are entering into these agreements. The primary reason cited for this is that they require access to markets in developed countries and they are often not fully aware of what they are signing away.[108] The US for example has made enhanced intellectual property standards a condition for developing countries to qualify for US trade preferences under the Caribbean Basin Initiative[109] and

---

[103] IT/GB-4/11/Inf. 6 – International Treaty on Plant Genetic Resources for Food and Agriculture, Fourth Session of the Governing Body, 14–18 March 2011, *Compilation of Views and Experiences on the Implementation of Farmers' Rights Submitted by Contracting Parties and Relevant Organizations, Note by the Secretary*, December 2010, 14.

[104] The G20 is a coalition of developing countries which was established on 20 August 2003 during the preparations to the Cancun Ministerial Conference of that year. Its central focus is on agriculture. It has 23 member countries from Africa, Asia and Latin America. See http://www.papda.org/article.php3?id_article=17 (last accessed 30 June 2012).

[105] Mayne, above n 94.

[106] Ibid at 5.

[107] GRAIN, above n 89, 16. See also Susan Sell, 'TRIPS was Never Enough: Vertical Forum Shifting, FTAs, ACTA, and TPP' (2011) 18 *Journal of Intellectual Property Law* 447.

[108] Drahos, above n 66, 29; Mayne, above n 94, 5.

[109] The Caribbean Basin Trade Partnership Act of 2000 is part of the Caribbean Basin Initiative launched in 1983. It entered into force on 1 October 2000 and continues until 30 September 2008 or an earlier date on which a free trade agreement enters into force between the US and a beneficiary country. Currently 19 countries of the region are partners in this initiative. See http://www.ustr.gov/Trade_Development/Preference_Programs/CBI/Section_Index.html (last accessed 30 June 2012).

Andean Trade Preferences Act.[110] Under the required standards these countries must provide levels of IPR protection as defined by the US.[111] Critics have pointed out that developing countries are paying for very limited access to these markets by signing away the flexibility they had under TRIPS.[112]

Bilateralism also has implications for multilateralism in international standard setting on intellectual property. The interaction of multilateralism and bilateralism in a way that is most advantageous to developed nations is evident in the operation of the Most Favoured Nation Treatment clause of the TRIPS Agreement found in Article 4. Under this provision any terms negotiated regionally or bilaterally must be made available to other WTO members on the same basis.[113] Therefore, for example, a developing country which agrees to higher levels of intellectual property protection in a bilateral agreement entered into with the US would be required to grant that same level of protection to all other member states of the TRIPS Agreement. This potentially makes further negotiations in the TRIPS Council irrelevant.

Therefore apart from fragmenting developing country alliances in fora such as the WTO and WIPO, TRIPS-plus provisions potentially undermine the multilateral system which carries at least a façade of agreement with consensus.[114] The combined effect of negotiations in both spheres also opens up the possibility that it would replace multilateral intellectual property standard setting which would become redundant.

It should be noted that there have been some examples of resistance to bilateralism, notably in the suspension of the negotiations of the Free Trade Area of the Americas. Similarly in 2005 Ecuador and Colombia refused to agree to TRIPS-plus measures in negotiations with the US, although Colombia subsequently gave in.[115] Much of the resistance is emanating from civil society groups and the public.[116] At the same time developing

---

[110] The Andean Trade Preference Act was enacted in 1991 to combat drug production and trafficking in the Andean countries: Bolivia, Colombia, Ecuador and Peru. It was expanded under the Trade Act of 2002, and is now called the Andean Trade Promotion and Drug Eradication Act. See http://www.ustr.gov/trade-topics/trade-development/preference-programs/andean-trade-preference-act-atpa (last accessed 30 June 2012).

[111] Mayne, above n 94, 6.

[112] Berne Declaration, above n 82.

[113] Commission on Intellectual Property Rights, above n 26, 162.

[114] Mayne, above n 94, 7.

[115] Sell, above n 102, 57.

[116] GRAIN, above n 89.

countries are uniting to push for reforms in the TRIPS Council.[117] It remains to be seen how successful this resistance will be.

CONCLUSION

The discussion above examined the operation of the international IPR and trade regime as it potentially applies to the patenting of plant varieties. The primary purpose of the regime is the development of higher intellectual property standards, the facilitation of processes for approving patent applications and the international upward harmonization of the rules relating to both. While this process does not relate to PGRFA alone, it will necessarily impact upon these resources, and much of the concerns raised by developing countries in this regard have been in relation to them. The substantive issues on plant variety protection are for the most part dealt with by TRIPS, which provides for minimum IPR standards, while leaving to countries a certain degree of flexibility to formulate their laws within this framework. UPOV deals specifically with plant breeders' rights over plant varieties and, as will be analyzed later in this book, its provisions have been linked to those of TRIPS in an attempt to enhance patent protection of PGRFA. The procedural aspects of intellectual property protection have been addressed in the WIPO by way of its patent agenda.

The debate on patenting of plant varieties has, for the most part, taken place in the TRIPS Council and in WIPO fora. WIPO can be considered as a somewhat more neutral forum than the former for developing countries to raise their concerns, since, being a UN organization, its mandate includes accelerating economic, social and cultural development in these countries. However, its patent harmonization agenda has been a cause for concern among them. To date, developing countries have resisted this process with some degree of success, and in turn have brought in their own proposals as counter measures. These include the development agenda in the WIPO and demands that requirements of IPRs be reviewed in order to prevent unjustified patent protection being granted over plant varieties and related traditional knowledge. Developing countries have also raised the same

---

[117] Third World Network, *TRIPS: Majority of WTO members now support disclosure proposal* 14 March 2008, available at http://www.twnside.org.sg/title2/wto.info/twninfo20080318.htm; Intellectual Property Watch, *TRIPS Council: Half of WTO Membership Backs Biodiversity Amendment* (14 March 2008), available at http://www.ip-watch.org/2008/03/14/trips-council-half-of-wto-membership-backs-biodiversity-amendment/ (both last accessed 30 June 2012).

issues in other fora including the CBD, and negotiations are continuing in these as well.

Developed countries in turn are now offsetting their failure to push their agenda through in multilateral fora by once again resorting to a bilateral strategy. This serves to effectively undermine the united front presented by developing countries in the WTO and WIPO, and further, by bypassing TRIPS, to strengthen intellectual property protection measures on a country by country basis. While they have been successful in this strategy to a large extent, they have encountered some resistance in this sphere.

As will be seen in the further discussions, the international IPR regime, consisting of these three institutions, has succeeded in instituting a system of intellectual property rights applicable to PGRFA, which enables the appropriation of crop plants and their removal from the public domain. While this process serves the interests of commercial plant breeders and agribusiness, it is inimical to the interests of farmers, indigenous and local communities, and national agricultural systems and food security, particularly in developing countries. The continuing debate on the issue reflects the attempts of developing countries to negotiate measures to counteract the negative impacts of this regime. The next chapter will analyze the provisions of these agreements on access to PGRFA, and the following chapters will continue the examination on the substantive issues which are being discussed in international fora.

8. The plant protection provisions of UPOV, the TRIPS Agreement and bilateral treaties

INTRODUCTION

The previous chapter provided a general overview of the workings of the international property rights regime in regard to PGRFA and this chapter will analyze its specific application to these resources. The development of property rights over new plant varieties, while having its roots in national laws, later expanded in the international sphere. The national and international developments have to a great extent influenced each other. The process has also resulted in the impetus at international level to make national legislation on such rights consistent with international regimes.

This chapter will provide a brief discussion of the development of plant protection laws in the national sphere and then examine the provisions of two international agreements which deal with the application of intellectual property rights (IPRs) to PGRFA, namely the UPOV Convention and the TRIPS Agreement. I will consider the impacts of IPRs on farmers and agricultural systems particularly in developing countries, and analyze the debate on the subject which is taking place in international fora.

FORMS OF PLANT PROTECTION

Two forms of monopolistic property rights are available to breeders of new varieties of plants – namely patents, and plant variety protection (PVP) or plant breeders' rights (PBRs). Both are forms of intellectual property rights. A patent, which is available for any industrial invention, gives the inventor the right to prevent any other person from using the invention in any way for a period of time, usually 20 years. The criteria for obtaining a patent on an invention are proof of novelty or non-obviousness, inventiveness, and utility or usefulness.

PVP or PBRs are unique forms of intellectual property rights, similar to patents, specifically designed to protect property rights over new varieties of plants, and available only to plant breeders. Currently, the criteria for PVP are novelty, distinctness, uniformity and stability of the plant variety.[1] PVP enables the breeder to prevent any other person from reproducing the plant variety for commercial purposes without his/her prior authorization. PVP is also subject to two exceptions, namely the farmers' exception and the breeders' exception. Consequently, it is viewed as a weaker form of patent.

DEVELOPMENTS IN PLANT PROTECTION IN THE NATIONAL SPHERE

The United States was one of the first countries to institutionalize private property rights over plant varieties.[2] While plants were initially excluded from the subject matter of standard utility patents,[3] in 1930 Congress passed the Plant Patent Act[4] in order to 'afford agriculture, so far as practicable, the same opportunity to participate in the benefits of the patent system as has been given to industry.'[5] Such patents were initially restricted to distinct and new varieties of asexually reproducing plants[6] and those reproducing sexually were excluded. In the next 40 years 2,700 plant patents were issued

---

1 See *International Convention for the Protection of New Varieties of Plants*, of 2 December 1961 as Revised at Geneva on 10 November 1972, on 23 October 1978, and on 19 March 1991 (hereinafter UPOV Act 1991); see Chapter III of the Act for explanations of these terms.

2 Anne E Crocker, 'Will Plants Finally Grow Into Full Patent Protection on an International Level? A Look at the History of US and International Patent Law regarding Patent Protection for Plants and the Likely Changes after the US Supreme Court's Decision in JEM Ag Supply v Pioneer Hi-Bred' (2003) 8 *Drake Journal of Agricultural Law* 251.

3 The exclusion of plant varieties from patentable material is based on the 'products of nature doctrine' which postulates that what exists in nature cannot be new – David G. Scalise and Daniel Nugent, 'International Intellectual Property Protections for Living Matter: Biotechnology, Multinational Conventions and the Exception for Agriculture' (1995) 27 *Case Western Reserve Journal of International Law* 83, 90. The authors criticize the restrictive application of plant patents based on this doctrine.

4 US Plant Patent Act, 35 USC §§ 161–164.

5 Cited in Patricia Lucia Cantuaria Marin, *Providing Protection for Plant Genetic Resources – Patents, Sui Generis Systems and Biopartnerships* (2002), Chapter 2.

6 That is, plants which reproduce by vegetative material such as tubers, grafts and cuttings and not by seeds.

under this Act.[7] In 1970, Congress passed the Plant Variety Protection Act (PVPA)[8] which extended protection to sexually reproducing plants if the breeder could show that the new variety had the attributes of novelty, uniformity, stability, and distinctness.[9] The second Act was largely motivated by the rise of the private hybrid seed industry, and the strengthening of plant variety protection laws in Europe.[10] The protection available under the PVPA was initially not as comprehensive as under the Plant Patent Act, and contained a 'farmers' privilege' exception which permitted farmers to save seeds produced by protected varieties and replant them without paying additional royalties. Farmers were also permitted to sell these seeds, but this right to sell was removed by a later amendment to the Act.[11]

The US courts also played an important role in furthering plant breeders' rights. The protection afforded to plant breeders by statute was substantially strengthened by judicial decisions beginning with that of *Diamond v Chakrabarthy*[12] in which the US Supreme Court extended standard utility patent protection to novel plant varieties.[13] In this case a genetically modified micro-organism which was capable of breaking down oil spills was initially rejected for patent protection by the patent office on the grounds that micro-organisms are a product of nature and living things are not patentable under the law. This ruling was overturned by the Supreme Court which disagreed with the contention that living things were not patentable, declaring that 'the relevant distinction was not between living and inanimate things, but between products of nature, whether living or not,

---

[7] David S Tilford, 'Saving the Blueprints: The International Legal Regime for Plant Resources' (1998) 30 *Case Western Reserve Journal of International Law* 373, 401.

[8] Plant Variety Protection Act of 1970 (PVPA), 7 USC §§ 2321–2582.

[9] See Section 41 of the Act for definitions of these terms. See also Jim Chen, 'The Parable of the Seeds: Interpreting the Plant Variety Protection Act in Furtherance of Innovation Policy' (2005) *Notre Dame Law Review* 105, 121.

[10] For an account of the development of PVP laws in Europe see Klaus Bosselmann, 'Plants and Politics: The International Legal Regime concerning Biotechnology and Biodiversity' (1996) 7 *Colorado Journal of International Environmental Law and Policy* 111. See also Crocker, above n 2.

[11] See below section on the farmers' privilege.

[12] *Diamond, Commissioner of Patents and Trademarks v Chakrabarty* (1980, United States Supreme Court) 447 US 303; 100 S Ct 2204; 65 L Ed 2d 144; 1980 US LEXIS 112; 206 USPQ (BNA) 193.

[13] For a more detailed account of US case law in relation to plant patenting see Marin, above n 5, Chapter 2.

and human-made inventions.'[14] In the present case, it held that the respondent's micro-organism was the result of human ingenuity and research, and thereby patentable.

Chakrabarty was followed by a series of decisions culminating in the cases of *Ex parte Hibberd*[15] where the US Patent Office for the first time addressed the granting of utility patents for plant varieties, and of *E.M. Ag Supply, Inc.* v *Pioneer Hi-Bred International, Inc*[16] in which the US Supreme Court conclusively held that sexually reproducing plants are eligible for protection under the PVPA as well as by utility patents under the Patents Act,[17] thus sealing the position that patents are now issuable on life forms.[18] Although the conditions for obtaining patents are more stringent and would be practically available only to genetically engineered plants and animals, the benefits obtained under the patent system would be greater, including that the invention would not be subject to the exceptions found in the PVP system under UPOV.[19]

Patents were used to some extent by some European countries around 1930, and in both Germany and the Netherlands national PVP systems were set up which became the forerunners to UPOV.[20] When the push for plant variety protection was initiated after the Second World War, the European seed industry was in fact asking for industrial patents on plants, since it was already developing a cross border trade in plant varieties. This proposal met with resistance, most notably from European governments which feared that industry would dominate the agricultural sector. Resistance also came from patent experts who were concerned that extending patents to plant varieties could undermine the credibility of patents.[21] The seed companies,

---

[14] 447 US 303, 313.

[15] *Ex parte Hibberd* 227 USPQ (BNA) 443 (1985).

[16] *E.M. Ag Supply, Inc.* v *Pioneer Hi-Bred International, Inc* (2001, United States Supreme Court) 534 US 124; 122 S Ct 593; 151 L Ed 2d 508; 2001 US LEXIS 10949; 70 USLW 4032; 60 USPQ.2D (BNA) 1865; 2001 Cal Daily Op Service 10239; 2001 Daily Journal DAR 12749; 15 Fla L Weekly Fed S 29.

[17] Chen, above n 9.

[18] Scalise and Nugent, above n 3, 97; Tilford, above n 7, 400; Marin, above n 5, Chapter 2.

[19] Scalise and Nugent, above n 3,100; Elisa Rives, 'Mother Nature and the Courts: Are Sexually Reproducing Plants and their Progeny Patentable under the Utility Patent Act of 1952?' (2001/2002) *Cumberland Law Review* 187.

[20] GRAIN, *The end of farm-saved seed? Industry's wish list for the next revision of UPOV* (2007), available at http://www.grain.org/briefings/?id=202 (last accessed 20 July 2012).

[21] 'Plants are living and evolving organisms and therefore cannot be exhaustively described in the way required by a patent – well enough to allow someone else

represented by the International Association for the Protection of Intellectual Property (AIPPI)[22] and the International Association of Plant Breeders (ASSINSEL)[23] therefore had to settle for a *sui generis* system of protection and together with the French government, initiated the process which was to result in the UPOV Convention.[24]

PLANT VARIETY PROTECTION UNDER UPOV

The progressive amendments of UPOV from 1961 to 1991 reflect the gradual strengthening of intellectual property rights (IPRs) over plant varieties, from a limited monopoly to one which is now similar to patent protection.[25] While the 1972 and 1978 revisions of UPOV made only minor changes to the Convention, the 1991 Act contained significant amendments.[26] It has been contended that the 1991 amendments to UPOV were largely brought about by the conventional plant breeders who were challenged by large biotechnology corporations armed with genetic engineering techniques. These techniques made it possible for their plant varieties to meet the criteria required for patents, (particularly the 'novelty' criterion). By this point the US Supreme Court had already ruled that patents were

---

to "repeat the invention" exactly. Thus patents on plants would require far-reaching exemptions from normal patent criteria' – GRAIN, ibid. Further, these interest groups also required the 'novelty' and 'inventive step' (or non-obviousness) criteria of patents to be relaxed for plants so that varieties reflecting merely incremental improvements on known varieties could also receive protection and this requirement could not be met – Graham Dutfield, *Intellectual Property, Biogenetic Resources and Traditional Knowledge* (2004), 33; Marin, above n 5.

22 AIPPI is the acronym for the Association Internationale pour la Protection de la Propriété Intellectuelle, see www.aippi.org (last accessed 20 July 2012).

23 ASSINSEL is the acronym for the Association Internationale des Sélectionneurs pour la Protection de Obentions Végétales. The organization merged in 2002 with the International Seed Trade Federation (FIS) and the two became the International Seed Federation, ISF, see http://www.worldseed.org/isf/home.html (last accessed 20 July 2012).

24 GRAIN, above n 20. See also GRAIN, *Seed companies want to ban farm-saved seed* (2007), available at <http://www.grain.org/briefings_files/upov-2007-summary-en.pdf (last accessed 20 July 2012); Dutfield, above n 21, 33.

25 GRAIN, above n 20.

26 Rolf Jördens, 'Progress of plant variety protection based on the International Convention for the Protection of New Varieties of Plants (UPOV Convention)' (2005) 27(3) *World Patent Information* 232, 234.

issuable on plant varieties. The 1991 amendments to UPOV thus gave the conventional plant breeders an expanded right which was very close to patents.[27]

UPOV Provisions

The UPOV Convention, including its amending Acts, established five main features in regard to plant variety protection, namely:

- the standard criteria for protection (distinctness, uniformity and stability, with the criterion of novelty being added in 1991);
- the minimum scope of protection;
- the minimum duration of protection;
- the minimum number of plant genera and species for which variety protection must be provided; and
- the rules for accession to the Convention, national treatment and priority of applications.[28]

In regard to the plants protected under the Convention, while the 1978 Act permitted states to determine which plants would be accorded protection,[29] the 1991 Act requires plant varieties of all genera and species to be protected,[30] thereby extending the rights afforded to the breeder. This also means that countries no longer have the discretion to decide which plant varieties they will protect.

The requirements for protection are now, novelty, distinctness, uniformity, stability and also variety of denomination.[31] Article 5 of the 1991 Act specifically states that the grant of the breeder's rights shall not be subject to any further or different conditions than these. This provision thus imposes an upper limit on the criteria for protection, thereby precluding countries from restricting the scope of the rights by requiring further conditions to be

---

[27] GRAIN, above n 20.

[28] Jördens, above n 26, 234.

[29] *International Convention for the Protection of New Varieties of Plants*, of 2 December 1961, as revised at Geneva on 10 November 1972 and on 23 October 1978 (hereinafter UPOV Act 1978), Article 2.

[30] UPOV Act 1991, Article 3.

[31] UPOV Act 1978, Article 6 and UPOV Act 1991, Chapter III and Article 20. For an explanation of these requirements see Mark Hannig, 'An Examination of the Possibility to Secure Intellectual Property Rights for Plant Genetic Resources Developed by Indigenous Peoples of the NAFTA States: Domestic Legislation under the International Convention for Protection of New Plant Varieties' (1996) *Arizona Journal of International and Comparative Law* 175.

satisfied, for example, disclosure of origin of the variety. This significant aspect will be discussed further in this book.

The 1991 Act extends the plant breeder's rights in regard to both term and scope of protection. The term of protection has been increased in the 1991 Act, from an original minimum of 15–18 years to a minimum of 20–25 years.[32] Under the 1978 Act, the breeder's prior authorization was required for the production of the variety for purposes of commercial marketing, the offering for sale, or the marketing of the reproductive or vegetative propagating material, as such.[33] This was maintained in the 1991 Act which prohibits the unauthorized production or reproduction (multiplication), conditioning for the purpose of propagation, offering for sale, selling or other marketing, exporting or importing, or stocking of the variety for any of the purposes mentioned above. In addition, a state may extend the range of acts which are so prohibited.[34] Further, in 1991 these restrictions were extended from propagating material only, to material harvested from the plant variety as well, again benefiting the breeder.[35]

The 1991 Act also lifted the restriction on dual protection included earlier. Under Article 2(1) of the 1978 Act a member state may provide protection to a breeder either by way of patent or a special title of protection. Any member state whose national laws provide for both forms of protection may use only one form in respect of one and the same botanical genus or species.[36] This prohibition has been omitted from the 1991 Act and consequently the breeder can now seek dual protection under two distinct regimes, reaping the benefits and avoiding the limitations of both. For example, the requirements of novelty and the 'inventive step' criteria of patents are not required for

---

[32] UPOV Act 1978, Article 8; UPOV Act 1991, Article 19.

[33] UPOV Act 1978, Article 5.

[34] UPOV Act 1991, Article 14(4).

[35] Marin explains this distinction with the following example. Under the 1978 Act if a person used the oil of a protected coconut variety to produce an anti-aging cream, he/she would not have violated the rights of the breeder. However, under the 1991 Act this would constitute a violation – Marin, above n 5, 32.

[36] However, it must be noted that the UPOV Act 1978, Article 37 titled 'Exceptional Rules for Protection under Two Forms' provides that notwithstanding the provisions of Article 2(1), a state which had provided for protection under different forms for one and the same genus or species, may continue to do so, if at the time of signing or ratifying this Act it notifies the Secretary-General of that fact. Marin states that this loophole was included to accommodate the US, since at that time its legislation permitted parallel protection. This was thus an important step in bringing international law in line with US domestic law – Marin, above n 5, 33.

breeders' rights,[37] while there are exceptions to breeders' rights (discussed below) which are not applicable under patent protection.

Other important aspects of UPOV include the amended provision in the 1991 Act which prohibits discrimination between nationals of a state and non-nationals. While Article 3 of the 1978 Act permitted states to limit the benefits of the protection accorded to a particular plant variety to nationals of states which also applied the Convention to that variety, the 1991 Act now requires that the nationals of all member states enjoy the same level of protection in each others' countries.[38] This is equivalent to the principle of national treatment under the TRIPS Agreement and means that UPOV was positioning itself to be truly international.

Exceptions to Plant Breeders' Rights (PBRs)

There are certain exceptions or limitations to PBRs which have been recognized in both domestic laws and international law, namely the farmers' privilege and the breeders' or research exception. These exceptions are significant since they constitute one factor which distinguishes PBRs from industrial patents.

The Farmers' Privilege

As discussed earlier, there is an age-old tradition among farmers of saving seed from one year's harvest for replanting in the succeeding year. Farmers also traditionally shared and exchanged seed, thus contributing to the development of new plant varieties. While this may appear to be an unwritten but obvious aspect of the agricultural process, it has in fact become a contentious legal issue, both in international and national law in the context of the propertization and commercialization of plant varieties.

The controversy surrounding what has come to be known as the 'farmers' privilege' or 'farmers' exception'[39] was actually triggered by the 1991

---

[37] While novelty as a criterion was added in UPOV Act 1991, the application of the term differs from that in the context of industrial patents – see UPOV Act 1991, Article 6.

[38] UPOV Act 1991, Article 4.

[39] Also called the crop exception. These terms are not actually found in the conventions. Some writers take the view that the term 'farmers' privilege' is a misnomer as what is permitted to the farmer is a right rather than a privilege. See Graham Dutfield, *Intellectual Property Rights, Trade and Biodiversity* (2000), 28. See also GRAIN, *Farmers Privilege under Attack* (2003), available at http://www.grain.org/briefings_files/bio-ipr-fp-june-2003-en.pdf (last accessed 20 July 2012).

UPOV Act. The 1978 Act makes no mention of the farmers' exception. It merely defines the scope of protection granted to the plant breeder with reference to the three acts mentioned above which require his/her prior authorization.[40] Farmers were thereby implicitly prohibited from violating plant breeders' rights by *selling* seed from one year's crop.[41] However, in the absence of a specific prohibition on *saving* and *sharing* seed, there was a de facto acceptance of the farmers' continued practice of doing so which was in fact upheld by many countries, although to varying extents.

The 1991 UPOV Act introduced a specific provision on the farmers' exception. This was done by defining it in the form of a limitation on the plant breeder's right and also by setting out its scope and extent. Article 15(2) reads:

> [*Optional exception*] Notwithstanding Article 14, each Contracting Party *may, within reasonable limits and subject to the safeguarding of the legitimate interests of the breeder*, (emphasis added) restrict the breeder's right in relation to any variety in order to permit farmers to use for propagating purposes, on their own holdings, the product of the harvest which they have obtained by planting, on their own holdings, the protected variety or a variety covered by Article 14(5)*(a)*(i) or (ii).

For the first time, therefore, what had been an unwritten, customary practice was now incorporated into the law, and restricted. This was done by making the farmers' exception an optional one and leaving it to national governments to implement it at their discretion but within 'reasonable limits.'

The farmers' exception was also introduced into the US Plant Variety Protection Act.[42] Under the PVPA a farmer was permitted to save and sell a limited amount of seed each year, and this would not violate the rights of the breeder. However, under a 1994 amendment to the PVPA[43] (which was in fact introduced to bring US domestic legislation in line with the 1991 UPOV Act), the right to sell seeds was removed and farmers can now only use saved seed on their own farms.[44]

---

40 See above n 33.

41 UPOV Act 1978, Article 5 (1).

42 Scalise and Nugent point out that prior to 1970 there was no need for a farmers' exemption as the patenting of sexually reproducing plants was not permitted – Scalise and Nugent, above n 3, 88.

43 Plant Variety Protection Act Amendments of 1994, Pub L No. 103–349, § 10, 108 Stat. 3136, 3142 (1994). See also Crocker, above n 2, 254.

44 Prior to the statutory amendment, the US Supreme Court had limited the ambit of the exception – Rives, above n 19. See also Crocker, above n 2.

The principle of the farmers' exception is among the most contentious in the discourse on rights to PGRFA. The saving, sharing and exchange of seed among farmers obviously erodes the profits of the seed companies as they will not be assured of a continual market for their products. The seed industry has made its opposition to the farmers' exception clear.[45] In a position paper on farm-saved seed, ASSINSEL claimed that plant breeders have developed cultivars used by an increasing number of farmers worldwide which contain increasing genetic variability and which, together with 'improved cultural practices,' has resulted in a dramatic increase in food production. Plant breeding is therefore no longer a 'by-product of agriculture' but a separate activity for which the breeders must get a return on large investments. ASSINSEL warns that its members oppose the farmer's privilege going beyond the 1991 Act:

> i.e. within reasonable limits in terms of acreage, quantity of seed and species concerned and subject to the safe-guarding of the legitimate interest of the breeders in terms of payment of a remuneration and information.

It also states that its members:

> consider that any national legislation authorizing farm saved seed without reasonable limit and without safeguarding the legitimate interest of the breeders is not in conformity with the 1991 Act of the UPOV convention. In addition it would not be an effective sui-generis system in the meaning of the article 27.3.b of the TRIP's agreement.[46]

Those in favour of the farmers' exception firstly emphasize that the farmers' right to save seed dates back millennia to the emergence of agricultural societies. While some writers take the view that this exception amounts to a servitude on the proprietary rights of the breeder,[47] it can be also pointed out that servitudes are acquired by prescription and long term use. Saving seed

---

[45] For an overview of the corporations which dominate the global seed industry see ETC Group, *Global Seed Industry Concentration – 2005* ETC Group Communiqué Issue #90 (September/October 2005), available at http://gmwatch.org/component/content/article/10558-the-worlds-top-ten-seed-companies-who-owns-nature (last accessed 20 July 2012).

[46] Position Papers, Statements and Motions adopted by FIS, ASSINSEL and ISF – Farm Saved Seed (adopted 31 May 2001), available at http://www.worldseed.org/cms/medias/file/PositionPapers/OnIntellectualProperty/Archives/Farm_Saved_Seed_(En)_Archives_20080701.pdf (last accessed 20 July 2012). See also the position papers of ISF, available at http://www.worldseed.org/isf/on_intellectual_property.html (last accessed 20 July 2012).

[47] Scalise and Nugent, above n 3. For an account of US court decisions restricting the farmers' exception under the PVPA see Peter J Goss 'Guiding the

has long pre-dated proprietary rights on seed varieties, and it has also been asserted that it constitutes a common law right.[48] It can therefore be counter argued that intellectual property rights over plant varieties constitute an unjustifiable restriction on the rights of farmers in this regard.

It should be noted at this point that UPOV's restrictions on the farmers' exception is in direct conflict with the provisions on farmers' rights in the FAO International Treaty on Plant Genetic Resources for Food and Agriculture (FAO Treaty). Article 9.3 of the Treaty states that:

> [n]othing in this Article shall be interpreted to limit any rights that farmers have to save, use, exchange and sell farm-saved seed/propagating material, subject to national law and as appropriate.

This is reinforced by several other provisions, both directly and indirectly.[49] However, the weakness in this Article lies in the fact that farmers' rights are made subject to national legislation rather than being enforceable in international fora. In view of the fact that under TRIPS countries are required to institute some form of plant variety protection, and the preferred form is UPOV style PBRs, this would be an unreliable source of protection for farmers' rights. Several countries have, in fact, UPOV style plant variety protection laws in place and there is now increasing pressure on others to conform to this system.[50]

The farmers' exception contained in UPOV has been consistently whittled down and in the light of subsequent technological developments in fact offers little protection to the interests of farmers in either developed or developing countries. Further advances in agricultural biotechnology and their implementation, particularly in regard to genetically engineered seeds

---

Hand That Feeds: Toward Socially Optimal Appropriability in Agricultural Biotechnology Innovation' (1996) *California Law Review* 1395; Neil D Hamilton, 'Why Own the Farm if You Can Own the Farmer (and the Crop)?: Contract Production and Intellectual Property Protection of Grain Crops' (1994) 73 *Nebraska Law Review* 48, 95.

48 Samantha M Ohlgart, 'The Terminator Gene: Intellectual Property Rights Vs The Farmers' Common Law Right to Save Seed' (2002) 7 *Drake Journal of Agricultural Law* 473.

49 See *International Treaty on Plant Genetic Resources for Food and Agriculture*, adopted at the 31st Session of the FAO Conference on 3 November 2001 available at http://www.fao.org/AG/cgrfa/itpgr.htm (last accessed 20 July 2012) and the website of the Treaty at http://www.planttreaty.org (last accessed 20 July 2012), (hereinafter FAO Treaty), Preamble Paragraph 8, Articles 5.1(c) and 6.1 (c) and (d).

50 GRAIN, *The International Treaty on Plant Genetic Resources, A Challenge for Asia* (2002), available at http://www.grain.org/docs/it-asia-feb2002-en.pdf (last accessed 20 July 2012).

and genetic use restriction technologies (GURTs), have also served to strengthen the hand of the plant breeders and possibly make the principle of the farmers' exception redundant.[51] The farmers' exception has also been the primary reason why the seed and biotechnology industries have sought utility patent protection, since patents do not provide for the exception.[52] These measures illustrate the concerted efforts taken by biotechnology corporations to safeguard their property in seeds whether by legislative or technological measures. These corporations will potentially make windfall profits when markets in developing countries, which are for the most part untapped, are opened up for their seeds.[53] However, if farmers were compelled to start planting protected plant varieties, they would inevitably be caught up in the cycle of the seed saving prohibition and this would potentially result in loss of autonomy and dependence on the biotechnological industry for agricultural inputs.[54]

---

[51] Seed companies' contracts with farmers also contain clauses prohibiting them from saving or selling seed – 2006 Monsanto Technology/Stewardship Agreement, available at http://www.worc.org/userfiles/Understanding%20 Monsanto's%20Technology%20Use%20Agreement%202–06.pdf (last accessed 20 July 2012). Seed companies have also been known to sue farmers whom they allege use their products illegally – Centre for Food Safety, *Monsanto v US Farmers* (2007), available at http://www.centerforfoodsafety.org/pubs/CFSM OnsantovsFarmerReport1.13.05.pdf (last accessed 20 July 2012); Peter Straub, 'Farmers in the IP Wrench – How Patents on Gene-modified Crops Violate the Right to Food in Developing Countries' (2006) *Hastings International and Comparative Law* 187, 191. The author cites the Canadian case of *Monsanto Canada* v *Schmeiser* [2004] SCR1 in this regard.

[52] Rives, above n 19, 228. Woods notes that over seven to eight years more than 10,000 utility patents have been granted for plants – Michael Woods, 'Food for Thought: The Biopiracy of Jasmine and Basmati Rice' (2002) 13 *Albany Law Journal of Science & Technology* 123, 126; Straub, above n 51,190.

[53] Devlin Kuyek, *Intellectual property rights: Ultimate Control of Agricultural R&D in Asia* (2001), available at http://www.grain.org/briefings_files/asiaipr.pdf (last accessed 20 July 2012). It has also been noted that a less well-known fact is that many rich and middle income countries also rely on a considerable amount of farm saved seed ranging from an average of 20–40 per cent but going up to 90 per cent in some countries. It has been estimated that if farm saved seed were made illegal the seed industry would gain by around $7 billion annually – GRAIN, above n 20. The conflict between plant breeders and developed country farmers can also be seen in the presentation made to UPOV by the International Seed Federation – UPOV/ ENFORCEMENT/05/3 – Meeting on Enforcement of Plant Breeders' Rights – *Presentation by the International Seed Federation (ISF)* – 4 October 2005.

[54] Straub, above n 51. For a discussion on the operations of global food corporations see ActionAid International, *Power Hungry – Six Reasons to Regulate*

The Breeders' or Research Exception

Competition can arise among plant breeders themselves, giving rise to conflicts over developing new varieties.[55] Breeders who have secured such protection over varieties would seek to prevent others from using them for research, or for further development of more varieties. This conflict finds expression in the provisions on what is known as the breeders' or research exception.

The breeders' or research exception imposes a limited restriction on PBRs to permit subsequent breeders to use previously protected varieties for further breeding and improvement. This exception appears in both the 1978 and 1991 UPOV Acts. Article 5(3) of the 1978 Act states that:

> [a]uthorisation by the breeder shall not be required either for the utilisation of the variety as an initial source of variation for the purpose of creating other varieties or for the marketing of such varieties. Such authorisation shall be required, however, when the repeated use of the variety is necessary for the commercial production of another variety.

Therefore the original rights of subsequent breeders were wide enough for them to carry on further research for developing a new variety.

The 1991 Act also contains the research exception but has limited its scope quite significantly. Article 15 of the 1991 Act states that the (original) breeder's right shall not extend to 'acts done for experimental purposes' and 'acts done for the purposes of breeding other varieties.' However, this section will apply only to 'other' varieties which are not 'essentially derived' from the original protected variety.[56] Therefore the scope of the research exception now revolves around the concept of 'essential derivation.'

UPOV has itself stated that breeders need access to all forms of breeding material to sustain progress in plant breeding.[57] However, the seed industry is as hostile to the research exception as it is to the farmers' exception. While it has acknowledged that it 'is essential for continued progress from

---

Global Food Corporations (2005) http://www.actionaid.org.uk/_content/documents/power_hungry.pdf (last accessed 20 July 2012).

[55] Fredrick H Buttel and Jill Belsky, 'Biotechnology, Plant Breeding and Intellectual Property – Social and Ethical Dimensions' (1997) 12(1) *Science, Technology and Human Values* 31.

[56] UPOV Act 1991, Article 14(5).

[57] *Access to Genetic Resources and Benefit-Sharing,* Reply of UPOV to the Notification of June 26, 2003, from the Executive Secretary of the Convention on Biological Diversity (CBD) adopted by the Council of UPOV at its Thirty-Seventh ordinary session on 23 October 2003.

plant breeding,' it has also expressed concern that it was being abused due to the assessment of distinctness based upon the 1978 Act, and that 'cosmetic modifications' were sufficient to protect a new variety. Therefore they claimed that the concept of 'essential derivation' was introduced into the 1991 Act in order to establish a minimum distance between two species so as to claim distinctness.[58]

The concept of 'essential derivation' is theoretically one of fact and such determination may be subjective, although both the 1991 Act and the seed industry have attempted to lay down guidelines to determine the issue. The industry strongly supports the concept because it has 'the potential to drastically decrease the risk of plagiarism in plant breeding.'[59]

That the industry intends to curtail the research exception as aggressively as it has done the farmers' exception is evident from its statement that:

> ISF considers that exception as meaning that a plant breeder can use, for further breeding, protected varieties in accordance with the UPOV Convention he has had access to lawfully. This does not mean that access and use of such protected varieties cannot be subject to restrictions under other international and/or national law.[60]

In all probability this matter will in fact be determined under national laws, many of which favour the plant breeder.[61] In addition, while the burden of proof would obviously be on the initial breeder to prove that a subsequent variety is essentially derived, the industry has also recommended that this burden should shift in specified circumstances.[62] It must also be noted that the essential derivation rule only applies to protected varieties and not to traditional varieties. Therefore a plant which is essentially derived from a

---

[58] See 'Essential Derivation and Dependence – Practical Information' Position papers, Statements and Motions adopted by FIS, ASSINSEL and ISF, available at http://www.worldseed.org/cms/medias/file/PositionPapers/OnIntellectualProperty/Essential_Derivation_from_a_Not_Yet_Protected_Variety_20050601_(En).pdf (last accessed 20 July 2012).

[59] International Seed Federation 'ISF View on Intellectual Property' (Bangalore, June 2003), available at http://www.worldseed.org/cms/medias/file/PositionPapers/OnIntellectualProperty/View_on_Intellectual_Property_2009.pdf (last accessed 20 July 2012).

[60] Ibid.

[61] For example, the same limitation on the research exception was incorporated into the PVPA of the US by its 1994 amendment – Plant Variety Protection Act Amendments of 1994, Pub L No 103–341, 108 Stat. 3136, 3136–3137. See also Mark D Janis and Jay P Kesan, 'US Plant Variety Protection: Sound and Fury?' (2002) *Houston Law Review* 727.

[62] International Seed Federation, above n 59.

landrace could be the subject of PVP, which in effect is what happened in the case of basmati and jasmine rice.[63]

Writers are of the opinion that the amendment will not benefit the seed industry to a great extent and will merely divert resources away from research towards litigation on the issue.[64] However, the establishment of the concept in itself has made subsequent breeders wary of accusations of infringements.[65] Helfer also agrees that while the concept is highly controversial, '[n]evertheless, the overall effect of this provision of the 1991 Act has been to narrow the breeders' exemption and expand the IPRs of first generation breeders.'[66]

Conclusion

Since the 1978 revision of UPOV, there have been unprecedented developments in plant biotechnology, which have potentially enormous commercial returns. However, ensuring those returns requires a strategy which both secures property rights over the end products and ensures a market in which to sell them. The 1991 revision of UPOV is guaranteed to achieve the first objective.

A fundamental objection to such propertization of seeds is the inequity resulting from PGRFA which was nurtured and developed by farmers and local communities being appropriated and subject to monopolistic corporate control. Many of the 'new' and 'modern' varieties of protected plants are based upon the species developed by traditional farmers who were not compensated for their use. Examples of the misappropriation of traditionally bred varieties of PGRFA have already been cited in Chapter 3. PBRs, like patents, do not recognize the previous actors in the process of plant variety development, or compensate those who developed the resource base from which modern varieties are derived.

Aside from the inequity of misappropriating varieties bred by traditional farmers in the past, the current economic impacts are also a matter of concern. The prohibition on saving and exchanging seed may obstruct farmers from carrying on their traditional activities of plant breeding and increase their production costs when buying fresh seeds every year. In

---

63 See Chapter 3.

64 Crocker, above n 2; Goss, above n 47, 1434; Janis and Kesan, above n 61.

65 International Seed Federation, above n 59.

66 Laurence R Helfer, *Intellectual Property Rights in Plant Varieties: An Overview with Options for National Governments,* FAO Legal Papers Online #31 (2002) 16, available at http://papers.ssrn.com/sol3/papers.cfm?abstract_id=711842 (last accessed 20 July 2012).

developing countries a high proportion of farming is in the hands of small scale subsistence farmers. They do not have the resources to continually buy new seeds, but rely on saving or exchanging seeds or cultivating wild varieties, and agriculture in these countries is still often grounded in the sharing and distribution of farmer saved seed. Further, higher costs for farmers would inevitably be passed on to the consumer, thus jeopardizing access to food, particularly in developing countries.

Commercial transactions in seed varieties have still not taken hold in these regions, and while for instance, the Asian seed market has immense potential for agricultural biotechnology corporations, it is still largely untapped. These corporations therefore need to get a foothold into these countries in order to sell their products with the potential to make windfall profits. The current practice of farmers of saving and exchanging their own seed varieties is hindering them from doing so. Therefore from the perspective of the biotechnological industry, restrictions on the farmers' right to save seed would be an effective strategy to change this situation. The governments of the countries concerned would also find themselves under pressure to provide for the legal framework to protect the interests of the breeders. The imposition of intellectual property laws on farmers and the restrictions on their traditional practices would thus have wider implications for biodiversity conservation, sustainable agriculture, and food security in developing countries.

The future directions of UPOV and PVP are closely linked to the workings of the TRIPS Agreement. While the 1991 amendments to UPOV were triggered by the stand-off between the conventional seed industry and the biotechnological corporations, that dimension no longer exists since the former has been largely bought up by the latter, resulting in a consolidation of the industry.[67] The common objective therefore is the extension of industrial patents to plant varieties. This process is taking place in the context of TRIPS as well as bilateral agreements.

---

[67] GRAIN, above n 20.

THE PLANT PATENT PROVISIONS OF THE TRIPS AGREEMENT AND CONCERNS OF DEVELOPING COUNTRIES

Introduction

The provisions of the TRIPS Agreement which impact upon PGRFA are those relating to patents, contained in Section 5, Articles 27 to 34. The present discussion will be confined to Article 27 entitled 'Patentable Subject Matter.'

According to Article 27.1, subject to the provisions of Articles 27.2 and 27.3:

> patents shall be available for any inventions, whether products or processes, in all fields of technology, provided that they are new, involve an inventive step and are capable of industrial application.

The Article does not define what constitutes an invention but merely demarcates what conditions one should meet in order to be patentable. The conditions reflect the generally accepted conditions of patentability which have now been incorporated into a global agreement.

Articles 27.2 and 27.3 specify the exceptions to patentability. According to Article 27.2 Members may exclude inventions from patentability if the commercial exploitation of those inventions within their territory should be prevented in the interests of:

> *ordre public* or morality, including to protect human, animal or plant life or health or to avoid serious prejudice to the environment, provided that such exclusion is not made merely because the exploitation is prohibited by their law.

According to Article 27.3 Members may also exclude from patentability, inter alia:

> plants and animals other than micro-organisms, and essentially biological processes for the production of plants or animals other than non-biological and microbiological processes.

However, a proviso to the section specifies that:

> [m]embers shall provide for the protection of plant varieties either by patents or by an effective *sui generis* system or by any combination thereof.[68]

Therefore TRIPS requires its contracting parties to protect inventions based upon plants in one of three ways – patents, a *sui generis* system or a combination of both. Although this gives member states some leeway in the type of protection they must provide, since more countries have acceded to TRIPS than to UPOV, it also ensures that plant variety protection has in fact been extended. Other factors which have contributed to TRIPS' influence on plant variety protection include its link to other international trade agreements, its widespread ratification by states in the industrialized and developing world, and its novel enforcement, review and dispute settlement provisions.[69]

The Potential Impact of TRIPS on Plant Breeding

While it has been argued that universal IPRs in general and the TRIPS Agreement in particular are, by and large, inimical to the interests of developing countries,[70] it is Article 27 and its impact on PGRFA and related traditional knowledge that has perhaps resulted in the most friction. The patent provisions of the TRIPS Agreement impact upon agricultural biodiversity both directly and indirectly. Until the Agreement, countries were

---

[68] Agreement on Trade-Related Aspects of Intellectual Property Rights, Annex 1C of the Marrakesh Agreement Establishing the World Trade Organization, signed in Marrakesh, Morocco on 15 April 1994, 1869 UNTS 299; 33 ILM 81 (1994). For an explanation of the negotiation of these sections see Daniel Gervais, *The TRIPS Agreement – Drafting History and Analysis* (2nd ed 2003), 220.

[69] Helfer, above n 66.

[70] UNCTAD Document UNCTAD/ITE/1 – *The TRIPS Agreement and Developing Countries* (1996); South Centre, The TRIPS Agreement: A Guide for the South. The Uruguay Round Agreement on Trade-Related Intellectual Property Rights (1997), available at http://www.southcentre.org/index.php?option=com_content&task=view&id=87&Itemid=67 (last accessed 20 July 2012); Commission on Intellectual Property Rights, Integrating Intellectual Property Rights and Development Policy (2002), available at http://www.iprcommission.org/papers/pdfs/final_report/CIPRfullfinal.pdf (last accessed 20 July 2012); Erin Kathleen Bender, 'North and South: The WTO, TRIPS, and the Scourge of Biopiracy' (2003) 11 *Tulsa Journal of Comparative & International Law* 281; Laurence R Helfer, 'Regime Shifting: The TRIPS Agreement and New Dynamics of International Intellectual Property Lawmaking' (2004) 29 *Yale Journal of International Law* 1; Farhana Yamin, 'Globalisation and the International Governance of Modern Biotechnology, IPRs, Biotechnology and Food Security' (date not available), available at http://ictsd.org/i/ip/29165/ (last accessed 20 July 2012).

free to decide on what would or would not be patentable, and the duration and scope of the rights. This flexibility which enabled countries to set their intellectual property (IP) standards according to their specific circumstances has been eliminated by TRIPS which now sets minimum, universal standards in this regard. Under TRIPS, all inventions, both products and processes are patentable. While 'plants and animals' may be excluded from patent protection, 'micro-organisms and essentially biological processes for the production of plants or animals' cannot be excluded unless they are 'non-biological and micro-biological processes.'[71] These have been cited as including isolated DNA sequences that code for certain proteins, isolated or purified proteins, seeds, plant cells and plants, plant varieties, including parent lines, hybrids, processes to genetically modify plants and processes to obtain hybrids.[72]

This broad coverage of patent protection could thus threaten commercial breeding of plants, particularly with broadly drafted patents. Further, if a process by which plants are produced is itself patented (for example, genetic engineering), all plants bred by way of that process would also be covered by the patent. The patent holder is further safeguarded by Article 34.1 which places the burden on a defendant to prove that the product was not obtained by way of that process.[73]

Exceptions to TRIPS Provisions

While TRIPS sets out the minimum standards of intellectual property protection to which every country must conform, some provisions of Article 27 appear to give countries a certain degree of flexibility in regard to implementing its plant patent provisions. These provisions include the lack of a definition as to what constitutes an invention, the exceptions to patentability found in Articles 27.2 and 27.3, and the discretion to decide on the form of plant variety protection. Further flexibilities are found in Article 30 entitled 'Exceptions to Rights Conferred,' which states:

---

71 TRIPS Agreement, above n 68, Article 27.3.

72 Mywish K Maredia, *Application of Intellectual Property Rights in Developing Countries: Implications for Public Policy and Agricultural Research Institutes (2001) Final Draft Submitted to the World Intellectual Property Organization December 2001*, 15, available at http://www.wipo.int/about-ip/en/studies/pdf/study_k_maredia.pdf (last accessed 20 July 2012).

73 Ibid.

> Members may provide limited exceptions to the exclusive rights conferred by a patent, provided that such exceptions do not unreasonably conflict with a normal exploitation of the patent and do not unreasonably prejudice the legitimate interests of the patent owner, taking account of the legitimate interest of third parties.

However, these flexibilities have in fact resulted in inconsistencies in the way TRIPS has been implemented by member states. For example, while most industrialized countries grant patents on life forms, others such as Brazil, Argentina and the Andean Pact countries specifically exclude them in regard to natural substances since they do not involve an invention.[74] Further, the conditions of patentability have not been defined in the Agreement, which may also result in inconsistencies in implementation.[75] The debate regarding plant patent provisions has been further intensified by the contention of developing countries that on the one hand, patents on life forms have moral and ethical implications and, on the other, by the argument that in any event an invention based on naturally occurring matter cannot *ipso facto* be an invention. These positions are reflected in the discussions in the TRIPS Council discussed below.

The TRIPS Debate on Genetic Resources and Traditional Knowledge

The TRIPS debate on genetic resources and traditional knowledge has taken place in the context of two issues. Firstly, Article 27.3(b) states that '[t]he provisions of this subparagraph shall be reviewed four years after the date of entry into force of the WTO Agreement,' which scheduled the review for 1999. This provision was included in part because of the differing views of the US and the European Union (EU) on patenting life forms. While some developed countries had supported the US position that such patents should be permitted, the EU supported the developing countries in holding that plants and animals should not be patentable. This was mainly due to the fact that it faced internal opposition to the patenting of living organisms.[76] The current draft was essentially a compromise, and conditional upon the review.

---

[74] Richard Gerster, 'Patents and Development A Non-Governmental Organization View Prior to Revision of the TRIPS Agreement' (1998) 1(4) *Journal of World Intellectual Property* 605, 612. The Andean Community countries are Bolivia, Colombia, Ecuador, Peru and Venezuela.

[75] For example, see the US definition of prior art in the context of novelty, below Chapter 12, which has given rise to accusations of biopiracy.

[76] Duncan Matthews, *Globalizing Intellectual Property Rights: The TRIPs Agreement* (2002), 58.

Dutfield comments that 1999 may be identified as the year that marked a shift in the balance of power in the WTO as developing countries became more proactive and assertive.[77] The developed countries, on the other hand, were seeking to use the review to raise intellectual property protection standards or 'improve' the protection offered by TRIPS, including by way of eliminating the patentability exceptions and incorporating key provisions of the UPOV Convention into it.

In 2001 the review took on a new dimension under Paragraph 19 of the 2001 Doha Declaration,[78] which stated that the TRIPS Council should also look at the relationship between the TRIPS Agreement and the CBD, at the protection of traditional knowledge and folklore and other relevant new developments that member governments raise in the review of the TRIPS Agreement.[79] A specific issue which arose in this regard was the disclosure of origin or source of biological material and associated traditional knowledge. Given the significance of this question, and in light of the fact that it is also being debated in other fora, this will be discussed in a separate chapter. The other elements of the Article 27.3(b) review and the TRIPS/CBD relationship are discussed in this section.

The Review of Article 27.3 (b)

Article 27.3(b) is the single provision in the Agreement that was made specifically subject to an early review, four years after its entry into force.[80] The topics raised in the TRIPS Council during the review included:[81]

- how to apply the existing TRIPS provisions on whether or not to patent plants and animals, and whether they need to be modified;

---

[77] Graham Dutfield, *Trade, Intellectual Property and Biogenetic Resources: A Guide to the International Regulatory Landscape* (2002) International Centre for Trade and Sustainable Development (ICTSD) and Centre for Policy Dialogue, Bangladesh, 20.

[78] WT/MIN(01)/DEC/1 – Ministerial Conference, Fourth Session, Doha, 9–14 November 2001, *Ministerial Declaration, Adopted on 14 November 2001*, 20 November 2001, paragraph 19.

[79] Ibid.

[80] Correa notes that the review was scheduled within the transitional period for implementation granted to developing countries under Article 65 – Carlos M Correa, 'The TRIPS Agreement: how much room for maneuver?' (2001) 2(1) *Journal of Human Development* 79, 97.

[81] See http://www.wto.org/English/tratop_e/trips_e/art27_3b_background_e.htm (last accessed 20 July 2012).

- the meaning of effective protection for new plant varieties (i.e. alternatives to patenting such as the 1978 and 1991 versions of UPOV). This included the flexibility that should be available, for example to allow traditional farmers to continue to save and exchange seeds that they harvest;
- how to handle moral and ethical issues, e.g. to what extent invented life forms should be eligible for protection;
- how to deal with the commercial use of traditional knowledge and genetic material by those other than the communities or countries where they originate, especially when they are the subject of patent applications; and
- how to ensure that the TRIPS Agreement and the CBD support each other.

The ongoing discussions on the Article 27.3(b) revisions have identified some specific issues for discussion.[82] These are general issues; scope of exceptions to patentability in Article 27.3(b); ethical exceptions to patentability and Article 27.2; and conditions of patentability in Article 27.1 and plant and animal inventions.

While the discussion cannot be reproduced in detail, some significant questions, which were raised, will be identified. The debate also focused to a great extent on questions of terminology, since TRIPS does not provide definitions of key terms and therefore there is considerable flexibility in applying its provisions. The continuing debate in the TRIPS Council illustrates the fact that this has worked largely to the advantage of patent applicants who have benefited from broad interpretations of these terms, which lower the threshold of patent criteria. This debate has been deadlocked along the lines of countries seeking to advance patent protection, and those trying to safeguard their genetic resources from being patented.

General Issues

The general question which goes to the heart of the TRIPS Agreement is whether plant and animal inventions should be patent protected in the first place, and the line between developed and developing countries has been blurred to some extent on this issue.[83] The arguments in favour include that

---

[82] IP/C/W/369/Rev.1 – TRIPS Council, *Review of the Provisions of Article 27.3(B) Summary of Issues Raised and Points Made*, 9 March 2006.

[83] For example the countries which have expressed support of such patent protection include Australia, Canada, China, the EU, Japan, Singapore, Switzerland and the US – see ibid, footnotes 1–5.

plant and animal as well as other biotechnological inventions should be accorded the same treatment as inventions in other fields. Therefore patent protection is necessary to further private sector investment in these activities for the general good. It is also necessary to have international rules in this regard, rather than relying on national laws. Alternatively, those opposed to such patents[84] have argued that patents on life forms 'give rise to a range of concerns, including in regard to development, food security, the environment, culture and morality.'[85]

The TRIPS review also considered the ways in which the mandated review of Article 27.3(b) should take place. The suggestions were grouped into four categories. These categories covered a range of positions from total prohibition on the patenting of life forms to unfettered patenting of plant and animal inventions. The US took the latter position arguing that the exceptions to patentability were unnecessary and it would urge other members also not to avail themselves of the exceptions allowed under Article 27.3(b).[86]

Bangladesh, India and African countries advocated the former position on the basis that Article 27.3(b) should be amended or clarified to prohibit the patenting of all life forms.[87] They also advocated prohibitions on the patenting of inventions based on traditional knowledge or those that violate Article 15 or other provisions of the CBD. These countries further urged that the review should permit unqualified exceptions for exclusions from patentability, along the lines of other WTO agreements that permit Members to take measures in the public interest, including on ethical and moral grounds, and that a universal standard on novelty should be introduced to stop piracy of traditional knowledge and other information. They also suggested that the obligation of developing countries to implement the Article should take effect five years after the review is completed.

The other categories of suggestions fell in between these two positions. One maintained that Article 27.3(b) is well balanced and maintains members' rights to decide whether or not to exclude plants and animals from patentability in the light of their specific national interests and needs. It was suggested that the process should be one of information sharing on how

---

84 Countries particularly vocal in the TRIPS council in this regard have been Brazil, India and the African Group of countries – see documents cited ibid.

85 Ibid.

86 IP/C/M/29 – TRIPS Council, *Minutes of Meeting from 27 to 30 November and 6 December 2000,* 6 March 2001, paragraph 185.

87 IP/C/W/369/Rev.1, above n 82, paragraph 9.

members have implemented the Article nationally.[88] The other suggestion was to retain the exceptions but provide clarifications and definitions of key terms, particularly the differences between plants, animals and micro-organisms.[89] These issues were further debated in the review process as can be seen from the discussions in the following sections.

The review has remained deadlocked. The African Group, expressing concern at the lack of progress, proposed that areas of possible agreement which would reflect an overall balance for all members could include the following points, i.e. members' rights and freedom to determine and adopt appropriate regimes to protect plant varieties by an effective *sui generis* system, including non-commercial use of plant varieties and the system of seed saving and exchange as well as selling among farmers; the TRIPS Agreement and the CBD as well as the FAO Treaty should be implemented in a mutually supportive and consistent manner; the TRIPS Agreement, being a minimum standards agreement, does not prevent members from protecting traditional knowledge, and the importance of documentation of genetic resources and traditional knowledge to help better patent examination.[90]

However, developed country members stood by their position that Article 27.3(b) provided sufficient flexibility for individual members to make exclusions to patentable subject matter, and refused to agree to further flexibilities. The US also emphasized that by the same token members were also free to provide patent protection for such subject matter, stating that it did so. It credited such measures with the subsequent development of its strong biotechnology industry.[91]

Scope of Exceptions to Patentability in Article 27.3(b)

The discussion on this subject has focused for the most part on the terminology used in Article 27.3(b), since what can or cannot be patented will depend on the nuances in these definitions. The clarifications were called for by developing countries which took the position that uncertainty

---

88 Countries which took this view included Australia, Brazil, Canada, China, Korea, the EU, Japan, Mexico, Singapore and Switzerland – ibid, footnotes 10–13.

89 Brazil, India, Peru, Thailand and Zimbabwe advocated this – ibid, footnote 14.

90 IP/C/W/404 – TRIPS Council, *Taking Forward the Review of Article 27.3(B) of the TRIPS Agreement Joint Communication from the African Group*, 26 June 2003.

91 IP/C/M/37/Add.1 – TRIPS Council, *Minutes of Meeting on 17–19 September 2002, Addendum*, 8 November 2002, paragraph 209.

in definitions would cause problems of legal uncertainty in the patenting process. However, as the position taken by countries promoting intellectual property protection for plants indicates, definitional ambiguity necessarily works to the advantage of those in favour of expanding patentable subject matter, and a concrete decision on this issue has not been achieved to date.

The term most in dispute was 'micro-organisms.'[92] Developing countries argued that there was no scientific or other rationale for distinguishing between plants and animals on the one hand, and micro-organisms on the other. Both are living things which can only be discovered and not invented, and should be excluded from patentable subject matter. Clarification was also asked for regarding 'plants and animals,'[93] and 'non-biological and micro-biological processes.'[94] In regard to 'plants and animals' for example, it was suggested that it should be made clear that parts of plants and animals are excludable from patentable subject matter. Further, the word 'plants' is ambiguous and cells, cell lines, genes and genomes should be excluded.

With regard to 'non-biological and micro-biological processes' it was pointed out that although TRIPS makes these processes patentable, it does not define the terms. In the absence of definitions there are artificial distinctions between 'essentially biologically processes' on the one hand, and 'micro-biological and non-biological processes' on the other, which should be removed. It has been argued that micro-biological processes are biological processes and should be treated as such in the TRIPS Agreement.

Responses to the developing country positions included that the issues are complex, and consensus on them would be impossible, that the World Intellectual Property Organization (WIPO) may be the more appropriate forum in which to raise them given the technical expertise available there, and the absence of clear definitions at the international level gives Members the flexibility to implement them at the national level.[95]

Ethical Exceptions to Patentability and Article 27.2

Further clarification was sought by developing countries in regard to ethical exceptions to patentability and Article 27.2. Some of these countries have

---

92 IP/C/W/369/Rev.1, above n 82, paragraph 21. See for example the position of Brazil as stated in IP/C/M/29, above n 86, paragraph 146 and IP/C/W/228 – TRIPS Council, *Review of Article 27.3(b) Communication from Brazil*, 24 November 2000.

93 IP/C/W/369/Rev.1, above n 82, paragraph 20.

94 Ibid, paragraph 26.

95 IP/C/M/37/Add.1, above n 91, paragraph 197.

suggested that some specific concerns should be taken into account, namely, those relating to public health, restrictions on research materials, limitations on competition as in the case of GURTs, human rights, agricultural security, biopiracy, traditional knowledge and farmers' rights, and the concern that the current provisions of Article 27.3(b) did not prevent the abuse of patent systems.[96]

A case was also made for the unconditional prohibition on the patenting of life forms on the grounds that it was unethical and harmful.[97] It was argued that the conditions imposed by Article 27.2 amount to re-defining morality for members, and is meaningless for members that consider patents on life forms 'to be immoral, contrary to the fabric of their society and culture.' These countries therefore suggested that the exception in Article 27.3 (b) should not restrict the exception in Article 27.2.[98] This position has most recently been reiterated by Bolivia which forcefully articulated its opposition to patenting life forms.[99] The submission set out the negative consequences of patenting life forms, including the concentration of the control of life forms in the private sector, particularly a few trans-national corporations in the developed world, which has negative impacts on sectors such as food, agriculture and health. Patents on life forms also enable the rights holders to restrict and even deny access to them, with serious consequences for food security and food sovereignty. This would particularly affect developing countries and their indigenous peoples. Bolivia also noted that such patents would affect the export and commercial activities of developing countries, and cited the patent on the Enola bean,[100] and Monsanto's patent on soya meal which were used to block exports to the US and Europe respectively. Bolivia also challenged the premise that patents are necessary to foster innovation arguing that 'this dominant model of innovation also frustrates innovation, stifles research and development and hinders science from fully benefiting the public.'

The Bolivian submission also pointed out that detrimental impacts of patenting life forms are particularly felt in the area of food and agriculture

---

96 IP/C/W/369/Rev.1, above n 82, paragraph 27.

97 IP/C/W/404, above n 90.

98 Ibid.

99 IP/C/W/554 – TRIPS Council, Article 27.3(B) and the Legalization of Biopiracy: Trends, Impacts and Why it Needs to be Amended, Communication from the Plurinational State of Bolivia, 28 March 2011. See also IP/C/W/545 – TRIPS Council, Review of Article 27.3(B) of TRIPS Agreement, Communication from Bolivia, 26 February 2010, which was withdrawn.

100 Gillian N Rattray, 'The Enola Bean Patent Controversy: Biopiracy, Novelty and Fish-and-Chips' (2002) *Duke Law & Technology Review* 1–8.

as it has given a few corporations dominance over the food chain. These corporations are profiting from the threat of climate change by patenting plants and parts of plants, which could prove detrimental to the very future of humanity.

The counter arguments included that Article 27.2 adequately takes ethical concerns into account insofar as patent law is concerned. Other ethical issues will have to be addressed by other laws such as those on environmental protection, public health and animal welfare. It was also said that Article 27.3 (b) is the result of a carefully negotiated balance and that:

> biological materials are research ingredients and that patents for these materials should be granted as long as the patentability requirements are met and the commercial exploitation of such living organisms does not go against public order.[101]

Conditions of Patentability in Article 27.1 and Plant and Animal Inventions

The way in which the conditions of patentability should be applied in the case of micro-organisms, micro-biological processes, and other plant and animal inventions, was also raised in the TRIPS Council. This issue also surfaced in the context of definitional uncertainties. India argued that the lack of clear definitions of the criteria have resulted in uncertainties in regard to the term 'invention' and the scope of patentable subject matter, and leaving the issue to the discretion of member states is unsuitable.[102] A related issue was the unduly low thresholds adopted by patent offices in meeting patent criteria, which Brazil claimed were undermining the patent system.[103]

One of the most disputed issues raised in regard to patentability criteria was the distinction to be made between discoveries and inventions and the requirement of inventive step.[104] The African Group argued that by providing for the patenting of micro-organisms and micro-biological processes, TRIPS 'violates the basic tenet of patent law,' i.e. that discoveries

---

[101] IP/C/W/369/Rev.1, above n 82, paragraph 33.

[102] IP/C/M/28 – TRIPS Council, *Minutes of Meeting on 21 and 22 September 2000*, 23 November 2000, paragraph 128.

[103] IP/C/W/228, above n 92, paragraph 9.

[104] IP/C/W/369/Rev.1, above n 82, paragraph 36. For a discussion of this issue see Graham Dutfield, 'Sharing the Benefits of Biodiversity. Is there a Role for the Patent System?' (2002) 5(6) *Journal of World Intellectual Property* 899, 905.

are not patentable.[105] A clearer understanding of which stages of research constitute discoveries and which constitute inventions was also necessary. It was alleged that some members classify the discovery of naturally occurring matter or the mere isolation of such matter as inventions, and thereby permit patents on life forms, and such patents do not satisfy the tests of non-obviousness and inventive step.[106]

Developed countries countered these positions by stating that mere discoveries not involving human intervention (including micro-organisms found in nature), are not patentable subject matter. However, naturally occurring matter such as chemical substances or micro-organisms which have been subject to sufficient human intervention such as isolation or purification, would constitute an invention.[107] 'Plants, animals or micro-organisms and other genetic resources would have to be altered by the hand of man or produced by means of a technical process to satisfy the criteria of patentability.'[108]

Developing countries also raised the issue of the criterion of novelty in the context of protecting traditional knowledge.[109] They have argued that some members define novelty so as to exclude information publicly available by way of oral traditions, but outside their national jurisdiction which has led to piracy of genetic resources and traditional knowledge.[110] This issue will be further discussed in Chapter 12.

The Relationship Between the TRIPS Agreement and the CBD

The discussion on the relationship between the TRIPS Agreement and the CBD, including the patentability of genetic materials, was essentially a duplication of the debate which took place in the context of the Article 27.3(b) review. The developing countries continued to reiterate their objections to patenting of genetic material. They argued that this in itself is inconsistent with the CBD because it limits access to this material and can conflict with the sovereign rights of countries over their genetic

---

[105] IP/C/W/163 – TRIPS Council, *Review of the Provisions of Article 27.3(b) Communication from Kenya on behalf of the African Group*, 8 November 1999; IP/C/W/206 - TRIPS Council, *Review of the Provisions of Article 27.3(b) Communication from Mauritius on behalf of the African Group,* 20 September 2000.

[106] IP/C/M/28, above n 102; IP/C/M/29, above n 86; IP/C/W/228, above n 92.

[107] See position of Japan in IP/C/M/29, above n 86, paragraph 151.

[108] IP/C/W/369/Rev.1, above n 82, paragraph 37.

[109] Ibid, paragraph 38; IP/C/M/40 – TRIPS Council, *Minutes of Meeting on 4–5 June 2003*, 22 August 2003.

[110] IP/C/M/28, above n 102, paragraph 126.

resources.[111] They also observed that inconsistencies between the two instruments can arise when countries do not follow closely enough the criteria for patentability as laid down in TRIPS, and grant over broad patents.[112] In this regard they reiterated their concerns that granting patents for micro-organisms amounted to patenting genetic materials in their natural state, and granting of patents over genetic material that has been merely isolated from nature and not modified in any other way gives rise to questions of inconsistency with the CBD. The same questions would arise in relation to the granting of erroneous patents based, directly or indirectly, on genetic resources or traditional knowledge that do not qualify as being novel or inventive.[113]

Developed countries continued to refute these arguments, stating that patents on inventions based on genetic resources do not hinder fulfilment of the sovereignty and prior informed consent and access provisions of the CBD, and repeated their position regarding patenting of micro-organisms. They further took the view that erroneously granted patents were the rare exception rather than the rule, and implementation of post-grant opposition or re-examination proceedings could be used to rectify such errors. They cited the cases of neem and turmeric, where US and EU patent offices had withdrawn patents on these plants on proof of non-compliance with the relevant criteria. Thus they argued that erroneously granted patents are the result of lack of information rather than inherent flaws in the patent system, and procedures such as searchable databases on the knowledge, innovations and practices of indigenous and local communities could be established to improve examination procedures.[114]

Developing countries objected to post-grant counter action, pointing out that this would be a burdensome and expensive process, since holders of genetic resources and traditional knowledge would have to initiate them in

---

[111] IP/C/W/368/Rev.1 – TRIPS Council, *The Relationship between the TRIPS Agreement and the Convention on Biological Diversity, Summary of Issues Raised and Points Made*, 8 February 2006, paragraph 19.

[112] IP/C/W/228, above n 92; IP/C/W/447 – TRIPS Council, *Article 27.3(b), Relationship between the TRIPS Agreement and the CBD and Protection of Traditional Knowledge and Folklore, Communication from Peru*, 8 June 2005.

[113] IP/C/W/368/Rev.1, above n 111, page 10. See below Chapter 12.

[114] Ibid, paragraph 23. See also Shayana Kadidal, 'Subject-Matter Imperialism? Biodiversity, Foreign Prior Art and the Neem Patent Controversy' (1997) 37 *IDEA* 371; John Tustin, 'Traditional Knowledge and Intellectual Property in Brazilian Biodiversity Law' (2006) *Texas Intellectual Property Law Journal* 131, 135.

different jurisdictions. Although misappropriation is an acknowledged problem, only a few patents have been challenged on this basis.[115]

Developing countries also expressed doubts as to the usefulness of searchable databases. They pointed out that in view of the vast store of traditional knowledge such a compilation could not be comprehensive, particularly when such knowledge is based on oral traditions or documented only in local languages. Based on experiences to date, information sharing on such issues has not been effective in preventing misappropriation. Further, use of such databases would be voluntary, and patent examiners cannot be compelled to use them. Another constraint would be the high cost involved. An important issue to also consider is the loss of confidentiality of traditional knowledge which is not in the public domain.[116]

TRIPS-PLUS PROVISIONS IN BILATERAL TREATIES AFFECTING PLANT GENETIC RESOURCES AND TRADITIONAL KNOWLEDGE

Bilateral treaties usually include provisions in regard to plant variety protection which go beyond the level provided for in TRIPS. TRIPS-plus measures in bilateral treaties have eroded the freedom of developing countries to exercise their prerogative under Articles 27.2 and 27.3 to

---

[115] They pointed out that the neem and turmeric patents were successfully challenged owing to the intervention of the government of India and a consortium of non-governmental organizations – IP/C/W/368/Rev.1, above n 111, paragraph 24. See also ETC Group, *Whatever Happened to the Enola Bean Patent Challenge?* (2005) Genotype, 21 December 2005, available at http://www.etcgroup.org/sites/www.etcgroup.org/files/publication/41/01/genotypeenola05.pdf (last accessed 20 July 2012) which describes how the workings of the US patent system has permitted a patent owner to use bureaucratic delays to continue the operation of a patent which had in fact been rejected.

[116] In this regard it is interesting to note that the United States had earlier suggested that such databases would also create sources of information that could be used by potential licensees in order to obtain leads to information on the uses of genetic resources. It was pointed out that this would help to meet the objectives of Article 8(j), i.e. to promote the wider application of the knowledge, innovations and practices of indigenous and local communities and encourage the equitable sharing of the benefits arising from them. It would appear that databases could also serve to promote misappropriation and may potentially be a double-edged sword. IP/C/W/368/Rev.1, above n 111, paragraph 23. See also the discussion in Chapter 12 below.

provide exceptions to plant patentablity. These treaties have been signed by these countries with the US,[117] the EU,[118] the EFTA[119] and Japan.[120]

A common provision in these treaties requires the latter countries to join UPOV 1978 or 1991 by a particular date, or within a given period.[121] As noted above, TRIPS does not require member states to join UPOV, which is merely one option for providing for plant variety protection.

By acceding to UPOV, developing countries eliminate their options to implement *sui generis* systems of plant variety protection which would be suited to their particular needs and circumstances. It has been noted that the level of protection currently being targeted is UPOV for plants per se, and patents for everything else (i.e. plant genes, animals, human genetic sequences and others). Transnational corporations require a homogenous and predictable environment of intellectual property protection, rather than multiple and diverse national systems, and it has been observed that ultimately they would prefer patenting to UPOV. Since provisions on patenting, particularly those restricting the flexibilities in this regard, have also been included in these treaties in all likelihood UPOV too would ultimately become irrelevant.[122] The end result of this process would be the

---

[117] US treaties include those with Bahrain (2004), Cambodia (1996), Singapore (2003) and Peru (2005). The North American Free Trade Association (NAFTA) agreement requires Mexico to take the same measures – GRAIN, *Bilateral agreements imposing TRIPS-plus intellectual property rights on biodiversity in developing countries* (2008), available at http://www.twnside.org.sg/title2/FTAs/Intellectual_Property/IP_and_other_Topics/BilateralAgreementsImposingTRIPS+IPRsOnBiodiversityInDevelop.PDF (last accessed 20 July 2012).

[118] EU treaties include those with Bangladesh (2001), Korea (2001), Syria (2004), Egypt (2001) and Algeria (2002) – GRAIN, ibid. See also South Centre and Centre for International Environmental Law, *Intellectual Property and Development: Overview of Developments in Multilateral, Plurilateral, and Bilateral Fora* (2004), available at http://www.ciel.org/Publications/IP_Update_3Q04.pdf (last accessed 20 July 2012).

[119] EFTA treaties include those with Jordan (2001), Chile (2003), Lebanon (2004) Morocco (2000) and Tunisia (2004) – GRAIN, above n 117.

[120] Treaties between Japan and Indonesia (2007) and Chile (2007) – GRAIN, above n 117. See also GRAIN, *Japan digs its claws into biodiversity through FTAs* (2007), available at http://www.grain.org/Articles_files/atg-11-en.pdf (last accessed 20 July 2012).

[121] EFTA-Jordan FTA (2001), EU-Lebanon FTA (2002), US-Bahrain FTA (2004), Japan-Indonesia FTA (2007), US-Singapore FTA (2003) – GRAIN, above n 117. See also GRAIN, above n 120.

[122] Berne Declaration, Switzerland, '*TRIPS – Plus' through EFTA's back door – How Free Trade Agreements concluded with EFTA-States impose much stronger*

upward harmonization of IPRs on plants at a far higher level than that which could have been achieved in the WTO.[123]

More specific provisions in these treaties seek to ensure that developing country partners provide stringent protection for plant varieties. Such provisions may require, for example, 'adequate and effective patent protection for inventions in all fields of technology on a level similar to that prevailing in the European Patent Convention,' which allows the patenting of transgenic plants and animals.[124] They may also state that '[t]he parties recognise the need to ensure adequate and effective protection of patents on plant varieties and on biotechnological inventions.'[125] Such wording thus eliminates the exclusion from patentability provided in TRIPS. Some agreements specifically ensure that developing countries do not exclude plants and animals from intellectual property protection as permitted under TRIPS.[126]

A common strategy adopted by both the US and the EU is to require the developing country concerned to implement the 'highest international standards' of intellectual property protection.[127] The EU-South Africa FTA for example states that:

> South Africa shall ensure adequate and effective protection for patents on biotechnological inventions. South Africa must also implement the 'highest international standards' of IPR protection and undertake to go beyond TRIPS standards of IPR protection.[128]

The term 'highest international standards' is ambiguous. By definition it assumes that there is no single applicable standard of intellectual property protection. It is also not clear that it is the TRIPS standards which are being

---

rules on developing countries for IPRs on life than the WTO, available at http://www.evb.ch/cm_data/Trips-plus_through_EFTAs_back_door_rev2.pdf (last accessed 20 July 2012).

[123] Yamin, above n 70, 44.

[124] EFTA treaties with Jordan (2001) and Morocco (2000) – GRAIN, above n 117.

[125] EU Cotonou Agreement of 2000 – GRAIN, ibid.

[126] US-Mongolia Agreement on Trade Relations (1991), US-Sri Lanka IPR Agreement (1991) and Free Trade Area of the Americas (negotiations suspended) – GRAIN, ibid.

[127] EFTA/Palestinian Authority FTA (1998), EU-Tunisia FTA (1998), EU/Mexico FTA (2000), EU-Sri Lanka Cooperation Agreement (1995) – GRAIN, ibid.

[128] EU/South Africa FTA of 1999 – GRAIN, ibid.

referred to.[129] While some writers have argued that it would exclude national standards,[130] others have expressed concern that, for example, US standards of patent protection could be cited as the benchmark for what constitutes the highest international standards.[131] Since these are among the most stringent, it would result in raising global standards of intellectual property protection.

Indigenous and local communities' traditional knowledge has also become a feature of bilateral agreements, particularly those currently negotiated by the US.[132] Arguably, the inclusion of traditional knowledge in such treaties is largely due to the debate whether to treat such knowledge as intellectual property which is subject to privatization, or as the collective heritage of communities and peoples which the state should not regulate or meddle with.[133] Developing countries attempt to insert provisions relating to traditional knowledge into bilateral treaties so as to prevent its misappropriation and remedy the current asymmetries in its protection. However, it has been argued that these efforts are generally unsuccessful and the wisdom of this strategy has been questioned.[134] In light of the failure to reach a global agreement on protection of both genetic resources and related traditional knowledge at a multilateral level, there is a danger that including traditional knowledge into bilateral treaties may in fact rebound on developing countries. For example, at the negotiations on the Free Trade Area of the Americas which are currently deadlocked, Andean countries have proposed disclosure of origin, prior informed consent and benefit sharing in relation to all biodiversity related patents granted by the signatories. These proposals have been rejected by the US.[135] Other agreements limit the

---

[129] Carlos M Correa, *Bilateral Investment Agreements: Agents of new global standards for the protection of intellectual property rights?* (2004) 20, available at http://www.grain.org/briefings_files/correa-bits-august-2004.pdf (last accessed 20 July 2012).

[130] Ibid at 20.

[131] GRAIN, *'TRIPS-plus' through the back door – How bilateral treaties impose much stronger rules for IPRs on life than the WTO* (2001) 9, available at http://www.grain.org/system/old/briefings_files/trips-plus-en.pdf (last accessed 20 July 2012).

[132] GRAIN, *FTAS: Trading Away Traditional Knowledge* (2006), available at http://www.grain.org/system/old/briefings_files/fta-tk-03–2006-en.pdf (last accessed 20 July 2012).

[133] Ibid.

[134] Ibid.

[135] Ibid.

implementation of disclosure requirements, thus preventing countries from passing and implementing their own laws in this regard.[136]

CONCLUSION

The debate on the review of Article 27.3(b) and the relationship between TRIPS and the CBD in relation to patentability of genetic material above, illustrates the inherently incompatible positions of the developing and developed countries on IPRs over genetic resources and related traditional knowledge. Developing countries view Article 27.3(b) as facilitating the misappropriation of these resources and enabling exclusive ownership over them to be retained by private interests. Their efforts to engineer a review have been two pronged. One strategy is to restrict the application of patents by pinning down the definitions of key terminology in order to prevent over liberal interpretations of these terms in granting them. The second strategy is the outright demand for a total prohibition on patents on all life forms and on inventions derived from traditional knowledge.

To date neither strategy has met with success in the context of the TRIPS review. The primary objective of the US in terms of the review was to attempt to strengthen intellectual property standards and eliminate the current flexibilities and exceptions contained in Article 27.3(b). The proposals of developing countries to make these standards more flexible and/or to prohibit the patenting of life forms were met with resistance to any amendments to TRIPS, which would restrict the patentability of inventions based upon genetic resources and/or traditional knowledge. Developed countries are taking the position that any country dissatisfied with the status quo is at liberty to address the situation under its national laws, but outside the patent system. They also argue that in the event a patent is granted in violation of the relevant criteria, post-grant measures could be instituted to address the situation.

Developed countries have further stated that the exceptions to patentability, and the flexibility accorded to members to make exceptions to patentable subject matter on specified grounds, constitute adequate safeguards for those countries to prevent misappropriation of their genetic resources and traditional knowledge. Further, contract measures if effectively implemented and enforced would be sufficient to ensure that conditions of prior informed consent and benefit sharing are met. The efficacy of these latter measures will be examined in the next chapter.

---

[136] See for example the US-Dominican Republic-Central America FTA (CAFTA) of 2004 – Ibid.

The strategy of developing countries in the TRIPS Council is also debatable. The simultaneous tabling of two proposals, which on the one hand demand a total prohibition on the patenting of life forms and on the other ask for restrictions on the application of such patents, appears inconsistent and contradictory. While developing countries have, to a large extent, presented a united front in the debates and a stronger opposition than might have been expected, this dual approach must necessarily weaken their position and cloud the issue.

It is argued that these countries should have ideally maintained the position that patents should not apply to life forms since genetic resources critical for human survival should remain in the public domain. There are several grounds on which this position could have been maintained. Some countries did point out the ethical issues involved in patenting life forms. The exceptions in Article 27.2 which permit member states to exclude inventions from patentability on the grounds of *ordre public* or morality, including on the grounds of protecting human, animal and plant life, and to avoid prejudice to the environment, could justifiably be applied to plant varieties. Issues of food security and loss of plant genetic diversity, particularly in the context of climate change, would be relevant in this regard. Developing countries could also have benefited from the definitional ambiguities discussed above, including the question of what constitutes inventions, arguing that life forms cannot amount to an invention. While these issues were raised, they were not adequately sustained. On the other hand, by simultaneously negotiating defensive measures to patent protection of plant varieties they appear to have compromised on their position.

In view of the fact that developing countries themselves have somewhat divergent positions on whether there should be a total prohibition on patenting life forms, they could have alternatively proposed that countries should at least have the individual flexibility to determine the scope of patentability in accordance with their own needs and objectives. Articles 27.2 and 26.3 in fact provide for member states to take their own decisions in this regard and some countries have done so. For example, as cited above, Brazil, Argentina and the Andean Pact countries exclude natural substances from patentability on the grounds that they do not constitute inventions. However, many countries are signing away this flexibility in bilateral agreements entered into with developed countries.

While developed countries have met with resistance in both WIPO and the TRIPS Council they are now using bilateral treaties to undermine the multilateral negotiations and raise standards of plant variety protection on an ad hoc basis. This is a disturbing trend and it remains to be seen whether this strategy will succeed in trumping the multilateral negotiations on this issue. In the meantime developing countries are continuing their attempts to achieve some degree of equity in the use of PGRFA and related traditional knowledge on the basis of positive measures to ensure access and benefit sharing of genetic resources, as well as defensive strategies to prevent their unjustifiable appropriation. These measures are discussed in the following chapters.

9. Access and benefit sharing measures

INTRODUCTION

Developing countries have taken a two-pronged approach in their efforts to protect rights over their natural resources and traditional knowledge, and to prevent their misappropriation. These two approaches have been classified as positive and defensive measures. Positive measures seek to put in place a system which ensures that the countries providing such resources are assured firstly, of a voice in how and to what extent they are accessed, and secondly, of a fair share in the benefits derived from them. This approach is implemented by means of mechanisms which regulate access to genetic resources by those seeking to exploit them for commercial purposes. These measures will be discussed in this chapter. The other form of positive measures to protect such rights is the systems of plant variety protection which countries are required to put in place by the TRIPS Agreement. This is done either by way of patents or by *sui generis* legislation. These systems will be discussed in the next chapter.

Defensive mechanisms of plant variety protection refer to pre-emptive measures intended to prevent the misappropriation and propertization of plant genetic resources for food and agriculture (PGFRA) and traditional knowledge, rather than to enable provider countries to gain any benefits from them. These measures will be considered separately in succeeding chapters.

ACCESS AND BENEFIT SHARING IN INTERNATIONAL LAW

Both the CBD and the FAO Treaty have been informed by the ongoing debate on germplasm flows from the southern to the northern hemisphere, and the inequities of access to, and sharing of the benefits arising out of these resources. A common factor of the two conventions is that they both represent a rejection of the doctrine of the common heritage of humankind as applied to genetic resources and as expressed in the International Undertaking on Plant Genetic Resources. Both treaties seek to establish frameworks for more equitable access to and sharing of these benefits, but they take two different approaches towards this objective. The CBD envisages a bilateral approach to access and benefit sharing (ABS) agreements which requires providers and users of the resources to enter into mutually agreed contracts in this regard. The FAO Treaty alternatively envisages a multilateral system of ABS in regard to the PGRFA specified in it.

ACCESS AND BENEFIT SHARING UNDER THE CBD

The CBD provisions on ABS are framed in very broad terms, contained in Article 15 which reads:

> Recognizing the sovereign rights of States over their natural resources, the authority to determine access to genetic resources rests with the national governments and is subject to national legislation.

The sovereign right of states is however, countered by an obligation to create conditions to facilitate access to such resources for environmentally sound uses by other parties, and to refrain from imposing restrictions that run counter to the objectives of the CBD.[1]

The framework of possible genetic resources access agreements has been addressed in broad terms within Article 15. It states that access where granted, shall be on mutually agreed terms (MATs) and subject to the provisions of the Article. It further states that genetic resources shall be subject to the prior informed consent (PIC) of the contracting parties providing such resources, unless otherwise determined by that party.

Article 15(6) deals with the issue of scientific research based upon genetic resources. Parties carrying out such research are required to ensure the participation of the providing countries and, where possible, must do so within such countries. The results of such research and development and the benefits arising out of the commercial utilization of such resources shall be shared with these countries.

Article 15, while attempting to set out the framework for ABS, is couched in ambiguous and repetitive language. As with many of the provisions of the CBD, its wording is merely exhortatory and it does not set out specific and enforceable rights and obligations. It has been interpreted and developed by

---

[1] *Convention on Biological Diversity* (1992) 31 ILM 818, (hereinafter CBD), Article 15(2): 'Each Contracting Party shall endeavour to create conditions to facilitate access to genetic resources for environmentally sound uses by other Contracting Parties and not to impose restrictions that run counter to the objectives of this Convention.'

the administrative mechanism of the Convention, specifically the Conference of the Parties (CoP) and subsidiary bodies of the CBD, and by national legislation.

THE ELEMENTS OF ACCESS AND BENEFIT SHARING SYSTEMS

The CBD CoP has analyzed the nature of ABS arrangements, pinpointing their salient features. It notes that an ABS agreement:

> consists of the relationships among participants in an ABS arrangement, as well as the formal legal agreement that records their understanding. In addition, the legal and institutional context for the arrangement is also important.[2]

A primary feature of such arrangements is that they involve long-term commitments or obligations since, on the one hand, access seekers will require additional samples as research progresses, and on the other, providers will also need to monitor the use of such resources to ensure that they receive a share of the benefits.

The CoP has also noted the possibility that there will be unequal bargaining power between those negotiating ABS agreements and stated that guidelines and technical assistance may be required in order to redress this imbalance. It has observed that:

> agreements will effectively accomplish the Convention's objectives only if all sides have access to adequate information and technical expertise, as reflected in the requirement for PIC contained in Article 15.[3]

The CoP has also pointed out that ABS agreements need not necessarily be encompassed in a single document, but could be contained in several, at different stages of negotiation. In addition, a single ABS arrangement could include different legal agreements in relation to the same resource, as for instance, with different parties involved in the process. While these arrangements can simplify the process, separate negotiations may also lead to inconsistencies in the agreements.[4]

---

[2] UNEP/CBD/COP/2/13 – CBD CoP, Second Meeting, 6–17 November 1995, Access to Genetic Resources and Benefit-Sharing: Legislation, Administrative and Policy Information, 6 October 1995, paragraph 21.

[3] Ibid, paragraph 22.

[4] Ibid, paragraphs 21–24.

In the light of these factors the various elements of ABS agreements will be analyzed with case studies of such agreements being discussed to determine how the process operates. This book takes the position that ABS agreements, where they exist, do not achieve their stated purposes and, in particular, sharing of the benefits which arise from the commercialization of plants is inadequate or negligible. The case studies also show that appropriation without the consent of those holding the resources, or the knowledge relating to them, continues unabated and there is a lack of accountability in this regard.

Access to Genetic Resources and Traditional Knowledge

The CBD does not contain a definition of the term 'access,' and it has been left to national legislation to define the term.[5] The CoP observes that:

> [n]ational measures might include definition of the term *access*, to clarify what kind of activity constitutes 'access'; for instance, physical taking, collection, exchange, etc.; definitions of the kind of use to which materials 'accessed' will be put, and the scope of the national legislation.

It notes that to date access is generally defined by geographical scope and the scope of the genetic resources covered, rather than the nature of the physical activity that constitutes it.[6]

The CoP has also pointed out that '[m]ost genetic-resource exchanges are not limited to a simple user/provider relationship.' Research and development on genetic resources for scientific and commercial purposes would involve numerous collaborators including academic, governmental, and industrial partners in several countries.[7] Contractual arrangements must be sufficiently flexible to allow for this aspect, and to address the rights and responsibilities of the parties throughout the duration of the contract.

---

[5] The Bonn Guidelines and the Nagoya Protocol do not have a definition either. The Bonn Guidelines on Access to Genetic Resources and Fair and Equitable Sharing of the Benefits Arising Out of their Utilization were adopted in 2002 to 'assist Parties when establishing administrative, legislative or policy measures on access and benefit-sharing and/or when negotiating contractual arrangements for access to genetic resources and benefit-sharing' – http://www.cbd.int/abs/background/ (last accessed 9 July 2012).

[6] UNEP/CBD/COP/3/20 – CBD CoP, Third Meeting, 4–15 November 1996, *Access to Genetic Resources*, 5 October 1996, paragraph 45.

[7] UNEP/COP/CBD/5/8 – CBD CoP, Fifth Meeting, 15–26 May 2000, *Report of the Panel of Experts on Access and Benefit-Sharing*, 2 November 1999, paragraph 67.

In regulating access, parties may also consider the reasons or purposes for which it is required, in particular making a distinction between research that is for scientific or academic purposes on the one hand, and research for commercial purposes on the other. It may not always be possible to make the distinction between the two types of research, as research that had been conducted on the basis that it is academic could be later used for commercial purposes. While over regulation of access may in fact operate to unduly restrict research to the detriment of the country concerned, abuse is also possible when academic research is used for commercial purposes. In spite of the difficulties in drawing boundaries in this regard, some countries have attempted to distinguish between the purposes of research.[8] Further, some laws also make nationality related distinctions, conferring different levels of access upon nationals and non-nationals.[9]

The Panel of Experts on ABS had noted fairly early that while contractual arrangements were the primary mechanism for enabling access, legislation was essential to ensure that they serve national policy goals and ensure the fulfillment of the ABS provisions of the CBD. It has observed that '[s]uch legislation should be clear and simple, to allow flexibility, transparency and reduce transaction costs, and will need to be tailored to the circumstances of individual countries,' and a legal framework should clarify property rights, including ownership of genetic resources, knowledge and innovations, and conservation and biosafety.[10] Such clarity and simplicity will be facilitated by receiving countries which take legislative, administrative, and policy measures to ensure to providers that the resources will be used in accordance with the CBD. The Panel observed that the CoP may wish to consider developing international guidelines in this regard.

The Nagoya Protocol is now the definitive document addressing questions of access and its provisions are weighted towards requiring provider countries to put the necessary legislation in place so as to facilitate it. It does not define the term 'access' although the Preamble recognizes 'the importance of providing legal certainty with respect to access to genetic resources and the fair and equitable sharing of benefits arising from their utilization.' Articles 6 and 7 deal with access to genetic resources and traditional knowledge respectively. Article 6 places the onus on developing countries to enact legislative, administrative and policy measures if it requires prior

---

8 UNEP/CBD/COP/3/20, above n 6, paragraph 44.

9 UNEP/CBD/COP/4/23 – CBD CoP, Fourth Meeting, 4–15 May 1998, Review of National, Regional and Sectoral Measures and Guidelines for the Implementation of Article 15, Note by the Executive Secretary, 19 February 1998, p. 11.

10 UNEP/COP/CBD/5/8, above n 7, paragraphs 94–95.

informed consent. Such an obligation was not required by the CBD, and as Nijar points out it seems to imply that where such measures are absent access can take place without consent, thus condoning biopiracy.[11] Given the fact that many developing countries do not have access laws in place, such a requirement puts such countries at a disadvantage. Article 6 also sets out in detail the elements of such measures, all of which are intended to facilitate access by the provider country. These provisions constrain the discretion of provider countries to enact such measures in their own best interests, and suited to their particular circumstances. For example, subsection 3(b) which requires 'fair and non-arbitrary rules and procedures' on access, would potentially restrict the right of countries to give different levels of access to different applicants, or for different purposes. Ultimately, such decision must rest with each country and cannot be governed by the Protocol.[12]

The onus placed upon provider countries to facilitate access to genetic resources is reinforced in Article 8 entitled 'Special Considerations.' Subsection (a) requires each Party, in developing and implementing its ABS legislation and regulations, to promote and encourage research, which contributes to the conservation and sustainable use of biodiversity, particularly in developing countries. It also requires simplified measures on access for non-commercial research purposes, 'taking into account the need to address a change of intent for such research.' As has been noted above, some countries have attempted to draw a distinction between non-commercial and commercial research, with different procedures and levels of access for the two categories, and this provision restricts this discretion. Subsection (c) of this Article also requires parties to 'consider the importance of genetic resources for food and agriculture and their special role in food security.' While it is important that the critical nature of PGRFA has been acknowledged in the Protocol, the wording of this provision is ambiguous and does not indicate how PGRFA should be accessed in this context. The opportunity to provide for effective benefit sharing of these resources has been missed.[13]

---

[11] Gurdial Singh Nijar, 'The Nagoya Protocol on Access and Benefit Sharing of Genetic Resources: Analysis and Implementation Options for Developing Countries', South Centre Research Papers 36, March 2011.

[12] Ibid.

[13] Article 8(b) must be viewed in the context of access to pathogens which have been provided to the World Health Organization by developing countries and their complaints that no benefit sharing has ensued for the vaccines developed from them. For a discussion on this point see Nijar above n11.

The onus placed on provider countries to facilitate access is further reinforced by Article 13 which requires them to designate national focal points and a competent national authority on access and benefit sharing. This must be done no later than the date of entry into force of the Protocol for that country. The focal point must make available all the necessary information on access measures, and the competent authority must grant access, issue written evidence that access requirements have been complied with and advise on the procedures for obtaining prior informed consent and entering into MATs. Parties are required to provide the Access and Benefit Sharing Clearing House[14] with all information relevant to the implementation of the Protocol, in particular, information on ABS measures and national focal points and competent authorities. The information also specifically includes permits or their equivalents as evidence of prior informed consent and MATs.

While these provisions are heavily weighted in favour of simplifying access procedures for the benefit of user countries, they must be contrasted with Article 15 of the Protocol which sets out the corresponding obligations of the latter countries in accessing these resources. The wording of this Article is merely exhortatory and user countries are only required to take 'appropriate, effective and proportionate' measures to ensure that genetic resources utilized within their boundaries have been accessed as required by the provider countries and that situations of non-compliance are addressed. User countries are required 'as far as possible and as appropriate' to co-operate in cases of alleged violations of these requirements. The weak wording of these provisions does not address the concerns of provider countries in regard to biopiracy. Further, there is no provision in the Protocol to designate focal points or competent authorities in user countries that would be responsible for ensuring that the entities functioning within their jurisdictions comply with the requirements and procedures of providing countries.

Prior Informed Consent (PIC)

Article 15(5) of the CBD simply states that 'access to genetic resources shall be subject to prior informed consent of the Contracting Party providing such resources, unless otherwise determined by that Party.' It does

[14] Article 14.

not contain an explanation or definition of the term.[15] The CoP has interpreted PIC to mean:

> consent to an activity that is given after receiving full disclosure regarding the reasons for the activity, the specific procedures the activity would entail, the potential risks involved, and the full implications that can realistically be foreseen.[16]

The CoP has observed that PIC is the trigger to benefit sharing, and the requirement to obtain it affords an opportunity for those whose consent is sought to reach MATs with those who seek access, and to stipulate the benefits to be shared.[17] However, it has also taken the position that while PIC is essential for access, Parties must endeavour to facilitate access, and thereby ensure the continued exchange of genetic resources. National measures must therefore strike a balance between the need to ensure fair and equitable benefit sharing on MATs, with the need to ensure that procedures facilitating PIC and benefit sharing do not obstruct such access.[18] This position is now reinforced in the Nagoya Protocol. The question is whether the requirement of PIC in the CBD does in fact ensure that genetic resources and traditional knowledge are obtained in a fair and equitable manner or whether it is merely a procedural device to give legitimacy to the acquisition and use of such resources and knowledge.[19]

---

[15] Other terms used are 'free, prior, informed consent' and 'advance informed agreement' – Indigenous Peoples Rights Act of 1997 of the Philippines; Joji Carino, 'Indigenous Peoples' Right to Free, Prior, Informed Consent: Reflections on Concepts and Practice' (2005) *Arizona Journal of International and Comparative Law* 19; Amanda Wolf, 'The Emergence and Implementation of the Advance Informed Agreement Procedure' in Philippe G Le Prestre (ed), *Governing Global Biodiversity: the evolution and implementation of the Convention on Biological Diversity* (2002), Chapter 6.

[16] UNEP/CBD/TKBD/1/2 – Workshop on Traditional Knowledge and Biological Diversity, 24–28 November 1997, *Traditional Knowledge and Biological Diversity*, 18 October 1997, paragraph 108.

[17] UNEP/CBD/COP/4/22 – CBD CoP, Fourth Meeting, 4–15 May 1998, Addressing the Fair and Equitable Sharing of the Benefits Arising out of Genetic Resources: Options for Assistance to Developing Country Parties to the Convention on Biological Diversity, 9 February 1998, paragraph 16–17.

[18] UNEP/CBD/COP/3/20, above n 6, paragraph 51. See also the Bonn Guidelines, Section 26.

[19] Donna Dickenson, 'Consent Commodification and Benefit-Sharing in Genetic Research' (2004) 4(2) Developing World Bioethics 109. The author discusses this issue in the context of human genetic research but it is equally applicable to genetic resources.

Who Gives Consent?

As noted by the CoP, the first step in defining PIC is to determine who has the right and the authority to give consent. This would depend on the property regime applicable to the resource in question.[20] At this point it is relevant to examine the ways in which the CBD, the Nagoya Protocol and national legislation address the issue and identify the stakeholders from whom PIC is required, as well as the methods of implementing the requirement. The wording of Article 15(5) of the CBD indicates that the contracting party has the discretion to determine all aspects of PIC including whether it can be dispensed with. This situation remains unchanged in the Nagoya Protocol.[21] It must then be determined who is encompassed within the phrase 'contracting party' in this context. In light of the fact that international agreements are entered into by and between states, and the CBD emphasizes state sovereignty over natural resources, it would appear that it is the state and its representative institutions which are covered by the term.

In practice however, the situation is more complex. Given the involvement in the issue of indigenous peoples, farmers and other communities, non-governmental organizations and citizens, the term 'contracting party' would, in reality, require a wider definition and inclusion of stakeholders, rights holders and beneficiaries within the state in regard to the commercial and other uses of genetic resources. As the CoP notes:

> [t]o date, Parties have defined a two-tiered set of authorities: (a) the Contracting Party, at the national level; and (b) at the local level, private individuals and groups, including indigenous and local communities.[22]

The CoP has further stated that while the PIC of Contracting Parties is essential, access legislation in different countries:

> should take into account the interest of different stakeholders, including local communities, indigenous groups, protected-area management boards, and owners, holders and administrators of land.

Other stakeholders whose PIC may be required include:

> departments of environment, development, science and technology, trade and industry, health, education and tourism in central or state Governments, regional

---

20 UNEP/CBD/TKBD/1/2, above n 16, paragraph 109.

21 See Article 6.

22 UNEP/CBD/TKBD/1/2, above n 16, paragraph 109.

> and local offices of Government, protected-area management boards, municipalities, *ex situ* collections, universities and research centres, and non-governmental and intergovernmental organizations.[23]

While the interests of all the groups cited above are important, it is the rights of indigenous peoples and local communities, which have been extensively addressed. Both the CBD CoP and national/regional measures enacted in the last decade have dealt with the issue of these groups as stakeholders whose PIC is an essential requirement for access to genetic resources and traditional knowledge.[24] This element has been reinforced by the human rights approach which emphasizes the rights of indigenous peoples to participatory decision making.[25] The CoP has also linked Articles 15 and 8(j) of the CBD in this regard noting that:

> [g]iven the connections between genetic resources and local and indigenous knowledge and innovations which has been recognised in Decision III/15, it is important that Article 8(j) is implemented in conjunction with Article 15 of the Convention. For example, procedures of prior informed consent as required in Article 15.5 might also provide that access seekers must obtain the informed consent, the approval, of local and indigenous communities.[26]

The Nagoya Protocol has addressed the question of who should give prior informed consent in several Articles. Article 6(2) states that '[i]n accordance with domestic law, each Party shall take measures, as appropriate, with the aim of ensuring that the prior informed consent or approval and involvement of indigenous and local communities is obtained for access to genetic resources where they have the established right to grant access to such resources.' However, this requirement is diffused by the fact that it must be 'in accordance with domestic law' and only 'where they have the established right to grant access to such resources,' thus reinforcing the control of the state over these resources. The Article also requires prior informed consent *or* approval and involvement of these groups. Article 7

---

[23] UNEP/CBD/COP/4/22, above n 17, paragraphs 18–19.

[24] For a comprehensive study of national and regional measures see Kathryn Garforth, Isabel López Noriega, Jorge Cabrera Medaglia, and Gabriel R Nemogá, *Overview of the National and Regional Implementation of Access to Genetic Resources and Benefit Sharing Measures* (2005), available at http://cisdl.org/public/docs/news/CISDL_ABS_Imp_Study_final.pdf (last accessed 9 July 2012).

[25] See for example *Convention Concerning Indigenous and Tribal Peoples in Independent Countries* (ILO No. 169), 72 ILO Official Bulletin 59 (entered into force 5 September 1991) (hereinafter ILO Convention 169) and the *UN Declaration on the Rights of Indigenous Peoples* 46 ILM 1013, 13 September 2007.

[26] UNEP/CBD/TKBD/1/2, above n 16, paragraph 30.

deals with access to traditional knowledge associated with genetic resources and this provision too requires prior informed consent *or* approval and involvement. The wording of the phrase is ambiguous and it is unclear whether the consent of these groups is essential or whether their mere involvement in the process is sufficient to satisfy the requirement. Further, both Articles require states parties to take measures 'as appropriate' to ensure that the indigenous and local communities have granted PIC for such access. The Protocol clearly intends that it is the state party that will have the final authority to grant consent.

A more problematic situation arises in instances where the same genetic resources or traditional knowledge is found *in situ* in more than one party's territory. Article 11 of the Protocol requires those parties to co-operate as appropriate with the involvement of the indigenous and local communities 'with a view to implementing the objective of the Protocol.' The term 'with the involvement' is ambiguous and open to interpretation but indicates that the consent of these communities is not essential.

Although this matter arose prior to the promulgation of the Nagoya Protocol, a relevant example of the problems arising in regard to obtaining prior informed consent in transboundary situations is that of the Hoodia plant of the San people of the Kalahari Desert in Southern Africa. The Hoodia is a plant used by the San people as a drink substitute and an appetite suppressant, among other things.[27] In 1998 the Council for Scientific and Industrial Research (CSIR), a South African state research institute, signed a licensing agreement with Phytopharm, a British company, granting it an exclusive worldwide licence to manufacture and market products related to the plant and to exploit the patents which had been granted to CSIR in relation to it. Phytopharm later patented P57, the appetite suppressing ingredient in the Hoodia plant. It also entered into an agreement with the pharmaceutical company Pfizer to commercialize the drug.

The prior informed consent of the San for the use of the plant or the knowledge they possessed regarding it had not been obtained, and their contribution to the possible benefits of the plant was not acknowledged. Efforts by non-governmental organizations and media publicity brought the matter to light, and finally compelled the CSIR to enter into benefit sharing agreements with them. This included recognition of the San as the originators of the ethnobotanical knowledge related to the plant.

---

27 Rachel Wynberg, 'Rhetoric, Realism and Benefit-Sharing. Use of Traditional Knowledge of Hoodia Species in the Development of an Appetite Suppressant' (2004) 7(6) *Journal of World Intellectual Property* 851.

Two important issues arose out of this situation. The first, related to identifying rights holders. The San people are dispersed across three countries, namely, South Africa, Namibia and Botswana. Since the CSIR was reluctant to negotiate with groups outside South Africa, the South African San Council was mandated to negotiate for all groups. A related issue which also arose was the fact that non-San communities which had also occupied areas in which Hoodia was found and who were also possibly aware of and used its properties, would be excluded from the process. It was also possible that not all groups of the San people had historically used the plant, but given their history of displacement, it was impossible for this to be confirmed.[28] Therefore the questions which arose were who had knowledge of the uses of the plant, and consequently who had jurisdiction to give prior informed consent.

The Nagoya Protocol now supposedly resolves such situations by the requirement in Article 11 that the relevant parties 'shall endeavor to co-operate', 'with the involvement' of the indigenous and local communities. This weak terminology paves the way for one state party out of several to give consent and further, will potentially eliminate the need for the informed consent of all the communities in question.

Article 10 of the Protocol also calls for parties to consider the need for a global multilateral benefit sharing mechanism to address issues of genetic resources and traditional knowledge found in a transboundary context where it is not possible to grant or obtain prior informed consent. While the modalities of such a mechanism would have to be worked out by the CoP, it is important to ensure that it is not used as a means to circumvent the requirement of PIC.

The Subject Matter of the PIC Process

The next question in regard to prior informed consent is over what specifically do the stakeholders have rights, and to what is their consent required? This question relates in particular to indigenous and local communities in the context of whether their PIC is required only when their traditional knowledge is accessed, or whether they also have rights in regard to genetic resources. The CBD has not addressed this question, although the Bonn Guidelines appear to take a broader view of such rights, recognizing:

---

28 Ibid.

established legal rights of indigenous and local communities associated with genetic resources being accessed or where traditional knowledge associated with these genetic resources is being accessed … [29]

The Nagoya Protocol gives a limited recognition to indigenous and local communities' rights over genetic resources, stating in Article 6 that parties shall take measures as appropriate to obtain the PIC of such communities where they have the established right to grant access to such resources. Therefore parties may determine firstly, whether there is such an established right and further, whether the measures taken to obtain such PIC are appropriate.

Some of the early legal and other measures on ABS emerged from countries such as the Philippines[30] and Costa Rica[31] and more recently South Africa[32] and India.[33] Regional measures include the Andean Pact Decision 391,[34] the OAU Model Law[35] and the draft ASEAN Framework Agreement on Access to Biological and Genetic Resources.[36] Although these laws are broadly similar, they vary significantly in their requirements of PIC, both as regards those who are entitled to grant or withhold it, and the extent to which it is applicable. While they unanimously recognize the sovereign rights of the state over biological/genetic resources,[37] in some countries these rights are not limited to the state per se, and the interests of

---

[29] Bonn Guidelines – Article 31.

[30] Executive Order No. 247 – Prescribing Guidelines and Establishing a Regulatory Framework for the Prospecting of Biological and Genetic Resources, Their By-products and Derivatives, for Scientific and Commercial purposes, and for Other Purposes (1995).

[31] Biodiversity Law (1998).

[32] National Environmental Management: Biodiversity Act, 2004.

[33] Biological Diversity Act, 2002. For an analysis of this Act see Rajesh Sagar, 'Intellectual Property, Benefit-Sharing and Traditional Knowledge. How Effective Is the Indian Biological Diversity Act, 2002?' (2005) 8(3) *Journal of World Intellectual Property* 383.

[34] Andean Community Decision 391: Common Regime on Access to Genetic Resources (1996).

[35] African Model Legislation for the Protection of the Rights of Local Communities, Farmers and Breeders, and for the Regulation of Access to Biological Resources (2000).

[36] (2000 draft).

[37] Biological Diversity Act of India – Preamble, Paragraph 4; ASEAN Framework Agreement – Article 1; OAU Model Law – Preamble; Biodiversity Law of Costa Rica – Article 2; Andean Community Decision 391 – Article 5.

defined groups and citizens within it are also acknowledged. The Philippines Executive Order 247, the OAU Model Law[38] and the draft ASEAN Framework Agreement[39] acknowledge the rights and interests of a range of stakeholders including citizens as a whole, indigenous peoples and local communities, farming communities, plant breeders and women.

Even where the rights of stakeholders are acknowledged, national laws may differ markedly on the requirement of PIC. While some require PIC in relation to both genetic resources and traditional knowledge, others give indigenous and local communities rights only over the latter. The OAU Model Law is among the strongest in recognizing the 'inalienable rights of local communities including farming communities over their biological resources, knowledge and technologies.'[40] Similarly the Philippines Indigenous Peoples Rights Act of 1997 permits access to biological and genetic resources and indigenous knowledge only with the PIC of the communities concerned, in accordance with their customary law.[41] The Andean Pact Decision 391 on the other hand is clear that jurisdiction over natural resources lies with the State, and limits the rights of 'native, Afro-American and local communities' to their 'know-how, innovations and traditional practices.'[42] The Indian Biodiversity Act also reserves the authority to grant

---

[38] OAU Model Law. The Preamble acknowledges that 'the State and its people exercise sovereign and inalienable rights over their biological resources,' and states that 'the rights of local communities over their biological resources, knowledge and technologies' are '*a priori* rights which take precedence over rights based on private interests.' The Preamble also states that 'it is the duty of the State and its people to regulate access to biological resources and to community knowledge and technologies,' thus equating the role of the State with citizens. It goes on to recognize the necessity of providing 'adequate mechanisms for guaranteeing the just, equitable and effective participation of its citizens in the protection of their collective and individual rights and in making decisions which affect its biological and intellectual resources as well as the activities and benefits derived from their utilization.' According to Part I, one of the specific objectives of the legislation is to 'recognize, protect and support the inalienable rights of local communities including farming communities over their biological resources, knowledge and technologies.'

[39] The Agreement, while respecting the sovereignty of each member state of its biological and genetic resource, is aware of the fundamental principle that the PIC of its indigenous peoples and local communities is a necessary precondition to access.

[40] OAU Model Law, Part 1 – Objectives.

[41] Section 35. For a discussion of this Act see T Fitschen, 'Protecting indigenous peoples and communities in the Philippines: the Indigenous Peoples Rights Act of 1997' (1998) 7(2) *International Journal of Cultural Property* 526.

[42] Article 7.

consent to the National and State Biodiversity Boards and does not give jurisdiction over this issue to local communities.[43]

Conclusion

The CoP has stated that PIC is the central procedural device enabling parties to fulfil the provisions of Article 15. It has further stated that parties must endeavor to facilitate access, and that national procedures including PIC should not block such access. In examining the way in which the requirement of PIC is implemented, the question which arises is whether it achieves the substantive objectives of fair and equitable access to genetic resources, or whether it is in fact merely a procedural device to legitimize what is inherently unjust and unethical. In view of the fact that there is more often than not, an imbalance between the parties seeking and providing such access, the equity of contracts based upon this consent would often be open to question. While the CoP may be attempting to strike a balance between divergent interests in genetic resources, in the light of centuries of free and unimpeded access to both genetic resources and traditional knowledge, and the current dominance of the IPR regime, it fails to acknowledge the inherent imbalance in the process.

At the national level the fundamental question in regard to PIC is who should have the authority to grant access and to what. While the CoP has recognized that there is a two-tiered set of authorities who can give consent, the involvement of indigenous and local communities or even the general public would, in reality, depend on the political environment of the state in question. The Nagoya Protocol has now unequivocally taken the position that the point of reference for PIC is the state and obtaining the consent of indigenous and local communities will be at state discretion. States have taken differing positions on this issue in regard to genetic resources and traditional knowledge, and in some instances communities have no rights of consent even over the latter. Under the circumstances it has again to be questioned whether PIC as a procedural device of implementing ABS arrangements, achieves the objective of equity where such communities or the general public are concerned.

Mutually Agreed Terms (MATs)

Article 15(4) of the CBD states that '[a]ccess, where granted, shall be on mutually agreed terms and subject to the provisions of this Article.' MATs

---

[43] Chapter 5.

essentially refer to the contract by which ABS measures are specified. Contractual arrangements are the norm in ABS agreements in view of the range and diversity of circumstances and actors involved in regard to each resource for which access is sought, necessitating case-by-case negotiations of terms and conditions. National and regional measures to govern them may also provide guidelines in this regard. While PIC is important at the point of determining whether a user can obtain access to genetic resources or traditional knowledge initially, the issue of MATs arises in the context of the conditions which determine the benefit sharing arrangements in relation to such resources. The phrase is premised upon the supposition that the contract in question has been negotiated by both parties operating on an equal footing, and its terms have been accepted by both.

The Bonn Guidelines have stated that PIC is linked to the requirement of MATs.[44] They have dealt with this topic in some detail and they set out the basic requirements for MATs and an indicative list of typical agreed terms.[45] The Guidelines have also noted that '[m]utually agreed terms could cover the conditions, obligations, procedures, types, timing, distribution and mechanisms of benefits to be shared. These will vary depending on what is regarded as fair and equitable in light of the circumstances.'[46]

The question in regard to contractual arrangements based upon MATs is whether they can in fact guarantee at least some degree of equity in ABS agreements. The concept presupposes that the process would achieve this objective, but this would depend on the actual parity of bargaining power and the capacity of the parties concerned. The need to negotiate each agreement on a case-by-case basis would have its pros and cons. The pros include flexibility to bargain for the most advantageous benefits in each instance. However, this flexibility would most likely benefit the party which holds the advantage in bargaining capacity. On the other hand, the ad hoc nature of such a process would also contribute to uncertainty in regard to access procedures and the identity of stakeholders, both state and non-state, from whom PIC is required.

Of particular concern to user parties are the high transaction costs which may be associated with the lack of legal and institutional certainty in the

---

44 Article 35.

45 Bonn Guidelines – Section IV (D). See also UNEP/CBD/COP/2/13, above n 2, paragraphs 90–92 and UNEP/CBD/COP/3/20, above n 6, paragraphs 46–50 and UNEP/CBD/TKBD/1/2, above n 16, paragraphs 103–106.

46 Bonn Guidelines – Article 45. The Guidelines also caution that 'Nothing in these Guidelines should be interpreted as affecting the rights and obligations relating to genetic resources arising out of the mutually agreed terms under which the resources were obtained from the country of origin' (Article I(6)).

process. High transaction costs may diminish the value of genetic resources as it decreases interest in their access and use. To avoid these effects the CoP has advocated a number of measures including legal certainty and clarity in regard to Governments' requirements for contractual arrangements, identification of national institutions and mechanisms to facilitate the process, umbrella arrangements under which repeat access could be facilitated, the use of standardized Material Transfer Agreements,[47] property stakeholder participation and provisions on use obligations.[48]

The Nagoya Protocol also seeks to simplify the process of arriving at MATs, requiring each party to encourage, as appropriate, the development, update and use of sectoral and cross-sectoral model contractual clauses for MATs. The CoP will periodically take stock of these clauses.[49] It has also indicated some terms which may be included in the contracts, namely (i) A dispute settlement clause; (ii) Terms on benefit sharing, including in relation to intellectual property rights; (iii) Terms on subsequent third-party use, if any; and (iv) Terms on changes of intent, where applicable. As Nijar has noted, the latter two clauses are of particular importance and may need to be re-negotiated if the need arises.[50] In addition, it requires parties to designate national focal points and competent national authorities to provide information and advice on PIC and MATs. The Protocol thus clearly puts the burden on provider countries to offer an efficient and low cost system to facilitate access to genetic resources and traditional knowledge for user countries.

Notwithstanding these attempts to standardize and facilitate the negotiation of MATs, questions have been raised as to whether these contracts are being entered into at all, and it has been noted that very few benefit sharing

---

47 Material Transfer Agreements (MTA) have been described as 'special types of contracts routinely used by the biotechnology industry and academic researchers in Northern countries to facilitate the sharing of biological research material for mutual gain. MTAs define the rights and obligations of all parties, including third parties, involved in a transfer of biological material. MTAs can be relatively concise documents, yet sufficiently flexible to be useful in a large number of research and development scenarios' – Daniel M Putterman, 'Model Material Transfer Agreements for Equitable Biodiversity Prospecting' (1996) 7 *Colorado Journal of International Environmental Law and Policy* 149, 150 and also for a discussion on possible terms of MTAs to ensure equity in ABS arrangements. See also UNEP/CBD/COP/6/6 – CBD CoP, Sixth meeting, 8–19 April 2002, *Report of the Ad Hoc Open-Ended Working Group on Access and Benefit-Sharing*, 31 October 2001 at p. 26 for suggestions for a standardized MTA.

48 UNEP/COP/CBD/5/8, above n 7, paragraphs 50–73.

49 Article 19 entitled 'Model Contractual Clauses.'

50 Nijar, above n 11, 4.

case studies have been documented.[51] In a study published by the Edmonds Institute,[52] the researcher has recorded a range of instances where genetic resources and traditional knowledge from Africa have been appropriated and/or patented by private corporations. In practically all instances the researcher has indicated that he was unable to find an ABS agreement relating to the acquisition. Even where such agreements have been documented, the question is whether they are equitable, and some examples are discussed below.

Fair and Equitable Sharing of Benefits

ABS arrangements for the use of genetic resources must necessarily be fair and equitable. The CBD refers to benefit sharing in several Articles in the context of genetic resources and TK, as well as in relation to the results of research and development, and technologies arising from their commercial or other uses.[53] The CoP has in fact interpreted the CBD as 'an instrument to promote the equitable exchange of access to genetic resources and associated knowledge for finance, technology and participation in research.'[54]

Although fair and equitable benefit sharing lies at the core of the CBD, the terms 'fair,' 'equitable,' 'benefit' or 'sharing' are not defined in the CBD, the Bonn Guidelines or the Nagoya Protocol. The CoP has noted that the lack of definitions and the 'use of language which softens any obligations,' give all parties considerable leeway in interpreting and implementing the provisions. The CoP also points out that given the multiplicity of stakeholders involved in the ABS process who are affected by the activities in question, and the complexity of the issue, benefit sharing can effectively succeed only when tailored to the specificity of each situation. Therefore

---

51 Elpidio V Peria, 'Benefit-Sharing from the Use of Genetic Resources: Real Myths or Mythical Realities?' in Beth Burrows (ed), *The Catch: Perspectives in Benefit Sharing* (The Edmonds Institute in co-operation with Third World Network 2008). See the website of the CBD at http://www.cbd.int/abs/pre-protocol/ (last accessed 9 July 2012) at 6 June 2008. See also Sarah Laird and Rachel Wynberg 'Access and Benefit Sharing in practice: Trends in Partnerships Across Sectors' Secretariat of the Convention on Biological Diversity', Technical Series No. 38 (2008).

52 Jay McGown, 'Out of Africa: Mysteries of Access and Benefit Sharing' (2006) Edmonds Institute in co-operation with African Centre for Biosafety, available at http://www.newscastmedia.com/4investors_africa.pdf (last accessed 9 July 2012).

53 CBD – Preamble, Pararaphs 12 and 20 and Articles 1, 8(j) and 15(7).

54 UNEP/CBD/COP/3/Inf.53 – Fair and Equitable Sharing of Benefits Arising from the Use of Genetic Resources, 4–15 November 1996, p. 2.

parties should be guided less by obligations under the CBD, and rather by the rationale for benefit sharing, i.e. equity and the conservation and sustainable use of biodiversity.[55]

Fair and Equitable

There is no absolute criterion for determining what is fair and equitable in the context of ABS and this issue necessarily depends upon the stakeholders involved. It is in such situations that the participation of non-state stakeholders is particularly important. PIC and MATs are obviously essential prerequisites for ensuring that ABS arrangements are fair and equitable. However, as argued above, in order for stakeholders to the agreement to ensure equity in sharing, there must also be equality of bargaining power which is essential at both national and international levels.

What Constitutes Benefits?

The CBD does not provide any indication as to what constitutes benefits, the mechanisms by which they should be shared or who should receive them. The Bonn Guidelines contain a list of possible benefits which are reproduced in the Nagoya Protocol. Both the CoP and national legislation have also elaborated on the more general benefits that may be claimed, both monetary/non-monetary and direct/indirect. Monetary benefits include various forms of fees, royalties and other payments. They could also include joint ownership of relevant IPRs. Non-monetary benefits could include education and training, institutional capacity building, contributions to the local economy and food and livelihood security benefits.[56] However, the range of potential benefits would vary across countries, stakeholders, circumstances, needs and other criteria and compiling an exhaustive list would not be possible.

Benefit Sharing Mechanisms

Article 15 (7) of the CBD requires Contracting Parties to take legislative, administrative or policy measures, with the aim of sharing in a fair and

---

55 Ibid, p. 3.

56 See for example UNEP/CBD/COP/2/13, above n 2, Section E and UNEP/COP/CBD/5/8 – CBD CoP, Fifth Meeting, 15–26 May 2000, *Report of the Panel of Experts on Access and Benefit-Sharing,* 2 November 1999, paragraphs 74–90. See also UNEP/CBD/COP/3/Inf.53, above n 54, and Appendix II of the Bonn Guidelines.

equitable way the results of research and development and the benefits arising from the commercial and other utilization of genetic resources with the contracting party providing such resources. Such sharing shall be upon mutually agreed terms. This is reiterated in Article 5 of the Nagoya Protocol. However, such terms would be of no avail in the absence of effective compliance measures by user countries.

Nijar comments that:

> For developing countries, compliance was at the 'core of the core' of the Protocol. Recurring reports of cases of biopiracy underlined their concern of the continuing expropriation of their resources without any sharing of benefits. At all stages of the negotiations, developing countries maintained that weak compliance provisions would mean an insignificant and unacceptable Protocol.[57]

However, their expectations that the Protocol would address these concerns did not materialize.

The Nagoya Protocol contains provisions for compliance which require user parties to take appropriate, effective and proportionate legislative, administrative and policy measures to ensure that genetic resources utilized within their jurisdiction comply with PIC and MAT requirements of the provider parties. User parties shall also take 'appropriate, effective and proportionate' measures to address issues of non-compliance and shall '*as far as possible and as appropriate*' (emphasis added) co-operate in case of alleged violations of these requirements.[58] The desultory wording of this provision falls far short of the specific measures that provider countries have been urging for violations of PIC and MAT requirements. These measures include revocation of patents.[59]

In regard to the recipients of the benefits, the Protocol clearly identifies such recipients as states parties. Article 5 of the Protocol states that such benefits 'shall be shared in a fair and equitable way with the Party providing such resources that is the country of origin of such resources or a Party that has acquired the genetic resources in accordance with the Convention.' In regard to indigenous and local communities, it is left to the party concerned to take legislative, administrative and policy measures, as appropriate, to ensure that benefits arising from the utilization of genetic resources are shared with such communities. However, this is only required in the case of *established rights* of such communities and excludes other rights based on customary uses of genetic resources. Once again, this weakens the position

---

[57] Nijar, above n 11, 5.

[58] Article 15.

[59] See Chapter 11.

of such communities as their claim to benefits is limited and such claims are subject to the discretion of the state party. Further, rights based on customary uses of such resource will be excluded.[60] The sharing of benefits arising from the traditional knowledge of indigenous and local communities are not subject to such rights being established, but again the requirement to take measures in this regard is qualified by the phrase 'as appropriate.' In a submission to the first intergovernmental meeting of the Protocol, indigenous communities argued that 'Any interpretation that undermines Indigenous rights would be inconsistent with "fair and equitable" benefit sharing. It would also be incompatible with the other legal requirements in the Protocol.'[61]

Some case studies documented by researchers indicate that the actual benefits flowing to either nations or communities from the commercialization of genetic resources vary widely. The benefit sharing arrangement, which was established between a research institute in Kerala, the Tropical Botanic Garden and Research Institute (TBGRI) and the Kani community in Kerala, has been cited as one where the benefits to the latter were doubtful at best. The Kanis used the fruit of a plant, *Trichopus zeylanicus travancoricus*, which they called *Aarogyappacha,* for its anti-fatigue properties. Scientists of the TBGRI, having discovered this, entered into an agreement with the Kanis and developed a drug called Jeevani from the plant. It has been claimed that Jeevani has a commercial value estimated to be around US$50 million to US$1 billion. The TBGRI had initially encouraged 50 Kani families to undertaken cultivation of the plant species, and the benefit to them was to be around Rs. 20,000 to 30,000 (very approximately US$350) per acre. The Kani people have received around US$12,000 as a one-time payment on the licensing of the product, and a royalty of US$5.[62]

Concerns as to the benefits received by the Kanis had been raised in several fora, including in the Kerala Legislative Assembly and the Kerala Institute for Research, Training and Development of Scheduled Castes and

---

[60] See Open-Ended Ad Hoc Intergovernmental Committee for the Nagoya Protocol on Access to Genetic Resources and the Fair and Equitable Sharing of Benefits Arising from their Utilization, 6–10 June 2011, *Nagoya Protocol on Access and Benefit Sharing: Substantive and Procedural Injustices relating to Indigenous Peoples' Human Rights*, paragraph 201.

[61] Ibid, paragraph 198.

[62] See Devinder Sharma, 'Selling Biodiversity: Benefit sharing is a dead concept' in Beth Burrows (ed), above n 51. See also Anil K Gupta, WIPO-UNEP Study on the Role of Intellectual Property Rights in the Sharing of Benefits Arising from the Use of Biological Resources and Associated Traditional Knowledge (2000) jointly produced by World Intellectual Property Organization (WIPO) and the United Nations Environment Programme (UNEP).

Scheduled Tribes (KIRTADS). This Institute believed that the Kanis had not been adequately involved in the negotiating process and that they 'should be encouraged to directly interact with wider society, and administer their medical knowledge according to terms set forth by them.' It observed that 'the only way tribal medicine can survive is by preserving its original form and premises, otherwise it is liable to be misused as a convenient resource base for other systems of medicine,' and 'TBGRI should consider ways and means to impart technical know-how to the Kanis to manufacture the drug, and thereby involve them further in the process.'[63]

In the case of the San people too, the nature of the ABS arrangement and the process by which it was negotiated was questioned. Under the agreement the San would receive only a fraction of the net sales of the product, i.e. between 0.03 and 1.2 per cent. This amount would be taken from royalty and milestone payments obtained by CSIR, while profits received by Phytopharm and its partners would remain untouched. The Agreement also protects Pfizer and Phytopharm from any further obligations to the San people.[64] It has been pointed out that the San were compensated for their traditional knowledge and not for any rights which they might have in the plant itself. In fact, it was the CSIR which gave consent for the use of the plant, not the San.[65]

Wynberg cites a more disturbing aspect of the agreement, which prevents the South African San from using their knowledge of the Hoodia plant in any other commercial applications. She notes that this prevents them from

---

63 RV Anuradha, Sharing with the Kanis: A case study from Kerala, India, available at www.cbd.int/doc/case-studies/abs/cs-abs-kanis.pdf (last accessed 9 July 2012); Salvin Paul, 'Biodiversity Associated Traditional Knowledge and Access and Benefit Sharing (ABS): A Critical Appraisal of Kani Experience from a Customary Law Perspective' (2010) 12(2) *Asian Biotechnology and Development Review* 37. See also Traci L McClellan, 'The Role of International Law in Protecting the Traditional Knowledge and Plant Life of Indigenous Peoples' (2001) 19 *Wisconsin International Law Journal* 249 for further examples. In addition to the negligible benefits accruing to the Kanis, as in the case of the San people, questions were raised regarding the validity of the consent granted to use the plant. It has been noted that the Kanis are not a cohesive unit or community, and while those from one area had imparted the knowledge of the plant, others from other areas had raised objections to the arrangements. This reflects the difficulties of identifying rights holders who can give consent as envisaged under the CBD and the Nagoya Protocol.

64 Wynberg, above n 27.

65 See Debra Harry and Le'a Malia Kanehe, 'The BS in Access and Benefit Sharing (ABS): Critical Questions for Indigenous Peoples' in Beth Burrows (ed), above n 51.

commercializing non-patented herbal medicines or from claiming the benefits from the dozens of Hoodia based products which have appeared on the market and which are being promoted on the basis of San traditional knowledge.[66] A second concern she cites is that the agreement is almost solely confined to monetary benefits, which are dependent on the successful commercialization of the end product. She notes:

> Yet commercialization is far from certain, highlighting the need for a more comprehensive and holistic approach to benefit-sharing that is not exclusively financial, is not contingent on successful drug development, and which provides immediate and tangible benefits to the San.[67]

Wynberg also notes that the San were faced with a dilemma in whether they should challenge the patent or adopt a more pragmatic approach and take a share of the benefits. She notes that in such communities sharing of knowledge is a culture and basic to their way of life and the idea of owning life is abhorrent. However, ultimately, considerations of necessity compelled them to compromise on this issue and accept a share of the royalties.[68]

Another question which arises is who in the country providing the resources should actually receive the benefits or the compensation? A WIPO study has documented an instance of the patenting of a gene, Xa21, of a wild rice variety, *Oryza longistaminata,* obtained from Mali.[69] The variety was originally accessed in Mali and transferred to a rice research programme in India where its resistance to bacterial rice blight was identified. A blight resistant specimen was transferred to the International Rice Research Institute (IRRI) in the Philippines where the locus called Xa21 which contained the resistance was identified, and then bred into cultivated rice varieties. One variety was acquired by the University of California, Davis (UC Davis), which mapped, sequenced and cloned the gene Xa21 and then obtained a patent on it.

Subsequently, a Genetic Resource Recognition Fund (GRRF) was established at UC Davis to share the benefits arising out of the commercialization of the patented gene with stakeholders in Mali and other developing countries. A certain percentage of the sales would be paid into the Fund for a certain number of years after the first year of commercialization. The Fund

---

66 Wynberg, above n 27.
67 Ibid at 866.
68 Ibid at 870.
69 Gupta, above n 62, 75.

would be used to provide fellowships to agriculture students and researchers from Mali and the Philippines for capacity building. The author notes that at the time of writing no money had yet been paid into the Fund. He also notes that there are presently no plans at UC Davis to mainstream this model of ABS. What is noteworthy is the fact that the farmers who grew and conserved this rice variety were not included as recipients of the benefits. They were in fact unaware of this particular value of the variety, and while some grew it for food, others considered it a weed. Nevertheless the question which arises is whether this lack of knowledge precludes them from sharing in the benefits of the discovery.

Benefit sharing arrangements which are often cited as being positive examples are those implemented in Costa Rica by the National Institute of Biodiversity (InBio). This was created 'as a private, but non-profit institution to coordinate the different activities of universities, private organizations, and government and to become a national focal point in the field of biodiversity.'[70] It has jurisdiction to bioprospect on state land, and therefore consent to such activities is provided by the state. This would facilitate the speed and efficiency with which ABS contracts could be concluded. The most well-known contract it has signed was in 1991 with the multinational Merck, Sharp and Dome, 'to collaborate in the investigation of the existing biodiversity in Costa Rica's tropical forests in order to establish its potential application to human health and animals.'[71] It has subsequently signed several agreements with a range of institutions including universities, multinational corporations and other groups. It has been observed that 'INBio provided unrestricted access to scout the tropical forests for a paltry fee. Costa Rica alone is home to five per cent of the world's biodiversity, with an estimated worth of several billion dollars, and all it has managed to get in return for its biodiversity is US $2.6 million.'[72]

Under the Merck agreement InBio received US$1 million from the first phase of the project, which has been extended many times since then. It also received non-monetary benefits in the form of laboratory equipment and material required for processing plant and micro-organism samples. While it is entitled to a percentage of royalties which may result from products derived from resources taken from the country, this information is kept confidential. Significantly, Merck has the exclusive rights to file patents over such products.

---

[70] Carmen Richerzhagen and Karin Holm-Mueller, 'The effectiveness of access and benefit sharing in Costa Rica: implications for national and international regimes' (2005) 53(4) *Ecological Economics* 445, 453.

[71] Sharma, above n 62, 7.

[72] Ibid at 8.

Dutfield cites a more positive benefit sharing agreement entered into between the Aguarunas people of Peru, and Searle the pharmaceutical division of Monsanto.[73] These peoples have negotiated a know-how license with Searle under which they will pass on medicinal knowledge and plants to the company and in return receive an annual license fee. The fee increases to reflect success in research and development. Further, the agreement does not affect the right of the Aguarunas to use, share or sell or otherwise transfer plants or knowledge. However, there is no indication as to what will happen in the event that a drug or other product is produced and marketed, i.e. who will own the patent on it and whether the income will be shared with the community.

While these examples of ABS agreements are not comprehensive, they raise several issues. The first is the difficulty of determining who should give consent to the preliminary accessing of the resource. Where the consent of communities is required, problems may arise when such communities are fragmented or widely dispersed, particularly across countries. This problem arose in the both the Kani and San cases.[74] Further problems would arise where one section of the community has revealed the knowledge and given consent for its use, which is opposed by other sections. In the case of the Aguarunas this would not happen since the agreement is non-exclusive and does not affect the rights of non-participating communities. While Article 11 of the Nagoya Protocol appears to address this question, it does not provide a framework for resolving it.

A second issue is that even within countries, the interests of various people and institutions in ABS arrangements would vary widely. In both the Kani and San cases, it was State sponsored research institutions within the country which accessed the resources and made use of the traditional knowledge relating to it. These institutions then entered into collaborative arrangements with other institutions including foreign companies to exploit the resource. It is clear that in both cases the interests of the communities in question was not a priority. Similarly, in Costa Rica, InBio has the authority to enter into ABS agreements in regard to biological resources on State land. Such resources would constitute the national heritage of the people of the country. Nevertheless, InBio does not appear to be accountable to the

---

[73] Graham Dutfield, *Intellectual Property Rights, Trade and Biodiversity* (2000), 43.

[74] The complexities of establishing the holders of traditional knowledge relating to a particular resource as well as negotiating the benefit sharing agreement are illustrated in the Hoodia case – Sarah Laird and Rachel Wynberg 'Access and Benefit Sharing in practice: Trends in Partnerships Across Sectors' Secretariat of the Convention on Biological Diversity', Technical Series No. 38, (2008).

general public as to the terms which it negotiates, and in fact many of the agreements are protected by confidentiality clauses. While InBio's ABS agreements have been generally cited as being exemplary, this would be largely unverifiable under the circumstances. Therefore the will or ability of states to protect their communities or natural resources, or to institute ABS arrangements in the public interest is called in question.

The benefits set out in ABS agreements are also a cause for concern. These benefits are categorized into monetary and non-monetary. The monetary benefits would include up-front payments and royalties from the possible commercialization of the end product, if any. As can be seen from the cases cited above, the monetary payments are often negligible. This was the case as regards both the Kani and San communities. Monetary benefits could also include joint ownership of the resulting patents, but as the case studies indicate, the multinational corporations' exclusive right to own the patent has generally been a feature of the agreements. Under the circumstances it is unlikely that communities would be able to insist on joint ownership of patents, and in any case, as noted above, many such communities have ethical problems in doing so. On the contrary, in the case of the San, the community was specifically prohibited from using the plant for any other purpose which may interfere with the patent holders' rights.

As cited by the Bonn Guidelines and the Nagoya Protocol, non-monetary benefits could include education and training, institutional capacity building, contributions to the local economy, and food and livelihood security benefits. Such benefits would often be negligible compared to the potential profits that would be made from the marketed product. This was the case in the San and Kani agreements. Writers also cite as an example, the agreement entered into between the University of Papua New Guinea and a consortium of research institutions including the US National Institute of Health and the University of Utah, where the former is executing a US$4 million project 'aimed at finding marine organisms and plant species that exhibit chemical properties useful in the treatment of tuberculosis, malaria, cancer, HIV, and other diseases.'[75] The uses of the $4 million payment include that:

> [l]ocal researchers will be taught to inventory plants, collect ethno-medicinal plant species, and prepare and screen extracts. They will also learn the process of economic valuation of natural products, develop intellectual property rights legislation, and conduct outreach programs to educate communities about the further sharing of their knowledge.[76]

---

[75] Sharma, above n 62, 5.
[76] Ibid at 6.

On the other hand, in the event that the drug discovery programme proves fruitful, it has been estimated that the partner organizations could make US$26 billion a year.[77] Even assuming that this is an overestimation, and taking into account the uncertainties of drug discovery and the possibility of marketing an end product, it must be questioned whether this kind of agreement benefits the country as a whole or only certain institutions within it, and also whether there is equitable sharing of the benefits.

Non-monetary benefits to communities would include enhancement of health and education, livelihood benefits and contributions to the local economy. However, these are all basic human rights in any case and communities should not need to sell their traditional knowledge to have them fulfilled at the behest of outsiders. Rather, as was pointed out in the Kani case, it would be more equitable to empower them to put their knowledge to commercial use.

Another point of concern is that communities are generally only compensated for the knowledge of the resources. For example, in the San case the community was compensated only for their knowledge and not for any rights they may have to the plants themselves. While it might be difficult to accept property rights of communities or anyone else over genetic resources, the role of communities in conserving them, should, where applicable, be compensated. This is further borne out by the case of the wild rice from Mali. In this instance, the local people were in fact unaware of the particular useful properties of the plant. However, they had been instrumental in conserving it. Nevertheless, the benefits which were proposed were intended for capacity building for academics and researchers and the community was overlooked. It must be noted that this situation could arise in the case of PGRFA, where farmers have conserved and developed plant varieties but may be unaware of a particular use of such variety, which is later discovered. In such a situation, the farmers, or the country in which such variety is found, could not be compensated for the knowledge of that use, and would probably not be compensated for developing and conserving the plant.

These case studies thus demonstrate that the ABS system as envisaged by the CBD has not resulted in equitable benefit sharing to the extent that it can be justifiably upheld. At the outset, issues of who should give consent to the process are highly complex. Even if this problem was resolved, there is a fundamental fallacy in the assumption that genetic resources which have immense potential commercial values can be compensated for by the type of 'benefits' that have been cited in the studies above.

---

[77] Ibid.

Conclusion

The bilateral system of ABS under the CBD gives rise to several questions. On the one hand, a bilateral contract based system for this purpose appears to be both necessary and inevitable as it gives each country the flexibility to negotiate its own contracts in accordance with its own context and requirements. On the other hand, the question of equality in bargaining power brings the equity of these contracts into question. These questions would arise in cases where the contracts are negotiated by government entities, but particularly so where they are negotiated by indigenous and local communities. Further, as noted earlier, the capacity of government entities to work in the best interests of these communities or in the national interest is also a debatable issue.

The enforceability of these contracts must also be considered. Many provider countries have enacted legislation to regulate these access contracts. However, the obligations of benefit sharing would fall on parties from user countries, usually non-state entities. In the absence of corresponding legislation in these countries with regard to ABS measures, enforcement of the terms, or remedies for their breach, would be difficult for the provider countries. A fundamental inequity in this regard is the fact that while IPRs, including on PGRFA, are being harmonized internationally and made enforceable, ABS arrangements in regard to these resources must still be negotiated on an ad hoc basis, with little enforceability outside the country of origin. Developing countries have raised these concerns in the TRIPS Council as discussed in the following chapters.

It must also be questioned whether the benefits, given to either countries or communities, can adequately compensate for the removal of genetic resources from the public domain. Monetary benefits in the form of fees, royalties and other payments, would realistically amount to only a very small proportion of the actual profits which may be derived from these resources. Non-monetary benefits also appear trifling when viewed in the light of the fact that foreign corporate entities are amassing huge profits in the development and marketing of new plant varieties and assuming control of agricultural systems in many countries. Handouts in any form cannot compensate for the fundamental inequity of the system.

The Nagoya Protocol did not fulfil the commitment made at the WSSD to negotiate an equitable international ABS regime. It maintains the status quo that provider countries must regulate the terms of benefit sharing agreements through their national laws and rules, and correspondingly the requirements on compliance by user countries set out in Articles 15 and 16 are couched in weak and qualified language. These provisions do not address developing country concerns on unjustified patents for genetic resources or traditional knowledge. At best it has the potential to provide at least a globally enforceable framework for ensuring that the resources are acquired in conformity with PIC and in accordance with MATs, and that some benefits are received by provider countries. It remains to be seen whether these expectations will be fulfilled.

THE MULTILATERAL SYSTEM OF ACCESS AND BENEFIT SHARING UNDER THE FAO TREATY

The multilateral system of 'facilitated access' to PGRFA under the FAO Treaty was brought about by the recognition of their special nature.[78] On the one hand the strong interdependence of all countries with regard to PGRFA means that their free flow is essential for global food security. On the other hand, the diffusion of major agricultural crops makes it difficult to trace their country of origin.[79] Therefore a bilateral system requiring case-by-case negotiations in regard to each crop, particularly where the country or community of origin has to be traced, is not the most efficient method of ensuring free access to essential germplasm. A multilateral system in which both a central point of access and a common contractual process are available would obviate the need to do so. It would also eliminate the transaction costs involved in negotiating ad hoc agreements.[80] A second purpose of a multilateral system is to keep designated germplasm in the public domain and prevent its propertization.[81] To this end, contracting parties have essentially agreed to place certain PGRFA in a common pool

[78] The term 'facilitated access' has been explained as the role of the Treaty in making easy or routine access or expediting access to the PGRFA with the system – Gerald Moore and Witold Tymowski, *Explanatory Guide to the International Treaty on Plant Genetic Resources for Food and Agriculture* (2005), 87.

[79] WIPO/GRTKF/IC/1/3 – Intergovernmental Committee on Intellectual Property and Genetic Resources, Traditional Knowledge and Folklore, First Session, 30 April–3 May 2001 *Matters Concerning Intellectual Property and Genetic Resources, Traditional Knowledge and Folklore – An Overview* 16 March 2001, p. 16.

[80] Moore and Tymowski, above n 78, 79; H David Cooper, 'The International Treaty on Plant Genetic Resources for Food and Agriculture' (2002) 11(1) *Review of European Community and International Environmental Law* 1.

[81] See Part IV of the Treaty. It has been argued that in this context the term 'in the public domain' can be interpreted to mean that which is not protected by intellectual property rights – Moore and Tymowski, above n 78, 84.

with open access to all. However, ensuring that the objectives of such a system as implemented by the FAO have, in fact, been achieved remains a challenge.

Access under the Multilateral System (MLS)

The multilateral system aims to facilitate open access to the PGRFA within its scope and to prevent the imposition of IPRs over them. Article 12 of the FAO Treaty sets out the conditions under which such access will be granted. A disputed provision in regard to IPRs is contained in Article 12.3 (d) which reads:

> Recipients shall not claim any intellectual property or other rights that limit the facilitated access to the plant genetic resources for food and agriculture, or their genetic parts or components, in the form received from the Multilateral System.

The controversy surrounds the phrase 'in the form received.' While the Material which is accessed cannot itself be patented, it is a debatable question as to whether a modified version of it or, for example, a gene isolated from it, can be.[82] It would be a question of fact as to whether there is sufficient modification of the original accession and sufficient distance between it and the patented version so as take it beyond 'the form received' from the MLS. This question would be analogous to the principle of 'essential derivation' under UPOV.

Secondly, only IPRs which limit *facilitated access* to the PGRFA in the MLS are prohibited. Here again, the fact that Materials in the MLS can be accessed, improved upon in however slight a form, commercialized, and free access restricted by IPRs, negates the fundamental premise of the Treaty that certain crops essential for food security must (presumably) in all their forms be freely available, including for further research and development.

It has been noted that this provision was essentially an agreement to disagree. Helfer states that while developing countries wanted the phrase 'or their genetic parts or components' retained and the phrase 'in the form' deleted, the US wanted the first deleted and the second retained. A

---

[82] An example of the latter is the gene isolated from the wild rice in Mali, and it must also be noted that UC Davis acquired the variety from the International Rice Research Institute in the Philippines.

compromise saw both clauses included in the final draft.[83] Countries with strong interests in intellectual property argued that Material subsequently developed from the original Material should not be precluded from patentability. Developing countries opposing IPRs over plant varieties argued for a total prohibition on patenting of such Materials. The ambiguities of this provision have yet to be resolved.

The Coverage of the Multilateral System (MLS)

The MLS covers PGRFA listed in Annex 1 of the FAO Treaty established according to criteria of food security and interdependence.[84] However, it has been noted that the inclusion of the crops was negotiated less on this basis than on the basis of the interests of Parties, and many crops important for food security have been excluded.[85] Further, the PGRFA included in the Annex are only those under the management and control of the Contracting Parties and in the public domain,[86] and which are held by the IARCs.

Therefore Material held by private entities would come within the MLS only if they voluntarily place them within it. However, while these entities have no obligation to place their Material within the MLS, they are not precluded from accessing the Material in it. Article 11.3 states that contracting parties will take appropriate measures to encourage natural and legal persons within their jurisdiction who hold PGRFA listed in Annex 1 to place it within the MLS. The Governing Body is required to assess progress in this regard within two years of the entry into force of the Treaty, and to decide whether access by those entities that have not done so should continue to be facilitated. At the Second Session of the Governing Body in 2007 it was noted that, since the First Session, no natural or legal persons have placed their collections in the MLS, although some inquiries have been made in

---

[83] Laurence R Helfer, *Intellectual property rights in plant varieties: International legal regimes and policy options for national governments* FAO Legislative Study 85 (2004) 89, available at ftp://ftp.fao.org/docrep/fao/007/y5714e/y5714e00.pdf (last accessed 9 July 2012). See also South Centre and Centre for International Environmental Law, *Intellectual Property and Development: Overview of Developments in Multilateral, Plurilateral, and Bilateral Fora* (2004) 5, available at http://www.ciel.org/Publications/IP_Update_3Q04.pdf (last accessed 9 July 2012).

[84] *International Treaty on Plant Genetic Resources for Food and Agriculture*, adopted at the 31st Session of the FAO Conference on 3 November 2001 available at http://www.fao.org/AG/cgrfa/itpgr.htm (last accessed 9 July 2012) and the website of the Treaty at http://www.planttreaty.org/ (last accessed 9 July 2012), Article 11.1.

[85] Moore and Tymowski, above n 78, 15.

[86] FAO Treaty – Article 11.2.

this regard. The Governing Body had, at its First Session, decided to defer assessment under Article 11.4 until its Third Session.[87] As at the Fourth Session of the Governing Body held in March 2011 there has not been any significant progress on this matter.[88]

Benefit Sharing under the MLS

According to Article 13.1, the contracting parties recognize that facilitated access to the PGRFA in itself constitutes a major benefit and agree that benefits accruing from the system should be shared fairly and equitably. The benefits shall be shared through the following mechanisms: the exchange of information, access to and transfer of technology, capacity-building, and the sharing of the benefits arising from commercialization. These mechanisms have been further fleshed out in the following subsections. Provisions for implementing the last mechanism, i.e. sharing the benefits arising from commercialization, will be incorporated into the Standard Material Transfer Agreement.[89]

The Access Provisions of the Standard Material Transfer Agreement

The Standard Material Transfer Agreement (SMTA) was adopted by Resolution 2/2006 at the First Session of the FAO Treaty Governing Body in June 2006.[90] The provisions of the SMTA reflect the provisions of the Treaty[91] and the ABS aspects are contained in Articles 5 and 6.[92]

---

[87] IT/GB-2/07/11 – International Treaty On Plant Genetic Resources For Food And Agriculture, Second Session Of The Governing Body, 29 October – 2 November 2007, *Progress In The Inclusion Of Plant Genetic Resources For Food And Agriculture In The Multilateral System.*

[88] IT/GB-4/11/12 – International Treaty on Plant Genetic Resources for Food and Agriculture,
Fourth Session of the Governing Body 14–18 March 2011, *Report on the Implementation of the Multilateral System of Access and Benefit Sharing* and IT/GB-4/11/13, Reviews and Assessments Under The Multilateral System, and of the Implementation and Operation of the Standard Material Transfer Agreement, Note by the Secretary.

[89] FAO Treaty – Article 13.2(d).

[90] IT/GB-1/06/6 – International Treaty on Plant Genetic Resources for Food and Agriculture, First Session of the Governing Body, 12–16 June 2006 – *Draft Standard Material Transfer Agreement*, Preamble.

[91] The Preamble to the SMTA refers in particular to Articles 4, 11, 12.4 and 12.5 of the FAO Treaty.

[92] For a discussion of the negotiation and drafting of the SMTA see Carlos M Correa, 'Considerations on the Standard Material Transfer Agreement under the

The access provisions generally relate to the provider and are contained in Article 5. The Provider is required to transfer the Material expeditiously and free of charge or at a minimal cost. All passport data and, subject to applicable law, all other associated and non-confidential descriptive information must also be provided.

Subclauses (c) and (d) restrict the free flow of Material in certain circumstances. Article 5 (c) states that:

> Access to Plant Genetic Resources for Food and Agriculture under Development, including material being developed by farmers, shall be at the discretion of its developer, during the period of its development.

The definition of 'PGRFA under Development' states that it is material:

> [d]erived from the Material, and hence distinct from it, that is not yet ready for commercialization and which the developer intends to further develop or to transfer to another person or entity for further development. The period of development for the Plant Genetic Resources for Food and Agriculture under Development shall be deemed to have ceased when those resources are commercialized as a Product.

This definition is applicable to material which is, in fact, intended to be developed and commercialized by private plant breeders who have the discretion whether to provide access to it or not. This discretion is operative until the period of development ends when the material is commercialized.

However, Article 5(c) and the definition read together would be more difficult to apply to material under development by farmers. Farmers are more likely to informally place developed varieties in the public domain rather than to commercialize them, thereby making it difficult to define the end of the development period under the SMTA. According to both the Treaty and the SMTA, after being placed in the public domain such material would be freely available for others to access. It appears therefore that the SMTA has been formulated on the basis of the way in which private plant breeders rather than traditional farmers operate, and that the reference to farmers in Article 5 (c) is merely a token gesture with little significance.[93]

Article 5 (d) further protects commercial plant breeders stating that:

FAO Treaty on Plant Genetic Resources for Food and Agriculture' (2006) 9(2) *Journal of World Intellectual Property* 137.

[93] It is the only occurrence of the word in the SMTA.

> [a]ccess to Plant Genetic Resources for Food and Agriculture protected by intellectual and other property rights shall be consistent with relevant international agreements, and with relevant national laws.

Therefore while plant breeders have free access to the PGRFA in the MLS, access to their own varieties protected by IPRs is restricted.

Conditions of Access

Conditions of access are included in Article 6 of the SMTA relating to the rights and obligations of the recipient. The recipient undertakes that the Material is used or conserved only for the purpose of research, breeding, and training for food and agriculture. Chemical, pharmaceutical and other non-food related industrial purposes are excluded.

Article 6.2 of the SMTA is almost identical to Article 12.3 (d) of the FAO Treaty and its critique will not be repeated. Under Articles 6.4 and 6.5 the recipient may re-transfer the Material or a PGRFA under development to a Subsequent Recipient under the terms of the SMTA. Beyond informing the Governing Body of such re-transfer, the recipient has no further obligation in this regard. It is unclear as to how compliance with the terms of the SMTA will be enforced and who has jurisdiction to do so. These Articles also appear to be beneficial to private entities in accessing, further developing, and commercializing Material in the MLS with little regulation under the Treaty or the SMTA.

The SMTA Benefit Sharing Provisions

Benefit sharing is an obligation of the recipient and comes within Article 6. Where the recipient commercializes a product that is a PGRFA and which incorporates Material from the MLS and that product is not available without restriction to others for further research and breeding, he/she is required a pay a fixed percentage of the sales of the product into the mechanism established by the Governing Body.[94] Where such a product is available the recipient is encouraged to make voluntary payments.[95]

---

[94] Article 6.7. Annex 2 of the SMTA sets out the amount payable and the terms under which payment should be made. Unavailability would generally occur when the movement of the seeds is restricted either by patents or by technological processes such as GURTs – Claudio Chiarolla, 'Plant Patenting, Benefit Sharing and the Law Applicable to the Food and Agriculture Organization Standard Material Transfer Agreement' (2008) 11 (1) *Journal of World Intellectual Property* 1, 5.

[95] Article 6.8.

The benefit sharing provisions of the SMTA are half-hearted. While Articles 6.7 and 6.8 appear to promote some degree of benefit sharing, it must be noted that payment is due only when the product is *not available for further research and breeding*. Therefore the SMTA appears to be premised on the tacit acceptance that Material in the MLS will, in fact, be further developed and commercialized and intellectual property protection obtained for the end product. However, in order to perpetuate the process of developing new plant varieties and ensure food security, it is essential that the varieties should remain in the public domain at all stages of improvement and development. By permitting the propertization of plant varieties which have been further developed from Material in the MLS, the collections in the public domain would potentially remain static at a particular stage of development.

Implementation of the SMTA

While there is a dispute settlement mechanism in the SMTA, it is extremely complex both in relation to the applicable law and the procedures involved, and has yet to be tested.[96] However, criticisms have been leveled at the implementation of the system aside from disputes which may arise. It has been argued that it is fundamentally unenforceable and several key issues have been cited in this regard. These include, that no signature indicating acceptance of the terms of the MTA is required; the Centres officially renounce responsibility to monitor compliance with the Agreement; Centres have been caught distributing designated germplasm without an MTA; and designated material distributed from the Centres has been directly appropriated under intellectual property regimes.[97]

It has also been contended that the 'no IPR' policy is unenforceable as it only applies to the germplasm accessions in the form in which they are received from the gene banks. It does not prevent components of the germplasm such as individual genes or derivatives, or modified germplasm

---

[96] SMTA – Articles 7 and 8. See Claudio Chiarolla, above n 94, for a detailed analysis of this mechanism.

[97] GRAIN, *Biopiracy by another name? A critique of the FAO-CGIAR trusteeship system*, Seedling October 2002, available at http://www.grain.org/bio-ipr/?id=52 (last accessed 9 July 2012). For examples of patent protection being granted to plant varieties acquired from CGIAR Centres see Patricia Lucia Cantuaria Marin, *Providing Protection for Plant Genetic Resources – Patents, Sui Generis Systems and Biopartnerships* (2002), 40.

from being subject to intellectual property rights.[98] Under the circumstances the CGIAR gene banks remain a resource for private interests to exert property rights over what is intended to be a global public good.

Conclusion

The Treaty has been in force for a decade but concerns have been raised as to whether its objectives are achievable or whether it has become 'the greatest case of institutional biopiracy ever seen.'[99] To what extent is this assessment justified?

The fact that private entities both natural and legal (including corporate) are permitted to access the Materials within the MLS while keeping their own Material out of it constitutes the fundamental flaw in its formulation. It is noteworthy that while the Governing Body is required by the Treaty to assess this situation within a given time frame, it has at present deferred this process to its Third Session.

The inequity of the situation above is further exacerbated by the fact that not only are corporate entities permitted to access Material in the public domain, they are also permitted to claim intellectual property protection over them, so long as it is not 'in the form received' from the collection. As noted above, whether the nature of the subsequent product is so far removed from that of the original acquisition so as to conform to this condition is a question of fact, and the Treaty does not contain a mechanism to adjudicate on this and to enforce its decision in the multilateral sphere. Another cause for concern is the fact that the person or entity originally accessing the Material may transfer it, or a PGRFA under Development, to a subsequent recipient. While Article 6.4 provides that this must also be done under the terms of the SMTA and the Governing Body notified, the recipient has no further obligations to ensure that the Subsequent Recipient in fact complies with these terms. Here again there is no indication as to who would have jurisdiction to do so. While there is a dispute settlement mechanism, again its viability has yet to be tested.

It can be argued therefore that the conceptualization of the MLS as maintaining critical germplasm in the public domain has been negated by its

---

[98] Modification, however, is open to interpretation and it has also been contended that slight modifications would probably be insufficient for the purpose of claiming IPRs over such germplasm. See GRAIN, *Interview with Carlos Correa*, Seedling, January 2003, available at http://www.grain.org/seedling/?id=223 (last accessed 9 July 2012).

[99] GRAIN, *Farmers call for suspension of Seed Treaty*, available at http://grain.org/bio-ipr/?id=531 (last accessed 9 July 2012).

legitimization of intellectual property rights on 'improved' material. Plant germplasm is in a constant process of development and improvement and must be maintained as international public goods at all stages of this process. The situation is further compounded by the fact that it is precisely the plants that are most critical to global food security that have been included in the MLS. These are also the plants that will for that reason have the most commercial value. Therefore facilitating their accession by private entities will result in global agriculture being possibly controlled by them.

There is a fundamental misconception in conceptualizing benefit sharing of PGRFA which is critical for global food security in terms of permitting monopoly control over them in the first place, and then claiming a minimal share of the profits derived in order to benefit humanity as a whole. It is particularly ironic that the farmers who have been singled out to receive these benefits are the category which has contributed immeasurably to develop this vast pool of resources.

On a more positive note it could be said that the MLS is the most promising of the strategies to emerge from international fora in order to enable the free flow of germplasm which will ultimately benefit developing countries. It has been noted that over 100,000 accessions are being exchanged annually through the SMTA though the bulk of this represents the collections of the IARCs and other international institutions and genebanks in developed countries.[100] The system is potentially open to abuse but given the strong international environment which is increasingly facilitating the privatization of PGRFA, it is important that significant *ex situ* collections of PGRFA were voluntarily placed in the public domain, and that the FAO Treaty and the multilateral system of access and benefit sharing that it has put in place was successfully negotiated. This is an important starting point to ensure free access to these resources and to counter measures to propertize them.

THE TRIPS AGREEMENT AND PRIOR INFORMED CONSENT/BENEFIT SHARING

The key issue under this topic is the concern that TRIPS may permit the patenting of inventions based on genetic material and traditional knowledge without ensuring that the CBD requirements of PIC and ABS have been complied with. In other words, TRIPS may facilitate biopiracy by granting

---

[100] IT/GB-3/09/13 – International Treaty on Plant Genetic Resources for Food and Agriculture, Third session of the Governing Body, 1–5 June 2009, *Review of the Implementation of the Multilateral System*, 11.

private property rights over genetic resources and traditional knowledge regardless of whether they were legally acquired. The three concerns which arise in this regard are to ensure that the key objectives of the CBD have been complied with in the patenting process, i.e. that access has been obtained with PIC, that there is equitable sharing of the benefits arising from the use of the genetic resources or traditional knowledge, and that the erroneous granting of unjustifiable patents is avoided.

Two approaches regarding the mutual supportiveness of the two Agreements were raised in the TRIPS Council. The first was to use national solutions, including legislation on ABS and contracts to deal with the problem, and this has been termed the national based approach. The other is the disclosure approach which advocates a requirement at the international level to disclose the origin or source of the genetic resources and/or traditional knowledge used in the invention. The first will be discussed in this section. The second has been simultaneously debated in other fora and will be discussed in Chapter 11.

The National Based Approach

The national based approach advocated by developed countries indicates their preference that access to genetic resources and traditional knowledge be based on an ad hoc bilateral contract system rather than by a comprehensive international regime which would lay down overriding rules in this regard. This is essentially the status quo under Article 15 of the CBD and remains unchanged by the Nagoya Protocol. Those advocating this approach[101] take the view that national legislation could efficiently address the three issues noted above by way of permits, contractual obligations, visa systems and civil and/or criminal penalties for non-compliance. Most significantly these national systems would be outside the intellectual property system. Therefore the granted patent would not per se be affected.

A contract system to prevent 'bad' patents has been justified on the basis that it would be sufficiently flexible so as to take account of the relative value attributable to the genetic resources and that attributable to the efforts of the inventor. It could also be appropriately tailored so as not to have unintended, negative consequences on the intellectual property system, but rather to provide for penalties against those few who might misappropriate

[101] The United States has advocated this approach most strongly in the discussions, see IP/C/W/368/Rev.1 – TRIPS Council, The Relationship between the TRIPS Agreement and the Convention on Biological Diversity, Summary of Issues Raised and Points Made, 8 February 2006, 14–27, footnotes in this section citing the submitted documents.

genetic resources. Such contracts could clarify definitions of key terms at the outset so as to achieve clarity in regard to the rights and obligations of all parties, and could be used to effectively control the collection of resources and ensure sharing of benefits from their use. A contract based system could be adaptable to each country's legal system without undermining the economic benefits of a strong IP system. It could also be put in place immediately and would not require waiting for the outcome of the discussions in the TRIPS Council and other fora. Such a system could also help to implement Article 19 of the CBD with regard to the handling of biotechnology and the distribution of its benefits.[102]

This proposal gives rise to the same questions raised earlier, namely the parity of bargaining power between the parties to these contracts and the equity of the resulting contracts which are negotiated. It also does not resolve the problem of misappropriation of resources and patents granted in relation to them. The fact that such contracts are not necessarily enforceable across borders also limits their effectiveness.[103]

The subsequent discussion in the TRIPS Council addressed four issues in relation to national based approaches, namely, the transboundary use of genetic resources and traditional knowledge, the bargaining power of parties to the contract, transaction costs, and the effectiveness of remedies proposed.[104]

In regard to the transboundary use of genetic resources and traditional knowledge, developing countries argued that the national based approach, including contracts, may be helpful and also required under the CBD, but cannot be the only solution to erroneously granted patents. In view of the transboundary nature of the problem where the material is located in one country and the patent is issued in the other, national measures would be insufficient to ensure transparency and would not deter those intent on acting in bad faith.[105] Further, there is no obligation in international law for Members to legislate on PIC and ABS, particularly those not party to the CBD. It was also noted that a commitment to negotiate an international ABS regime was made at the World Summit on Sustainable Development at

---

102 Ibid at 14.

103 IP/C/W/443 – TRIPS Council, The Relationship Between The TRIPS Agreement And The Convention On Biological Diversity (CBD) And The Protection Of Traditional Knowledge, Technical Observations On Issues Raised In A Communication By The United States (IP/C/W/434) Submission from Brazil and India, 18 March 2005, 3.

104 IP/C/W/368/Rev.1, above n 101, 24.

105 Ibid at 24–25.

Johannesburg in 2002 and a national based approach may not be reconcilable with this.[106] Developing countries also pointed out that if voluntary contracts are considered sufficient to ensure respect of countries/communities of origin of genetic resources and traditional knowledge, they should also be considered sufficient to ensure respect of the protection of intellectual property. Therefore it could also be countered that national patent laws are sufficient to protect IPRs, and international agreements such as TRIPS are not necessary.

The responses to these concerns were made primarily by the United States.[107] It observed that the reference to national laws does not imply that international norms are irrelevant or that the proposed solutions are not international in character. It cited the Bonn Guidelines and the work of the WIPO IGC which may be helpful in achieving the shared objectives. It further stated that a national contract based system can be international in outlook and can include provisions to resolve transboundary enforcement or dispute issues. It reiterated that cases of misappropriation are the exception rather than the norm and a contractual system would in fact apply to the vast majority of those seeking access. Cases where a contract has not been concluded and access is in violation of national laws could be dealt with under criminal/civil national systems. The US also argued that countries would promote and encourage PIC and ABS on MATs without being a party to the CBD, and these countries have ensured that bioprospectors and researchers within their jurisdiction have been made aware of such systems in other countries.

In regard to bargaining power, developing countries protested that indigenous and local communities did not have the capacity to negotiate equitable terms, and most owners of genetic resources were unaware of the benefits to be obtained from them. This unequal bargaining power could lead to unfair results since developed countries could compel developing countries (or communities) to accept unfair contracts.[108] Further, the lack of

---

[106] Ibid at 25; IP/C/M/48 – TRIPS Council, *Minutes of Meeting*, 14–15 June 2005, 15 September 2005, paragraph 55.

[107] IP/C/W/368/Rev.1, above n 101, footnotes in paragraph 61.

[108] An often cited example of a dubious benefit sharing arrangement is that of the patent issued by the US Patent and Trademark Office to the United States Department of Health and Human Services on a virus found in the blood of a Hagahai tribesman of Papua New Guinea. The tribesman was infected with a virus which causes cancer in humans but had not contracted the disease and his DNA was therefore important for medical research. The researchers had in fact obtained permission from the tribe and had agreed that it would receive 50 per cent of the patent royalties – Valentina Tejera, 'Tripping over Property Rights: Is it Possible to

an obligation to enter into or enforce these contracts makes them difficult to enforce outside the country of origin. These arguments were countered by the US which pointed out that member states may regulate the terms of agreements through their national laws or rules and determine the terms of collection. The seeking of information by outsiders on knowledge, innovations and practices would help to educate communities in acquiring the expertise with which to market them, and also give such communities an opportunity to indicate that they do not want this knowledge shared with others. This would also be an opportunity to educate such communities on trade secret laws in this regard.[109]

Developing countries also protested that a fragmented nation-by-nation system with no common denominator could not ensure transparency and predictability in access and benefit sharing, including prior informed consent. It could not regulate relationships between entities, persons, and activities in different counties and ensure transparency and predictability in the system. The transaction costs of doing so would also be too high. Further, such a system could not deal with the long term nature of research and development activities in regard to genetic resources. These arguments were disputed, and in response it was said that such a system need not entail high transaction costs if implemented efficiently and need not become fragmented. There was also adequate flexibility in the system to address long term research and development issues.[110]

Finally developing countries argued that the civil and criminal remedies proposed for violations of conditions will not be an effective deterrent to prevent illegal use in third countries where the prospecting and use of the resources has taken place without the authorization of the competent national authority. This was countered by the contention that violations were rare exceptions and could be dealt with by criminal and civil sanctions similar to those in areas of law such as environmental, health and safety and others in which governments have a regulatory interest.[111]

Conclusion

The above discussions in the TRIPS Council indicate that while developed countries have enforced a multilateral regime in regard to the protection of IPRs, they are resistant to a similar system being implemented in regard to

Reconcile the Convention on Biological Diversity with Article 27 of the TRIPS Agreement?' (1999) 33 *New England Law Review* 967.

[109] IP/C/W/368/Rev.1, above n 101, paragraphs 63–64.

[110] Ibid, paragraphs 65–66.

[111] Ibid, paragraphs 67–68.

equitable benefit sharing of genetic resources and traditional knowledge, preferring instead a national contract based system. In the absence of an internationally applicable regulatory framework, the latter system is intrinsically disadvantageous to developing countries and their indigenous and local communities. Negotiation of such contracts on an ad hoc basis makes it more difficult to ensure fair and equitable terms of benefit sharing. Further, non-compliance must also be addressed by the provider countries as these contracts are not enforceable across borders, and here again developed countries have resisted measures to make them so. They have also maintained that sanctions in the event of abuse of the system or erroneously granted patents, must be remedied by civil and criminal law, but should leave the patent intact. The requirement of the Nagoya Protocol that user countries enact measures to address issues of non-compliance with legislative and regulatory measures in regard to access and equitable benefit sharing, are unlikely to include remedies for unjustifiable patents. The conservation regime has again failed to address the concerns of developing countries in regard to equity in the use of these resources.

10. *Sui generis* legislation

INTRODUCTION

Article 27.3(b) of the Agreement on Trade Related Aspects of Intellectual Property Rights (TRIPS Agreement) states that members shall provide for the protection of plant varieties either by patents or by an effective *sui generis* system, or by any combination thereof. Therefore while countries are required to formulate a legal framework to protect new plant varieties, this need not be based on patents. A *sui generis* system permitted for this purpose would be one tailored to the specific context, situation and needs of each country as opposed to one that would be applicable globally.

The debate on this requirement has taken place in the TRIPS Council in the context of the review of Article 27.3(b). While *sui generis* legislation is contained in the TRIPS Agreement in relation to plant variety protection, its application has been expanded to cover traditional knowledge and expressions of folklore. Developing countries have taken up issues of *sui generis* legislation for the protection of traditional knowledge in relation to plants and their uses in the TRIPS Council, and also in various fora of the CBD in the context of Article 8 (j). In the World Intellectual Property Organization (WIPO), the topic has been discussed in the Intergovernmental Committee on Intellectual Property and Genetic Resources, Traditional Knowledge and Folklore (IGC).

There has been considerable debate in international fora as to the nature of *sui generis* measures and what elements they should comprise. These elements would differ in regard to the protection of plants on the one hand, and traditional knowledge on the other. One of the primary issues to be considered is to what extent *sui generis* legislation should be based on intellectual property systems in regard to protection of both plant varieties and traditional knowledge. The second issue which has been discussed in the TRIPS Council is what constitutes 'effective protection' of plant varieties in terms of Article 27.3(b). Developed and developing countries have again taken diametrically opposing views on this question.

Concurrently with the discussions taking place in international fora, several countries have unilaterally enacted legislation to protect both plants and traditional knowledge, tailored to suit their particular situations and needs. There have also been regional initiatives in this regard, and to date five regions have developed or are developing regional agreements, frameworks, or model laws on *sui generis* systems which are based on customary laws for the protection of traditional knowledge.[1]

Although *sui generis* systems to protect plant varieties on the one hand and traditional knowledge on the other are necessarily connected, the strategies to do so will differ. Therefore they will be discussed separately.

OPTIONS UNDER TRIPS FOR THE PROTECTION OF PLANT VARIETIES

Developing countries have three options in meeting their obligations under TRIPS to protect plant varieties, namely, patents, legislation based on the International Convention for the Protection of New Varieties of Plants (UPOV Convention), and a different form of *sui generis* legislation.

There are divergent views as to whether a *sui generis* system to protect plant varieties should be compatible with a system of intellectual property rights, i.e. either patents or plant breeders' rights, the latter being based on the UPOV model. The question which arises is whether such a system will serve the interests of developing countries and their farming and local communities which are negatively impacted by the propertization of plant varieties. On the one hand it can be argued that there appears to be an inherent contradiction in using an IPR based approach to protect plant varieties and traditional knowledge from being subject to IPRs. On the other, it can be also argued that the most effective way in which to afford this protection is, in fact, to use such an approach. The pros and cons of whether to base *sui generis* systems on IPRs have been raised in the TRIPS Council.

Plant Variety Protection Based on Patents

In the TRIPS Council the US has taken the position that in order to be effective a *sui generis* system 'should possess the same basic characteristics as those that generally apply in relation to the protection of property rights,

---

[1] UNEP/CBD/WG-ABS/5/3 – Ad Hoc Open-Ended Working Group On Access And Benefit-Sharing, 8–12 October 2007, *Analysis Of Gaps In Existing National, Regional And International Legal And Other Instruments Relating To Access And Benefit-Sharing*, 13 September 2007, paragraph 120.

whether real, tangible or intangible.'[2] This would include intellectual property rights, and more specifically patents. The EU on the other hand has taken a more flexible approach, stating that Members could design a protection regime that is appropriate to their specific national situation. They can take account of, for instance, overall agricultural development policy objectives or the need to protect the rights of small or subsistence farmers in doing so.[3]

Not surprisingly, developing countries have insisted on the flexibility to design their own systems in accordance with their specific needs and situations. For example the African Group has stated that:

> Members have the right and the freedom to determine and adopt appropriate regimes in satisfying the requirement to protect plant varieties by effective *sui generis* systems ... The appropriate and beneficial approach is to have systems of protection which can address the local realities and needs.[4]

Plant Variety Protection Based on UPOV or Plant Breeders' Rights

There is no provision in the TRIPS Agreement which suggests that UPOV is the model of choice for a *sui generis* system of plant variety protection. However, developed countries are strongly in favour of a UPOV style system being adopted in this regard as an alternative to patent protection. The reasons given for this position are that the UPOV system is the most favourable for encouraging the development of new plant varieties in all WTO member countries, and the uniformity provided by this system would facilitate trade in such plants. Further, a growing number of countries have signed onto UPOV and the number of protected varieties under it is increasing. In view of the difficulties associated with creating and administering *sui generis* systems to protect plant varieties, the most efficient way to implement Article 27.3(b) would be to rely on an already existing and harmonized system which could possibly be adapted to meet national needs. In regard to the concerns expressed about its impact on farmers' and

---

[2] IP/C/W/369/Rev.1 – TRIPS Council, *Review of the Provisions of Article 27.3(B) Summary of Issues Raised and Points Made*, 9 March 2006, paragraph 51.

[3] IP/C/W/383 – TRIPS Council, *Communication from the European Communities and their Member States, Review of Article 27.3(b) of the TRIPS Agreement, and the Relationship between the TRIPS Agreement and the Convention on Biological Diversity (CBD) and the Protection of Traditional Knowledge and Folklore, 'A Concept Paper,'* 17 October 2002, paragraph 73.

[4] IP/C/W/404 – TRIPS Council, *Taking Forward the Review of Article 27.3(B) of the TRIPS Agreement, Joint Communication from the African Group*, 26 June 2003, p. 2.

plant breeders' rights, especially in developing countries, it has been argued that the UPOV system was flexible enough to allow countries to address these issues by way of, for example, the farmers' privilege and the breeders' exemption.[5]

Developing countries countered that firstly, Article 27.3(b) does not bind members to adopt UPOV as a model, and members are free to choose other models such as those based on the International Undertaking on Plant Genetic Resources or the CBD. They have also argued that UPOV is designed to protect plant breeders in developed countries rather than users in developing countries.[6]

The merits of the two UPOV conventions were discussed in the TRIPS Council.[7] While UPOV 1978 is still in force, most countries are in the process of ratifying UPOV 1991. Unsurprisingly, developed countries favour the latter, stating that it achieves the proper balance of rights and obligations which work for the benefit of all countries, and provides the most appropriate system and level of protection. They have also made the point that UPOV 1991 does not limit the plant species eligible for protection and those that would not have been protected under UPOV 1978 would now be eligible. They have also argued that most members who responded to the questionnaire regarding the implementation of Article 27.3(b) have adopted UPOV 1991, and its membership is increasing.

Some developing countries have stated that many countries are resisting signing UPOV 1991 in view of its limited flexibility compared with the 1978 Act.[8] Their objections are primarily based on the restrictions in UPOV 1991 on farmers' rights. Developed countries' response is that the farmers' exemption can be justified under either Article 27.3(b) or Article 30[9] of the TRIPS Agreement, and there is no need to change its wording to accommodate this.[10]

---

[5] IP/C/W/369/Rev.1, above n 2, paragraph 61. See also the position of Switzerland in IP/C/M/30 – TRIPS Council, *Minutes of Meeting from 2 to 5 April 2001*, 1 June 2001, paragraph 166.

[6] IP/C/W/369/Rev.1, above n 2, paragraph 62.

[7] Ibid, paragraph 64.

[8] See for example IP/C/W/228 – TRIPS Council, *Review of Article 27.3(b) Communication from Brazil*, 24 November 2000, p. 3.

[9] Article 30 states: 'Members may provide limited exceptions to the exclusive rights conferred by a patent, provided that such exceptions do not unreasonably conflict with a normal exploitation of the patent and do not unreasonably prejudice the legitimate interests of the patent owner, taking account of the legitimate interests of third parties.'

[10] IP/C/W/369/Rev.1, above n 2, paragraphs 65–66. Commentators have noted that for example, in Asia the seed industry is aggressively pushing for UPOV 1991

Other Forms of *Sui Generis* Protection

If a *sui generis* system is not based on patents or PBRs, the question arises as to how it should be constructed. While Article 27.3(b) requires member countries to devise and implement an 'effective' *sui generis* system of plant variety protection, TRIPS does not define this term. Two views have been expressed in the Council in regard to this question. These are that (i) there are specific criteria available to judge the effectiveness of a *sui generis* system; and (ii) the TRIPS Agreement does not specify criteria by which to judge whether a *sui generis* system is effective, and therefore this should be left to members to decide.[11]

Since developing countries have, in general, not been amenable to the suggestion that UPOV constitutes an 'effective' form of *sui generis* protection, many have taken initiatives to formulate their own systems in accordance with their own specific needs. However, in this debate too, developed countries have specified what they believe should be the minimum required criteria of such a system.[12] Accordingly, they argue that it must have provision for a legally defined and enforceable right over plants, it must

---

style protection for plants and Asia is fast conforming to this type of legislation. While the need to conform to TRIPS is one reason for doing so, a more fundamental reason is the pressure from industry to privatize resources and knowledge. The study notes that while Asian countries have taken the *sui generis* option seriously and attempted to protect their farming communities, the overriding trend is towards harmonization rather than *sui generis* systems tailored to specific situations. This process has also been exacerbated by the trend in bilateral treaties, many of which require the signatory country concerned to adhere to UPOV 1991. A similar process is taking place in Africa – Devlin Kuyek, *Intellectual Property Rights: Ultimate Control of Agricultural R&D in Asia* (2001) 6, available at http://www.grain.org/briefings_files/asiaipr.pdf (last accessed 9 July 2012); Devlin Kuyek, *Intellectual Property Rights in African Agriculture – Implications for Small Farmers* (2002), available at http://www.grain.org/briefings_files/africa-ipr-2002-en.pdf (last accessed 9 July 2012). It has also been noted that the UPOV Secretariat is also strongly advocating the UPOV Convention as the appropriate form of *sui generis* protection – Biswajit Dhar, *Sui Generis Systems for Plant Variety Protection – Options under TRIPS* (2002) Quaker United Nations Office, Chapter 2, available at http://www.geneva.quno.info/pdf/sgcol1.pdf (last accessed 9 July 2012).

[11] IP/C/W/369/Rev.1, above n 2, paragraph 50.

[12] IP/C/W/383, above n 3, paragraph 77; IP/C/W/209 – TRIPS Council, *Review of the Provisions of Article 27.3(b) Further Views of the United States, Communication from the United States*, 3 October 2000, Section 2. See also IP/C/W/122 – TRIPS Council, *Review of the Provisions of Article 27.3(b), Illustrative List of Questions*, 22 December 1998 and IP/C/M/29 – TRIPS Council, *Minutes of Meeting from 27 to 30 November and 6 December 2000*, 6 March 2001, para 162.

include the principles of national treatment and most favoured nation treatment, and it must provide for the effective enforcement of rights under the TRIPS Agreement. These provisions would essentially result in bringing *sui generis* systems in line with TRIPS, and thus an 'effective' system is one that is TRIPS compliant.[13] Specifying such criteria at the outset imposes constraints on countries in formulating their own systems and these pre-conditions have been resisted. It must however, be noted that the final arbiter of what constitutes an effective system would be the dispute resolution mechanism of TRIPS.

Alternate views as to what an effective *sui generis* system should comprise encompass a wide range of issues. The UK IPR Commission has for example, emphasized such aspects as the rights of farmers to save and plant seed, including the possibility of informal sale and exchange.[14] The International Plant Genetic Resources Institute (IPGRI) has also produced a checklist for developing *sui generis* systems, noting that a system of IPRs suitable for industrialized export oriented agriculture would not necessarily be suitable for one based on subsistence farming. It has also emphasized that appropriate mechanisms should be used to prevent the monopolist effects of IPRs, especially patents.[15] The various aspects that must be addressed in such a system and the differing views of developed and developing countries expressed in the TRIPS Council, are discussed below.[16]

---

[13] Dwijen Rangnekar, *Access to Genetic Resources, Gene-based Inventions and Agriculture* Commission on Intellectual Property Rights Study Paper 3a (2002) 33, available at http://www.iprcommission.org/papers/pdfs/study_papers/sp3a_rangnekar_study.pdf (last accessed 9 July 2012); Geoff Tansey, *Trade, Intellectual Property, Food and Biodiversity – Key issues and options for the 1999 review of Article 27.3(b) of the TRIPS Agreement* (1999) 8, available at http://www.quno.org/geneva/pdf/economic/Discussion/Trade-IP-Food-Biodiversity-English.pdf (last accessed 9 July 2012).

[14] Commission on Intellectual Property Rights, *Integrating Intellectual Property Rights and Development Policy* (2002) 66, available at http://www.iprcommission.org/papers/pdfs/final_report/CIPRfullfinal.pdf (last accessed 9 July 2012).

[15] Tansey, above n 13, 10–11.

[16] For a discussion on the possible aspects of a *sui generis* system see Philippe Cullet, 'Revision of the TRIPS Agreement concerning the Protection of Plant Varieties: Lessons from India concerning the Development of a *Sui generis* System' (1999) 2(4) *Journal of World Intellectual Property* 617, 652.

The Nature and Extent of the Protectable Subject Matter

Developed countries have stated that the protectable subject matter (i.e. plant varieties) must be clearly defined, including the characteristics or qualities it must possess to qualify for protection. The US view is that it is in members' interests to include as many varieties as possible since this will encourage investment in developing new plant varieties from among the widest possible range of genera and species. Therefore protection should apply to plant varieties throughout the plant kingdom.

This position has been countered on the basis that Article 27.3(b) does not specify which plant varieties should be protected and even UPOV does not require protection of the entire plant kingdom.[17] It has also been suggested that in the absence of a definition of a plant variety in TRIPS, developing countries are free to produce their own definition which could cover both 'modern' varieties as well as landraces. While the modern varieties could be protected under a UPOV like legislation on the basis of novelty, distinctness, uniformity and stability, farmers' varieties could be protected under more flexible criteria such as sufficient identification and distinctness.[18]

The Criteria to Qualify for Protection

Developed countries have insisted that the conditions for granting protection must be clearly defined. The EU has stated that in the context of plant varieties, novelty is an essential condition for protection. The US has also argued that to qualify for protection the plant must meet the requirements of novelty, distinctiveness, uniformity and stability. Novelty is a criterion of patents and establishes a high threshold which the product in question must meet to qualify for protection. Farmers' varieties would not generally meet this criterion. Developing countries have counter argued that these requirements go beyond the determinants contained in existing models, and for example under UPOV, novelty is not strictly speaking, a criterion.[19] India has pointed out that members might wish to protect farmers' varieties under their *sui generis* laws, and while such varieties may not be new, they may be the result of further improvement. Such protection might, on the other hand,

---

[17] IP/C/W/369/Rev.1, above n 2, paragraph 52.

[18] Rangnekar, above n 13, 29; Michael Blakeney, *Access to Genetic Resources, Gene-based Inventions and Agriculture* (2002) Commission on Intellectual Property Rights, Study Paper 3b, 11, available at http://www.iprcommission.org/papers/pdfs/study_papers/sp3b_blakeney_study.pdf (last accessed 9 July 2012).

[19] IP/C/W/369/Rev.1, above n 2, paragraph 53.

be based on other *sui generis* systems like the International Undertaking (now the FAO Treaty) or the CBD.[20]

While patent type criteria of protection would not be in the interests of developing countries, applying PVP standards as under UPOV may also be unsatisfactory. PVP laws have lower thresholds than the standards required for patents and there is no requirement of non-obviousness (i.e. inventive step or novelty), or utility. As a result such laws may allow breeders to protect varieties with very similar characteristics and lacking genuine improvement. This too could prove detrimental to farmers' varieties as negligible improvements could be made to them and protection obtained.[21] It appears therefore that either the presence or absence of novelty as a criterion for protection would be problematic.

It has been suggested that developing countries should raise the threshold of novelty so that only varieties with significant innovations with particular characteristics are accorded protection. These characteristics would be those that are considered socially beneficial, for example yield increases, or traits of nutritional value. Therefore the criteria of distinctness could be strengthened and other criteria formulated to ensure the social and economic utility of the varieties.[22]

The Nature of the Protection

There was extensive discussion in the TRIPS Council as to the nature and duration of the rights to plant varieties, as well as the exceptions to them. The EU argued that the rights holder should at least be able to prevent third parties from carrying out certain acts in relation to the subject matter over a specified period of time. The law should also provide for national treatment and most favoured nation treatment.[23] The US stated that the system must establish the period during which the rights are in force and the circumstances, if any, in which they may expire early or be extended, the former ideally being at least 20 years from the date the rights are granted, with some varieties being granted a period of 25 years. The US was prepared to accept that certain limitations on these rights may be expressly provided for. These include non-commercial use, experimental use and use of a variety for the purpose of breeding other varieties. It would also accept a provision

---

20 IP/C/M/29, above n 12, paragraph 162.

21 Commission on Intellectual Property Rights, above n 14, 61.

22 Ibid at 61.

23 IP/C/W/383, above n 3, paragraph 77.

which permits farmers to save seed from the harvest of a protected variety to re-seed their own holdings for the following year.[24]

African countries have responded that, regardless of what *sui generis* systems are adopted certain exceptions must be included as a matter of public policy to address, inter alia, issues of 'food security, health, rural development and equity for local communities whose traditional knowledge systems have produced staple varieties, including varieties that have medicinal and biodiversity value.'[25] These exceptions include the non-commercial use of plant varieties and the farmers' system of seed saving, exchange and selling of seeds. They have also taken the position that any *sui generis* system to protect plant varieties must also be consistent with the provisions of the CBD and the FAO Treaty.[26]

Who can obtain Property Rights over the Subject Matter?

An effective law must also establish who is entitled to the property rights over plant varieties. According to the US view such rights would be limited to breeders or others specifically entitled to them either through contract or the law of succession. However, this would preclude the recognition of farmers' rights that have arisen through tradition rather than through contracts or succession. Developed countries have responded that protecting farmers' rights would not be precluded but would not be an obligation under the TRIPS Agreement.[27] The EU has however, accepted that the farmers' exemption can be justified under Article 27.3(b) of TRIPS depending on the scope of the exemption.[28]

While the inclusion of farmers' and breeders' exemptions in a patent or PVP system of plant protection would protect the rights of these groups to some extent, a *sui generis* system to positively ensure farmers' rights would be more effective. Certain issues would have to be considered in formulating such a system. One based on IPRs would not be effective in protecting farmers' varieties. Firstly, they would not meet the criterion of protection required under IPRs, particularly the requirement that a new variety is

---

24 IP/C/W/209, above n 12, 3. See also the EU position in IP/C/W/383, above n 3, paragraph 77 and IP/C/W/369/Rev.1, above n 2, paragraphs 55–57.

25 IP/C/W/206 – TRIPS Council, *Review of the Provisions of Article 27.3(b) Communication from Mauritius on behalf of the African Group 20 September 2000*, 2.

26 IP/C/W/404, above n 4, 3.

27 IP/C/W/369/Rev.1, above n 2, paragraph 54.

28 IP/C/W/383, above n 3, paragraph 86.

distinct from 'varieties of common knowledge.'[29] Secondly, varieties developed by farmers cannot generally be attributed to an identifiable individual or individuals, thus making it more difficult to assign the rights. As Blakeney notes, the *sui generis* systems which are most relevant to developing countries are those which protect farmers' varieties and landraces, combining one of the versions of UPOV with the access principles of the CBD.[30] He cites the OAU Model Law as one such law which is based on UPOV 1991, but notes that most national systems prefer legislation based on UPOV 1978.[31]

CONCLUSION

The provision in the TRIPS Agreement which permits member states to provide for plant variety protection by way of patents, an effective *sui generis* system, or any combination thereof gives developing countries the opportunity to devise unique systems tailored to their specific needs. The question that arises is whether these countries can, and will, make optimum use of this flexibility.

The debate in the TRIPS Council indicates that developed countries are attempting to negate this flexibility by insisting that a *sui generis* system must necessarily be based on a form of intellectual property rights, and to this end they are advocating a UPOV style system, which is very similar to patents. It is in the interests of developed countries to have a uniform and efficient system of plant variety protection, which is specifically tailored to recognize and reward the processes and end products of modern plant breeders working in laboratories. The question is whether such a system would provide developing countries and their farmers with the same protection and advantages.

In regard to the protection of farmers' varieties, it can be argued that IPRs would not achieve this objective since patent criteria of novelty, distinctness, uniformity and stability would be difficult to apply to landraces. Also, given the community based processes of breeding carried out by farmers, it would also be nearly impossible to identify the recipient or recipients of the patent. Further, farmers are involved not only in breeding, but also in

---

29 Blakeney, above n 18, 3.

30 Ibid at 3–4.

31 Ibid at 36. See African Model Law, 2000. Examples of the latter are the Andean Community's Common System on Access to Genetic Resources, 1996, Biodiversity Law of Costa Rica, 1998, Community Intellectual Property Rights Act of India, 1999 and the Seeds and Plant Varieties Act of Kenya, 1975.

conserving and nurturing crop diversity, and this cannot be recognized or rewarded under an IPR system. An IPR system applied to plant variety protection will in fact reduce crop diversity as its purpose is to protect a few specific varieties with particular characteristics marketed as beneficial. Therefore the drawback of such a system for developing countries is that it does not recognize the work of farmers in the field, whose breeding processes are different but result in equally valuable products.

A *sui generis* system for developing countries should ideally be one which neutralizes the impacts of IPRs, on farmers, as well as on national agricultural systems. The primary objective of such a mechanism should be to ensure that PGRFA is maintained in the public domain to the greatest extent possible. Therefore rather than extending a system of privatization to farmers' varieties, it would be more effective to put in place a system which would prevent farmers' landraces, or aspects of them which may be of value, from being appropriated.

Such a system would have to be devised within the boundaries of the TRIPS Agreement, but there are sufficient flexibilities contained in Articles 27.2 and 27.3, which could be made use of for this purpose. Currently, the liberal application of the novelty standard in effect permits plants with minimal variation to be patented, and also permits discoveries to be interpreted as inventions. As suggested by the UK IPR Commission, developing countries should raise the threshold of novelty so that only varieties, which are clearly distinct and innovative, would be accorded protection. This would prevent negligible variations on farmers' varieties from being accorded patent protection. Further, they should strictly interpret the terms 'inventions' and 'discoveries' in order to prevent, for example, genes that are isolated from existing varieties from being patented. Instances such as the patenting of basmati and jasmine rice, discussed in Chapter 3, and the gene isolated from the wild rice variety in Mali discussed in Chapter 9, would need to be prevented in the future. Further, developing countries should maintain the position that TRIPS does not define what is meant by an 'effective' system of protection, and member states have the flexibility to interpret this term to suit their particular requirements.

The second aspect of a *sui generis* system should be to obviate the effects of the monopolistic control of plant varieties on farmers and agriculture in developing countries. An important aspect of negating this control is to maintain the rights of farmers to save and re-use seed, and also to protect their role as breeders of new varieties. Since UPOV 1991 has further restricted the rights of farmers and breeders to do so, adherence to this agreement would not be in the interests of developing countries. A system which is more conducive to furthering these interests, particularly in regard to farmers' and breeders' rights, can be found in the UPOV 1978 Act which is considerably less stringent than that contained in UPOV 1991 or in a patent system. A *sui generis* system could also take advantage of the flexibilities in TRIPS, particularly those which permit inventions to be excluded from patentability in the interests of *ordre public* and morality, including to protect human, animal or plant life or health, or to avoid serious prejudice to the environment.

Although implementing *sui generis* systems of plant protection has been cited as a positive measure to protect the biological resources of developing countries, it seems that it would need to be formulated rather as a defensive strategy against the impacts of IPRs. As noted earlier, the question is to what extent developing countries can in fact put *sui generis* systems in place. TRIPS is sufficiently flexible to permit them to introduce measures protecting their interests within the framework of the Agreement. Nevertheless the majority of such countries have not done so, and the debate on the nature of such a system is continuing in the TRIPS Council. Concurrently with the debate, provisions in bilateral treaties are requiring many such countries to adopt UPOV 1978 or UPOV 1991. This would of course, effectively pre-empt any further attempts by such countries to formulate their independent systems.

SUI GENERIS PROTECTION OF TRADITIONAL KNOWLEDGE

As noted earlier both defensive and positive measures are required to protect traditional knowledge from misappropriation, and *sui generis* protection of traditional knowledge has been cited as a form of positive protection. *Sui generis* protection of traditional knowledge is not specifically mentioned in any of the international environmental documents, and the issue has evolved in relation to the traditional knowledge associated with plant varieties which often serves to provide leads to their uses.

The questions which need to be considered in *sui generis* systems to protect traditional knowledge include what is to be protected and from whom, for what purpose, for whose benefit and in what form.[32] Three broad objectives have been identified in this regard, namely, preservation, protection and promotion.[33] It has also been suggested that specific regimes may

---

[32] Surinder Kaur Verma, 'Protecting Traditional Knowledge: Is a *Sui generis* System an Answer?' (2004) 7(6) *Journal of World Intellectual Property* 765, 766.

[33] Sophia Twarog, 'Preserving, Protecting and Promoting Traditional Knowledge: National Actions and International Dimensions' in UNCTAD/DITC/TED/10

have to be created for specific components of traditional knowledge, such as artistic creations, including expressions of folklore, PGRFA and associated knowledge, and traditional medicine.[34] This section will consider traditional knowledge in relation to PGRFA.

Whatever the form and content of such a system, an overriding question is whether such measures should go beyond merely preventing the misappropriation of traditional knowledge and ensuring the sharing of the benefits derived from it, or whether it should take a more holistic approach to the issue, promoting its further development and conservation in the interests of the communities which hold it.[35] Several Declarations of indigenous peoples have, for example, demanded the right to control the development and manipulation of traditional knowledge, and the right to define for themselves their own intellectual property.[36] Indigenous peoples have also declared that the protection of traditional knowledge must be linked to their rights to self-determination and territory.[37] They have also

Sophia Twarog and Promila Kapoor (eds) (2004) *Protecting And Promoting Traditional Knowledge: Systems, National Experiences And International Dimensions*, 61at 63.

[34] Carlos M Correa, *Issues and options surrounding the protection of traditional knowledge* (2001) Quaker United Nations Office Geneva, 14, available at http://www.geneva.quno.info/pdf/tkcol3.pdf (last accessed 9 July 2012).

[35] See TD/B/COM.1/EM.13/2 – United Nations Conference on Trade and Development, *Systems and National Experiences for Protecting Traditional Knowledge, Innovations and Practices*, 22 August 2000 for a list of objectives to be considered when designing systems to protect TK.

[36] See for example the *Mataatua Declaration on Cultural and Intellectual Property Rights of Indigenous Peoples* – First International Conference on the Cultural & Intellectual Property Rights of Indigenous Peoples (1993), available at http://www.ankn.uaf.edu/IKS/mataatua.html (last accessed 9 July 2012); *Charter of the Indigenous and Tribal Peoples of the Tropical Forests* – Statement of the International Alliance of the Indigenous and Tribal Peoples of the Tropical Forests (Established Penang, Malaysia, 15 February 1992) (Revised Nairobi, Kenya, 22 November 2002), available at www.international-alliance.org/documents/charter_eng. doc (last accessed 9 July 2012); *Jalayinbul Statement on Indigenous Property Rights*, 1993 cited in WIPO/IPTK/RT/99/3 – World Intellectual Property Organization, *Roundtable on Intellectual Property and Traditional Knowledge, November 1 and 2, 1999, What Is Traditional Knowledge? Why Should It Be Protected? Who Should Protect It? For Whom?: Understanding The Value Chain, Prepared by Professor Michael Blakeney, Centre for Commercial Law Studies Queen Mary and Westfield College, University of London*. See also UN Declaration on Indigenous Peoples 2007 – Article 31.

[37] Michael Halewood, 'Indigenous and Local Knowledge in International Law: A Preface to *Sui generis* Intellectual Property Protection' (1999) 44 *McGill Law Journal* 953.

stated that they have a fundamental right to practice their culture and to use their customary laws to maintain and protect their knowledge, and a fundamental right to participate in decision-making processes that affect their well-being.[38]

The United Nations Conference on Trade and Development (UNCTAD) takes a more holistic approach to the protection of traditional knowledge than that taken in the discourse on biological resources and PGRFA, and acknowledges its importance in enhancing the socio-economic development of its holders. UNCTAD has also noted that *sui generis* systems are in fact only one possible option to protect traditional knowledge, other measures being strengthening customary law, IPR protection including existing IPR instruments, prior informed consent and access and benefit-sharing mechanisms, documentation of traditional knowledge, and other measures to strengthen and develop traditional knowledge protection systems.[39]

Prior informed consent and access and benefit sharing methods have already been discussed. Documentation of traditional knowledge falls under the category of defensive mechanisms of protection and will be discussed in Chapter 12. *Sui generis* systems in relation to customary law and IPRs will be considered here.

Sui Generis Systems for the Protection of Traditional Knowledge Based on Intellectual Property Rights

One question which has been debated is whether intellectual property rights, particularly patents, can provide adequate positive protection for traditional knowledge. Developing countries and indigenous communities have generally taken the position that they cannot, and several reasons have been cited in this regard. First, IPRs protect individual property rights while traditional knowledge is created, improved and transmitted collectively. Second, traditional knowledge is developed over a period of time and either codified in texts or retained in oral traditions over generations. Therefore the conditions of novelty and innovative steps necessary for the granting of patents may be questionable. Third, knowledge is often held by different independent communities and this would make it difficult to identify a

---

38 UNCTAD/DITC/TED/10 – Sophia Twarog and Promila Kapoor (eds) *Protecting and Promoting Traditional Knowledge: Systems, National Experiences And International Dimensions* (2004) 83. See also Rosemary J Coombe, 'Protecting Traditional Environmental Knowledge and New Social Movements in the Americas: Intellectual Property, Human Right, or Claims to an Alternative Form of Sustainable Development?' (2005) *Florida Journal of International Law* 115, 122.

39 TD/B/COM.1/EM.13/2, above n 35, 10.

single holder of that knowledge. Fourth, patents grant protection for a limited period of time whereas traditional knowledge is passed on from generation to generation.[40]

While it has also been suggested that other forms of IPRs such as copyrights, trade secrets, trademarks and geographical indications may be useful in protecting traditional knowledge, the general consensus is that they too are not appropriate mechanisms to do so.[41] As a study of the United Nations Permanent Forum on Indigenous Issues (UNPFII) has noted:

> [i]ndigenous traditional knowledge is not simply a different type of intellectual property; it is a completely different entity. This is a distinction that is not generally appreciated, and as long as it remains unrecognized, questions will persist about the appropriateness of existing intellectual property regimes to protect indigenous interests.[42]

The UNPFII has commented that the question whether IPRs can be used or adapted to protect traditional knowledge is controversial. It points out that firstly they were never designed to protect traditional knowledge, and secondly the matter is difficult to separate from related issues such as the extent to which such IPRs would encroach on the public domain and in fact create incentives for the privatization of public goods. As in the case of the protection of genetic resources, IPRs would not seem to be an appropriate mechanism for this purpose.[43]

---

[40] IP/C/W/347/Add.1 – TRIPS Council, *Review of the Provisions of Article 27.3(b), Relationship between the TRIPS Agreement and the Convention on Biological Diversity and Protection of Traditional Knowledge and Folklore, Information from Intergovernmental Organizations*, 10 June 2002, 6. See also Eliana Torelly de Carvalho, 'Protection of Traditional Biodiversity-Related Knowledge: Analysis of Proposals for the Adoption of a Sui generis System' (2003) 11 *Missouri Environmental Law & Policy Review* 38.

[41] Graham Dutfield, *Intellectual Property, Biogenetic Resources and Traditional Knowledge* (2004) Chapter 10.

[42] E/C.19/2007/10 – Economic and Social Council, Permanent Forum on Indigenous Issues, Sixth session, 14–25 May 2007, Implementation of recommendations on the six mandated areas of the Forum and on the Millennium Development Goals Report of the Secretariat on Indigenous traditional knowledge, 8.

[43] TD/B/COM.1/EM.13/2, above n 35, 11. See also UNEP/CBD/WG8J/5/INF/12 – Ad Hoc Open-Ended Inter-Sessional Working Group on Article 8(J) and Related Provisions of the Convention on Biological Diversity, Fifth meeting, 15–19 October 2007, *UNPFII Study on Customary Laws Pertaining to Indigenous Traditional Knowledge and on to What Extent Such Customary Laws should be*

Sui Generis Systems for the Protection of Traditional Knowledge, Based on Customary Laws and Community Rights

An alternative option to IPR based *sui generis* systems to protect traditional knowledge is one based on customary laws and community rights. It has been pointed out that access to, and use of, traditional knowledge, both within and outside communities, is governed by a diversity of unwritten, customary laws which carry responsibilities as well as customary rights.[44] In countries where such laws already exist and are granted recognition along with the mainstream legal systems, perhaps the most appropriate method of protection would be to strengthen and implement them. UNCTAD has noted that giving customary laws even minimal recognition would still help to challenge the assumption that traditional knowledge is in the public domain and therefore open access to all. It observes:

> All too often TK is misappropriated because it is conveniently assumed that since it has been publicly disclosed, communities have given up all claims over it. In fact, it is possible that the acts of disclosure and subsequent commercial use contravened customary law. Before considering the applicability of conventional IPRs or *sui generis* systems, consideration should be given to enhancing the status of the established laws of the TK-holding communities.[45]

Reflected in International and National Standards Addressing Traditional Knowledge, paragraph 21. For a discussion on the issue see Bernard O'Connor, 'Protecting Traditional Knowledge. An Overview of a Developing Area of Intellectual Property Law' (2003) 6(5) *Journal of World Intellectual Property* 677. For a comprehensive analysis of *sui generis* intellectual property laws to protect traditional knowledge see The Crucible II Group, *Seeding solutions Volume 2. Options for national laws governing control over genetic resources and biological innovations* (2001). See also Halewood, above n 37.

[44] TD/B/COM.1/EM.13/2, above n 35, 5. See also WIPO/GRTKF/IC/8/6 – Intergovernmental Committee on Intellectual Property and Genetic Resources, Traditional Knowledge and Folklore, Eighth Session, June 6 to 10, 2005, *Practical Means of Giving Effect to the International Dimension of the Committee's Work*, paragraph 13; UNEP/CBD/WG8J/6/2/Add.1 – Ad Hoc Open-Ended Inter-Sessional Working Group on Article 8(J) and Related Provisions of the Convention on Biological Diversity, Sixth meeting, 2–6 November 2009 *Advice on how Article 10 (C) Can Be Further Advanced and Implemented as a Priority Note by the Executive Secretary* 2.

[45] TD/B/COM.1/EM.13/2, above n 35, 10. For definitions of terminology related to *sui generis* systems see UNEP/CBD/WG8J/7/INF/1/Add.1 – Ad Hoc Open-Ended Inter-Sessional Working Group on Article 8(J) and Related Provisions of the Convention on Biological Diversity, Seventh meeting, 31 October – 4 November 2011, *Extracts covering the evolution of the issue of definitions within*

In 2006 the UNPFII recommended that the Forum should commission a study on customary laws pertaining to traditional knowledge in order to investigate the extent to which they should be reflected in international and national laws. The study should include an analysis of such laws as a potential *sui generis* system for protecting traditional knowledge.[46] Principles of customary law relevant to genetic resources and traditional knowledge constitute *sui generis* systems for managing such resources and knowledge.[47] The Working Group on Article 8(j) (WG8J) has also stated that the scope of such systems 'should consider the collective nature of indigenous and local communities and their holistic approach to resource use and management, including its ideology and relationship to local environment.'[48]

The WG8J goes on to note that in practice no single overarching international, regional or national *sui generis* system can embrace all the aspects of traditional knowledge in its original cultural context and its related customary law, in view of the diversity of the world's indigenous communities. Therefore it is essential that such systems be local in nature but supported by national and international frameworks and guidelines.[49]

Customary laws would necessarily encompass community rights which go beyond protection of traditional knowledge. The term 'community rights' refers to the collective rights of communities over their traditional knowledge and biological resources. A community rights system could be all encompassing or address specific issues. The term includes more specific definitions, as for example, 'community intellectual property rights,' 'community intellectual rights,' 'community based property rights'

---

the sui generis agenda item from the Working group on Article 8(J) and Related Provisions, Note by the Executive Secretary, 6 July 2011.

[46] E/C.19/2006/2 – United Nations Economic and Social Council, Fifth session, 15–26 May 2006 *Report of the International Technical Workshop on Indigenous Traditional Knowledge*, 15 December 2005, 12. This recommendation was adopted – E/C.19/2006/11 – United Nations Permanent Forum on Indigenous Issues, *Report on the fifth session,* 15–26 May 2006.

[47] E/C.19/2007/8 – United Nations Economic and Social Council, Sixth Session, *Report of the International Expert Group Meeting on the International Regime on Access and Benefit-Sharing and Indigenous Peoples' Human Rights of the Convention on Biological Diversity*, 14 March 2007, paragraphs 43–44.

[48] UNEP/CBD/WG8J/5/6 – Ad Hoc Open-Ended Inter-Sessional Working Group On Article 8(J) And Related Provisions Of The Convention On Biological Diversity, 15–19 October 2007, *Development Of Elements Of Sui generis Systems For The Protection Of Traditional Knowledge, Innovations And Practices To Identify Priority Elements*, 20 September 2007, paragraph 15.

[49] Ibid, paragraph 15.

(CBPR) and 'traditional resource rights (TRR).' While there are points of difference between these terms, they generally take a holistic approach to the question of indigenous rights and are not restricted to issues of traditional knowledge alone. Community rights have been incorporated in many national and regional laws and the point in issue is less the terminology used than the rights which have been acknowledged in them.

The concept of traditional resource rights is perhaps the most all encompassing of community rights, covering the gamut of human rights including resource rights. Traditional resource rights have been defined as:

> an integrated rights concept that recognises the inextricable link between cultural and biological diversity and sees no contradiction between the human rights of indigenous and local communities including the right to development and environmental conservation. Indeed, they are mutually supportive since the destiny of traditional peoples largely determines, and is determined by, the state of the world's biological diversity. TRR includes overlapping and mutually supporting bundles of rights.[50]

Community based property rights (CBPR) are:

> by *definition* emanate from and are enforced by communities. The *distinguishing feature* of CBPRs is that they derive their authority from the community in which they operate, not from the nation-state where they are located. Formal legal recognition or grant of CBPRs by the state, however, is generally desirable and can help to ensure that CBPRs are respected and used in pursuit of the public interest.[51]

The term community intellectual property rights deals most directly with the issue of traditional knowledge protection. As noted it 'would enable farmers to assert their "rights to seed" by claiming that any corporation using local knowledge or local resources without the permission of local communities is engaging in intellectual piracy.'[52] Community intellectual property rights would need to be included in national legislation with reciprocal recognition in other countries, an international database would have to be created for trading the germplasm, and an institutional

---

[50] Darrell A Posey and Graham Dutfield, *Beyond intellectual property: toward traditional resource rights for indigenous peoples and local communities* (1996) Chapter 9.

[51] Center for International Environment Law (CIEL) *Whose Resources? Whose Common Good? Towards a New Paradigm of Environmental Justice and the National Interest in Indonesia* (2002) Chapter 1, available at http://www.ciel.org/Publications/Whose_Resources_3–27–02.pdf (last accessed 9 July 2012).

[52] Posey and Dutfield, above n 50, Chapter 9.

mechanism would be required to address conflicts.[53] However, such rights are essentially an adaptation of mainstream IPRs and the concept has met with some opposition. GRAIN notes that in recent years the word 'property' has been dropped from the phrase because the concept was found to be inimical to community views and the term has been rephrased as 'community intellectual rights.'[54]

Community rights have been incorporated in various forms in the national legislation of several countries as well as in regional frameworks. At present five regions have developed or are developing regional agreements, frameworks or model laws for *sui generis* systems based on customary laws to protect traditional knowledge.[55] The national legislation includes special intellectual property regimes, community intellectual property rights protection Acts, and indigenous peoples' rights Acts.[56]

A good example of community rights is found in Part IV of the OAU Model Law entitled 'Community Rights.' Under Article 16 of the Law the State recognizes the rights of communities over the following:

i) their biological resources;
ii) the right to collectively benefit from the use of their biological resources;
iii) their innovations, practices, knowledge and technologies acquired through generations;

---

53 Ibid.

54 GRAIN, *Signposts to Sui Generis Rights: 3 – Strategy Ideas for the 1999 TRIPS Review & Beyond*, available at http://www.grain.org/briefings/?id=176 (last accessed 9 July 2012).

55 These include the African Union, the Andean Community, ASEAN, Latin America and the Pacific Forum. See also International Centre for Trade and Sustainable Development, *WIPO Committee on Genetic Resources, Traditional Knowledge Inconclusive Thus Far* (2007), available at http://ictsd.org/i/ip/39615/ (last accessed 9 July 2012); Kathryn Garforth, Isabel López Noriega, Jorge Cabrera Medaglia, Kent Nnadozie and Gabriel R Nemogá *Overview of the National and Regional Implementation of Access to Genetic Resources and Benefit Sharing Measures* (3rd ed 2005), available at http://cisdl.org/public/docs/news/CISDL_ABS_Imp_Study_final.pdf (last accessed 9 July 2012).

56 UNEP/CBD/WG-ABS/5/3, above n 1, paragraph 120. See also the measures taken by Australia regarding elements of *sui generis* systems to protect traditional knowledge – UNEP/CBD/WG8J/7/INF/1– Ad Hoc Open-Ended Inter-Sessional Working Group on Article 8(J) and Related Provisions of the Convention on Biological Diversity, Seventh meeting, 31 October – 4 November 2011, *Compilation of Views on Elements of* Sui Generis *Systems for the Protection of Traditional Knowledge, Note by the Executive Secretary,* 8 July 2011.

iv) the right to collectively benefit from the utilization of their innovations, practices, knowledge and technologies;
v) their rights to use their innovations, practices, knowledge and technologies in the conservation and sustainable use of biological diversity;
vi) the exercise of collective rights as legitimate custodians and users of their biological resources.

These rights will be protected as they are enshrined under the norms, practices and customary laws of the communities whether written or not.[57]

The Third World Network has drafted a Model Draft Intellectual Rights Act, which is also based on the custodianship of traditional knowledge. This Model Act deals with 'innovations' which include any collective and cumulative knowledge or technology of the use, properties, values and processes of any biological material. The local community shall be the lawful and sole custodian of such innovation in perpetuity and their rights in this regard shall not be impaired. Any exclusive monopoly right in respect of such innovation shall constitute an impairment of these rights.[58]

The Biodiversity Law of Costa Rica[59] also recognizes *sui generis* community intellectual rights stating that the right:

> exists and is legally recognised by the mere existence of the cultural practice or knowledge related to genetic resources and biochemicals; it does not require prior declaration, explicit recognition nor official registration; therefore it can include practices which in the future acquire such status.

It goes on to state that '[t]his recognition implies that no form of intellectual or industrial property rights protection regulated in this chapter, in special laws and in international law shall affect such historic practices.'[60]

The Pacific Community Regional Framework[61] is also based on a similar principle. It recognizes the concept of traditional cultural rights and states that '[t]he traditional owners of traditional knowledge or expressions of

---

[57] Article 17.

[58] Community Intellectual Rights Act developed by the Third World Network, available at http://www.biotech-monitor.nl/3606.htm (last accessed 9 July 2012).

[59] Biodiversity Law No. 7788 of 1998.

[60] Article 83.

[61] Regional Framework for the Protection of Traditional Knowledge and Expressions of Culture, Secretariat of the Pacific Community: Model Law for the Protection of Traditional Knowledge and Expressions of Culture (2005) 12 *International Journal of Cultural Property* 459.

culture are the holders of the traditional cultural rights in the traditional knowledge or expressions of culture.' Such rights exist whether or not those expressions of culture are in material form: they are inalienable and continue in force in perpetuity.

The common theme in these laws is that the rights of communities over traditional knowledge is presumed without explicit recognition or articulation, and by that fact the imposition by others of IPRs over such knowledge is precluded. This is in essence a defensive measure against the propertization of such knowledge.

THE INTERNATIONAL DEBATE ON *SUI GENERIS* SYSTEMS TO PROTECT TRADITIONAL KNOWLEDGE

While the debate on *sui generis* systems to protect traditional knowledge emerged out of the debate on the propertization of PGRFA, it is important to note that its protection cannot be viewed only in the light of the latter. While it is necessary to protect traditional knowledge from claims of third parties to IPRs and this is in fact the primary problem regarding the issue, it must also be borne in mind that traditional knowledge which is held by indigenous and local communities is an intrinsic component of their lives, culture and rights. Therefore its protection cannot be isolated from these aspects and a more holistic approach must be taken in resolving the problems. As can be seen from the discussion in this section, indigenous peoples have consistently urged this position in international fora.

The debate on *sui generis* systems to protect traditional knowledge has taken place in several international fora including the WIPO IGC, TRIPS Council and the CBD as well as in other UN agencies such as the Permanent Forum on Indigenous Issues. While none of these fora has succeeded to date in producing specific proposals on either the nature or scope of such a system, with the exception of the Permanent Forum on Indigenous Issues the emphasis has been on traditional knowledge protection in the context of IPRs rather than on a holistic consideration of indigenous rights.

The WIPO IGC

In the WIPO it is the Intergovernmental Committee on Intellectual Property and Genetic Resources, Traditional Knowledge and Folklore (IGC) which has a specific mandate to address the issue of traditional knowledge protection including *sui generis* systems. The discussion in the IGC has revolved around locating traditional knowledge protection within the IPR system, focusing on such issues as disclosure obligations as protection from misappropriation rather than emphasizing *sui generis* measures.[62] There is substantive indigenous peoples' and non-governmental participation in the IGC and these groups have expressed concern at the trends of the discussions. The issues they have raised include the inadequacy of the IPR system to protect traditional knowledge, the possible substance of a legally binding document, the recognition of customary laws, and mutual supportiveness with other agreements.[63]

While several developing countries have urged the formulation of a legally binding instrument to protect traditional knowledge,[64] indigenous groups have cautioned that it should recognize issues outside of the IPR debate. These include that indigenous peoples must be recognized as custodians and owners of their knowledge and natural resources, and have exclusive rights of control over them; States should affirm that the land and territorial rights of indigenous peoples are fundamental to the retention of indigenous knowledge and cultural practices pursuant to the implementation of relevant international obligations; an international regime should expressly affirm the right of indigenous peoples to restrict and/or exclude access to their knowledge and natural resources; an international regime must ensure that the right to prior informed consent of indigenous peoples is guaranteed and protected as a fundamental principle in the exercise of self-determination and sovereignty, and the right of PIC must be maintained throughout any ABS arrangement; an international regime must enable the effective implementation, application and enforcement of indigenous customary laws and cultural practices; and in the event of a conflict, indigenous

---

62 See for example WIPO/GRTKF/IC/12/7 – Intergovernmental Committee on Intellectual Property and Genetic Resources, Traditional Knowledge and Folklore, Twelfth Session, 25–29 February 2008, *Recognition of Traditional Knowledge Within the Patent System*, 12 February 2008.

63 South Centre and CIEL, *The Proposed WIPO Framework on Traditional Knowledge: Does It Meet Indigenous Peoples' Demands?* Quarterly Update Second Quarter 2007, available at http://www.ciel.org/Publications/IP_Update_2Q07.pdf (last accessed 9 July 2012), 4 April 2008. See also WIPO/GRTKF/IC/12/6 – Intergovernmental Committee on Intellectual Property and Genetic Resources, Traditional Knowledge and Folklore Twelfth Session, 25–29 February 2008, *Summary of Options for the International Dimension of the Committee's Work*, 6 December 2007.

64 See for example WIPO/GRTKF/IC/9/14 Prov 2. – Intergovernmental Committee on Intellectual Property and Genetic Resources, Traditional Knowledge and Folklore, Ninth Session, April 24 to 28, 2006, *Draft Report (Second Draft)*.

customary laws and cultural practices should prevail over domestic law or an international regime.[65]

The discussion on this topic is ongoing and has currently been carried into the Twenty-First Session of the IGC in April 2012. The draft Policy Objectives and Core Principles (which include general guiding principles and substantive principles) for the protection of traditional knowledge are still being negotiated, reflecting the difficulties in reaching consensus on these issues.[66] The current draft articles on the protection of traditional knowledge still fall short of indigenous peoples' demands for a holistic approach to the issue, and they remain located in the discourse on access to and sharing of the benefits arising from the use of such knowledge.

The Forty-Ninth Session of the WIPO General Assembly in 2011 agreed to extend the mandate of the IGC for the 2012–2013 biennium. During this period the text based negotiations will be expedited in order to reach agreement on international legal instruments on genetic resources, traditional knowledge and traditional cultural expressions. The Twenty-First Session of the IGC in April 2012 will consider traditional knowledge and will address four articles on Subject Matter of Protection, Beneficiaries, Scope of Protection and Limitations and Exceptions.[67]

The TRIPS Council

In the TRIPS Council, developing countries have stated that defensive measures to prevent the misappropriation of traditional knowledge are insufficient, and the Council may have to consider 'proposals regarding an international framework to provide *positive* protection of traditional knowledge, which would recognize protection of traditional knowledge at the national and regional levels.'[68] Some of the essential components of a

---

[65] See for example WIPO/GRTKF/IC/6/14 – Intergovernmental Committee on Intellectual Property and Genetic Resources, Traditional Knowledge and Folklore Sixth Session, 15–19 March 2004, *Report*, April 14, 2004, paragraph 228.

[66] See WIPO/GRTKF/IC/18/5 – Intergovernmental Committee on Intellectual Property and Genetic Resources, Traditional Knowledge and Folklore, Eighteenth Session, 9–13 May 2011, *The Protection Of Traditional Knowledge: Revised Objectives And Principles*.

[67] WO/GA/40/7 – WIPO General Assembly, Fortieth (20th Ordinary) Session, 26 September–5 October 2011, Matters Concerning the Intergovernmental Committee on Intellectual Property and Genetic Resources, Traditional Knowledge and Folklore (IGC), Document prepared by the Secretariat, 4.

[68] IP/C/W/356 – TRIPS Council, *The Relationship between the TRIPS Agreement and the Convention on Biological Diversity and the Protection of Traditional Knowledge*, 24 June 2002, paragraph 16.

framework for international recognition of various *sui generis* systems, customary law and others for protection of traditional knowledge were identified as:

- local protection to the rights of traditional knowledge holders through national level *sui generis* regimes including customary laws as well as others, and its effective enforcement inter alia through systems such as positive comity of protection systems for traditional knowledge;
- protection of traditional knowledge through registers of traditional knowledge databases in order to avoid misappropriation;
- a procedure whereby the use of traditional knowledge from one country is allowed, particularly for seeking IPR protection or commercialization, only after the competent national authority of the country of origin gives a certificate that source of origin is disclosed and prior informed consent, including acceptance of benefit sharing conditions, obtained; and
- an internationally agreed instrument that recognizes such national level protection.

This would not only prevent misappropriation but also ensure that national level benefit sharing mechanisms and laws are respected worldwide.[69]

Developing countries have also advocated 'a system of protection of traditional knowledge that provides proprietary rights [and] can ensure that market forces will operate to generate fairness and equity.'[70] The African Group has proposed that traditional knowledge be recognized as a category of IPRs but has also stated that Members may adopt *sui generis* systems for more extensive protection.[71] Given the fact that the discourse in the TRIPS Council is in fact grounded in the IPR system this approach is perhaps inevitable, but may undermine the alternate approach which requires a more holistic view of the issue.[72]

---

69 Ibid, paragraph 16.

70 IP/C/W/370/Rev.1 – TRIPS Council, *The Protection of Traditional Knowledge and Folklore – Summary of Issues Raised and Points Made*, 9 March 2006, paragraph 33.

71 IP/C/W/404, above n 4.

72 For a criticism of this approach see GRAIN, *The TRIPS review at a turning point?* (2003), available at http://www.grain.org/briefings_files/trips-july-2003-en.pdf (last accessed 9 July 2012).

The CBD

Article 8 (j) of the CBD deals with the protection of traditional knowledge and this Article has been taken up in several fora including the WG8J, the Ad Hoc Open-Ended Working Group on Access and Benefit-Sharing (WG-ABS), and the Conference of the Parties to the CBD (CoP), with the primary mandate being with the first forum. To date, the work has mostly been confined to compiling views and information on the issue.

The WG8J was mandated to identify the priority elements of *sui generis* systems. This forum too has prioritized the protection of traditional knowledge, innovations, and practices of indigenous peoples in the context of access and benefit sharing of such knowledge and the conservation and sustainable use of biological diversity,[73] and sustainable development and poverty alleviation have been identified merely as possible side benefits of such systems.[74] It has also emphasized that such systems may focus on preservation and promotion in addition to protection and this would ensure that the system to be established is within the mandate of the Convention.[75] It has stated that:

> Sui *generis* systems could also promote a clear, transparent and effective system of traditional knowledge protection, which increases legal certainty and predictability to the benefit not only of knowledge holders, but also of society as a whole, including firms and research institutions, who are potential partners of knowledge holders in the pursuit of the goals of the Convention. By promoting such transparency and efficiency, *sui generis* systems would aim to lower transaction costs for local and indigenous communities for protecting their traditional knowledge or for those using it for commercial or non-commercial purposes.[76]

---

73 UNEP/CBD/WG8J/5/6 above n 48, for example, paragraphs 7 and 13. UNEP/CBD/WG8J/6/5 – Ad Hoc Open-Ended Inter-Sessional Working Group on Article 8(J) and Related Provisions of the Convention on Biological Diversity, 2–5 November 2009, *Elements of Sui Generis Systems for the Protection of Traditional Knowledge, Innovations and Practices Note by the Executive Secretary*; UNEP/CBD/WG8J/7/3 – Ad Hoc Open-Ended Inter-Sessional Working Group on Article 8(J) and Related Provisions of the Convention on Biological Diversity, Seventh meeting, 31 October – 4 November 2011, *Elements of Sui Generis Systems for the Protection of Traditional Knowledge, Innovations and Practices, Note by the Executive Secretary*.

74 UNEP/CBD/WG8J/7/3, above n 73, paragraph 21.

75 Ibid, paragraph 17.

76 Ibid, paragraph 9.

The WG8J clearly views *sui generis* systems as primarily furthering the objectives of the CBD. Nevertheless there are some positive aspects in its work on *sui generis* systems. It has acknowledged the 'holistic nature of traditional knowledge and the need to respect its cultural context'[77] and 'the important link between protecting traditional knowledge and securing tenure and/or access over lands and waters traditionally occupied or used by indigenous and local communities.'[78] Significantly the WG8J has recognized the importance of customary law and community protocols as the basis of *sui generis* systems at the local level, noting that 'It is important for *sui generis* systems at the local level to be based on the relevant customary laws of the communities concerned.'[79] This wording goes beyond the weak wording of the Nagoya Protocol which merely requires that 'Parties shall in accordance with domestic law take into consideration indigenous and local communities' customary laws, community protocols and procedures, as applicable, with respect to traditional knowledge associated with genetic resources.'[80]

The WG8J also goes beyond the Nagoya Protocol in addressing the issue of transboundary occurrences of genetic resources and traditional knowledge. The Protocol provides for a global multilateral benefit sharing option to address such situations, or for those where it is not possible to obtain prior informed consent. It also provides that where the same genetic resources or traditional knowledge is found *in situ* in the territory of more than one party 'those Parties shall endeavour to cooperate, as appropriate, with the involvement of indigenous and local communities concerned, where applicable, with a view to implementing this Protocol.'[81] The WG8J on the other hand, states that in the case of transboundary occurrences of both genetic resources and traditional knowledge, as well as its occurrence among different indigenous and local communities within the same country:

> ownership of shared knowledge and resources should be seen as joint ownership and consent should be required from all parties involved according to their respective community protocols. Research and development of traditional knowledge could then be coordinated and profits should be shared equitably and according to the relevant customary laws.[82]

---

77 Ibid, paragraph 22.
78 Ibid, paragraph 25.
79 Ibid, paragraphs 29–34.
80 Nagoya Protocol Article 12.
81 Ibid, Articles 10–11.
82 UNEP/CBD/WG8J/7/3, above n 73, paragraph 35.

This position is significant for the situations which arose in the case of both the San people in southern Africa and the Kani in India discussed previously. Thus while the work of the WG8J is based primarily on implementing the purposes and objectives of the CBD in regard to access and benefit sharing, it has also acknowledged the wider issues concerning indigenous peoples and traditional knowledge which are not articulated in the CBD or the Nagoya Protocol. However, whether this recognition will evolve into substantive measures to provide for comprehensive protection of traditional knowledge beyond these objectives remains to be seen.

The United Nations Permanent Forum on Indigenous Issues (UNPFII)

It is in fora such as the UNPFII that the issue of indigenous traditional knowledge has been approached most comprehensively.[83] For example, at this forum it was noted that:

> indigenous traditional knowledge raises a range of policy, procedural, conceptual, political and practical challenges in a wide variety of areas, such as the conservation of biological diversity, intellectual property, trade negotiations, agricultural policies, education, the environment, science, climate change, sustainable development, private sector activities, health, cultural policies, gender issues and human rights.[84]

Indigenous participants at the forum also emphasized that adequate protection of their traditional knowledge demands respect for their human rights as a whole, including to territories and resources and the rights to self-determination. It was generally agreed that while intellectual property issues were important, they constitute only a limited part of the debate on indigenous traditional knowledge issues, but have been taking up a disproportionate amount of attention to the detriment of other issues. This was however, understandable given the concerns of such communities in regard to this problem. It was agreed that since this was a multi-faceted and complex question, indigenous communities needed to carefully identify their needs and objectives and formulate strategies to deal with it.

---

83 E/C.19/2006/2 – United Nations Economic and Social Council, Fifth session, 15–26 May 2006 Report of the International Technical Workshop on Indigenous Traditional Knowledge, 15 December 2005.

84 Ibid, paragraph 31.

CONCLUSION

The need to protect traditional knowledge, whether by 'positive' or 'defensive' mechanisms, has arisen as a result of its unauthorized appropriation and privatization by way of IPRs. Since it may not always be possible (or appropriate) to prevent the use of traditional knowledge by others, particularly knowledge which is widely known, the objective of a protection mechanism would be, to prevent it from being appropriated by the application of intellectual property rights over it. Several issues arise in determining what strategies would be most effective in this regard.

As noted in Chapter 6, there are two categories of knowledge relevant to this problem, i.e. knowledge that is in the public domain (i.e. nationally or regionally) or what could be called common knowledge, and that which is specific to a particular community. The debates on the matter have not always made this distinction clear, and the question of whether the knowledge is generally known or not, would be relevant in defining the strategies to be adopted to protect it. As in the case of genetic resources, again the question arises as to whether a *sui generis* system based upon some form of IPRs would be the most appropriate way to prevent traditional knowledge from being appropriated.

Much of the debate in international fora has centred upon *sui generis* measures to protect community based traditional knowledge, which would not be generally in the public domain. Views are divided between addressing the question as a distinct issue, or dealing with it on the basis that the knowledge of indigenous communities is inseparable from the totality of their lifestyles, cultures and rights. The second approach, generally taken by indigenous groups particularly in the WIPO IGC and the UNPFII, views traditional knowledge in the context of indigenous rights and as an indivisible component of them. It also argues that the primary entitlements to traditional knowledge are vested in the respective communities for their use and benefit, and to further promote and develop their cultures. The commodification of such knowledge by outsiders is one threat among many, to the development and maintenance of their cultural systems. Therefore the discourse on this topic is not confined to issues of trade and IPRs but is rooted in that of indigenous peoples' rights.

The holistic approach to traditional knowledge protection has been mainly supported by human rights fora, as for example the UNPFII whose mandate is to take a comprehensive view of indigenous rights. This forum is not constrained either by trade and IPR issues, or by issues of biodiversity conservation and benefit sharing. It is therefore desirable that the current debate on traditional knowledge protection is extended to these fora and their input also incorporated in an international document on this subject.

Nevertheless there is also an immediate need to ensure that traditional knowledge whether within or outside the public domain is protected from privatization, although the strategies to do so may need to vary. Knowledge in the public domain, including traditional agricultural knowledge, can be addressed as a separate topic since it will not give rise to wider questions of rights and culture, as does community based knowledge. Where such knowledge is concerned the important issue would be to prevent its appropriation by way of the IPR system, and it would be within the jurisdiction of States to do so. In the case of community based knowledge, wider issues including confidentiality and secrecy would need to be considered. A further discussion on such measures is found in Chapter 12. Again, it can be argued that as in the case of protecting genetic resources from privatization, *sui generis* systems to protect traditional knowledge must also be essentially devised to counteract the effects of IPRs.

The approaches of the various international fora to the debate on traditional knowledge protection are rooted in their own aims and objectives. Not surprisingly the trade and IPR fora have been unenthusiastic about promoting holistic protection since it would restrict, at least to some extent, their access to the knowledge. This is evident in the proceedings of the TRIPS Council and the WIPO which have failed to reach agreement on either the nature or scope of such measures. The CBD has not progressed much further and again is rooted in its primary objective of sharing the benefits arising from such knowledge. In all three fora, despite the urgings of developing countries, no progress has been made towards an international agreement in this regard, binding or otherwise.

Notwithstanding the failure of international law to address the issue, several countries and regional groupings have taken their own legislative measures to regulate access to traditional knowledge. However, these countries have continued to argue that national and regional measures must be supported by binding international rules. Although this element continues to be discussed, in the face of opposition by developed countries which maintain that ultimately protection of traditional knowledge is best carried out at the national level, the prospects of such an agreement are not promising.

11. Disclosure of origin of genetic resources and traditional knowledge

INTRODUCTION

While the previous two chapters focused on positive measures to protect rights over genetic resources and traditional knowledge and the equitable sharing of their benefits, the next two chapters will deal with defensive measures to prevent their misappropriation. Disclosure of origin of these resources is one such strategy advocated by developing countries to prevent such misappropriation. The other, discussed in the next chapter, is the recognition of traditional knowledge as prior art for the purposes of establishing novelty in a patent application in order to forestall the patenting of such knowledge. The significance of these proposals is that they attempt to use elements of patent law for this purpose.

Disclosure is a core requirement of patent law since, until full disclosure regarding all relevant aspects of the invention is made, it is not possible to determine whether it fulfils the criteria of patentability. Article 29.1 of the TRIPS Agreement states:

> Members shall require that an applicant for a patent shall disclose the invention in a manner sufficiently clear and complete for the invention to be carried out by a person skilled in the art and may require the applicant to indicate the best mode for carrying out the invention known to the inventor at the filing date or, where priority is claimed, at the priority date of the application.

Developing countries have been advocating, as a defensive strategy against misappropriation of genetic resources and traditional knowledge, a different aspect of disclosure in regard to the subject matter of the patent application. This is the mandatory requirement that patent applications should disclose the origin of these resources, and, where relevant, the traditional knowledge relating to them. The aim of these countries in requiring such disclosure is to monitor the commercial use of the biological resources and associated traditional knowledge extracted from them (knowingly or unknowingly) by prospective inventors, in order to ensure that they receive a fair share of the benefits accruing from them.

The principle of disclosure of origin is a complex one, and several issues would have to be clarified before it can be effectively implemented. Some general points as raised by authors on the topic will be discussed first. Thereafter, the specific proposals and the debates in the various fora will be considered.

DEFINITION OF DISCLOSURE OF ORIGIN

According to Dutfield, disclosure of origin 'has become a collective term for certain requirements to be incorporated into patent law.' While these requirements vary widely in terms of the obligations imposed on patent applicants, the most promising version is that of 'proof of legal acquisition.' This essentially requires patent applicants to provide proof that genetic resources, and where relevant traditional knowledge, acquired from provider countries was done in accordance with access and benefit sharing (ABS) regulations, including prior informed consent (PIC), and on mutually agreed terms between the parties.[1] More specifically, the requirement would address the following aspects:

- disclosure of the country of origin, and legal source of the biological resources and traditional knowledge used or incorporated in the invention;
- evidence of prior informed consent and approval by national biodiversity authorities when relevant;
- evidence of prior informed consent and approval by national authorities in relation to traditional knowledge; and
- evidence of fair and equitable benefit sharing in accordance with national laws.[2]

---

1 Graham Dutfield, *Protecting Traditional Knowledge: Pathways to the Future* (2006) ICTSD Issue Paper No. 16, available at http://www.iprsonline.org/unctadictsd/docs/Graham%20final.pdf (last accessed 9 July 2012).

2 David Vivas-Eugui and Manuel Ruiz, 'Toward an effective disclosure mechanism: justification, scope and legal effects' (2005) in Martha Chouchena-Rojas, Manuel Ruiz Muller, David Vivas and Sebastian Winkler (eds), *Disclosure Requirements: Ensuring mutual supportiveness between the WTO TRIPS Agreement and the CBD*, 24, available at http://www.iprsonline.org/resources/docs/Disclosure_req_book.pdf (last accessed 9 July 2012).

OBJECTIVES AND SCOPE OF A DISCLOSURE OF ORIGIN MECHANISM

From the perspective of developing countries, the primary objective of the disclosure of origin requirement is to ensure transparency and equity in the granting of patents based on genetic resources and related traditional knowledge, and to prevent misappropriation of these resources. These countries have argued that such a requirement will improve the patent examination process and help to prevent biopiracy and the granting of 'bad' patents. They point out that the defence of patent examiners for granting unjustified patents is largely based upon the argument that information on relevant state of the art was not available during the examination process. Mechanisms for making this information available have been mooted, but will not in themselves be adequate to resolve the problem.[3] Therefore a legally binding obligation to disclose the source and origin of the resources and the knowledge in question will help the patent examiners to determine this issue, and also decide whether the invention is one that is excludable under Articles 27.2 and 27.3 of the TRIPS Agreement.[4]

It has also been noted that such a system would create a favourable environment among providers and users, and facilitate the flow of genetic resources at all levels.[5] Therefore amending the patent system to ensure transparency and eliminate misappropriation of these resources would have the ripple effect of increasing access to them as envisaged in the CBD.

The scope of the disclosure of origin mechanism relates to what, in fact, should be disclosed, and what should trigger the requirement. In regard to the latter, developing countries have advocated that:

> any use, the disclosure of which is necessary to determine the existence of prior art, inventorship or entitlement to the claimed invention, the scope of the claim and/or is necessary for understanding or carrying out the invention, would be sufficient to trigger the disclosure obligation.[6]

---

3 IP/C/W/368/Rev.1 – TRIPS Council, *The Relationship between the TRIPS Agreement and the Convention on Biological Diversity Summary of Issues Raised and Points Made*, 8 February 2006, 12.

4 IP/C/W/429/Rev.1 – TRIPS Council, *Elements of the Obligation to Disclose the Source and Country of Origin of the Biological Resources and/or Traditional Knowledge Used in an invention Submission from Brazil, Cuba, Ecuador, India, Pakistan, Peru, Thailand, and Venezuela, Revision*, 27 September 2004.

5 Vivas-Eugui and Ruiz, above n 2, 25.

6 IP/C/W/429/Rev.1, above n 4, paragraph 8.

This would apply even where the use was only incidental. Examples of uses which would trigger the obligation would include, where the genetic resources or knowledge in question is used (a) to form part of the claimed invention; (b) during the process of developing the claimed invention; (c) as a necessary prerequisite for the development of the invention; (d) to facilitate the development of the invention; and (e) as necessary background material for the development of the invention.[7]

In regard to what should be disclosed, firstly, the definition could require disclosure of the geographical origin (i.e. the country, region, or community) of the resources. In addition, it should also disclose the legal source of the resources, i.e. proof of legality of access. Several countries have specifically demanded that proof of PIC, and access and benefit sharing measures, should also be provided.[8] This formulation of the requirement therefore takes the concept beyond disclosure of sources to a requirement of proving equitable and legal access to them.

PROCEDURAL ASPECTS OF A DISCLOSURE OF ORIGIN MECHANISM

In order to ensure the effective implementation of a disclosure of origin mechanism, it is essential to have a workable procedure in place. The most practical method is that the patent application form should include a request/requirement for such disclosure. However, in view of the fact that disclosure of certain information may well result in non-issuance of the patent, it may be unrealistic to formulate a procedure based upon the bona fides of the applicant, and other safeguards would need to be put in place to prevent incomplete disclosures, fraud and misrepresentation. International co-operation among intellectual property and biodiversity offices, improved databases and other sources of information will be necessary to accommodate the developing countries' suggestions in this regard. The option of interested parties to present additional information would also be important.[9] Monitoring of patent applications by civil society groups and

---

[7] Ibid, paragraph 8. For a critique of this requirement see Graham Dutfield, 'Disclosure of Origin: Time for a Reality Check?' (2005) in Chouchena-Rojas et al, above n2.

[8] IP/C/W/429/Rev.1, above n 4, paragraph 15.

[9] Vivas-Eugui and Ruiz, above n 2, 27.

interested persons would, in fact, be an effective strategy to prevent fraudulent or incomplete disclosures.

The actual information required would depend on the country in question, but at a minimum would obviously include the elements discussed above. Ensuring proper disclosure of the sources of genetic resources, and also proof of PIC and ABS measures would be relatively easy, since documentation could be asked for. However, rather different issues would arise in the case of traditional knowledge where enforcing disclosure may be difficult, as it goes directly to the criterion of novelty and state of the art.

While some developing countries have the necessary laws in place to ensure such disclosure, in the absence of similar laws in developed countries these would not be effective due to the transnational nature of the use of genetic resources and associated traditional knowledge, and the grant of patent applications for inventions based upon them.[10] In as much as the territorial nature of intellectual property laws limits their efficacy in the international sphere, the territoriality of disclosure of origin laws would have the same effect. Therefore internationalizing the principle, like intellectual property itself, is essential to ensure its effectiveness.

LEGAL EFFECTS OF A DISCLOSURE OF ORIGIN MECHANISM

The most contentious issue in the debates taking place in international fora on the subject of disclosure of origin relate to the proposed legal consequences of a patent applicant not disclosing the origin of genetic resources or traditional knowledge. The legal effects would depend on the form of the requirement, and there are three possible options in this regard.[11] Disclosure as an optional requirement would mean that non-compliance would not

---

[10] Ibid at 24.

[11] UNEP/CBD/WG-ABS/2/INF/2 – Ad Hoc Open-Ended Working Group on Access and Benefit-Sharing, Second meeting, 1–5 December 2003, *Measures, Including Consideration of Their Feasibility, Practicality and Costs, to Support Compliance with Prior Informed Consent of the Contracting Party Providing Genetic Resources and Mutually Agreed Terms on which Access was Granted in Contracting Parties with Users of Such Resources under Their Jurisdiction – 'Disclosure of Origin and Prior Informed Consent for Applications of Intellectual Property Rights Based on Genetic Resources: A Technical Study of Implementation Issues' Final Report by Cynthia M. Ho,* July 2003. See also Michael A Gollin, 'Feasibility of National Disclosure of Origin Requirements' (2005) ICTSD/CIEL/IDDRI/IUCN/QUNO Dialogue on Disclosure Requirements: Incorporating the CBD Principles in the TRIPS Agreement on the Road to Hong Kong WTO Public

incur any sanctions. A mandatory requirement would either result in the loss of the patent or, while keeping the patent intact, merely incur administrative, civil and/or criminal sanctions.

The consequences of non-disclosure could include the presumption of abandonment of the application if full disclosure is not made. If the disclosure is incomplete the application could be suspended, while the applicant's priority rights are safeguarded, with an opportunity to rectify any defects in the application. In the case of fraudulent non-disclosure detected after the grant of the patent, some claims could be invalidated or the application suspended while the situation is rectified. The most severe sanction would be to revoke the patent and where necessary to also enable the complaining party to initiate legal action for violation of other laws including ABS requirements, and for damages.

While developing countries have advocated a mandatory requirement with loss of the patent as the penalty for non-compliance, developed countries have advocated one of the other two options.

NATIONAL MEASURES ON DISCLOSURE OF ORIGIN

The moves to conceptualize the disclosure of origin requirement began with the Andean Community Decision 391.[12] While it initially met with scepticism, it gradually gained both interest and support from a range of groups including some indigenous peoples, civil society and policy makers. Several countries (both developed and developing) have also unilaterally incorporated it into their national laws in varying forms. These include the Andean Community countries, Belgium, Brazil, Costa Rica, Denmark, India, Nepal, Norway and the African Union (53 African countries). These provisions have been incorporated in either intellectual property legislation or in laws dealing with access and benefit sharing of genetic resources and

Symposium, Geneva, 21 April 2005, available at http://www.iprsonline.org/ictsd/docs/DOO3_Gollin.pdf (last accessed 9 July 2012).

[12] Andean Community Decision 391: Common Regime on Access to Genetic Resources (1996).

traditional knowledge.[13] In addition, regional agreements also include such provisions, the most significant being the Andean Community Decision 391 and the European Directive on Biotechnological Inventions.[14]

The effectiveness of these national and regional endeavours to implement the obligation has been categorized into weak, medium and strong.[15] The characteristics of the weak measures[16] generally include that they are not mandatory, the disclosure is limited in relation to the information required,[17] and the patent application and patent rights are not affected by the disclosure. Medium disclosure requirements generally require greater disclosure including evidence of PIC. However, non-compliance will not invalidate the patent application although penalties under other laws may be imposed.[18] Strong disclosure measures generally result in patent applications being refused on grounds of non-compliance, have a wide scope which includes genetic resources and derivatives or 'innovations involving elements of biodiversity,'[19] and require submission of licenses and ABS contracts.[20]

---

[13] Chouchena-Rojas et al, above n2. See also Michael Blakeney, *Proposals for the Disclosure of Origin of Genetic Resources in Patent Applications* (date not available), available at http://www.economia.uniroma2.it/conferenze/icabr2005/papers/Blakeney.pdf (last accessed 9 July 2012); Alison L Hoare and Richard G Tarasofsky, 'Asking and Telling: Can "Disclosure of Origin" Requirements in Patent Applications Make a Difference?' (2007) 10(2) *Journal of World Intellectual Property* 149.

[14] No. 96/9/EC of 11 March 1996. See also IP/C/W/368/Rev.1, above n 3, 38–41.

[15] Blakeney, above n 13. See also Commission on Intellectual Property Rights, *Integrating Intellectual Property Rights and Development Policy* (2002) 86, available at http://www.iprcommission.org/papers/pdfs/final_report/CIPRfullfinal.pdf (last accessed 9 July 2012).

[16] Blakeney cites countries with weak measures such as Egypt, the European Union, Germany, Romania, Spain and Sweden – Blakeney, above n 13, 6.

[17] For example, the European Union Directive only requires disclosure of geographical source – Blakeney, above note 13, 6.

[18] Countries with medium legislation include Denmark, Norway, Switzerland and New Zealand – Blakeney, above n 13, 9.

[19] Biodiversity Law of Costa Rica, Article 81.

[20] Countries with strong measures include the Andean Community countries, Belgium, Brazil, Costa Rica, India and Peru – Blakeney, above n 13, 11.

THE INTERNATIONAL DEBATE ON DISCLOSURE OF ORIGIN

Developing countries with strong disclosure measures have been in the forefront of the drive to put these requirements on the international patent agenda. Coalitions of developing countries have also collectively called for such recognition. For example, the Cancun Declaration of 2002 issued by the Group of Like Minded Megadiverse Countries[21] states that one of its objectives is the creation of an international regime to promote the fair and equitable use of genetic resources, which would include:

> certification of the legal provenance of biological materials, prior informed consent and mutually agreed terms for the transfer of genetic material, as requirements for the application and granting of patents, strictly in accordance with the conditions of access agreed by the countries of origin.[22]

The disclosure of origin would help to fulfil three main functions of the patent system. First, it would facilitate the substantive examination of patent applications, including determining the question of prior art. Second, it would also improve the determination of inventorship. Third, it would facilitate the actual execution of the invention, for example where a biological material is endemic to a particular location. If the demands of developing countries that proof of compliance with access legislation are

---

[21] The Group of Like Minded Megadiverse Countries (LMMC) established in 2002 comprises 17 countries whose stated objective is to consolidate consultation and co-operation and to develop strategies to conserve biological diversity and to ensure the sustainable use of its components for the benefits of their countries and peoples. The countries are Bolivia, Brazil, China, Colombia, Costa Rica, Democratic Republic of Congo, Ecuador, India, Indonesia, Kenya, Madagascar, Malaysia, Mexico, Peru, Philippines, South Africa and Venezuela. Seventy per cent of all biodiversity and 45 per cent of the global population is located within these countries. See the New Delhi Ministerial Declaration of Like Minded Megadiverse Countries on Access and Benefit Sharing.

[22] Cancun Declaration of Like-Minded Megadiversity Countries, 18 February 2002, Article 1(h), available at http://www.weltvertrag.org/e375/e719/e1045/CancunDeclarationonLike-MindedMegadiversityCountries_2002_ger.pdf (last accessed 9 July 2012). See also the Cusco Declaration on Access to Genetic Resources, Traditional Knowledge and Intellectual Property Rights of Like-minded Megadiverse Countries, 29 November 2002, available at http://pe.biosafetyclearinghouse.net/actividades/2009/grouplmmc.pdf (last accessed 9 July 2012).

also included in disclosure of origin obligations, it could also serve possible functions outside patent law, which would fulfil the purposes of the CBD.[23]

The debate on disclosure of origin requirements has taken place in several fora including the TRIPS Council,[24] WIPO,[25] and the CBD.[26] Proposals for implementing the principle have been formulated by both developing and developed countries and have sometimes been submitted in two or more fora simultaneously. For the sake of clarity, the various proposals in the relevant fora will be discussed separately.

The discussions have given rise to several suggestions on how the concept should be implemented. The most significant are the TRIPS disclosure proposal, the PCT disclosure proposal and the mandatory disclosure proposal.[27] The first was submitted by several developing countries to the TRIPS Council.[28] In addition, Norway also submitted a separate proposal to the TRIPS Council. The PCT disclosure proposal was submitted by Switzerland, and envisages that the Regulations under the WIPO PCT will be amended to enable the national patent legislation of Member countries to

---

[23] Carlos M Correa, *Establishing a Disclosure of Origin Obligation in the TRIPS Agreement* (2003) Quaker United Nations Office Occasional Paper, 12, available at http://www.quno.org/geneva/pdf/economic/Occassional/Dec-of-Origin.pdf (last accessed 9 July 2012).

[24] Carlos M Correa, *The politics and practicalities of a disclosure of origin obligation* (2005) QUNO Occasional Paper 16, footnote 2, available at http://www.quno.org/geneva/pdf/economic/Occassional/Politics-of-Dec-of-Origin.pdf (last accessed 9 July 2012).

[25] WIPO's work on disclosure of origin has taken place largely in the IGC but has also been addressed in the SCP and the Working Group on the Reform of the PCT – WIPO/GRTKF/IC/1/3 – Intergovernmental Committee On Intellectual Property And Genetic Resources, Traditional Knowledge And Folklore, First Session, 30 April–3 May 2001 *Matters Concerning Intellectual Property And Genetic Resources, Traditional Knowledge And Folklore – An Overview,* 16 March 2001.

[26] The CBD has discussed it in the CoP, the Ad Hoc Open-Ended Inter-Sessional Working Group on Access and Benefit Sharing and the Ad Hoc Open-Ended Inter-Sessional Working Group on Article 8(j) and Related Provisions. The CBD discussions are considered below.

[27] IP/C/W/368/Rev.1, above n 3, 27.

[28] This proposal was initiated by developing countries including, the African Group, the Andean Community, Brazil, China, Colombia, Ecuador, India, Indonesia, Kenya, Pakistan, Thailand, Venezuela and Zimbabwe. Brazil and India were particularly strong proponents of the proposal. See IP/C/W/368/Rev.1, above n 3, documents cited in footnotes 135–156.

require the disclosure of origin of genetic resources and traditional knowledge in patent applications.[29] The mandatory disclosure proposal was submitted by the European Union (EU) to the WIPO Intergovernmental Committee on Intellectual Property and Genetic Resources, Traditional Knowledge and Folklore (IGC).

PROPOSALS IN THE TRIPS COUNCIL

Developing Country Proposals

The disclosure of origin debate in the TRIPS Council originated in the context of the discussion on the review of Article 27.3(b), and the relationship between the TRIPS Agreement and the CBD principles of access and benefit sharing of genetic resources.[30] According to the TRIPS disclosure proposal, the TRIPS Agreement should be amended to make it mandatory for member states to require that a patent application relating to biological materials or traditional knowledge must include the following information:

- the source and country of origin of the biological resource and of the traditional knowledge used in the invention;
- evidence of prior informed consent from the authorities under the relevant national regime; and
- evidence of fair and equitable benefit sharing under the relevant national regime.

The TRIPS disclosure proposal of the developing countries goes beyond simply disclosing the source or origin of the invention. Rather, the countries putting forward the proposal have sought to formulate a mechanism which achieves two objectives – first, to combat the misappropriation of genetic resources and traditional knowledge which they claim has been facilitated

---

[29] See the following documents – IP/C/W/400/Rev.1 – TRIPS Council, *Article 27.3(b), The Relationship Between the TRIPS Agreement, and the Convention on Biological Diversity, and the Protection of Traditional Knowledge, Communication from Switzerland Revision*, 18 June 2003; IP/C/W/423 – TRIPS Council, *Additional Comments by Switzerland on its Proposals Submitted to WIPO Regarding the Declaration of the Source of Genetic Resources and Traditional Knowledge in Patent Applications, Communication from Switzerland*, 14 June 2004; IP/C/W/433 – TRIPS Council, *Further Observations by Switzerland on its Proposals Regarding the Declaration of the Source of Genetic Resources and Traditional Knowledge in Patent Applications Communication from Switzerland*, 25 November 2004.

[30] IP/C/W/368/Rev.1, above note 3.

by the patent system,[31] and second as a strategy by which the ABS obligations of the CBD, including that of prior informed consent would be fleshed out and incorporated in the TRIPS Agreement as conditions of patentability.[32]

As can be seen from the requirements below, several elements of the proposal attempt to compensate for anticipated inadequacies in legislative and other capacities in countries and communities where genetic resources and traditional knowledge originate.

The obligation to prove PIC will be a positive obligation on the applicant on whom the burden of proof will rest. The applicant would have to provide evidence that the genetic resources and/or traditional knowledge on which the invention is based were obtained with the approval or consent of the national authorities of the country and/or the community concerned. The burden would be discharged by a declaration to this effect. Where relevant, actual evidence of the consent in the form of a certificate or duly certified contract between the parties would also be submitted. It was argued that given the other information that a patent applicant has to submit, this additional requirement would not be unduly burdensome.[33]

A high degree of proof has been proposed in regard to proving ABS. Proof is required of an existing or future benefit sharing arrangement that is based upon mutually agreed terms and is fair and equitable under the

---

[31] See IP/C/W/470 – TRIPS Council, *Submission in response to the communication from Switzerland (IP/C/W/446), Communication from Bolivia, Cuba, Ecuador, India, Sri Lanka and Thailand*, 21 March 2006; IP/C/W/441/Rev.1 – Article 27.3(B), *Relationship Between the TRIPS Agreement and the CBD and Protection of Traditional Knowledge and Folklore, Communication from Peru, Revision*, 19 May 2005; IP/C/W/458 – *Analysis of Potential Cases of Biopiracy, Communication from Peru*, 7 November 2005; IP/C/W/484 – *Response to Comments Contained in Document IP/C/W/469, Relating to the Peruvian Communication IP/C/W/458, Communication from Peru*, 2 November 2006.

[32] See the issues raised in IP/C/W/420 – TRIPS Council, *The Relationship between the TRIPS Agreement and the Convention on Biological Diversity (CBD) Checklist of Issues, Submission from Brazil, Cuba, Ecuador, India, Peru, Thailand and Venezuela*, 2 March 2004. See also IP/C/W/429 – *Elements of the Obligation to Disclose the Source and Country of Origin of Biological Resource and/or Traditional Knowledge Used in an Invention, Submission from Brazil, India, Pakistan, Peru, Thailand, and Venezuela*, 21 September 2004.

[33] For specific proposals regarding disclosure of prior informed consent see IP/C/W/438 – TRIPS Council, *The Relationship Between the TRIPS Agreement and the Convention on Biological Diversity (CBD) and the Protection of Traditional Knowledge-Elements of the Obligation to Disclose Evidence of Prior Informed Consent under the Relevant National Regime, Submission from Bolivia, Brazil, Cuba, Ecuador, India, Pakistan, Peru, Thailand and Venezuela*, 10 December 2004.

circumstances.[34] The agreed terms would cover issues relating to the conditions, obligations, procedures, types, timing, distribution, and mechanisms of the benefits to be shared, and the patent application would also have to show how the other party would enforce the terms. However, the applicant would only be required to provide information that is known or should have been known to him/her. Further, on the premise that traditional communities may not have the capacity to negotiate and enforce such agreements, any such agreement primarily negotiated with them should be subsequently confirmed by the national regulatory authority. The CBD principles of PIC and benefit sharing would have to be respected, even where the country of origin has not set up benefit sharing regimes, and in such cases the applicant would be required to state that fact and indicate that there has at least been consent from the relevant authority or community in compliance with other relevant laws of the country.[35]

The legal effects of non-disclosure or inadequate or fraudulent disclosure have been formulated to provide sufficient deterrence. At the stage of processing the patent, the process would be delayed until the requirements are satisfactorily complied with, within given time limits and with penalties. At the post grant stage the patent would be revoked. In addition, criminal and/or administrative sanctions could also be imposed. Where disclosure shows that the inventor is in fact another person, community or agency, a full or partial transfer of rights to the latter will take place. The scope of the claims would also be affected where a part of the patentable subject matter is affected by lack of novelty or by fraudulent disclosure. These remedies would also possibly be subject to judicial review. While there is flexibility in these legal effects, members are obliged to ensure that there is sufficient deterrent, compensatory and equity value. Remedies should also be retrospective so as to cover past use.[36] The burden of proof in demonstrating disclosure will be on the patent applicant.

Peru had specifically identified the US, the EU and Japan as countries that should incorporate disclosure of origin requirements in their patent

---

[34] While there may not be a straightforward way of determining what is fair and equitable, developing countries have noted some factors which could be used to do so – see IP/C/W/442 – TRIPS Council, *The Relationship Between the TRIPS Agreement and the Convention on Biological Diversity (CBD) and the Protection of Traditional Knowledge – Elements of the Obligation to Disclose Evidence of Benefit-Sharing under the Relevant National Regime, Submission from Bolivia, Brazil, Colombia, Cuba, Dominican Republic Ecuador, India, Peru and Thailand*, 18 March 2005.

[35] IP/C/W/368/Rev.1, above n 3, 28.

[36] Ibid at 29. See also IP/C/W/429/Rev.1, above n 4.

legislation, while observing that a first step would be the inclusion of these requirements in the text of the TRIPS Agreement.[37] This should be done either as an exception to patentability under Article 27.3(b), or as an element of patentability under Article 29.[38]

Specific suggestions for the text were initially proposed by several countries in 2006.[39] After the adoption of the Nagoya Protocol a revised text for a draft Article to amend the TRIPS Agreement was submitted to the TRIPS Council.[40] The Preamble to the proposal referred to Article 17 of the Protocol which requires parties to take measures as appropriate, to monitor and to enhance transparency about the utilization of genetic resources. The draft Article 29bis entitled 'Disclosure of Origin of Genetic Resources and/or Associated Traditional Knowledge' sets out the modalities for an implementing requirement which would also achieve compatibility between TRIPS and the CBD. These include that where the subject matter of a patent application involves utilization of genetic resources and/or associated traditional knowledge, Members shall require applicants to disclose the country of origin of such resources and the source in the country providing the resources and/or knowledge. Applicants must provide a copy of an Internationally Recognized Certificate of Compliance (IRCC)[41] and the information must be published jointly with the application or grant of the patent. Patent applications must not be processed without compliance with these obligations. In the event of non-compliance or fraud, the draft Article also calls for sanctions, including revocation of the patent. However, this proposal continues to be resisted by developed countries and discussions are continuing.

---

[37] IP/C/W/447 – *Article 27.3(b), Relationship between the TRIPS Agreement and the CBD and Protection of Traditional Knowledge and Folklore, Communication from Peru*, 8 June 2005.

[38] IP/C/W/368/Rev.1, above n 3, 30.

[39] IP/C/W/474 – General Council, Trade Negotiations Committee, TRIPS Council, *Doha Work Programme – The Outstanding Implementation Issue on the Relationship Between the TRIPS Agreement and the Convention on Biological Diversity, Communication from Brazil, China, Colombia, Cuba, India, Pakistan, Peru, Thailand and Tanzania, Revision*, 5 July 2006; IP/C/W/475 – TRIPS Council, *Response to Questions Raised on the Draft Amendment to TRIPS – Article 29bis, Communication From Brazil*, 26 July 2006.

[40] TN/C/W/59 – World Trade Organization, Trade Negotiations Committee, *Draft Decision to Enhance Mutual Supportiveness Between the TRIPS Agreement and the Convention on Biological Diversity, Communication from Brazil, China, Colombia, Ecuador, India, Indonesia, Peru, Thailand, the ACP Group, and the African Group*, 19 April 2011.

[41] This is provided for in Article 17 of the Nagoya Protocol.

Norway's Proposal

Of the developed countries, a concrete proposal on disclosure of origin was submitted by Norway in the TRIPS Council.[42] Norway proposed that a binding international obligation which would apply to all patent applications (international, regional and national) should be introduced to include information on the supplier country (and the country of origin, if known and different) of genetic resources and traditional knowledge in such applications. If the supplier country or country of origin requires consent for access under its national law, the application must indicate whether such consent was obtained. If the country of origin is unknown, this must be disclosed. The application would not proceed if the applicant is unable to, or refuses to provide, the required information.

While these elements of the proposal appear to prima facie support the developing country position, it is made ineffective by the lack of post grant invalidation of the patent due to incorrect or incomplete information being originally submitted. Norway has emphasized that a post grant discovery of breach of the obligation would not affect the validity of the patent, which would only be subject to sanctions outside the patent system. As can be seen from other developed country proposals submitted to other fora, there has been a consistent refusal to accept invalidation of the patent as a sanction for incorrect information, even where it may have been due to fraud.

The Debate in the World Intellectual Property Organization

As noted earlier, in WIPO, discussions on developing countries' concerns on the misappropriation of genetic resources and traditional knowledge and the equitable sharing of these resources were moved to the IGC which was established for this purpose. The topics taken up for discussion included the

---

42 IP/C/W/167 – TRIPS Council, *Review of the Provisions of Article 27.3(b), Communication from Norway*, 3 November 1999; IP/C/W/473 – TRIPS Council, *The Relationship Between the TRIPS Agreement, the Convention on Biological Diversity and the Protection of Traditional Knowledge – Amending the TRIPS Agreement to Introduce an Obligation to Disclose the Origin of Genetic Resources and Traditional Knowledge in Patent Applications, Communication from Norway*, 14 June 2006; IP/C/W/491 – TRIPS Council, *The Relationship Between the TRIPS Agreement, the Convention on Biological Diversity and the Protection of Traditional Knowledge, Amending the TRIPS Agreement to Introduce an Obligation to Disclose the Origin of Genetic Resources and Traditional Knowledge in Patent Applications, Answers from Norway to Questions Posed by Switzerland in the TRIPS Council, Communication from Norway*, 7 May 2007.

requirement for disclosure of origin.[43] Subsequently, the issue has also been taken up in several other WIPO fora. However, apart from producing information and studies on the question, Parties have not reached agreement on substantive issues.[44]

The disclosure of origin obligation was also raised in the negotiations of the Substantive Patent Law Treaty (SPLT). In this forum too countries have been divided over proposed provisions which enable or require contracting parties to comply with international obligations and applicable laws on protection of genetic resources and traditional knowledge. Developed countries have generally supported the view that the draft SPLT should be limited to provisions relating to the definition of prior art, grace period, novelty and inventive step. Other delegations took the view that all provisions of the draft should be examined as a whole 'taking into account their interdependent nature and recalling the importance they attached to other matters' including disclosure of origin of genetic resources and traditional knowledge. There was also disagreement as to whether the Standing Committee on the Law of Patents (SCP) should deal with these latter issues.[45] As at the Seventeenth SCP Session held in December 2011 this matter had not been resolved.

---

[43] For an update of the international developments on genetic resources including disclosure of origin see WIPO/GRTKF/IC/11/8 (b) – Intergovernmental Committee on Intellectual Property and Genetic Resources, Traditional Knowledge and Folklore Eleventh Session, 3–12 July, 2007, *Genetic Resources: Factual Update of International Developments, Document prepared by the Secretariat*, 30 May 2007.

[44] For an account of WIPO's work on disclosure see WIPO/GRTKF/IC/7/10 – Intergovernmental Committee on Intellectual Property and Genetic Resources, Traditional Knowledge and Folklore, Seventh Session, 1–5 November 2004, *Patent Disclosure Requirements Relating to Genetic Resources and Traditional Knowledge: Update*, 15 October 2004. WIPO was also invited by the CBD CoP to submit a report on disclosure methods within its treaties – see UNEP/CBD/COP/7/INF/17 – CBD CoP, Seventh Meeting, 9–20 and 27 February 2004, *Technical Study on Disclosure Requirements Related to Genetic Resources and Traditional Knowledge, Submission by the World Intellectual Property Organization (WIPO)* 15 December 2003. Also referenced as WIPO Document – *Technical Study on Disclosure Requirements in Patent Systems Related to Genetic Resources and Traditional Knowledge, Study No. 3* and UNEP/CBD/COP/8/INF/7 – CoP, Seventh Meeting, 9–20 and 27 February 2004, *Interrelation of Access to Genetic Resources and Disclosure Requirements in Applications for Intellectual Property Rights: Report of the World Intellectual Property Organization (WIPO)*, 16 January 2006.

[45] WIPO/IP/GR/05/01 – *Examination of Issues Relating to the Interrelation of Access to Genetic Resources and Disclosure Requirements in Intellectual Property Rights Applications, First Draft,* 31 January 2005, p. 15. See also WIPO SCP/12/3 –

Switzerland's Proposal

Switzerland had initially submitted its proposal on disclosure of origin to the WIPO Working Group on Reform of the Patent Cooperation Treaty in May 2003.[46] The most updated document in this regard was submitted to the Eleventh Session of the IGC in 2007.[47]

At the outset the Swiss proposal commented that there was a need to prevent the granting of 'bad' patents which it claimed occurs due to the unavailability of sufficient data on prior art. One way to improve this situation would be to collect traditional knowledge in databases, and both the PCT and the Patent Law Treaty (PLT) would be amended to accommodate the obligation.[48] The proposal envisages that the PCT Regulations will be amended so as to:

Standing Committee on the Law of Patents Twelfth Session, 23–27 June, 2008, Report on the International Patent System, 15 April 2008.

[46] PCT/R/WG/4/13 – Working Group on Reform of the Patent Cooperation Treaty (PCT) Fourth Session, 19–23 May 2003, *Proposals by Switzerland Regarding the Declaration of the Source of Genetic Resources and Traditional Knowledge in Patent Applications*, 5 May 2003; PCT/R/WG/6/11 – Working Group on Reform of the Patent Cooperation Treaty (PCT), Sixth Session, 3–7 May 2004, *Additional Comments by Switzerland on its Proposals Regarding the Declaration of the Source of Genetic Resources and Traditional Knowledge in Patent Applications*, 21 April 2004; PCT/R/WG/7/9 – Working Group on Reform of the Patent Cooperation Treaty (PCT) Seventh Session, 25–31 May 2005, *Further Observations by Switzerland on its Proposals Regarding the Declaration of the Source of Genetic Resources and Traditional Knowledge in Patent Applications*, 5 April 2005; PCT/R/WG/8/7 – Working Group on Reform of the Patent Cooperation Treaty (PCT), Eighth Session, 8–12 May 2006, *Declaration of the Source of Genetic Resources and Traditional Knowledge in Patent Applications, Proposals Submitted by Switzerland*, 21 April 2006; PCT/R/WG/9/5 – Working Group on Reform of the Patent Cooperation Treaty (PCT) Ninth Session, 23–27 April 2007, *Declaration of the Source of Genetic Resources and Traditional Knowledge in Patent Applications, Proposals Submitted by Switzerland*, 7 March 2007. For a comment on the role of Switzerland in international IPR negotiations see Richard Gerster, 'Patents and Development, A Non-Governmental Organization View Prior to Revision of the TRIPS Agreement' (1998) 1(4) Journal of World Intellectual Property 605.

[47] WIPO/GRTKF/IC/11/10 – Intergovernmental Committee on Intellectual Property and Genetic Resources, Traditional Knowledge and Folklore Eleventh Session, 3–12 July 2007 *Declaration of the Source of Genetic Resources and Traditional Knowledge in Patent Applications: Proposals by Switzerland*, 6 June 2007.

[48] Ibid, Annex, paragraphs 9–10.

> explicitly enable the Contracting Parties of the PCT to require patent applicants, upon or after entry of the international application into the national phase of the PCT procedure, to declare the source of genetic resources and/or traditional knowledge, if an invention is directly based on such resource or knowledge.[49]

Further, applicants will be afforded the possibility of satisfying this requirement at the time of filing an international application, or later during the international phase. Such a declaration would be included in the publication of the international application. If the international application does not contain the required declaration, national law may prevent its further processing until the information is submitted. This process would also be linked to the PLT, and Parties to the latter would be enabled to require in their national patent laws that applicants declare the source of genetic resources and/or traditional knowledge.[50]

There are several weaknesses in the Swiss proposal from the developing countries' perspective. To begin with it would be optional for countries to introduce disclosure legislation. The optional approach has been defended on several grounds. First, since a final decision has not been made on the issue, faster progress can be obtained by such an approach rather than a mandatory one. Second, it would enable those countries who wish to introduce such legislation to do so, and the international community would gain experience in the matter without prejudice to further international efforts. This again appears to be a stalling measure. Third, the optional approach would not oblige developing countries, especially least developed countries, to introduce such a measure, since they most likely lack the capacity to implement it. Since most patent applications are applied for in developed countries, introducing such measures would not benefit developing countries.[51] This last argument essentially accepts the position that developing countries are unable to defend themselves against misappropriation of their resources. Therefore there is even greater reason for implementing defensive measures at international level for this purpose.

Aside from being optional the enforcement of the proposed process is weak. If the national laws require the declaration, the PCT rules will be amended to require the national Office to give the applicant at least two months to comply with the requirement. In the case of failure to do so, the Office may refuse the application or consider it withdrawn. However, if the applicant submitted the declaration with the international application or

---

[49] Ibid, Annex, paragraph 13.

[50] Ibid, Annex, paragraph 14.

[51] Ibid at 6.

during the international phase, the national office must accept the declaration and not require any further evidence regarding the source. Again this provides the patent applicant with a loophole to avoid compliance. Finally, as in all developed country proposals, post grant invalidation/revocation of the patent is not a penalty, except in the case of fraudulent intention which would need to be proved.[52]

The European Community's Proposal

The European Community submitted a document to the Eighth Session of the IGC in 2005.[53] While this proposal appears to be a broad acceptance of developing country requirements, certain clauses limit its efficacy.

At the outset the EU proposal states that a mandatory requirement should be introduced to disclose the country of origin or source of genetic resources in patent applications, and the requirement should apply to all international, regional and national patent applications at the earliest stage possible. In order to achieve this objective the PLT, PCT and regional agreements such as the European Patent Convention would need to be amended.[54]

The applicant should declare the country of origin or, if unknown, the source of the specific genetic resource to which the inventor has had physical access, and which is still known to him/her. The applicant is required to disclose the specific source of traditional knowledge that is associated with the genetic resource only if he/she is aware that the invention is directly based on such traditional knowledge. This gives an applicant a broad loophole to bypass this requirement.

The loophole is further widened by the contention that:

> there are concerns about the possibly unclear scope of the term 'traditional knowledge'. In order to achieve the necessary legal certainty, a further in-depth discussion of the concept of TK is necessary.[55]

The applicant is only required to give a positive or negative response to the question as to whether the invention is based on genetic resources or

---

[52] Ibid, paragraphs 26–27.

[53] WIPO/GRTKF/IC/8/11 – Intergovernmental Committee on Intellectual Property and Genetic Resources, Traditional Knowledge and Folklore, Eighth Session, 6–10 June 2005, *Disclosure of Origin or Source of Genetic Resources and Associated Traditional Knowledge in Patent Applications, Document submitted by the European Community and its Member States,* 17 May 2005.

[54] The TRIPS Agreement is a notable exception to this requirement.

[55] WIPO/GRTKF/IC/8/11, above n 53, 3.

traditional knowledge. If the response is negative, no further information is necessary. In the event of a fraudulent declaration the proposal states that:

> [w]here it is proved that the patent applicant has disclosed incorrect or incomplete information, effective, proportionate and dissuasive sanctions *outside the field of patent law* should be imposed on the patent applicant or holder [emphasis added]

and:

> [f]or reasons of legal certainty, the submission of incorrect or incomplete information should not have any effect on the validity of the granted patent or on its enforceability against patent infringers.

Therefore even in the case of a fraudulently obtained patent, the rights of the patent holder remain intact and compensation is sought in ways other than the revocation of the patent.[56]

Recent Developments

At the Seventeenth Session of the IGC in December 2010, the African Group submitted a proposal on genetic resources and future work. The proposal was compiled taking into consideration the various documents on genetic resources within the IGC, and the objectives and principles of the CBD and the Nagoya Protocol. The document was based on the proposal that the work of the IGC should be mutually supportive of the CBD and the Nagoya Protocol, and should be without prejudice to the negotiations in the WTO on the mandatory disclosure proposal in the context of the relationship between the CBD and the TRIPS agreement. The African Group proposed that negotiations on genetic resources in the IGC should be based on a mandatory disclosure requirement and an appropriate way to ensure PIC and fair and equitable benefit sharing in line with the Nagoya Protocol. The draft text for negotiations would be based on the proposals of Switzerland and the EU proposal. The objectives would be to amend the PCT and the PLT to reflect a mandatory disclosure of the origin of the genetic resource, the incorporation of the 'internationally recognized certificate of

[56] The EU has also reiterated this position in the TRIPS Council – IP/C/M/39 – *Minutes of Meeting on 18–19 February 2003*, 21 March 2003, paragraph 127.

compliance' as provided for in the Nagoya Protocol[57] and any other submission that may be tabled by member countries.[58]

Subsequently, the Group of Like Minded Megadverse Countries in their contribution to the draft articles on the protection of traditional knowledge proposed that contracting parties shall ensure that the beneficiaries have the exclusive collective rights to, inter alia 'require, in the application for IP rights involving the use of their traditional knowledge, the mandatory disclosure of traditional knowledge holders and their country of origin as well as evidence of compliance with prior and informed consent and benefit-sharing requirements in accordance with domestic laws or requirements of country of origin,' and 'prevent the use of traditional knowledge without acknowledging the source and origin of that traditional knowledge; acknowledging and attributing the traditional knowledge holders where known; and respecting the cultural norms and practices of its holders.'[59] These negotiations are ongoing.

Developments in the CBD

In the CBD the issue of disclosure of origin was taken up by the Sixth CoP in 2002.[60] The concept was incorporated in the Bonn Guidelines adopted by the Sixth CoP by Decision VI/24 A.[61] The Sixth CoP also took Decision VI/24 C on the 'Role of intellectual property rights in the implementation of access and benefit-sharing arrangements.' By this Decision the CoP invited:

> Parties and Governments to encourage the disclosure of origin of genetic resources and traditional knowledge in patent applications as a possible contribution to tracking compliance with PIC and MATs in regard to access to those resources and knowledge.

---

57 Article 17.

58 WIPO/GRTKF/IC/20/INF/12 – Intergovernmental Committee on Intellectual Property and Genetic Resources, Traditional Knowledge and Folklore, Twentieth Session, 14–22 February 2012, *Proposal of the African Group on Genetic Resources and Future Work, Document prepared by the Secretariat*, 17 October 2011.

59 WIPO/GRTKF/ IC/21/5 – Intergovernmental Committee on Intellectual Property and Genetic Resources, Traditional Knowledge and Folklore, Twenty-First Session, 16–20 April 2012, *Like-Minded Countries Contribution to the Draft Articles on the Protection of Traditional Knowledge*, 18 January 2012.

60 See Decisions VI/10 F – paragraphs, 31, 46 and VI/24 C entitled 'Role of intellectual property rights in the implementation of access and benefit-sharing arrangements.'

61 UNEP/CBD/COP/6/20 – *Report of the Sixth Meeting of the Conference of the Parties to the Convention on Biological Diversity* – 27 May 2002.

The Decision also resolved to undertake further information gathering and analysis in this regard with the help of WIPO and other CBD institutions. In relation to disclosure requirements and patent applications the issues to be studied included:

- the consistency and applicability of requirements for disclosure of country of origin and prior informed consent in the context of international legal obligations;
- the efficacy of country of origin and prior informed consent disclosures in assisting the examination of intellectual property rights applications and the re-examination of intellectual property rights granted as well as in monitoring compliance with access provisions;
- the feasibility of an internationally recognized certificate of origin system as evidence of prior informed consent and mutually agreed terms; and
- the role of oral evidence of prior art in the examination, granting and maintenance of intellectual property rights.

Notwithstanding this Decision which held out some promise that the issue of disclosure of origin would be effectively addressed in the CBD where it had failed in the intellectual property regimes, it has been conspicuously absent in both the Bonn Guidelines of 2002 and the Nagoya Protocol of 2010.

The Bonn Guidelines do not make any significant contribution to the debate on disclosure of origin obligations. They merely reiterate the CBD position that implementation of PIC and ABS provisions, including monitoring and enforcement, should be achieved by way of national legislation and contractual measures, though these measures have not proved effective. Therefore it puts the onus on provider countries to ensure that PIC and ABS laws are complied with, with no corresponding obligation on user countries. Further, it proposes that verification mechanisms, including a system of certification, should be merely voluntary.[62]

---

[62] It should be noted that an UNCTAD analysis on disclosure requirements which was submitted to the CoP in response to Decision VIII/19 is unequivocal in its contention that there is a need for an international system of mandatory disclosure of origin – See UNEP/CBD/COP/8/INF/25 – CBD CoP, Eighth Meeting, 20–31 March 2006, *Analysis of Options for Implementing Disclosure of Origin Requirements in Intellectual Property Applications – Submission by UNCTAD*, 9 February 2006. A caveat to the document states that the views of the authors do not necessarily reflect that of the UNCTAD Secretariat.

The Nagoya Protocol evolved from the draft International Regime on Access and Benefit Sharing, and unlike the Bonn Guidelines it is a legally binding agreement. In the light of the failure of the intellectual property fora to come to grips with the issue of compliance including disclosure of origin, it initially held out the greatest promise of including effective measures to ensure that PIC and mutually agreed terms were an integral part of the benefit sharing process. However, this potential does not appear to have materialized.

The issue of compliance including disclosure of origin and a certificate of compliance was intensely negotiated from the fifth to the ninth meetings of the Ad Hoc Open-Ended Working Group on Access and Benefit-Sharing (WG-ABS). While the developed/user countries pushed for facilitating access to genetic resources and related traditional knowledge, developing/provider countries emphasized the need for compliance and disclosure provisions and the need for effective checkpoints which they argued were at the heart of the Protocol.[63] At the ninth meeting of the WG-ABS the African Group in particular argued that Africa wanted strong checkpoints in the international regime which would ensure that biological resources effectively carried passports when they left Africa's national borders.[64] Indonesia too urged that as a megadiverse country it wanted the international regime to be a single legally binding instrument which should contain principles relating to compliance and enforcement measures with binding provisions to prevent biopiracy.[65]

The draft became progressively diluted as negotiations continued. The final draft of the international regime submitted by the WG-ABS at the second resumed session of its ninth meeting in October 2010 still included provisions on a (possibly) mandatory disclosure provision and a certificate of compliance.[66] However, penalties for non-compliance were weak and did not include revocation of patents.[67]

The final text of the Nagoya Protocol, which was adopted at the Tenth CoP in October 2010, did not meet the demands of provider countries in

---

63 UNEP/CBD/WG-ABS/9/3 – Ad Hoc Open-Ended Working Group on Access and Benefit-Sharing Ninth meeting, 22–28 March 2010, *Report of the First Part of the Ninth Meeting of the Ad Hoc Open-Ended Working Group on Access and Benefit-Sharing*, 26 April 2010.

64 Ibid at 8.

65 Ibid at 11.

66 UNEP/CBD/WG-ABS/9/ING/1 – Ad Hoc Open-Ended Working Group on Access and Benefit-Sharing, Ninth meeting (second resumed session), 16 October 2010, *Meeting of the Interregional Negotiating Group*, Article 13.

67 Ibid, Article 13 *bis*.

regard to disclosure or compliance measures. The word 'disclosure' does not occur anywhere in the text. Measures on compliance are found in Article 17 entitled 'Monitoring the utilization of genetic resources.' Article 17 requires each party to take measures, as appropriate, to monitor and enhance transparency about the utilization of genetic resources, but makes no mention of traditional knowledge. This omission is significant as many instances of misappropriation relate to traditional knowledge.

The compliance measures to be taken by parties are primarily the designation and operation of checkpoints. These designated checkpoints would collect or receive, as appropriate, relevant information about the accessing and use of genetic resources. These include PIC, the sources of the genetic resources, mutually agreed terms, and/or the utilization of the resources. According to Article 17(a)(ii) each party shall, as appropriate, and depending on the characteristics of a designated checkpoint, require users to provide this information and initiate the procedures by which this would be done. The relevant information, including from internationally recognized certificates of compliance where they are available, shall be provided to relevant national authorities, to the party providing PIC and to the Access and Benefit Sharing Clearing House as appropriate. This must be done without prejudice to the protection of confidential information.[68]

The provisions are couched in weak and ineffective language, interspersed with vague phrases such as 'as appropriate' and requiring parties to take measures which are 'effective' and 'relevant.' The onus is on provider countries to enforce these requirements and the demands of these countries that there should be an international regime to ensure compliance, and enforcement were therefore not met. Rather, it is left to each party to put its own measures in place, including dealing with situations of non-compliance, which will necessarily make the process inconsistent and difficult to enforce.

Nijar states that a point of contention between developed and developing countries was the designation of the checkpoints.[69] He notes that developing countries argued that user countries must establish effective checkpoints where users would be required to go for research and development on the resource, to claim a right in relation to the innovation made from such research and development, and for the commercialization of the end product. The user would have to provide information which would include the country of origin of the resource or the traditional knowledge, that PIC of

---

[68] Article 17 (1) (iii).

[69] Gurdial Singh Nijar, *The Nagoya Protocol on Access and Benefit Sharing of Genetic Resources: Analysis and Implementation Options for Developing Countries*, South Centre (2011) at 8.

the country had been obtained and MAT had been established, and its terms adhered to. Developing countries proposed that disclosure of such information should be mandatory at intellectual property offices, at offices involved in the commercialization of products, research institutions subject to public funding and institutions publishing research on the utilization of genetic resources.[70]

Developed countries were not amenable to these suggestions and the final wording is a diluted version of these proposals. The provisions again are couched in weak language with little scope for enforcement. Parties are required to take measures 'as appropriate' to collect or receive the information. The obligation of parties to require users to provide such information shall be 'as appropriate' and depends on the particular characteristic of the checkpoint. Most disappointingly, situations of non-compliance shall be dealt with by 'appropriate, effective and proportionate measures.'

Article 17 (2) of the protocol states that a permit or its equivalent issued in accordance with Article 6(3)(e) shall constitute an internationally recognized certificate of compliance. Such a certificate shall serve as evidence that the genetic resource that it covers has been accessed in accordance with PIC and in accordance with mutually agreed terms as required by the Party providing PIC.[71] This serves to protect a user from allegations of misappropriation of the genetic resource. This definition of such a certificate falls short of developing countries' demands for an international certificate of origin/source/legal provenance which should be a pre-condition of patentability.

The Governing Body of the FAO Treaty

The Interim Secretariat of the FAO Treaty has collaborated with WIPO mainly in regard to the work of the IGC. The issues under discussion of direct relevance to the Treaty include the possible role of a certificate of origin/source/legal provenance of genetic resources, in relation to patent applications. The Interim Secretariat has noted that in the event that such an instrument comes into force, the origin of materials from the Multilateral System of access and benefit sharing should be declared as the Multilateral System. The Standard Material Transfer Agreement would serve the role of such a certificate.[72]

---

[70] Ibid at 8.

[71] Article 17 (2).

[72] IT/GB-1/06/Inf.4 – International Treaty on Plant Genetic Resources for Food and Agriculture, First Session of the Governing Body, 12–16 June 2006, *Report on the Status of Cooperation With Other International Organizations,* May 2006;

UPOV

The UPOV position on disclosure of origin is contained in its reply to the notification of the CBD in June 2003. In regard to both disclosure of origin requirements and the obligation to prove PIC, its stance is that additional conditions to the grant of plant variety protection rights are not acceptable.[73]

CONCLUSION

It can be argued that there is no inherent obstacle to a mandatory disclosure requirement being incorporated into patent law, nor would it be incompatible with the elements of the patent system. Patent law is not static, and has undergone changes over time, both in regard to its substantive elements and the way in which it has been interpreted and implemented. For example, there are notable differences in the way in which plant patent laws have been implemented in the US and the EU, both in regard to the criteria and subject matter of patentability. Under the circumstances it is possible for patent and plant variety protection laws to be further adapted to incorporate measures to prevent the misappropriation of patentable subject matter.

However, the actual workings of the disclosure requirement and the information to be required will need to be closely examined. Mere disclosure of the source or origin of either the genetic resource or the knowledge related to it would not necessarily prevent their misappropriation. The internationally recognized Certificate of Compliance in Article 17 of the Nagoya Protocol which has been cited in the proposed amendment to the TRIPS Agreement, requires confirmation of PIC and mutually agreed

IT/GB-2/07/17 – International Treaty on Plant Genetic Resources for Food and Agriculture, Second Session of the Governing Body, 29 October – 2 November 2007, *Report on the Status of Cooperation With Other International Organizations, Including Agreements Between the Governing Body and the International Agricultural Research Centers of the Consultative Group on International Agricultural Research and Other Relevant International Institutions*, paragraph 25.

[73] *Access To Genetic Resources And Benefit-Sharing, Reply of UPOV to the Notification of June 26, 2003, from the Executive Secretary of the Convention on Biological Diversity (CBD)* adopted by the Council of UPOV at its thirty-seventh ordinary session on 23 October 2003. See also UNEP/CBD/WG-ABS/5/4/Add.1 – Ad Hoc Open-Ended Working Group on Access and Benefit-Sharing, *Overview of Recent Developments at the International Level Relating to Access and Benefit-Sharing*, 30 August 2007.

terms. Thus this requirement would be more inclusive than a requirement limited to only disclosing origin or source.

Determining questions of PIC and ensuring ABS would not be easy, even with the requirement of proof of legal acquisition. For instance, as shown in the case studies discussed in Chapter 9, the resource may be first acquired by one institution, which may often be located in the country of origin, and then licensed to another, which may be the patent applicant for the end product based in another country. This took place in the case of the Hoodia plant of the San people. In the case of the wild rice from Mali, the University of Utah which patented the gene in question, acquired the rice variety in which the gene was incorporated from the International Rice Research Institute (IRRI) in the Philippines, although the original source of the gene was the variety conserved by farming communities in Mali. Therefore, while the patent applicant would be able to prove legal acquisition from the immediate source from which it was acquired, this would not always ensure equity for countries or communities which are the origin of the resource. In order to be effective the requirement would have to be rigorously implemented so as to provide a comprehensive history of the movement of such resources, which would be relevant to their final patentability.

It must also be noted that while disclosure of traditional knowledge must also be required, other issues would also arise in cases where traditional knowledge of the uses of the resource has been utilized. It would be difficult to prove that such knowledge was in fact used for the purpose, and also such disclosure is more easily avoided. In any case, the issue in relation to traditional knowledge is the fact that the existence of such knowledge, per se negates a fundamental criterion of patentability, that of novelty. Therefore a different strategy would also be necessary to address issues of traditional knowledge, and this is discussed in the next chapter.

It is clear that proof of legal acquisition as a condition of patentability would not necessarily ensure greater equity in the use of the benefits of genetic resources or traditional knowledge, or resolve all the problems related to their appropriation and propertization. It is nevertheless a strategy which could be used to resolve some of the problems relating to this issue. However, in order to be effective, it is essential that non-compliance must result in the failure of the patent application, or at the post grant stage, the revocation of the patent. It is this requirement which is the stumbling block to its acceptance by developed countries. Some of these countries have been ostensibly supportive of the developing country concerns and have submitted several proposals for implementing the obligation. These proposals have in fact recommended that the obligation be made mandatory and have suggested amendments to patent treaties, specifically the TRIPS Agreement, the PCT and the PLT, to formalize it. Nevertheless, these countries have also been adamant that the obligation should effectively operate only at the patent application processing stage and it should not have any effect on patents already granted. This position has been justified on the grounds that it would cause uncertainty in the patenting process. However, given the complexities of the movement of genetic resources, it is possible that many facts may not come to light until a later stage, or may be suppressed initially. The Hoodia case is an example of this. Therefore the deterrent element must continue to be operative at all stages of obtaining and keeping a patent.

The Nagoya Protocol did not meet the expectations of developing countries in regard to implementing an effective disclosure provision, and in its aftermath the matter has forum shifted back to the TRIPS Council and the WIPO IGC. Proposals in both these fora urge consistency in the relationship between the CBD and the Nagoya Protocol on the one hand, and patent law on the other, particularly in regard to PIC and fair and equitable benefit sharing. It remains to be seen how the negotiations will progress. In the meantime bilateral agreements are concurrently undermining efforts in the international sphere to introduce a disclosure provision into patent laws. For example, Peru, while being one of the strongest advocates for these measures in the TRIPS Council, has in the US-Peru Free Trade Agreement of 2006 permitted the patenting of genetic resources and traditional knowledge. The FTA also does not require patent applicants to disclose the origin of plants or obtain permission before using traditional knowledge. In view of the opposition of developed countries to revocation of patents, the prospects for adopting and implementing the requirement of proof of legal acquisition are not promising.

12. The recognition of traditional knowledge as prior art

ISSUES OF TRADITIONAL KNOWLEDGE IN PATENTABLE INVENTIONS

Issues of traditional knowledge (TK) may arise in regard to claimed inventions which may be based on it, may be derived from it, or may be guided by or make use of it.[1] WIPO has noted that traditional knowledge may be potentially relevant to an invention's novelty or inventiveness (non-obviousness), to an applicant's declaration of identity of the true inventor(s), to an applicant's obligation to declare all known prior art relevant to an invention's patentability or to the applicant's claim of entitlement to apply for an invention.[2]

One of the conditions of patentability is that a claimed invention must be novel/inventive, and this criterion is assessed in relation to what is already known or exists. This body of existing knowledge is termed state of the art or prior art.[3] Developing countries have alleged that the patent system facilitates the misappropriation of traditional knowledge by granting patents on inventions based upon it, since the intellectual property rights (IPR) system does not recognize this body of knowledge as prior art.

---

[1] WIPO/GRTKF/IC/11/7 – Intergovernmental Committee on Intellectual Property and Genetic Resources, Traditional Knowledge and Folklore Eleventh Session, 3–12 July 2007, *Recognition of Traditional Knowledge within the Patent System*, 6 June 2007, 1. For an overview of WIPO's work on TK see Shakeel T. Bhatti, 'Intellectual Property and Traditional Knowledge: The Work and Role of the World Intellectual Property Organization (WIPO)' in UNCTAD/DITC/TED/10 Sophia Twarog and Promila Kapoor (eds) *Protecting and Promoting Traditional Knowledge: Systems, National Experiences and International Dimensions*, (2004) 121.

[2] WIPO/GRTKF/IC/11/7 above n 1, 1.

[3] For example Article 54 (1) entitled 'Novelty' of the European Patent Convention states that 'An invention shall be considered to be new if it does not form part of the state of the art' – *Convention on the Grant of European Patents* (European Patent Convention) 13 ILM 268 (1974).

The discussions in the TRIPS Council have put concerns about the misappropriation of traditional knowledge into two categories:

- concern about the granting of patents or other IPRs covering traditional knowledge to persons other than those indigenous peoples or communities who have originated and legitimately control the traditional knowledge;
- concern that traditional knowledge is being used without the authorization of the indigenous peoples or communities who have originated and legitimately control it and without proper sharing of the benefits that accrue from such use.[4]

Peru has articulated these concerns more specifically, stating that:

> One of the main concerns of Peru and various other countries (including the Group of Like-Minded Megadiverse Countries) is the fact that the patent system, as currently operated, frequently gives rise to situations in which inventions based directly or indirectly on genetic resources of Peruvian origin or the traditional knowledge of Peruvian communities pass the novelty or inventiveness tests when they should not do so or, alternatively, that these resources or knowledge could have been obtained in an unauthorized or patently illegal manner.[5]

The second issue raised in this statement, namely the possibility that these resources or knowledge have been obtained in an unauthorized or illegal manner, has already been discussed in the previous chapter on disclosure of origin of genetic resources and traditional knowledge. The first issue, that inventions based directly or indirectly on genetic resources or traditional knowledge pass the novelty or inventiveness test, will be discussed here. The concerns of developing countries have been summed up by Peru in the

---

[4] IP/C/W/370/Rev.1– TRIPS Council, *The Protection of Traditional Knowledge and Folklore – Summary of Issues Raised and Points Made*, 9 March 2006, 3. See also the position of the African Group – IP/C/W/404 – TRIPS Council, *Taking Forward the Review of Article 27.3(B) of the TRIPS Agreement Joint Communication from the African Group*, 26 June 2003.

[5] IP/C/W/447 – TRIPS Council, *Article 27.3(b), Relationship between the TRIPS Agreement and the CBD and Protection of Traditional Knowledge and Folklore, Communication from Peru*, 8 June 2005, 2. See also IP/C/W/493 – TRIPS Council, *Combating Biopiracy – The Peruvian Experience, Communication from Peru*, 19 September 2007 where Peru has documented several cases of inventions being patented in spite of evidence of prior art in relation to them.

following terms: '[a]re the patents granted "good" patents in the sense that the inventions are actually new and involve an inventive step?'[6]

Strategies for addressing these concerns and protecting traditional knowledge within the patent system are an aspect of defensive protection. The defensive protection of traditional knowledge does not envisage granting patent protection to this body of knowledge and would not necessarily prevent others from using it. Rather, it seeks to ensure that inventions based upon it are not themselves granted patent protection unjustifiably and illegally. The method by which this objective is to be achieved is to ensure that it is recognized as forming part of the state of the art or prior art so as to negate a claim of novelty in patent applications.

The WIPO IGC has explained this strategy in the following terms and set out its components:

> 'Defensive protection' of TK refers to strategies to prevent the acquisition of intellectual property rights over TK or genetic resources by parties other than the customary custodians of the knowledge or resources. Defensive protection has both legal and practical aspects. The legal aspect concerns whether TK is recognized as relevant prior art under the patent law of the jurisdiction concerned. Legal questions may include, for instance, recognition of orally transmitted knowledge, establishing a clear date of public disclosure of written or oral knowledge, and determining whether the TK was disclosed in such a way as to enable the reader to put the technology into effect. The practical aspect includes entails [*sic*] ensuring that information is actually available to search authorities and patent examiners, and is effectively accessible to patent authorities (such as being indexed or classified), so that it is much more likely to be found in a search for relevant prior art.[7]

These two aspects, the legal and the practical, are considered below.

It should be noted that while disclosure of origin requirements discussed in the previous chapter also facilitate defensive mechanisms to protect genetic resources and traditional knowledge, traditional knowledge being an intangible resource requires more specific action. However, the two mechanisms are inter-linked since disclosing the traditional knowledge in question would be the first step in determining whether it is prior art under the circumstances.

---

6 IP/C/W/447, above n 5, 4.

7 Ibid, paragraph 13.

THE LEGAL ASPECT OF INTEGRATING TRADITIONAL KNOWLEDGE AND PRIOR ART

The legal aspect of protecting traditional knowledge is based on the requirement that it be recognized in national and international patent law as part of the body of prior art, against which an invention would have to be measured for novelty and inventiveness. Since traditional knowledge is by and large an unwritten body of knowledge, the fundamental problem is whether oral traditions and knowledge can be legally and practically recognized as such when examining patent applications.

At the international level, the question of what constitutes prior art is found in the WIPO treaties. As noted earlier, prior art as a condition of patentability was raised in the discussions on the draft Substantive Patent Law Treaty (SPLT). The draft provision contained in Article 8(1) in fact appears promising for protection of traditional knowledge. It states:

> (1) [*Definition*] The prior art with respect to a claimed invention shall consist of all information which has been made available to the public anywhere in the world in any form [as prescribed in the Regulations] before the priority date of the claimed invention.[8]

This includes both written and unwritten knowledge. However, in view of the fact that the SPLT has not been finalized, the Patent Cooperation Treaty (PCT) would be currently applicable at the international level for this purpose. The provisions of the PCT are more restrictive in this respect than those in the draft SPLT.

The PCT states that '[t]he objective of the international search is to discover relevant prior art.'[9] The definition of prior art is found in Rule 33.1 (a) of the Regulations of the PCT, which states:

> For the purposes of Article 15(2), relevant prior art shall consist of everything which has been made available to the public anywhere in the world by means of written disclosure (including drawings and other illustrations) and which is capable of being of assistance in determining that the claimed invention is or is not new and that it does or does not involve an inventive step (i.e., that it is or is not obvious), provided that the making available to the public occurred prior to the international filing date.[10]

---

8 SCP/10/4 – Standing Committee on the Law of Patents, Tenth Session, May 10–14, 2004, *Draft Substantive Patent Law Treaty*, 30 September 2003, Article 8.

9 Article 15 (2) of the PCT.

10 WIPO Regulations under the Patent Cooperation Treaty (as in force from 1 July 2012). Similarly, Rule 64.1 (a) states '[f]or the purposes of Article 33(2) and

Unlike the draft SPLT, this provision excludes oral information and traditions from the purview of the PCT. In addition the IGC has stated that:

> this rule only directly concerns the non-binding international search and examination, and the applicable rules for determining what prior art is relevant can vary according to national or regional laws. A strategy for defensive protection clearly needs to take account of the legal situation that applies in any particular country of interest.[11]

The IGC therefore takes the position that national laws are the final arbiter on this issue. In view of the wide divergence in domestic laws in the potential recognition they accord to traditional knowledge, this would be disadvantageous to those countries trying to prevent its misappropriation. The US for example does not recognize foreign uses of claimed inventions, and also requires documentation of the knowledge in question whether within or outside the US.[12] Under the US Patent Act,[13] novelty is not established if:

> the invention was *known or used by others in this country,* or patented or described in a *printed publication* in this or a foreign country, before the invention thereof by the applicant for patent [emphasis added]

or:

> the invention was patented or described in a *printed publication* in this or a foreign country or in *public use* or on sale *in this country*, more than one year

(3), everything made available to the public anywhere in the world by means of written disclosure (including drawings and other illustrations) shall be considered prior art provided that such making available occurred prior to the relevant date.'

11 WIPO/GRTKF/IC/5/6 – Intergovernmental Committee on Intellectual Property and Genetic Resources, Traditional Knowledge and Folklore, Fifth Session, 7–15 July 2003, *Practical Mechanisms for the Defensive Protection of Traditional Knowledge and Genetic Resources within the Patent System*, 14 May 2003, 2. See also Manuel Ruiz, *The International Debate on Traditional Knowledge as Prior Art in the Patent System: Issues and Options for Developing Countries* South Centre, T.R.A.D.E. Series Occasional Paper 9 (2002), available at http://www.ciel.org/Publications/PriorArt_ManuelRuiz_Oct02.pdf (last accessed 30 June 2012).

12 Shayana Kadidal, 'Subject-Matter Imperialism? Biodiversity, Foreign Prior Art and the Neem Patent Controversy' (1997) 37 *IDEA* 371; Leanne M Fecteau, 'The Ayahuasca Patent Revocation: Raising Questions about Current US Patent Policy' (2001) 21 *Boston College Third World Law Journal* 69 for a discussion of US law.

13 35 U.S.C Sections 102 (a) and (b).

> prior to the date of the application for patent in the United States .... [emphasis added]

The US position is similar to the approach taken in the PCT which requires written proof of prior art.[14] The European Patent Convention in contrast has a wider definition of prior art, which encompasses everything made available to the public in any way.[15]

Restrictive national definitions of prior art have resulted in several conflicts on issues of genetic resources and traditional knowledge both internationally and within countries.[16] These have included patents granted for products based on the uses of the neem tree,[17] the medicinal properties of turmeric, the ayahuasca vine of the Amazon Basin[18] and the hoodia plant of the Kalahari desert.[19] These controversies revolved around the issue of whether traditional but undocumented knowledge of the beneficial properties of these plants would constitute 'prior art' within its meaning in national laws. In the case of neem and turmeric the patents were revoked only when ancient Sanskrit texts which documented their uses, were discovered.[20]

---

[14] Although one of the primary purposes of the PCT was to standardize the procedure for examining the criterion of prior art in patent applications, it categorically acknowledged that its provisions regarding prior art are exclusively for the purposes of international procedure. Consequently any country is free to apply the criteria of its national law in respect of this and other conditions of patentability not constituting requirements as to form and contents of applications – PCT, Article 27 (5).

[15] 'The state of the art shall be held to comprise everything made available to the public by means of a written or oral description, by use, or in any other way, before the date of filing of the European patent application' – *European Patent Convention*, above n 3, Article 54 (2).

[16] Commission on Intellectual Property Rights, *Integrating Intellectual Property Rights and Development Policy* (2002) 76, available at http://www.iprcommission.org/papers/pdfs/final_report/CIPRfullfinal.pdf (last accessed 30 June 2012). See also the discussion on biopiracy in Chapter 3.

[17] Kadidal, above n 12; Emily Marden, 'The Neem Tree Patent: International Conflict over the Commodification of Life' (1999) 22 *Boston College International and Comparative Law Review* 279.

[18] Fecteau, above n 12.

[19] Rachel Wynberg, 'Rhetoric, Realism and Benefit-Sharing: Use of Traditional Knowledge of Hoodia Species in the Development of an Appetite Suppressant' (2004) 7(6) *Journal of World Intellectual Property* 851.

[20] GRAIN, *One global patent system? WIPO's Substantive Patent Law Treaty* (2003), available at http://www.grain.org/briefings_files/wipo-splt-2003-en.pdf; see also http://www.tkdl.res.in/tkdl/langdefault/common/Biopiracy.asp?GL=Eng (both last accessed 30 June 2012); Report of the Commission on Intellectual Property Rights, above n 16, 76. See also Cynthia M Ho, 'Biopiracy and Beyond: A

The US has argued in the TRIPS Council that the problem lies not with its laws but with the knowledge systems in question which:

> often depend upon face-to-face communication, thereby limiting access to the information to persons in direct contact with one another. The public at large does not benefit from the knowledge nor can the knowledge be built upon.[21]

It has further stated that:

> In addition, if information is not written down, that information is completely inaccessible to patent examiners everywhere as prior art when they are examining patent applications. It is possible, therefore, for a patent to be issued claiming as an invention technology that is known to a particular indigenous community. The fault lies not with the patent system, however, but with the inaccessibility of the knowledge involved beyond the indigenous community.[22]

While the inaccessibility of traditional knowledge, particularly oral traditions, does constitute a practical difficulty in defining it as prior art, it can still be argued that the first step in defensive protection is to grant it legal recognition whether written or unwritten. Thereafter the practical problems of implementing the provisions can be addressed. Therefore the US position is not tenable. International recognition of non-written disclosures should not be left to the discretion of individual countries and a uniform standard should be made applicable. This position has been endorsed by the UK IPR Commission which has stated that it must be recognized that:

> much traditional knowledge will continue to be undocumented. The concept of absolute novelty whereby any disclosure including through use, anywhere in the world, is sufficient to destroy the novelty of an invention therefore remains a necessary safeguard. Without this safeguard, patents could continue to be granted for traditional knowledge that is already in the public domain, albeit not through written disclosure. Some countries do not include use outside their country as 'prior art.'
>
> Those countries that only include domestic use in their definition of prior art, should give equal treatment to users of knowledge in other countries. In addition,

Consideration of Socio-Cultural Conflicts With Global Patent Policies' (2006) *University of Michigan Journal of Law Reform* 433, 449; and John Tustin, 'Traditional Knowledge and Intellectual Property in Brazilian Biodiversity Law' (2006) *Texas Intellectual Property Law Journal* 131.

[21] IP/C/W/209 – TRIPS Council, *Review of the Provisions of Article 27.3(b) Further Views of the United States, Communication from the United States*, 3 October 2000, p. 4.

[22] Ibid.

> account should be taken of the unwritten nature of much traditional knowledge in any attempts to develop further the patent system internationally.[23]

The WIPO IGC has also acknowledged that one possible means to improve defensive protection of traditional knowledge within the patent system is to clarify the legal criteria applicable to prior art. It notes the differences in national and regional standards in this regard, including whether the prior art was made available to the public, the circumstances or extent of its disclosure and whether it was disclosed in oral or written form. The IGC notes that at the international level, this might entail harmonization of substantive patent law in this regard[24] and has also observed that 'in view of the increasing operational cooperation among patent offices, a universal understanding of the definition of prior art is the basis for a common understanding with respect to novelty and inventive step.'[25]

The IGC has in fact acknowledged that recognition of orally disclosed information is a further means of enhancing defensive strategies to protect traditional knowledge, since non-recognition of such information would prejudice the interests of communities with a stronger oral tradition.[26] It goes on to note that:

> [f]rom the legal perspective, it is possible to recognize orally disclosed material as being relevant prior art, and this recognition may be universal, in the sense that knowledge disclosed by any means, in any geographical location, may be considered as prior art relevant to the novelty of a claimed invention. Recognizing its legal status as relevant to the determination of validity of patent claims would clearly increase the legal basis for defensive protection, without necessarily requiring TK holders to disclose or publish their TK in violation of the principle of prior informed consent.

---

[23] Report of the Commission on Intellectual Property Rights, above n 16, 83.

[24] WIPO/GRTKF/IC/5/6, above n 11, paragraph 80.

[25] WIPO/GRTKF/IC/17/INF/8 – Intergovernmental Committee on Intellectual Property and Genetic Resources, Traditional Knowledge and Folklore, Seventeenth Session, 6–10 December 2010, *Note on the Meanings of the Term 'Public Domain' in the Intellectual Property System with special reference to the Protection of Traditional Knowledge and Traditional Cultural Expressions/Expressions of Folklore, Document prepared by the Secretariat*, 14.

[26] WIPO/GRTKF/IC/6/8 – Intergovernmental Committee on Intellectual Property and Genetic Resources, Traditional Knowledge and Folklore, Sixth Session, 15–19 March 2004, *Defensive Protection Measures Relating to Intellectual Property, Genetic Resources and Traditional Knowledge: An Update*, 15 December 2003, paragraph 17.

The EC has been more amenable to the principle of defensive protection of traditional knowledge through the patent system. It has noted in the TRIPS Council that an effective way in which to prevent misappropriation would be make sure that traditional knowledge would always be duly recognized as prior art.[27] However, in view of the fact that the negotiations on the draft SPLT and the revision of the TRIPS Agreement are currently deadlocked, it is uncertain as to how this would be achieved.

THE PRACTICAL ASPECT OF INTEGRATING TRADITIONAL KNOWLEDGE AND PRIOR ART

Defensive Publication of Traditional Knowledge

Even assuming that the concept of prior art is extended to traditional knowledge in national and international legislation, the practical problem remains as to how measures would be implemented to ensure that it is taken into consideration. The argument of patent applicants is that traditional knowledge is simply not available for examination for this purpose. Therefore if traditional knowledge is to be made available as prior art in order to pre-empt patent claims, it may need to be recorded and published. This could be both beneficial and detrimental to the communities which possess it.

The Ad Hoc Open-Ended Inter-Sessional Working Group on Article 8(j) and Related Provisions of the Convention on Biological Diversity (WG8J) has pointed out that the protection aimed at by documenting and recording traditional knowledge can be 'protection from extinction, protection from privatization and unjust enrichment, protection from unauthorized use, and protection for access and benefit sharing, among others.'

On the other hand making information on traditional knowledge widely available would also give rise to some potential problems which could be detrimental to the communities concerned.[28] The WG8J has gone on to note that:

---

[27] IP/C/W/383 – TRIPS Council, *Communication from the European Communities and their member states, Review of Article 27.3(b) of the TRIPS agreement, and the relationship between the TRIPS agreement and the Convention on Biological Diversity (CBD) and the protection of Traditional Knowledge and Folklore, 'A Concept Paper,'* 17 October 2002, paragraph 65.

[28] For a discussion of the potential problems involved in documenting traditional knowledge see UNEP/CBD/WG8J/4/INF/9 – Ad Hoc Open-Ended Inter-Sessional Working Group on Article 8(J) and Related Provisions of the Convention

> despite the potential benefits of documenting and recording traditional knowledge, the topic has been controversial, namely in terms of whether documenting traditional knowledge may itself constitute a threat to the preservation and nature of traditional knowledge and of whether it may, in practice, facilitate misuse and unauthorized use of such knowledge.[29]

India has submitted a proposal to the TRIPS Council, suggesting three possible methods of protection. These are: (i) documentation of traditional knowledge; (ii) registration and innovation patent system (*sic*); and (iii) development of a *sui generis* system.[30] This proposal also notes the same advantages and disadvantages of documenting and publishing traditional knowledge as cited above.

The first method, i.e. documentation of traditional knowledge, could give rise to two possible scenarios. India has pointed out that on the one hand it is believed that proper documentation of traditional knowledge would help in checking biopiracy since such documentation would be available to patent examiners in order to check traditional knowledge as possible prior art. Further, India has observed that '[i]t is also hoped that such documentation would facilitate tracing of indigenous communities with whom benefits of commercialization of such materials/knowledge has to be shared.' However, there are also apprehensions that documentation may in fact facilitate biopiracy. India points out that:

> a trade secret of an indigenous community would be maintained only until it is closely held by the community – as soon as it is put on paper, it will become accessible to pirates and would be purloined. This dilemma is the subject of discussions in national and international debates on benefit sharing. Some suggest the empowerment of the indigenous communities themselves so that

---

on Biological Diversity, Fourth meeting, 23–27 January 2006, *Composite Report on the Status and Trends Regarding the Knowledge, Innovations and Practices of Indigenous and Local Communities, The Advantages and Limitations of Registers,* 21 December 2005; UNEP/CBD/WG8J/5/3/Add.2 – Ad Hoc Open-Ended Inter-Sessional Working Group on Article 8(J) and Related Provisions of the Convention on Biological Diversity, Fifth meeting, 15–19 October 2007 – *Considerations for Developing Technical Guidelines for Recording and Documenting Traditional Knowledge and the Potential Threat of Such Documentation,* 28 July 2007.

[29] UNEP/CBD/WG8J/5/3/Add.2, above n 28, 2. This document provides a comprehensive analysis of the issues to be considered in documenting TK, including draft recommendations on the possibility of developing technical guidelines for doing so.

[30] IP/C/W/198 (WT/CTE/W/156) – Committee on Trade and Environment and TRIPS Council, *Protection of Biodiversity and Traditional Knowledge – The Indian Experience, Submission by India,* 14 July 2000.

> they are able to get legal protection for closely-held knowledge without the involvement of outside agencies. Nevertheless, documentation has one clear benefit. It would check patents based on TK in the public domain that are today difficult to prevent due to lack of availability of information with patent examiners.[31]

India has set out certain measures that it has taken in regard to documentation of traditional knowledge. These include Community Biodiversity Registers and Peoples' Biodiversity Registers with the involvement of a range of stakeholders including non-governmental organizations. The Traditional Knowledge Digital Library is a navigable computerized database of documented traditional knowledge relating to the use of medicinal and other plants, such knowledge being already in the public domain.[32]

However, India has reiterated that documentation is only one means of giving recognition to knowledge holders. It will not ensure that the benefits accruing from the use of such knowledge will be shared with them.[33] In fact a report submitted to the WG8J has cautioned that countries must be circumspect in resorting to databases as a means of protecting traditional knowledge. It states that:

> [m]any of the functions of traditional knowledge databases conflict with one another such that the benefits achieved for one function can produce costs for other goals. Other conflicts involve significant differences in how traditional knowledge is defined and regulated within the communities and externally in national and international jurisdictions. Knowledge for indigenous and local communities has multiple dimensions, such as cosmological, spiritual, ritual, kinship, inherited, and practical. Traditional knowledge is generally regulated under customary law and locally specific rules, taboos, and social and spiritual obligations that may differ greatly from national norms. Customary law regulates what can properly be stored in traditional knowledge databases, how this knowledge should be used, defines the benefits and harms from the distribution of this knowledge outside of its normal context.[34]

The second method, i.e. the registration and innovation patent system, involves creating a system of registration of innovations by inventors. This registration will give inventors the right to challenge any use of the

---

31 Ibid at 3.

32 See http://www.tkdl.res.in/tkdl/langdefault/common/Home.asp?GL=Eng (last accessed 30 June 2012). For a description of various TK databases see UNEP/CBD/WG8J/4/INF/9, above n 28.

33 IP/C/W/198, above n 30, 5.

34 UNEP/CBD/WG8J/4/INF/9, above n 28.

innovation without prior permission. The HoneyBee data base in India has been cited as an example. It was stated that:

> The network has probably the world's largest database on grassroot innovations, having now about 10,000 innovations, with names and addresses of the innovators (individuals or communities). Through the HoneyBee Newsletter, grassroots innovations have been disseminated to more than 75 countries. For example, this database has entries on traditional use of fish and fish products, improving crop productivity, etc.[35]

In regard to the third suggestion, i.e. the development of a *sui generis* system, India has stated that:

> Some experts have suggested that a *sui generis* system separate from the existing IPR system should be designed to protect knowledge, innovations and practices associated with biological resources. However, the parameters, elements and modalities of a *sui generis* system are still being worked out. This is in addition to the *sui generis* system of protection for plant varieties.

It appears therefore that documentation and registration of traditional knowledge will be necessary in order to bring it within the body of available prior art. However, as noted, the primary concern regarding this strategy is whether it may facilitate piracy rather than protecting it. In the context of this problem, knowledge that is in the public domain and that which is not, has been distinguished.[36] Several countries have noted this distinction in making suggestions for defensive measures. For example, at the outset of the deliberations of the IGC, the Asian Group and China noted that:

> [w]hen documenting the traditional knowledge, governments may take into account existing intellectual property standards and distinguish between traditional knowledge which is in the public domain and traditional knowledge which is not in the public domain. Based on this distinction, Member States may:
>
> as appropriate, compile databases of traditional knowledge which is in the public domain and make these databases available to patent-granting authorities for the

---

[35] IP/C/W/198, above n 30, 6. See http://www.sristi.org/hbnew/ (last accessed 30 June 2012).

[36] For an analysis of the contested domain of knowledge see Anil K Gupta, *WIPO-UNEP Study on the Role of Intellectual Property Rights in the Sharing of Benefits Arising From the Use of Biological Resources and Associated Traditional Knowledge*, (2000) jointly produced by the World Intellectual Property Organization (WIPO) and the United Nations Environment Programme (UNEP), Section A.

purposes of prior art searches, in order to prevent the grant of any intellectual property rights over such public domain knowledge;

establish registers of traditional knowledge elements which are not in the public domain and keep the contents of the registers undisclosed, pending the possible establishment of new protection standards for the traditional knowledge elements contained in the registers.[37]

The Asian Group subsequently submitted a further document detailing the experiences of Asian countries with the use of data bases and registries in regard to traditional knowledge and genetic resources.[38] The document noted inter alia, that the purpose of databases and registries is not to put undisclosed traditional knowledge and genetic resources into the public domain and their objectives include defensive and positive legal protection in respect of their contents.[39] There are risks involved in the compilation and digitization of traditional knowledge which may lead to its ready access and unauthorized exploitation in the absence of clear international legal principles. This factor must be addressed.

These concerns regarding documenting of traditional knowledge have also been expressed by the IGC which has cautioned that the objectives of defensive protection should be carefully considered. It has identified some points that traditional knowledge holders would need to take into consideration. It has noted that such defensive measures would often entail the first publication of traditional knowledge or information about genetic resources. This would mean that traditional knowledge holders may then forego patent rights over any innovations disclosed thereby, effectively precluding positive protection. Defensive protection would also make material more readily available, thus potentially enabling third parties to gain access to it and use it to the detriment of the holders. The IGC points out that:

---

[37] WIPO/GRTKF/IC/2/10 – Intergovernmental Committee on Intellectual Property and Genetic Resources, Traditional Knowledge and Folklore, Second Session, 10–14 December 2001, *Position Paper of the Asian Group and China, Document submitted by the Asian Group and China*, 3 December 2001, 3.

[38] WIPO/GRTKF/IC/4/14 – Intergovernmental Committee on Intellectual Property and Genetic Resources, Traditional Knowledge and Folklore, Fourth Session, 9–17 December 2002, *Technical Proposals on Databases and Registries of Traditional Knowledge and Biological/Genetic Resources, Document submitted by the Asian Group*, 6 December 2002, 2.

[39] The full range of proposed objectives is set out in ibid, Appendix of the Annexure.

For this reason, it is essential to consider carefully whether defensive protection is really what is intended, and whether the community or institution concerned would actually prefer to pursue a positive protection strategy or a combined positive and defensive approach. It would be important to secure the prior informed consent of any party providing information or material that would be disclosed in a defensive protection mechanism: this consent may need to be based on a full description of the implications of disclosure.[40]

ENFORCEMENT OF SEARCH AND DISCLOSURE MEASURES

The documentation of traditional knowledge would serve no purpose if patent examination processes did not take them into account, and this aspect also needs to be strengthened. Therefore such documentation must be made available to patent examiners, and measures to ensure that they are duly considered must also be put in place. This must be done at both national and international levels.

In regard to facilitating the implementation of the practical aspects of defensive protection, WIPO has cited two outcomes suggested by the IGC, namely:

- Amendments to international patent systems that are administered by WIPO. These amendments rely upon changes to rules and systems established by international IP treaties; and
- Practical products and tools for stakeholders. These tools do not amend existing systems, but allow TK holders and custodians of genetic resources to use these systems more effectively for their purposes.[41]

In regard to the first outcome WIPO has proposed the expansion of the international search process under the PCT to include documentation of traditional knowledge. Article 15(4) of the PCT provides that:

> [t]he International Searching Authority referred to in Article 16 shall endeavor to discover as much of the relevant prior art as its facilities permit, and shall, in any case, consult the documentation specified in the Regulations.

---

[40] WIPO/GRTKF/IC/5/6, above n 11, 10. The need for prior informed consent of the communities concerned has also been cited in other fora – see for example IP/C/W/228 – TRIPS Council, *Review of Article 27.3(b) Communication from Brazil*, 24 November 2000, paragraph 40.

[41] WIPO/GRTKF/IC/5/6, above n 11, 14.

The documentation in question is that contained in Rule 34 of the PCT Regulations entitled 'Minimum Documentation.' This includes national patent documents, the published international (PCT) applications, the published regional applications for patents and inventors' certificates, and the published regional patents and inventors' certificates and such other published items of non-patent literature as the International Searching Authorities shall agree upon, and which shall be published in a list by the International Bureau when agreed upon for the first time and whenever changed. The IGC has proposed that published traditional knowledge would be integrated into the PCT minimum documentation in order to ensure that traditional knowledge is considered in the international search and examination process, and necessary changes would be made in this regard.[42] However, this still does not address the question of oral traditions as prior art.

In regard to the second outcome the IGC has agreed on such steps as the compilation of a non-exhaustive Inventory of Traditional Knowledge-related Periodical, a non-exhaustive Inventory of Traditional Knowledge-related Databases, and the establishment of the WIPO Task Force on Classification of Traditional Knowledge. The practical products and tools for stakeholders include a Toolkit for IP Management, an Online Portal of Registries and Databases of Traditional Knowledge and Genetic Resources, a sample database of Ayurvedic traditional medicine from South Asia, a Questionnaire on Databases and Registries of Traditional Knowledge and Genetic Resources, and Technical Proposals Concerning Databases and Registries of Traditional Knowledge and Biological/Genetic Resources.[43]

CONCLUSION

This discussion highlights the fact that traditional knowledge is inherently incompatible with the patent system and cannot be brought under its aegis. While IPRs may be used to appropriate traditional knowledge, they cannot effectively protect it either by positive or negative mechanisms. Also, many traditional knowledge holders do not wish to use the IPR system to give positive protection to their body of knowledge even if they have created inventions which are practically patentable. Their concerns are rather to

---

[42] WIPO/GRTKF/IC/5/6, above n 11, paragraphs 31–43; WIPO/GRTKF/IC/6/8, above n 26, paragraphs 10–15; WIPO/GRTKF/IC/11/7, paragraph 48.

[43] WIPO/GRTKF/IC/5/6, above n 11, 20.

prevent others from using such knowledge in inventions and patenting them, in other words, protecting their knowledge heritage from the IPR system.

However, it appears that the best defensive measure in this regard is, in fact, to use that very system. Unlike in the case of the disclosure of origin requirement, which is not currently an aspect of patent law, the requirement of novelty is, and it is in fact the most fundamental condition of patentability. Therefore in this instance, the point in issue is to make that condition enforceable in relation to traditional knowledge. The first aspect of doing so, the legal aspect, entails introducing and enforcing a universal novelty standard. The divergent national standards and criteria for recognizing what is prior art should be harmonized at international level and national law brought into conformity with such criteria.

The practical, aspect of establishing what constitutes prior art has to be addressed very carefully. Documenting and publishing traditional knowledge may, in fact result in exposing it to the very threats from which the knowledge holders seek protection. Therefore a system needs to be carefully worked out which will prevent, or at least minimize this possibility. In doing so a distinction can be made between knowledge which is common knowledge where the issue would not arise, and knowledge which is not in the public domain. In the case of the latter a possibility is to document such knowledge but keep it undisclosed until further protection standards have been worked out.

As in the case of disclosure of origin, in regard to issues of novelty, it is likely that many 'bad' patents will slip through the net. Therefore, firstly, search and disclosure measures must be strictly enforced. One possible measure in this regard is to make the patent application public for a certain period of time in order that further information may be obtained from interested persons or communities. This would help to prevent unjustified patents from being granted. Nevertheless it is essential that post grant revocation of patents be made a feature of the system. There is even greater justification for doing so in this instance, since it can be argued that an invention which fails the novelty test should be rendered void *ab initio*.

13. Conclusion

Historically PGRFA were in the public domain, a public good accessible to all. The development of biotechnology and the expansion of intellectual property rights over these resources resulted in the enclosure of this global commons and a contest over access to and equitable sharing of their benefits. The conflict over plant varieties in the last two decades can be conceptualized by which property regime should be applied to them. The international trade and IPR regime, consisting of the TRIPS Agreement, UPOV and the several WIPO treaties provide the framework for private property rights. The CBD was negotiated on the basis of state sovereignty over biological resources, to a large extent as a counter measure to the former. The most recent agreement, the FAO Treaty, provides for specified crop plants to be placed in the public domain as an open access system. This too was intended as a foil to private property rights over plant varieties. The current debate as explored in this book revolves around the question as to whether one or all of these property systems can ensure equity in the uses of PGRFA. The following points have emerged from the analysis.

This book has taken the position that it is the private property regime, which has become the dominant paradigm by which PGRFA is regulated. This position has been entrenched by the application to these resources of plant breeders' rights under the 1978 and 1991 UPOV Acts, and patents under the TRIPS Agreement of 1994. Over the last two decades developing countries have been compelled to enforce IPRs over plant varieties by a combination of agreements adopted in a cycle of bilateral and multilateral negotiations. In recent years developed countries have pushed for the upward harmonization of IPRs which would also impact on the propertization of PGRFA. Where they have failed to achieve their objective in multilateral fora, they are increasingly resorting to bilateral agreements to do so. Thus, developed countries have succeeded in anchoring an international private property regime, which importantly, is enforceable by way of sanctions.

Given this reality, the debate on PGRFA and related issues has revolved around the strategies of developing countries to, if not prevent the patenting of crop plants, at least to alleviate the impacts of doing so. Developing countries have been essentially fighting a defensive action in this regard, and this book has concluded that their strategies have been generally unsuccessful. While some seemingly positive measures have been instituted in agreements such as the CBD and the FAO Treaty in regard to benefit sharing of the uses of these resources, these measures have in reality proved to be ineffective in the face of the dominance exerted by developed countries and corporate interests supported by the legal framework on IPRs.

The negotiations of the CBD were premised upon the principle of state sovereignty over natural resources, mainly at the insistence of developing countries. This provision refuted the earlier position that PGRFA constitute the common heritage of humankind. However, the driving force behind the CBD are the provisions for equitable access to and benefit sharing of biological resources which include PGRFA *in situ,* as well as the traditional knowledge related to it. The intrinsic problem with this concept is that measures to ensure equitable access and benefit sharing are to be negotiated on a bilateral basis. While bilateral negotiations may be inevitable in view of the divergences in resources and the circumstances in which they may be accessed, given the intrinsic imbalance in contractual capacity between providers (particularly communities), and those seeking access to these resources, the ABS system of the CBD is inherently disadvantageous to developing countries and their communities. As the case studies cited in Chapter 9 illustrate, the implementation of the system often does not guarantee that conditions of access and benefit sharing such as obtaining prior informed consent or negotiating mutually agreed terms are fulfilled.

The injustice is reinforced by the fact that unlike intellectual property rights ABS agreements are not enforceable across borders. Critics of the system have therefore questioned whether the principles of prior informed consent and mutually agreed terms are merely intended to legitimize what is innately unjust. In any event, as far as benefit sharing is concerned, it must be questioned whether the propertization of food plant varieties and their removal from the public domain can be adequately compensated for by the types of benefits which have been advocated in this regard. In this sense the conceptualization of the CBD is fundamentally flawed.

The most recent agreement in regard to PGRFA is the FAO Treaty of 2001. This Treaty deals with the *ex situ* collections of plants which are in the possession of countries throughout the world. It is founded on the principle of open access or no property in relation to crop plants, and has put in place a multilateral system of access to the varieties, which have been brought within its ambit. Since the process is regulated by the mechanisms of the Treaty, it obviates the need for ad hoc agreements between users and providers. The Treaty thus ensures the free flow of germplasm in a more efficient and cost effective way, at least as regards the varieties in their original form, and developing countries have undoubtedly benefited by this system. However, as discussed in Chapter 9, it does not prevent these resources from being acquired for further development, and the modified form of the plants from being appropriated. Thus the structure of the multilateral system may in fact facilitate the acquisition of these plants and their removal, at least of modified or enhanced versions, from the public domain. In any event, the provisions of the Treaty are applicable only to the crop varieties, which have been listed in Annex 1 to the Treaty or which are in the public domain and therefore its ambit is limited to this extent.

Equitable benefit sharing will in any case be limited by the imposition of IPRs on genetic resources and developing countries have not relied solely on the provisions of the CBD and the FAO Treaty in their strategies to craft a global framework to ensure equity in the use of PGRFA. They have also attempted to negotiate amendments to the patent system to prevent or restrict the patenting of plant varieties. In the TRIPS Council in the context of the review of Article 27.3(b) of the TRIPS Agreement, and the negotiations on the relationship between TRIPS and the CBD, they have asked for, on the one hand, a total prohibition on the patenting of life forms, and on the other hand, restrictions on such patenting. Neither demand has been achieved to date. The response of developed countries has been that any problems or injustice caused by the status quo must be addressed by national legislation but outside the patent system. Further, in regard to the requirement in TRIPS that countries must provide for plant protection, including by a *sui generis* system, some developed countries have attempted to push for a system that is either a UPOV style model or one which is TRIPS compliant.

As discussed in Chapters 11 and 12 specific defensive mechanisms to prevent the unauthorized appropriation and patenting of genetic resources and their attendant traditional knowledge have also been proposed by developing countries in several fora. The first is the requirement to disclose the origin of the genetic resources and traditional knowledge used in a patentable invention, and also to adduce proof that they were legally acquired with the consent of the provider country or community. Penalties for violation of this condition would include the revocation of the patent. Unsurprisingly, developed countries vetoed these proposals, once again arguing that any problems that may arise in this regard must be addressed outside the patent system and by national legislation. A similar resistance was shown to the proposal that traditional knowledge be recognized as constituting part of the state of the art so as to defeat the novelty criterion of a patentable invention, which is based on it. While developed countries appear to concur with developing countries' concerns about piracy of these resources, they are inflexible in their position so that the patent system remains intact.

At present the debate on this point remains deadlocked at international level. While developing countries have stalled the negotiations of the Substantive Patent Law Treaty in WIPO, they have not been successful in pressing their own case in the TRIPS Council. In the meantime some developing countries are bargaining away their positions in bilateral agreements. The most recent development in this narrative, the long awaited Nagoya Protocol, has not yet come into force, but a preliminary analysis of its provisions does not hold out much promise for any significant change in the status quo. The question to be now asked is, what lies ahead?

It was noted in Chapter 8 that in the debate in the TRIPS Council on Article 27.3(b) and the relationship between TRIPS and the CBD, developing countries had called for a total prohibition on patents on all life forms. In view of the fact that negotiations to ensure equitable benefit sharing have proved to be ineffective, and efforts to negate abuses of the patent system have also failed in the international IPR and biodiversity spheres, the demand for a total prohibition on life forms and a legal framework which keeps PGRFA in the public domain should be renewed. Since free access to PGRFA is critical to the fulfilment of the right to food and nutrition, such negotiations could now be forum shifted to the human rights sphere.

The monopolization of PGRFA and the corporate control of agricultural systems necessarily have negative impacts on the food and nutrition security of all peoples. This dimension has taken on a greater significance since the food crisis of 2007–2008, when the number of undernourished people worldwide increased to almost 1 billion. Since June 2010 the rise in food prices has again driven another 44 million people into extreme poverty. This has set back the achievement of the Millennium Development Goals, particularly the need to eradicate extreme poverty and hunger. There is now a renewed urgency in alleviating global hunger, developing sustainable agricultural systems particularly in adapting to climate change, and fulfilling the human right to food. Free and unrestricted access to crop diversity is of critical importance to achieving these goals. On the other hand, these very factors may serve as incentives for corporate interests to push for even wider monopolies on food crops. For example, it has been alleged that the six largest agrochemical and seed corporations are filing sweeping patents on climate ready crops in a bid to control the future supply of food in the face of climate change.[1] In view of these trends developing countries would

---

[1] ETC Group, 'Gene Giants Stockpile Patents on "Climate-ready" Crops in Bid to become "Biomassters": Patent Grab Threatens Biodiversity, Food Sovereignty' available at http://foodfreedom.wordpress.com/2010/10/25/gene-giants-stockpile-patents-on-climate-ready-crops-in-bid-to-become-biomassters/ (last accessed 30 June 2012); IP/C/W/554, TRIPS Council, *Article 27.3(B) and the Legalization of*

need to re-visit their point of reference in the negotiations on access to and equitable benefit sharing of the uses of PGRFA.

The human right to adequate food and freedom from hunger is a universal right set out in the International Covenant on Economic, Social and Cultural Rights (ICESCR).[2] The Rome Declaration on World Food Security of 1996 has also reaffirmed 'the right of everyone to have access to safe and nutritious food, consistent with the right to adequate food and the fundamental right of everyone to be free from hunger.' The Declaration has also reiterated that 'Food should not be used as an instrument for political and economic pressure.'[3]

The primary obligation of fulfilling this right rests with States. The Committee on Economic, Social and Cultural Rights in its General Comment 12 on the Right to Food notes that States must take steps to progressively achieve the full realization of the right.[4] The Rome Declaration also reiterates that 'Attaining food security is a complex task for which the primary responsibility rests with individual governments.' There are, therefore positive state obligations to fulfil this right. The Special Rapporteur on the Right to Food while also pointing out that States have an obligation to respect existing access to adequate food and an obligation to protect and fulfil the right to food, has further observed that 'These obligations apply both to the regulation of commercial seed systems and to the preservation and enhancement of informal or traditional farmers' seed systems.' He has further declared that the ICESCR 'could be relied upon in order to justify recognizing a right of access of farmers to seeds which are not in open access.'[5]

It is not difficult to argue that free access to PGRFA is fundamental to the progressive realization of the right to food since the fulfillment of this state obligation would include developing and protecting sustainable agricultural systems. Conversely, it could also be argued that permitting patents on plants would amount to States violating their obligations to protect and fulfil this right not only among their own people but also globally. As

---

Biopiracy: Trends, Impacts and Why It Needs To Be Amended, Communication from the Plurinational State of Bolivia, 28 March 2011.

[2] Article 15.

[3] See http://www.fao.org/docrep/003/w3613e/w3613e00.htm (last accessed 20 July 2012).

[4] See http://www.unhchr.ch/tbs/doc.nsf/0/3d02758c707031d58025677f003b73b9 (last accessed 20 July 2012).

[5] A/64/170 – *The right to food – Seed policies and the right to food: enhancing agrobiodiversity and encouraging innovation, Note by the Secretary-General*, 23 July 2009, 4.

pointed out earlier no country is self-sufficient in PGRFA, and all rely on non-indegenous crops to meet their food needs. The Special Rapporteur has reiterated that crop genetic diversity should be viewed as a global public good, noting that 'it has been concluded that domesticated plant genetic resources should be treated as a common pool, rather than as "property" of any particular State or local community.'[6] He has recommended that 'States should not allow patents on plants and should establish research exemptions in legislation protecting plant breeders' rights'. If States do allow patents on plants, they should establish research exemptions based on article 30 of the TRIPS Agreement.' The FAO Voluntary Guidelines to Support the Progressive Realization of the Right to Adequate Food in the Context of National Food Security has also said that 'States Parties should respect existing access to adequate food by not taking any measures that result in preventing such access, and should protect the right of everyone to adequate food by taking steps so that enterprises and individuals do not deprive individuals of their access to adequate food.'[7]

These human rights obligations conflict with states' obligations under IPR and trade law. While it is beyond the scope of this book to analyze this issue in depth, it can be argued that in the event of inconsistencies in states' obligations in different spheres of international law, the protection of human rights must be prioritized. Therefore clearly, states' obligations under IPR regimes cannot result in the violation of these rights. Activitsts have also called for states to 'Ensure that existing environmental and agricultural agreements which preserve agricultural biodiversity have precedence over trade agreements, where these conflict,' and to 'Prohibit patents on genetic resources for food and agriculture, to ensure the "free flow" of agricultural biodiversity without threats of privatisation through patents, and other intellectual property rights that restrict access to plant, animal and aquatic genetic resources.'[8]

---

6 This frame of reference has been reiterated in a new paradigm of 'the common goods of humanity.' The author states that the notion encompasses the indispensable elements of life such as water and seeds which are now being privatized. François Houtart, *From 'Common Goods' to the 'Common Good of Humanity'*, Rosa Luxemburg Foundation (2011).

7 CL127/10-Sup.1 – Report – Intergovernmental Working Group for the Elaboration of a Set of Voluntary Guidelines to Support the Progressive Realization of the Right to Adequate Food in the Context of National Food Security, 23 September 2004, *Final Report of the Chair*.

8 Intermediate Technology Development Group (ITDG), 'Preserving the web of life', available at http://www.ukabc.org/weboflife.htm (last accessed 30 June 2012).

The issue of universal free access to PGRFA has been raised again in a recent submission to the TRIPS Council where the Plurinational State of Bolivia has renewed the demand for a total prohibition on patents on seeds.[9] It points out the ethical and moral concerns in the patenting process and notes the negative impacts and consequences on food security and food sovereignty. Having declared that 'Allowing the patenting of life forms and parts thereof is simply unacceptable' it states 'For all these reasons, Bolivia proposes to amend Article 27.3 (b) to prohibit all forms of patenting of life and parts thereof as an essential part of the mandate in the Doha Development Round and as an important contribution of the WTO to the development objectives.' While this proposal has not progressed in the TRIPS Council, it is an encouraging sign that efforts to negating the enclosure of a critical global commons are being revived. To date developing countries have been largely reactive in their strategies to mitigate the effects of the IPR system on PGRFA and these have been unsuccessful. A proactive stance located within the international human rights discourse will give a renewed impetus to crafting an international legal framework which prohibits patents on plant varieties and maintains these resources in the public domain.

[9] IP/C/W/554, above n 1.

Index